CAROL CARTER   JOYCE BISHOP   SARAH LYMAN KRAVITS   PETER J. MAURIN

FIFTH CANADIAN EDITION

Keys to Success

Building successful

intelligence

and achieving

your goals

Pearson Canada
Toronto

Library and Archives Canada Cataloguing in Publication

Keys to success : building successful intelligence and achieving your goals / Carol Carter ... [et al.]. — 5th Canadian ed.

Includes index.
ISBN 978-0-13-501659-6

1. College student orientation—Canada—Handbooks, manuals, etc. 2. Study skills—Handbooks, manuals, etc. 3. College students—Canada—Life skills guides. I. Carter, Carol

LB2343.34.C3K48 2010   378.1'98   C2008-905788-0

Copyright © 2010, 2007, 2004, 2001, 1998 Pearson Education Canada, a division of Pearson Canada Inc., Toronto, Ontario.

Pearson Prentice Hall. All rights reserved. This publication is protected by copyright and permission should be obtained from the publisher prior to any prohibited reproduction, storage in a retrieval system, or transmission in any form or by any means, electronic, mechanical, photocopying, recording, or likewise. For information regarding permission, write to the Permissions Department.

Original edition published by Pearson Education, Inc., Upper Saddle River, New Jersey, USA. Copyright © 2009. This edition is authorized for sale only in Canada.

ISBN-13: 978-0-13-501659-6
ISBN-10: 0-13-501659-2

Vice President, Editorial Director: Gary Bennett
Editor-in-Chief: Ky Pruesse
Acquisitions Editor: David S. Le Gallais
Sponsoring Editor: Carolin Sweig
Marketing Manager: Loula March
Senior Developmental Editor: Jennifer Murray
Production Editor: Kevin Leung
Copy Editor: Lenore Latta
Proofreader: Robert Giannetto
Production Coordinator: Janis Raisen
Composition: Macmillan Publishing Solutions
Art Director: Julia Hall
Cover Design: Anthony Leung
Cover Image: Masaaki Toyoura/GettyImages

For permission to reproduce copyrighted material, the publisher gratefully acknowledges the copyright holders listed on page 403, which are considered an extension of this copyright page.

Statistics Canada information is used with the permission of Statistics Canada. Users are forbidden to copy the data and redisseminate them, in an original or modified form, for commercial purposes, without permission from Statistics Canada. Information on the availability of the wide range of data from Statistics Canada can be obtained from Statistics Canada's Regional Offices, its World Wide Web site at http://www.statcan.ca, and its toll-free access number 1-800-263-1136.

1 2 3 4 5   13 12 11 10 09

Printed and bound in the United States of America.

BRIEF CONTENTS

CONTENTS

Chapter 4
Analytical, Creative, and Practical Thinking 98

Chapter 5
Reading and Studying 136

Chapter 6
Listening, Note Taking, and Memory   168

Chapter 7
Test Taking   200

Chapter 8
Researching and Writing 232

Chapter 9
Relating to Others 272

Chapter 10
Personal Wellness 302

Chapter 11
Managing Career and Money   332

Chapter 12
Creating Your Life   366

MISSION STATEMENT

Our mission is to help students know and believe in themselves, take advantage of resources and opportunities, set and achieve their goals, learn throughout their lives, discover careers that fulfill and support them, build fruitful and satisfying relationships with others from all backgrounds and walks of life, and experience the challenges and rewards that make life meaningful.

PREFACE

Many students beginning college or university—or returning to school after many years—wonder if they have what it takes to succeed. What is the recipe for postsecondary success and beyond? Does a straight-A report card or high IQ predict success? Do low grades or scores signal that you'll stumble?

Among the ideas presented by the many people who have researched this question, one approach stands out from the rest. Psychologist Robert Sternberg coined the term *successful intelligence* to indicate that intelligence is much, much more than the kind of "book smarts" that can be measured by IQ or similar tests. Rather, it is the ability to use a combination of **analytical, creative,** and **practical** abilities to reach your most important goals.

What are the analytical, creative, and practical processes that underlie intelligence?

This Is Intelligence: Analysis

Analytical intelligence is highly valued as a crucial component of academic success. More commonly known as critical thinking, it is the ability to assess, analyze, compare, and evaluate information.

This Is Intelligence: Creativity

Creative intelligence is the ability to innovate, generate a variety of ideas in response to problems, or think out of the box. It also involves shifting perspectives and risk taking.

This Is Intelligence: Practical Application

Practical intelligence is more than "street smarts" or common sense. It also includes an awareness of oneself and others in situations and the translation of that knowledge into action. It is developed primarily through experience, observation, and practice.

Keys to Success Focuses on Successful Intelligence

Why is successful intelligence such an effective theme for a student success text? Here are some key reasons:

- It delivers strategies that work for *all kinds of students,* not just those with strong analytical skills who tend to do well in school.
- Research proves that teaching and learning with successful intelligence *improves achievement* across cultures, socioeconomic status, age, and gender.[1]

- It recognizes that *intelligence is dynamic* and can be developed, which *encourages lifelong learning,* a key ingredient for success in the modern world.
- It *promotes goal achievement* in college and beyond, supporting our tried-and-true emphasis on success in college, career, and life.

Having introduced successful intelligence as its theme in the last edition, *Keys to Success: Fifth Canadian Edition* takes its integration to new heights this time around, with tools in each chapter to help you build analytical, creative, and practical intelligence:

- New! At the beginning of the chapter, a mind map preview surveys the successful intelligence skills you will be working on. These will act as learning objectives for each chapter.
- Revised! Throughout the chapter, **Get Analytical, Get Creative,** and **Get Practical** exercises build those specific skills in the context of chapter material.
- New! As you finish the chapter, a **Successful Intelligence Wrap-Up** hits the high points of what you explored and accomplished.
- Revised! Each end-of-chapter exercise set begins with **Successful Intelligence: Think, Create, Apply,** an exercise that synthesizes the three aspects of successful intelligence by applying them to chapter content.
- New! Each chapter has a link to **Successful Intelligence Connections Online,** an audio feature on the text's Companion Website that will help you apply successful intelligence to specific chapter topics.

Keys to Success **Features Help You Grow**

Complementing the successful intelligence theme, additional features of this text will help you achieve your goals in college, career, and life.

Practical Strategies and Advice. Practical intelligence is in high demand in college and in the workplace. Instructors and students all over the country said they wanted more practical advice and application—and here it is in the form of topics and text features:

- Reflecting psychologist Daniel Goleman's latest research on social intelligence as well as his ongoing work with emotional intelligence, *Keys to Success* offers practical tools to help you master your feelings and make the most out of your relationships with others. New material on social intelligence, and expanded material on emotional intelligence, is highlighted in chapters 1, 4, and 11, and both social and emotional intelligence are referenced throughout the text.
- In this information age, **information literacy** is crucial for success. Chapter 4 has a new analytical thinking example showing different ways in which to critically evaluate information, and chapter 8 contains an updated segment on research, with comprehensive information about evaluating any kind of material you encounter in the library or on the Internet.
- Getting ready for exams, dealing with math anxiety and dealing with oral exams are high on the list of important practical skills. At the end

of each of the three parts in *Keys to Success,* a **Study Break** will help you build these crucial skills.

- At the end of every third chapter, a **Personal Triumph case study** showcases an extraordinary student who overcame adversity to achieve success. Accompanying these stories are art pieces created by students who have overcome challenges of their own.

A Text-Wide Focus on How You Learn. This text gives you tools to find out how you learn best, as well as strategies for applying this information in practical ways:

- The first of **chapter 3's self-assessments** helps you explore your strengths in eight ability areas that psychologist Howard Gardner calls the **multiple intelligences:** verbal-linguistic, logical-mathematical, bodily-kinesthetic, visual-spatial, interpersonal, intrapersonal, musical, and naturalistic. The other, the MBTI-based **Personality Spectrum,** helps you explore how you relate to others.

- In chapters 5 through 11, you will find **Multiple Intelligence Strategies grids** with strategies, related to a chapter topic, geared toward each of the eight intelligences. Enhanced for this edition, each grid has a new column that demonstrates possible ways to apply multiple intelligence-based strategies to a particular academic discipline (each chapter features a different discipline).

- Beyond the Multiple Intelligence Strategies grids, material in other chapters (particularly chapters 9 and 11) shows how you can apply what you know about how you learn to situations such as career exploration and communication.

End-of-Chapter Exercises. In addition to the **Successful Intelligence: Think, Create, Apply** synthesis exercise, the end-of-chapter exercises promote development of a skillset necessary to compete in a knowledge economy and global marketplace: group problem solving (**Teamwork: Create Solutions Together**), journaling and practical writing (**Writing: Journal and Put Skills to Work**), and preparing for a successful career (**Personal Portfolio: Prepare for Career Success**).

Keys to Success Is Better Than Ever

The new edition of *Keys to Success* includes improved presentations of critical college, career, and life success topics. Highlights include the following:

- **Quick Start to College and University** has been focused even more tightly on helpful information to get you in the groove as you begin school.

- An overhaul of **chapter 1 (Welcome to Your Post Secondary Career)** involves an expanded introduction of successful intelligence, three successful intelligence self-assessments, and careful selection of supporting topics such as academic integrity and working with others.

- **Chapter 3 (Learning How You Learn)** is newly streamlined in its explanations of multiple intelligences and the personality spectrum, clearer in its treatment of the accompanying assessments, and more practical in helping you apply what you learn from the assessments to school, work, and life.

- **Chapter 4 (Critical, Creative, and Practical Thinking)** has been strengthened to help you understand and use the different aspects of successful intelligence.
- Study skills enhancements in **chapters 5 through 8 (Reading and Studying; Listening, Note Taking, and Memory; Test Taking; and Researching and Writing)** include revised coverage of SQ3R, memory, and test taking; new material on text notes and highlighting and on combining text and class notes; and a streamlined writing chapter with a new writing sample.
- The latest health and fitness information appears in **chapter 10 (Personal Wellness),** notably in the sections on eating well, immunizations, staying safe, and drugs.
- **Chapter 11 (Managing Money and Career)** has a new emphasis on the most practical money management and career planning advice.
  - In each chapter, Canadian students offer their suggestions on how to make your transition to post secondary life easier.
  - Throughout the textbook, The Conference Board of Canada's Employability Skills 2000+ are highlighted to help students develop their own unique skills for career and life success.

Keys to Success Is Your Tool for Life

Broadening your definition of intelligence may change how you view your abilities and what you expect of yourself in college, in the workplace, and in your personal life. Successful intelligence can empower you with tools you never knew you had. Take action with what you learn about yourself and success in this text. Think and act analytically, creatively, and practically in the coming years as you work hard to achieve your goals and find a learning path that is uniquely your own.

Students and instructors: Many of our best suggestions come from you. Send your questions, comments, and ideas about *Keys to Success* to Carol Carter at *caroljcarter@lifebound.com* and to the Canadian author Peter J. Maurin at *peter.maurin@mohawkcollege.ca*. We look forward to hearing from you, and we are grateful for the opportunity to work with you.

Note

1. E.L. Grigorenko, L. Jarvin, and R.J. Sternberg, "School-Based Tests of the Triarchic Theory: Three Settings, Three Samples, Three Syllabi." *Contemporary Educational Psychology,* 27, April 2002, pp. 167–208.

ACKNOWLEDGMENTS

- We would like to thank all those students across the country who helped us (and their fellow students) by providing *Stressbuster* tips: Alejandra Gonzalez, Michael Murray, Kevin Forseth, Gabriel Schroedter, Claire Douglas, Anna Griffin, Alicia Brett, Stephanie Jack, Nancy E. Shaw, Soumik Kanungo, Sonya Beel, and Jennifer Armour. We would also like to thank the many instructors from across Canada who assisted us with the preparation of the *Stressbuster* tips: Sue Ann Cairns, Kwantlen University College; Sharon Cameron, Algonquin College; William Christian, Guelph University; Les Hanson, Red River College; Selia Karsten, Seneca College; Gail McClintock, Champlain College; Trudy McCormack, St. Francis Xavier University; Joan McKibbon, St. Lawrence College; and Doug McLean, Sprott-Shaw Community College.

- Thanks also to our reviewers, whose comments and suggestions have helped us in the preparation of this Fifth Canadian Edition: Jennifer Auld-Cameron, Nova Scotia Community College; Marc Belanger, Vanier College; Elizabeth Bishop, Confederation College; Rosa Fracassa, George Brown College, Jane Guzar, Mohawk College; Jerry Mays, Mohawk College; Joseph Murphy, CDI College; Sonia Perna, SAIT Polytechnic; Lynn Redford, Malaspina University-College; Barbara Ritchie, Humber College; Gladys Woodburn, triOS College.

- Thanks to the staff at Pearson Education Canada: Carolin Sweig, Sponsoring Editor; Jennifer Murray, Developmental Editor; and Kevin Leung, Production Editor.

- While I am the Canadian author for this, the fifth Canadian edition of *Keys to Success,* the contents of the book are really the product of years of teaching at several institutions. Thanks to my current and former students at Mohawk College and to the many former students at Brock University and Niagara College. Whether it was Communications, Media, or Sociology, you always taught me something in the process.

- Finally, to my gifted crew at home—Kim, Sonja, and Joshua: You are my "keys to success." Thanks for your love, patience, and understanding. I love you all very much.

Peter J. Maurin, M.A.

ABOUT THE AUTHORS

Carol Carter is founder of LifeBound, a career coaching company that offers individual coaching sessions and seminars for high school students, college students, and career seekers. She has written *Majoring in the Rest of Your Life: Career Secrets for College Students*, and *Majoring in High School*. She has also co-authored *Keys to Preparing for College, Keys to College Studying, The Career Tool Kit, Keys to Career Success, Keys to Study Skills, Keys to Thinking and Learning*, and *Keys to Success*. She has taught welfare-to-work classes, team taught in the La Familia Scholars Program at the Community College of Denver, and conducted numerous workshops for students and faculty around the country. Carol is a national college and career expert and is interviewed regularly for print, radio, and television news programs. In addition to working with students of all ages, Carol thrives on foreign travel and culture; she is fortunate enough to have been a guest in more than 40 foreign countries. Please visit her website and write her at www.lifebound.com.

Joyce Bishop holds a Ph.D. in psychology and has taught for more than 20 years, receiving a number of honours, including Teacher of the Year for 1995 and 2000. For five years she has been voted "favorite teacher" by the student body and Honor Society at Golden West College, Huntington Beach, California, where she has taught since 1987 and is a tenured professor. She worked with a federal grant to establish Learning Communities and Workplace Learning in her district, and she has developed workshops and trained faculty in cooperative learning, active learning, multiple intelligences, workplace relevancy, learning styles, authentic assessment, team building, and the development of learning communities. Joyce is currently teaching on-line and multimedia classes, and she trains other faculty to teach on-line in her district and region of 21 colleges. She co-authored *Keys to College Studying, Keys to Success, Keys to Thinking and Learning*, and *Keys to Study Skills*. Joyce is the lead academic of the Keys to Lifelong Learning Telecourse, distributed by Dallas Telelearning.

Sarah Lyman Kravits comes from a family of educators and has long cultivated an interest in educational development. She co-authored *Keys to College Studying, The Career Tool Kit, Keys to Success, Keys to Thinking and Learning*, and *Keys to Study Skills*, and has served as program director for LifeSkills, Inc., a non-profit organization that aims to further the career and personal development of high school students. In that capacity she helped to formulate both curricular and organizational elements of the program, working closely with instructors as well as members of the business community. She has also given faculty workshops in critical thinking. Sarah holds a B.A. in English and drama from the University of Virginia, where she was a Jefferson Scholar; and an M.F.A. from Catholic University.

Peter J. Maurin received his Master's degree in sociology from McMaster University in 1992. He currently teaches in the Media Studies Department at Mohawk College in Hamilton, Ontario. He has been a student advisor for the General Arts and Science Program at Mohawk, and has taught at Seneca College, Niagara College, and Brock University. The fifth Canadian edition of *Keys to Success* is Peter's tenth book for Pearson Education. Besides teaching, Peter is a professional communicator: He is a freelance writer and broadcaster, logging more than 20 years on the air for several radio stations in Ontario. He's also an old rock and roller. His weekly radio show "Oldies Without Borders" can be heard Sundays from 10 a.m. until noon online at http://www.mohawkcollege.ca/msa/cioi/.

SUPPLEMENTAL RESOURCES

Instructor Supplements: A Complete Instructional Package!

Pearson Education Canada is committed to preparing the best quality supplements for its textbooks. The following supplements provide an outstanding array of resources.

Instructor Resource CD-ROM This CD pulls together all of the supplements available to instructors, including the Instructor's Resource Manual, PowerPoint Presentations and Test Item File.

Instructor's Manual Each chapter of the Manual includes a chapter outline, learning objectives, facilitation questions, and Building Skills For Academic, Career and Life Success, which are activities focused on team building, journaling and the development of a career portfolio. This instructor resource also contains essay and short answer questions and quotations that can be used in a variety of classroom activities such as group discovery and public speaking.

PowerPoint Presentations The PowerPoint presentation created for this text provides dozens of ready-to-use graphics and images to guide and enhance lecture presentation.

Test Item File The Test Item File is comprised of over 600 questions including multiple-choice, true or false and essay formats.

MyTest A powerful assessment generation program, MyTest helps instructors easily create and print quizzes, tests and exams. Questions and tests can all be authored online, allowing flexibility and the ability to efficiently manage assessments at anytime, from anywhere. The MyTest can be accessed by visiting **www.pearsonmytest.com.**

Technology Specialists Pearson's Technology Specialists work with faculty and campus course designers to ensure that Pearson technology products, assessment tools, and online course materials are tailored to meet your specific needs. This highly qualified team is dedicated to helping schools take full advantage of a wide range of educational resources, by assisting in the integration of a variety of instructional materials and media formats. Your local Pearson Education sales representative can provide you with more details on this service program.

CourseSmart CourseSmart is a new way for instructors and students to access textbooks online anytime from anywhere. With thousands of titles across hundreds of courses, CourseSmart helps instructors choose the best textbook for their class and give their students a new option for buying the assigned textbook as a lower cost eTextbook. For more information, visit www.coursesmart.com.

Student Supplements: An Integrated Learning System!

Building on the study aids found in the text, Pearson Education Canada also offers supplements for students.

Companion Website (www.pearsoned.ca/carter) The text-specific website includes chapter objectives, practice quizzes, destinations and podcasts from the authors. In addition, the new website contains:

- *Online Learning Style Assessment Quiz:* This interactive quiz will allow students to determine their dominant learning style and will provide them with tips and strategies for maximizing their study time.

- *StudyLife:* Looking for a study partner to help you improve your grades in this course and others? *StudyLife* is a new social network from Pearson Canada that will help you make new connections and get better grades. You can also visit the site at www.studylife.ca

Quick Start to College and University

Helpful Information and Advice As You Begin Your Journey

Welcome, or welcome back, to your post secondary education! Ahead of you are opportunities to learn more than you can imagine. Over the next years, you will explore the world of ideas, acquire information, and develop skills that will last a lifetime.

With these wonderful opportunities comes the challenge of adjusting to the realities of college. It may help you to know that nearly every college student—no matter what age or level of experience—feels overwhelmed as college begins.

Quick Start to College and University is designed to help you feel in control as you start the most important educational journey of your life. As you read, consult your school handbook and/or website to learn about its specific resources, policies, and practices. The exercises interspersed throughout *Quick Start* will also help you focus on your school.

Remember that you, along with instructors, advisors, administrators, support personnel, and fellow students, are a full participant in the educational process. Take the first steps toward a future filled with opportunity by

- taking an active role in your courses from the first day of class.
- being in charge of your learning, which involves setting goals, managing your time, completing assignments on schedule, and seeking help, if necessary.
- striving to do your best and making a commitment to quality.
- being an advocate for yourself as you relate to others.
- taking care of your mind, body, and relationships.
- getting involved in activities that interest you and that help develop your talents.
- deciding what you want to study—what you are passionate about.
- pursuing meaningful academic goals (honours or awards, involvement in academic organizations, internships, or other work experiences that support your academic path).

One of the first steps in creating your own success is learning what your college expects of you—and what you have a right to expect in return as a consumer of higher education.

How colleges and universities are structured

Think of your school as a large organization made up of arms that perform specific functions and that is run by hundreds and sometimes thousands of people. The two primary functional arms of your school focus on teaching and administration.

Teaching takes centre stage

The primary mission of most colleges and universities is teaching—communicating to students the knowledge and thinking skills needed to become lifelong learners. Although the term "instructor" is used in this text, teachers have official titles that show their rank within your college. Instructors with the highest status are *full professors*. Moving down from these are *associate professors, assistant professors, lecturers, instructors,* and *assistant instructors,* more commonly known as *teaching assistants* or *TAs.* (Remember that titles may vary from school to school and from college to university.) *Adjuncts* may teach several courses, but are not official staff members. Later in *Quick Start,* you will see how to communicate with and get help from your instructors.

Administrators provide support

The administrative staff enables your school—and the student body—to function. *Vice-presidents* deal with the nuts and bolts of operations; they make sure buildings are repaired, instructors are hired, students are registered, tuition is collected. *Deans,* in contrast, are in charge of operations and issues that directly involve students—for example, a Dean of Student Affairs and a Dean of Admissions. (These divisions and titles do not always apply, so learn the system at your school.)

Large institutions may be divided into *schools* that have separate administrative structures and staffs—for example, a School of Business or a School of Social Work. Each school normally has its own dean, and each department has a *chair* or *chairperson*—an instructor named to head the department.

One of the most important administrative offices for students is the *Office of the Dean of Student Affairs,* which, in many schools, is the centre for student services. Staff members try to answer your questions or direct you to others who can help. Learn how the student-help system works so you can identify specific people to turn to in case of a problem.

Administrative offices dealing with tuition issues and registration

Among the first administrators you will meet are those involved with tuition payments, financial aid, and registration.

The *bursar's office* (also called the *office of finance,* the *accounting office,* and *cashiering services*) issues bills for tuition and room and board and collects payments from students and financial aid sources. Direct your questions about tuition payments to this office.

The *financial aid office* helps students apply for financial aid and understand the eligibility requirements of different programs. The three main sources of financial aid are student loans, grants, and scholarships. You will learn more about these sources below.

The *registrar's office* (also called the *admissions office* in many community colleges) handles course registration, sends grades at the end of the semester, and compiles your official transcript, which is a comprehensive record of your courses and grades. Graduate schools require a copy of your official transcript before considering you for admission, as do many employers before considering you for a job. Transcripts are requested through the registrar's office.

Administrative services for students

A host of services is designed to help students adjust to and succeed in school and to deal with problems that arise. Here are some services you are likely to find:

Academic enhancement centres, including reading, writing, math, and study-skills centres. These centres offer consultations and tutoring to help students improve skills at all levels and become more confident. Don't be shy or embarrassed about using these services. If you find yourself struggling at the start of term, get help as soon as possible.

Academic computer centre. Most schools have sophisticated computer facilities equipped with computers, software, printers, and other equipment. At many schools, these facilities are open every day, and are staffed by technicians who can assist you with computer-related problems. Many facilities also offer training workshops.

Student housing or commuter affairs office. Most colleges and universities provide on-campus housing for undergraduate students. The housing office handles room and roommate placement, establishes behavioural standards, and deals with special situations and problems (e.g., an allergic student's need for a room air conditioner). Schools with commuting students may have programs to assist students with transportation and parking.

Health services. Your school's health centre is staffed with medical professionals who may include physicians, nurse practitioners, registered nurses, and support staff. If you are not feeling well, visit the clinic for help. Available services generally include prescriptions for common medicines, routine diagnostic tests, vaccinations, and first aid. All clinics are affiliated with nearby hospitals for emergency care. In addition, psychological counselling is sometimes offered through the health clinic, or it may have a separate facility. Remember that, although services are available, it is up to you to seek them out.

Career services. This office helps students find part-time and full-time jobs, as well as summer jobs and internships. Career offices have reference files on specific careers and employers. They also introduce students to the job-search process, helping them learn to write a résumé and cover letter and use the Internet to find job opportunities. Career offices often invite employers to interview students on campus and hold career fairs to introduce different companies and organizations. Summer internships and jobs are snapped up quickly, so check the office early and often to improve your chances. Visit the career office during your first year to begin developing an effective long-term career strategy.

Services for students with disabilities. Colleges and universities must provide disabled students with full access to facilities and programs. For students with documented disabilities, federal law requires that assistance be provided in the form of appropriate accommodations and aids. These range from interpreters for the hearing-impaired to readers and note-takers for the visually impaired to ramps for students in wheelchairs. If you have a disability, visit the Office of Students with Disabilities to learn what is offered. Remember, also, that this office is your advocate if you encounter problems.

Parking. Campus parking spaces can be scarce, with the best choices often going to students with seniority. (Disabled students are always given priority privileges.) Students with cars are generally required to register vehicles annually with campus security and get a parking sticker.

How to get academic help

Attending college or university is one of the best decisions you've made. However, deadlines, academic and social pressures, and simply being in new surroundings can make the experience stressful at times. (Chapter 10 talks more about stress management.) Understanding that help is available is the first step in helping yourself. Step two is actually *seeking* help from those who can give it. This requires knowing where to go and what assistance you can reasonably expect.

Before turning to others, try to find the answers you need on your own. For general guidance, check your college calendar, handbook, and website.

Help from instructors and teaching assistants

When you want to speak personally with an instructor for longer than a minute or two, choose your time carefully. Before or after class is usually not the best time for anything more than a quick question—instructors may be thinking about their lecture or be surrounded by other students with questions. When you need your instructor's full attention, there are three ways to communicate effectively—make an appointment during office hours, send email, and leave voice-mail messages.

Office hours. Instructors are required to keep regular office hours during which students can schedule personal conferences. Generally, these are posted during the first class, on instructors' office doors, and on instructors' or departmental websites. Always make an appointment for a conference; if you show up unannounced, there's a good chance your instructor will be busy. Face-to-face conferences are ideal for working through ideas and problems—for example, deciding on a term paper topic. Conferences are also the best setting to ask for advice—if, for example, you are considering majoring in the instructor's field and need guidance on courses.

Email. Use email to clarify assignments and assignment deadlines, to ask specific questions about lectures or readings, and to clarify what will be covered on a test. Try not to wait until the last minute to ask test-related questions; your instructor may not have time to respond. Instructors' email addresses are generally posted on the first day of class and may also be found in your student handbook or syllabus, which is a detailed description of what you will learn in the course. Links may also be available on your school's homepage. Some instructors also have ICQ or Windows Messenger in order to communicate with students.

Voice mail. If something comes up at the last minute, you can also leave a message in your instructor's office voice-mail box. Make your message short, but specific. Tell the instructor your reason for calling (*"This is Rick Jones from your ten o'clock Intro to Psychology class. I'm supposed to present my project today, but I'm sick in bed with a fever."*) and avoid general messages (*"This is Rick Jones from your ten o'clock class. Please call me at 555-5555."*). Avoid calling instructors at home unless they give specific permission to do so.

If you are taking a large lecture course, you may have a primary instructor plus a teaching assistant (TA) who meets with a small group of students on a regular basis. It is a good idea to approach your TA with course-related questions and problems before approaching the instructor. Because TAs deal with fewer students, they have more time to devote to specific issues.

Help from academic advisors

In most colleges and some universities, every student is assigned an advisor who is the student's personal liaison with the institution. (At some schools, students receive help at an advising centre.) Your advisor will help you choose courses every semester, plan your overall academic program, and understand college regulations including graduation requirements. He or she will point out possible consequences of your decisions (*"If you put off taking biology this semester, you're facing two lab courses next semester."*), help you shape your educational goals, and monitor your academic progress. Your advisor also knows about tutoring and personal counselling programs and may write recommendations when you are searching for a job.

It is important to remember that you, not your advisor, are responsible for your progress—for fully understanding graduation requirements, including credit requirements, and choosing the courses you need. Your advisor is there to help you with these critical decisions.

Help from a mentor

If you are fortunate, you will find a mentor at school—a trusted counsellor or guide who takes a special interest in helping you reach your goals. Mentoring relationships demand time and energy on both sides. A mentor can give you a private audience for questions and problems, advice tailored to your needs, support, guidance, and trust. A mentor cares about you enough to be devoted to your development. In return, you owe it to a mentor to be open to his or her ideas and, respectfully, to take advice into consideration. You and your mentor can learn from each other, receive positive energy from your relationship, and grow together.

Your mentor might be your faculty advisor, an instructor in your major or minor field of study, or an academic support instructor. You may also be drawn to someone outside school—a long-time friend whose judgment and experience you admire or a supervisor at work. Some schools have faculty or peer mentoring programs to match students with people who can help them. Check your student handbook or website or ask your faculty advisor if this is offered at your school.

Help from learning specialists

Almost everyone has difficulty in some aspect of learning, and you may view your struggles as simply an area of weakness. In contrast, people with diagnosed learning differences have conditions that make certain kinds of learning difficult. Some learning disabilities cause reading problems, some create difficulties in math, and still others make it difficult for students to process the language they hear.

If you have a learning disability, know that you are one of many. Colleges and universities are filled with students with diagnosed learning problems who get help, develop coping skills, and excel in their chosen fields. To succeed on your own terms, you have a responsibility to understand your disability, to become an advocate for your rights as a student with special needs, and to do your best to overcome your condition.

Identify your needs and seek assistance. If you are officially diagnosed with a learning disability, you are legally entitled to aid, and, in fact, the law requires schools to hire specialists to help you one-on-one. Armed with your test results and documentation, speak with your advisor about getting support that will help you learn. Among the services that may be available are testing accommodations (e.g., having extended time, working on a computer, or taking oral rather than written exams); books on tape; note-taking assistance (e.g., having a fellow student take notes for you or having access to the instructor's notes); taking a reduced course load; and auditing a course before you take it for credit.

What your school expects of you

Y ou are a full participant in your relationship with your post-secondary education. Much is expected of you, and you have the right to expect much in return. The specific expectations described in this section involve understanding financial aid, curriculum, and graduation requirements; choosing and registering for classes; following procedures; pursuing academic excellence; understanding and following your school's academic integrity policy or honour code; learning your school's computer system; and getting involved in extracurricular activities. Do your best to understand how to proceed in all these areas and, if you still have problems, ask for help—from instructors, administrators, advisors, mentors, experienced classmates, and family members.

Understand and apply for financial aid

Let's face it: post-secondary education in Canada isn't cheap. As a result, many students need some sort of financial help. Most sources of financial aid don't seek out recipients. It is up to you to learn how you (or you and your parents, if they currently help to support you) can finance your education. Visit your school's financial aid office, research what's available, weigh the pros and cons of each option, decide what works best, then apply early. Above all, think critically. Never assume that you are not eligible for aid. The types of aid available are student loans, grants, and scholarships.

Student loans

As the recipient of a student loan, you are responsible for paying back the amount you borrow, plus interest, according to a predetermined payment schedule that may stretch over a number of years. The amount you borrow is known as the loan *principal,* and *interest* is the fee that you pay for the privilege of using money that belongs to someone else.

The federal government administers or oversees most student loans. To receive aid from any federal program, you must be a citizen or eligible non-citizen and be enrolled in a program that meets government requirements. The federal government recently took over control of the Canada Student Loans Program. Applying for assistance, no matter what province you live in, is done with a single application form. Your application is evaluated for eligibility for several programs, including the Canada Millennium Scholarship Program, provincial loans, plus any bursaries and grants you may be entitled to. For information regarding student loans in Canada, get an application form from your school. You can also contact the Canada Student Loans Program, administered through Human Resources Development Canada at

Canada Student Loans Program
Human Resources Development Canada
P.O. Box 2090, Station "D"
Ottawa, ON K1P 6C6

You can also call them at 1-800-O CANADA (1-800-622-6232) or you can go to http://www.hrsdc.gc.ca/en/gateways/topics/cxp-gxr.shtml for the latest information available. There are many helpful online references for student loans, some of which enable you to apply online. Be sure to apply early. Get your application at least 2–3 months prior to the start of your studies to ensure it will have time to be processed.

Grants and scholarships

Unlike student loans, neither grants nor scholarships require repayment. Grants, funded by governments as well as private organizations, are awarded to students who show financial need. Scholarships may be financed by government or private organizations, schools, or individuals, and are awarded to students who show talent or ability in specified areas.

Even if you did not receive a grant or scholarship in your first year, you may be eligible for opportunities in other years of study. These opportunities are often based on grades and campus leadership and may be given by individual departments.

If you are receiving aid from your school, follow all the rules and regulations, including meeting application deadlines and remaining in good academic standing. In most cases, you will be required to reapply for aid every year.

Scholarships. Scholarships are given for various abilities and talents. They may reward academic achievement, exceptional abilities in sports or the arts, citizenship, or leadership. Certain scholarships are sponsored by government agencies. If you display exceptional ability and are disabled, female, of an ethnic background classified as a minority, or a child of someone who draws government benefits, you might find federal scholarship opportunities geared toward you.

All kinds of organizations offer scholarships. You may receive scholarships from individual departments at your school or from your school's independent scholarship funds, local organizations such as the Rotary Club, or privately operated aid foundations. Labour unions and companies may offer scholarships for children of employees. Membership groups, such as Scouting organizations or the YMCA/YWCA, might offer scholarships, and religious organizations are another source of money.

Researching grants and scholarships. It can take work to locate scholarships and work-study programs because many aren't widely advertised. Start digging at your financial aid office and visit your library, bookstore, and the Internet. Two good places to start looking are www.studentawards.com and www.scholarshipscanada.ca.

Understand curriculum and graduation requirements

Every school has requirements for diplomas and/or degrees that are stated in the calendar or on a website. Among the requirements you may encounter at your school are the following:

- The number of credits needed to graduate, including credits required in major and minor fields.
- Curriculum requirements, including specific course requirements. Your school may require a specified number of course hours or credits in the humanities, social sciences, and natural sciences, plus a foreign language and a computer-literacy course.
- Departmental major requirements, including the cumulative average needed for acceptance as a major in the department. For example,

you may be automatically accepted if your average is at least 60 per cent. Those with a lower average may require special approval and may be turned down.

Your goal is to remain in *good academic standing* throughout your post-secondary career as you pursue your academic goal.

Choose and register for classes

Choosing and registering for classes is challenging, especially the first time. Among the things you should consider as you scan your school's calendar and make your course selections are the following:

- Core/general requirements for graduation. You have to take these classes no matter what your major or program.

- Your major or minor or courses in departments you are considering as a major or minor.

- Electives you want to take because they sound interesting, even though they are out of your field. These include classes and teachers that the grapevine says are not to be missed.

In most schools, you can choose to attend a class without earning academic credit by *auditing* the class. Because tuition and fees are generally the same and seats are given on a space-available basis, why would you make this choice? The main reason is to explore different areas without worrying about a grade.

Once you decide on courses, but before you register, create a schedule that shows daily class times. If the first class meets at 8 a.m., ask yourself if you will be at your best at that early hour. It is always a good idea to create a back-up schedule, or even several alternatives, because you may be closed out of some classes. Show your ideas to your advisor for input and approval.

Actual course registration varies from school to school. Registration may take place through your school's computer network, via touch-tone phone, or in the school gym or student union. When you register, you may be asked to pay your tuition and other fees. If you are receiving financial aid, it is up to you to make sure that cheques from all aid sources have arrived at the school before registration. If they haven't, you'll probably need to get on the phone to expedite the payment.

Follow procedures

Your school is a bureaucratic organization, which means that you have to follow established rules and regulations. Normally, procedures are clear and not excessively burdensome, but they can still seem stressful the first time you do them. Among the most common procedures you will encounter are the following:

- Adding or dropping a class. This should be done within the first few days of the semester if you find that a course is not right for you or that there are better choices. Your advisor can tell you how to follow your school's drop/add procedures, which involve completing a form. Late-semester unexcused withdrawals (i.e., any withdrawal after a predetermined date) receive a failing grade. However, course withdrawals that are approved for medical problems, a death in the family, or other special circumstances have no impact on your average.

- **Taking an Incomplete.** If you can't finish your work due to circumstances beyond your control—an illness or injury, for example—many colleges and universities allow you to take a grade of *Incomplete* and make the work up at a later, specified time. You'll need approval from your instructor, and you'll also need to commit to making up the work during vacation or semester break.

- **Transferring schools.** If you are a student at a community college and intend to transfer to a university, or vice versa, be sure to take the courses required for admission to that school. In addition, be sure all your courses are transferable, which means they will be counted toward your degree at the university or community college. Schools generally have advisors to help students work through this process.

- **Taking a leave of absence.** There are many reasons students take a leave of absence for a semester or a year and then return. You may want time away from academics to think through your long-term goals, or you may be needed for a family emergency. If you are in good standing at your school, leaves are generally granted in consultation with your dean and advisor. In contrast, students with academic or disciplinary problems who take a leave may have to reapply for admission when their leave is complete. Check with your advisor regarding details.

Read your school's handbook about the various procedures used at your school. If you still have questions, speak with your advisor.

Pursue academic excellence

Your instructors expect you to do your best in their classes. Doing your best means that you attend every class with a positive attitude, arrive on time, complete assignments on schedule, listen attentively and participate in discussions, value honest scholarship, and seek help if you need it. In return for your efforts, you will learn a great deal and you will receive a course grade. Think of your instructor as the manager of a company. If you want to get the best performance review and the highest pay raise, you'll need to over-deliver on his or her expectations of you.

It is important to remember that your *work*—and not *you*—receives the grades. A *D* or an *F* does not diminish you as a person, but rather tells you that your efforts or work products are below what the instructor expects. Similarly, an *A* does not inflate your value as a person, but recognizes the superb quality of your academic performance.

Have academic integrity

Your school's academic integrity policy should be printed in your student handbook. This code defines the standards of ethical behaviour that are expected of you in your academic work and in your relationships with faculty, administrators, and fellow students. As you will see in Chapter 2, academic integrity is a commitment to five fundamental values: honesty, trust, fairness, respect, and responsibility. As a student enrolled in your school, you have agreed to abide by your school's honour code.

You have also agreed to suffer the consequences should you be discovered violating a core value. Different schools have different ways of dealing with alleged violations. In most cases, students are brought before a committee of instructors or a jury of students to determine whether the offence actually occurred. What happens to a student found guilty varies from school to school. Some penalties include expulsion, suspension, grade reduction, or course failure, depending on the offence.

Master the school's computer system

A large part of the communication and work that you do in college or university involves the computer. Here are some examples:

- Registering for classes.
- Accessing a web-based course syllabus and required-readings list.
- Emailing instructors and students for assignment clarification; receiving email responses.
- Tapping into library databases and the Internet for research.
- Completing assignments and writing papers on your word processor.
- Submitting papers via email to instructors.
- Creating spreadsheets for math and science classes.
- Emailing classmates to schedule group/team meetings.
- Receiving school-wide announcements via the school's computer network.
- Taking interactive quizzes.
- Downloading the latest plane/train/bus schedule via the Internet as you plan your trip home during a school break.

In most colleges and universities, it is no longer possible to manage without a computer—either your own, one borrowed from school, or one accessed in computer labs. Most residence rooms are now wired for computers, which gives students access to the campus network, including the library database.

Here are some suggestions for using your computer effectively:

- **Get trained.** Start by getting help to connect to your school's network. Then, take training classes to master word processing, data and spreadsheets, and the Internet. In some schools, these classes are required. If your typing skills are weak, take a course or use a software program to develop your skills.
- **Use computers to get information.** If you have specific questions about your school, check for answers on your school's website. You may find the information or the email address of a contact person. You must also learn to use the Internet for academic library research (see Chapter 7 for more information).

- **Be a safe and cautious user.** Although computers seem to be the answer to everything, they sometimes fail. To safeguard your work, use your computer carefully and with respect, especially if it belongs to someone else or your school. Second, create regular backups by saving your work onto the computer hard drive every few minutes. In addition, don't just rely on the hard drive; periodically back up your work in a secondary location such as on a diskette, a CD, or your pocket size USB drive.

- **Use computers for appropriate tasks.** A quick diversion to internet surfing or a computer game can help refresh you, but it can get out of hand. Try to stay away from these distractions altogether during study time and set strict time limits at other times to keep your academic focus. Remaining focused is especially important when you are using the computer lab and others are waiting their turn.

- **Protect yourself from trouble.** The following strategies will help:
  - Run virus checks on your personal machine and install and update an anti-virus program.
  - Don't reveal personal data, including financial data, to strangers you meet on the Internet.
  - Be reluctant to take part in chat rooms that are not part of your school's network. Locate chat rooms made up of fellow students and spend downtime visiting with others in cyberspace.
  - If you encounter a technical problem, talk to technicians in the computer lab. Their help can save you hours of time and frustration.

A special word about email

You may be required to communicate with your instructor, submit home-work, and even take exams via email. Every student who has access to email should spend time becoming proficient in electronic communication. Following are some important suggestions.

- **Use your school's email system.** Register for an email account at your school as soon as possible, even if you have a personal email address through another Internet service provider. Without this connection, you may not be able to receive school-wide emails or access electronic files at the school library.

- **Be careful of miscommunication.** Body language (vocal tone, facial expression, body position) can account for over 75 per cent of what you communicate face to face. With email, however, your words stand alone, forcing you to be careful about your content and tone. Try to be diplomatic and pleasant, and think before you respond to messages that upset you. If you write back too quickly, you may be sorry later.

- **Use effective writing techniques.** Your email tells a lot about you. To make the best impression—especially when communicating with an instructor or administrator—take the time to find the right words. Organize your thoughts and use proper spelling, punctuation, and grammar. Here are some additional tips that will make your emails easy to read: get to the point in the first paragraph, use short paragraphs, use headings to divide long emails into digestible sections, and use numbered and bulleted lists. Always proofread before hitting "send."

- **Rein in social emailing.** Prioritize your emailing. Respond to the most important and time-sensitive requests first, especially school-related ones. Save personal and conversational email for when you have down time.

The computer skills you learn in college or university will be invaluable at work and in your personal and community activities. Most of today's jobs require computer literacy, as well as the ability to continue to learn as technology changes.

Get involved

The post-secondary lifestyle gives you the opportunity to become involved in activities outside class. These activities enable you to meet people who share your interests and to develop teamwork and leadership skills. They also give you the chance to develop skills that may be important in your career. For example, you might join the Spanish Club to improve your language skills. Being connected to friends and a supportive network of people is one of the main reasons people stay in school instead of dropping out.

Choose activities you genuinely enjoy, and then decide on your level of involvement. Do you want to attend meetings from time to time or become a group leader? As a first-year student, you may want to try several activities before deciding on those that are right for you.

Some first-year students take on more than they can comfortably handle and neglect their studies. If you see that your grades are dropping, it may be time to reduce your activities and focus on your work. You should seek balance in your post-secondary life; too much of anything is not effective time management.

You are beginning the journey of your post-secondary education. The work you do in this course and in the remaining pages of *Keys to Success* will help you achieve your goals in your studies and in your personal life and career. As you move forward, think about the words Josh Billings, a 19th-century American writer, said over 100 years ago: *"Everyone who does the best he can do is a hero."* From this day forward, be your own personal hero.

WELCOME TO YOUR POST-SECONDARY CAREER

Opening Doors to Success

1

SUCCESSFUL INTELLIGENCE

PRACTICAL · CREATIVE · ANALYTICAL

"Successfully intelligent people . . . have a can-do attitude. They realize that the limits to what they can accomplish are often in what they tell themselves they cannot do, rather than in what they really cannot do."

ROBERT J. STERNBERG

You and your fellow students are embarking on a new phase of life—one that offers ideas, information, and skills in exchange for hard work and dedication. The tools you acquire in your post-secondary career will help you succeed in an ever-changing world where technology and the global marketplace are transforming the way you live and work. *Keys to Success* will help you learn successfully, graduate, and reap the personal and professional rewards of a solid education. This chapter gets you started with an overview of how being a "successfully intelligent," responsible, and forward-thinking student will help you face challenges head-on and achieve more than you ever imagined.

In this chapter you will explore answers to the following questions:

- Where are you now—and where can your education take you? 4

- How can successful intelligence help you achieve your goals? 8

- How can this book help you build successful intelligence? 10

- What actions will prepare you for post-secondary success? 13

- How can what you learn now help you succeed in school, work, and life? 19

- Successful Intelligence Wrap-Up 24

Chapter 1's
Successful Intelligence Skills

Analytical

- Evaluating your starting point as you begin post-secondary education
- Analyzing how successful intelligence can help you achieve goals
- Considering how specific actions promote success in post-secondary education

Creative

- Creating new ideas about post-secondary goals
- Developing a fresh understanding of your ability to grow
- Creating ways to benefit from failure

Practical

- How to follow the code of academic integrity
- How to work with others effectively
- How to become a lifelong learner

Where are you now—and where can your education take you?

GLOBAL MARKETPLACE

An interconnected marketplace, where companies do business without regard to time zones and boundaries, and where companies from all over the world compete directly for business.

Reflect on the road that brought you to this day. You completed high school or its equivalent, or perhaps you are upgrading your high school equivalency. You may have built life skills from experience as a partner or parent. You may have been employed in one or more jobs. You have enrolled in post-secondary education, found a way to pay for it, signed up for courses, and shown up for class. And, in deciding to pursue a degree or diploma, you chose to believe in your ability to accomplish goals.

To make the most of college, first understand its value. College or university is the ideal time to acquire skills that will serve you in the **global marketplace**, where workers in Canada work seamlessly with people in other parts of the world. Thomas Friedman, author of *The World Is Flat*, explains how the digital revolution has transformed the working environment you will enter after college: "It is now possible for more people than ever to collaborate and compete in real time with more other people on more different kinds of work from more different corners of the planet and on a more equal footing than in any previous time in the history of the world—using computers, e-mail, networks, teleconferencing, and dynamic new software."[1] This means that you may be doing *knowledge work* and other jobs in conjunction with, or in competition with, highly trained and motivated people from around the world. Reaching your potential has never been more crucial to your success. You will be up to the task of succeeding in the global marketplace if you do the following:

- Acquire solid study skills
- Commit to lifelong learning and job training
- Persevere despite obstacles
- Perform high-quality work on a consistent basis
- Embrace change as a way of life

If your work in college or university helped you succeed only in the classroom, the benefit of your learning wouldn't last beyond graduation day. However, learning is a tool for life, and a post-secondary education is designed to serve you far beyond the classroom. Here are a few important "life success goals" that post-secondary education can help you achieve:

Life Success Goal: Increased employability and earning potential. Getting a degree greatly increases your chances of finding and keeping a high-level, well-paying job. According to Statistics Canada, "higher education is a gateway to higher earnings."[2] Statistically speaking, the more education you have, the more you earn (see Key 1.1).

Education and income.

Median annual income of persons by their highest degree attained, 2000

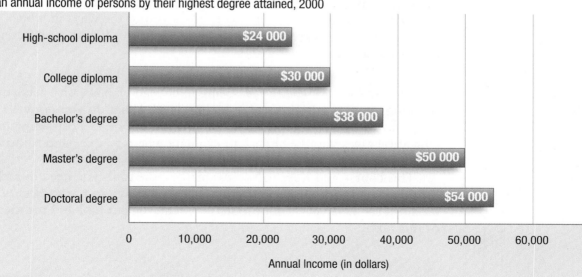

Source: Statistics Canada, "Education in Canada 2000," p. 124.

Life Success Goal: Preparation for career success. Your coursework will give you the knowledge and hands-on skills you need to achieve your career goals. It will also expose you to a variety of careers related to your intended course of study, whether that means working toward a certificate, diploma, or degree. Completing college and/or university will open career doors that are otherwise closed.

This book will frequently refer to *Employability Skills 2000+*, a profile developed by the Conference Board of Canada. The Conference Board is a research organization whose members include Canadian corporations and the government. "Employability skills" are defined as "the skills you need to enter, stay in, and progress in the world of work—whether you work on your own or as part of a team."[3] Many Canadian companies helped to determine which skills were preferred by Canadian businesses. These were broken down into three categories: fundamental skills, personal management skills, and teamwork skills (see Key 1.2). This book will place skills learned in the classroom into the broader context of employability skills. These skills you will learn are not just skills specific to your field of study—they are transferable skills useful in almost all career choices.

Life Success Goal: Smart personal health choices. The more educated you are, the more likely you are to take care of your physical and mental health. A post-secondary education prepares you with health-related information that you will use over your lifetime, helping you to practise wellness through positive actions and to avoid practices with the potential to harm.

Life Success Goal: Active community involvement and an appreciation of different cultures. Going to college prepares you to understand complex political, economic, and social forces that affect you and others. This understanding is the basis for good citizenship and encourages community involvement. Your education also exposes you to the ways in which people and cultures are different and the ways in which these differences affect world affairs.

Life Success Goal: Self-knowledge. Being in college or university gets you thinking about yourself on a big picture level. What do you do well? What do you want out of life? What can you improve? Post-secondary education gives you the chance to evaluate where you are and to decide where you want to be.

This course and *Keys to Success* provide the tools you need to kick off this exploration. Especially crucial is your ability to use *successful intelligence*—your most important goal-achievement tool and the theme of this text.

Employability skills 2000+.

The skills you need to enter, stay in, and progress in the world of work—whether you work on your own or as a part of a team.

These skills can also be applied and used beyond the workplace in a range of daily activities.

Fundamental Skills	**Personal Management Skills**	**Teamwork Skills**
The skills needed as a base for further development	The personal skills, attitudes, and behaviours that drive one's potential for growth	The skills and attributes needed to contribute productively

You will be better prepared to progress in the world of work when you can:

Communicate
- read and understand information presented in a variety of forms (e. g., words, graphs, charts, diagrams)
- write and speak so others pay attention and understand
- listen and ask questions to understand and appreciate the points of view of others
- share information using a range of information and communications technologies (e.g., voice, e-mail, computers)
- use relevant scientific, technological, and mathematical knowledge and skills to explain or clarify ideas

Manage Information
- locate, gather, and organize information using appropriate technology and information systems
- access, analyze, and apply knowledge and skills from various disciplines (e. g., the arts, languages, science, technology, mathematics, social sciences, and the humanities)

Use Numbers
- decide what needs to be measured or calculated
- observe and record data using appropriate methods, tools, and technology
- make estimates and verify calculations

Think & Solve Problems
- assess situations and identify problems
- seek different points of view and evaluate them based on facts
- recognize the human, interpersonal, technical, scientific, and mathematical dimensions of a problem
- identify the root cause of a problem
- be creative and innovative in exploring possible solutions
- readily use science, technology, and mathematics as ways to think, gain, and share knowledge, solve problems, and make decisions
- evaluate solutions to make recommendations or decisions
- implement solutions
- check to see if a solution works, and act on opportunities for improvement

You will be able to offer yourself greater possibilities for achievement when you can:

Demonstrate Positive Attitudes & Behaviours
- feel good about yourself and be confident
- deal with people, problems, and situations with honesty, integrity, and personal ethics
- recognize your own and other people's good efforts
- take care of your personal health
- show interest, initiative, and effort

Be Responsible
- set goals and priorities balancing work and personal life
- plan and manage time, money, and other resources to achieve goals
- assess, weigh, and manage risk
- be accountable for your actions and the actions of your group
- be socially responsible and contribute to your community

Be Adaptable
- work independently or as a part of a team
- carry out multiple tasks or projects
- be innovative and resourceful: identify and suggest alternative ways to achieve goals and get the job done
- be open and respond constructively to change
- learn from your mistakes and accept feedback
- cope with uncertainty

Learn Continuously
- be willing to learn and grow continuously
- assess personal strengths and areas for development
- set your own learning goals
- identify and access learning sources and opportunities
- plan for and achieve your learning goals

Work Safely
- be aware of personal and group health and safety practices and procedures, and act in accordance with these

You will be better prepared to add value to the outcomes of a task, project, or team when you can:

Work with Others
- understand and work within the dynamics of a group
- ensure that a team's purpose and objectives are clear
- be flexible: respect and be open to and supportive of the thoughts, opinions, and contributions of others in a group
- recognize and respect people's diversity, individual differences, and perspectives
- accept and provide feedback in a constructive and considerate manner
- contribute to a team by sharing information and expertise
- lead or support when appropriate, motivating a group for high performance
- understand the role of conflict in a group to reach solutions
- manage and resolve conflict when appropriate

Participate in Projects & Tasks
- plan, design, or carry out a project or task from start to finish with well-defined objectives and outcomes
- develop a plan, seek feedback, test, revise, and implement
- work to agreed quality standards and specifications
- select and use appropriate tools and technology for a task or project
- adapt to changing requirements and information
- continuously monitor the success of a project or task and identify ways to improve

255 Smyth Road, Ottawa
ON K1H 8M7 Canada
Tel. (613) 526-3280
Fax (613) 526-4857
Internet: www.conferenceboard.ca/education

Source: Conference Board of Canada, Employability Skills 2000+ Profile, **www.conferenceboard.ca/education/learning-tools/pdfs/esp2000.pdf.**

How can *successful intelligence* help you achieve your goals?

Think about how you would define *intelligence*. Chances are that you, like many people, believe that people are born with a certain, unchangeable amount of intelligence and that this has a significant effect on the ability to succeed. Another fairly common belief is that standardized tests, such as IQ (intelligence quotient) tests, accurately measure a person's intelligence and are predictors of success.

Psychologist and Yale professor Robert J. Sternberg views intelligence differently. His life experiences convinced him that traditional intelligence measurements lock people into poor performances and often do not accurately reflect their potential for life success. When test anxiety caused Sternberg to score poorly on IQ and other standardized tests during elementary school, he delivered exactly what was expected of him—very little. In Grade 4, a teacher saw something in him. By letting him know that she expected more than he had ever shown he could give, she provided a spark that turned his life around.

According to Sternberg, standardized tests measure **inert intelligence**—that is, they require passive repetition rather than goal-directed thinking. He further explains that those who score well on tests may have strong recall and analytical skills but do not necessarily have the power to make things happen in the real world.[4] That power to put information to work is critical to your success. No matter how high you score on a library science test, for example, your knowledge won't serve you unless you can use it to research a topic successfully.

Sternberg is also convinced that intelligence is *not* a fixed quantity; people have the capacity to increase intelligence as they learn and grow. Recent studies support this perspective, showing that the brain continues to develop throughout life if you continue to learn new things.[5] To make this development happen, you need to actively challenge yourself and believe in your ability to grow. Psychologist Carol Dweck says that "people with a growth mindset thrive when they're stretching themselves."[6] Conversely, people who shy away from challenge will experience less growth. Challenge yourself, and your value to yourself and to others will grow.

INERT INTELLIGENCE

Passive recall and analysis of learned information rather than goal-directed thinking linked to real-world activities.

Defining successful intelligence

In his book *Successful Intelligence: How Practical and Creative Intelligence Determine Success in Life*, Sternberg focuses on what he calls *successful intelligence*—"the kind of intelligence used to achieve important goals."[7] Successful intelligence better predicts life success than any IQ test because it focuses largely on actions—what you do to achieve your goals—instead of just on recall and analysis.

Sternberg uses this story to illustrate the impact of successful intelligence:

Two boys are walking in a forest. They are quite different. The first boy's teachers think he is smart, his parents think he is smart, and as a result, he thinks he is smart. He has good test scores, good grades, and other good paper credentials that will get him far in his scholastic life. Few people consider the second boy smart. His test scores are nothing great, his grades aren't so good, and his other paper credentials are, in general, marginal. At best, people would call him shrewd or street smart.

As the two boys walk along in the forest, they encounter a problem—a huge, furious, hungry-looking grizzly bear, charging straight at them. The first boy, calculating that the grizzly bear will overtake them in 17.3 seconds, panics. In this state, he looks at the second boy, who is calmly taking off his hiking boots and putting on his jogging shoes. The first boy says to the second boy, "You must be crazy. There is no way you are going to outrun that grizzly bear!" The second boy replies, "That's true. But all I have to do is outrun you!"[8]

This story shows that successful problem solving and decision making require more than book smarts. When confronted with a problem, using only analytical thinking put the first boy at a disadvantage. On the other hand, the second boy thought in different ways; he analyzed the situation, creatively considered the options, and took practical action. He asked and answered questions. He knew his purpose. And he lived to tell the tale.

Sternberg breaks successful intelligence into three parts or abilities: *Analytical* thinking, *creative* thinking, and *practical* thinking.

- *Analytical thinking*—commonly known as critical thinking—involves analyzing and evaluating information, often in order to work through a problem or decision. Analytical thinking is largely responsible for school success and is recognized and measured through traditional testing methods.
- *Creative thinking* involves generating new and different ideas and approaches to problems, and, often, viewing the world in ways that disregard convention.
- *Practical thinking* means putting what you've learned into action in order to solve a problem or make a decision. Practical thinking enables you to accomplish goals despite real-world obstacles.

These ways of thinking work together to move you toward a goal, as Sternberg describes:

> Analytical thinking is required to solve problems and to judge the quality of ideas. Creative intelligence is required to formulate good problems and ideas in the first place. Practical intelligence is needed to use the ideas and their analysis in an effective way in one's everyday life.[9]

Here are two examples that illustrate how this works.

Successful intelligence in a study group—reaching for the goal of helping each other learn

- **Analyze** the concepts you must learn, including how they relate to what you already know.

- **Create** humorous memory games to help you remember key concepts.
- **Think practically** about who in the group does what best, and assign tasks according to what you discover.

Successful intelligence in considering an academic path—reaching for the goal of declaring a major in university or a program of study in college

- **Analyze** what you do well, what you like to do. Then analyze the course offerings in your college catalogue until you come up with one or more that seem to match up with your strengths.
- **Create** a dream career, then work backward to come up with majors and programs that might support it. For example, if you want to be a science writer, consider majoring in biology and minoring in journalism.
- **Think practically** about your major or program of study by talking with students and instructors in the department, looking at course requirements, and interviewing professionals in the fields that interest you.

© neoblues—Fotolia.com

Why is successful intelligence your key to success? It helps you understand how learning propels you toward goals, boosting your desire to learn. It gives you ways to move toward those goals, increasing your willingness to work hard. It helps you to maximize strengths and compensate for weaknesses, leading to a greater ability to capitalize on who you are and what you can do. It also increases your value in school and on the job: *People with highly developed critical, creative, and practical thinking skills are in demand because they can apply what they know to new situations, innovate, and accomplish their goals.*

The three elements of successful intelligence can give all kinds of learners a more positive outlook on their abilities. Students who have trouble with tests and other analytical skills can see that creative and practical thinking also plays a significant role in success. Students who test well but have trouble using their knowledge to innovate and make things happen can develop a team approach to success as they work to improve their creative and practical skills. Everyone can find room, and ways, to grow.

How can this book help you build *successful intelligence?*

Chapter content

Each chapter incorporates successful intelligence with the following:

- A visual overview of the analytical, creative, and practical tools that you will gather in the chapter

- Contextual connections to analytical, creative, and practical thinking
- Accounts and examples from students, professors, and professionals that show how people use various analytical, creative, and practical skills to accomplish goals
- A *Successful Intelligence Wrap-Up* that summarizes the analytical, creative, and practical skills you have explored

In addition, Chapter 4—the chapter on thinking—goes into more detail about all three skills.

In-chapter activities

Within the text of each chapter, you will find three activities that help you build your successful intelligence skills:

- *Get Analytical* gives you an opportunity to develop your own analytical skills through your analysis of a chapter topic.
- *Get Creative* prompts you to develop your own creative skills as you think innovatively about chapter material.
- *Get Practical* provides you with a chance to develop your own practical skills through the experience of applying an idea from the chapter.

In this chapter, these exercises take the form of mini-assessments, tools that will help you get to know yourself as an analytical, creative, and practical thinker. With self-knowledge as the starting point, you will develop your successful intelligence throughout this book. Chapter 12 will provide an opportunity for you to assess yourself once again and consider how you have grown in each area.

End-of-chapter exercises

Here you have the opportunity to combine what you have learned and apply it to important tasks in several ways, as follows:

- *Successful Intelligence: Think, Create, Apply* unites the three aspects of successful intelligence.
- *Teamwork: Create Solutions Together* encourages you to apply various successful intelligence elements to a group setting.
- *Writing: Journal and Put Skills to Work* provides an opportunity to put analysis, creative thoughts, and practical ideas down in words.
- *Personal Portfolio: Prepare for Career Success* builds practical skills and a portfolio of information that promote career success.

Although successful intelligence is the overarching framework of how you will achieve college and life goals, many specific elements move you toward those goals day by day. Explore attitudes and actions that prepare you for success.

Assess Yourself as an Analytical Thinker

For each statement, circle the number that feels right to you, from 1 for "not at all true for me" to 5 for "very true for me."

1. I recognize and define problems effectively. 1 2 3 4 5

2. I see myself as a "thinker," "analytical," "studious." 1 2 3 4 5

3. When working on a problem in a group setting, I like to break down the problem into its components and evaluate them. 1 2 3 4 5

4. I need to see convincing evidence before accepting information as fact. 1 2 3 4 5

5. I weigh the pros and cons of plans and ideas before taking action. 1 2 3 4 5

6. I tend to make connections among pieces of information by categorizing them. 1 2 3 4 5

7. Impulsive, spontaneous decision making worries me. 1 2 3 4 5

8. I like to analyze causes and effects when making a decision. 1 2 3 4 5

9. I monitor my progress toward goals. 1 2 3 4 5

10. Once I reach a goal, I evaluate the process to see how effective it was. 1 2 3 4 5

Total your answers here: _____

If your total ranges from 38–50, you consider your analytical thinking skills to be *strong*.

If your total ranges from 24–37, you consider your analytical thinking skills to be *average*.

If your total ranges from 10–23, you consider your analytical thinking skills to be *weak*.

Remember that you can improve your analytical thinking skills with focus and practice.

What actions will prepare you for post-secondary success?

Preparing for post-secondary success is as much a state of mind as it is making sure you take specific actions. The following section points to the basics you need—in actions as well as attitude—to achieve your goals. Always remember that you are your own manager, in charge of meeting your obligations and making decisions that move you toward your goals.

Get motivated

Success is a process, not a fixed mark—and **motivation** is what keeps the process in motion. Motivation is the energy that fuels your drive to achieve. Successful people are those who can consistently motivate themselves to learn, grow, and work toward goals.

Post-secondary education provides an opportunity for you to discover the goals most important to you and build the motivation it takes to achieve them. Wherever you start, and whatever obstacles you encounter on the way, your motivation can help lead you to the future you envision.

What motivates you? People have all kinds of different *motivators*—goals or ideas that move them forward. For example, some potential motivators for attending school could be learning a marketable skill, supporting a family, or self-improvement. Furthermore, motivators can change with time or with different situations. A student might begin work on a course feeling motivated by a desire to earn a particular grade, and later, becoming interested in the subject, he or she becomes motivated by a desire to master the material.

From time to time, everyone experiences a loss of motivation, whether in the short term or for a longer spell. How can you build motivation or renew lost motivation? First, start on the path. Just beginning makes you feel better as you work toward your goals. Newton's first law of motion, a law of physics, says that things in motion tend to stay in motion and things at rest tend to stay at rest. Be a thing in motion.

Second, explore the following motivation-boosting strategies—making a commitment, developing positive habits, being responsible, building self-esteem, and facing your fears. Explore them, and experiment to see what helps most. You might use them in combination, focus on the ones that have the most positive effects on you, or try them out one by one.

Finally, reading and thinking about the Stressbuster stories in each chapter will give you real-world insight into what it takes to sustain motivation in the face of difficult obstacles. Even if you have never experienced such obstacles, let the courage of the people profiled inspire you to have confidence about your own life. If they can leap their hurdles successfully, so can you.

> **MOTIVATION**
>
> A force that moves a person to action; often inspired by an idea, a fact, an event, or a goal.

> ### Successful Intelligence Connections Online
>
> Listen to author Sarah Kravits describe how to use analytical, creative, and practical intelligence to build and sustain motivation.
>
> Go to the *Keys to Success* Companion Website at www.pearsoned.ca/carter to listen or download as a podcast.

Make a commitment

COMMITMENT

1. A pledge or promise to do something, or
2. dedication to a long-term course of action.

How do you focus the energy of motivation? Make a **commitment.** Commitment means that you do what you say you will do. When you honour a commitment to an academic goal, a career dream, or a self-improvement task, you prove to yourself and others that your intentions can be trusted. Commitment often stretches over a period of time; you hold yourself to a promise for as long as necessary to reach your goal.

How do you go about making and keeping a commitment?

- State your commitment concretely. Set a clear goal and break it into manageable pieces. Be specific; for example, say, "I'm going to turn in the weekly essay assignments on time," rather than "I'm going to do my best work in this course." Emphasize to yourself what you will gain from this commitment.

- Take the first step. Sometimes, feeling overwhelmed can immobilize you. Decide on the first step of your commitment and take it today. Then continue a day at a time, breaking tasks into small steps.

- Stay aware of each commitment. Keep a list of commitments in your planner, on your refrigerator, or on your computer. If they involve events or projects that take place on specific dates, note them on a calendar. Talk about them with someone you trust to help you stay on track.

- Keep an eye on your progress. You're not a failure if you lose steam; it's normal. Recharge by reflecting on the positive effects of your commitment and what you have already achieved.

- Reward yourself as you move ahead. Rewards help you feel good about what you've accomplished so far and can help keep you going. Treat yourself to dinner with a friend, a new music download or DVD, or a movie night.

For example, you might make this commitment: "I will write in my journal every night before going to sleep." You make journal entries for two weeks and then evaluate what positive effects this daily practice has had on your writing ability. If you stop writing for a time, you can renew your commitment by reminding yourself of how keeping a journal has improved your writing ability and relieved your stress. You might boost your commitment by telling a partner or housemate to check on you.

Making commitments helps you keep a steady focus on your most important goals. It gives you a sense of accomplishment as you experience gradual growth and progress.

Develop positive habits

HABIT

A preference for a particular action that you do a certain way, and often on a regular basis or at certain times.

People have all kinds of **habits**—some you may consider "bad" and others "good." Bad habits stall motivation and prevent you from reaching important goals. Some bad habits, such as chronic lateness, cause obvious problems. Other habits, such as surfing the internet, may not seem bad until you realize that you needed to spend those hours studying.

Good habits are those that bring the kind of positive effects that keep motivation high. You often have to wait longer and work harder to see a reward for good habits, which makes them harder to maintain. If you reduce your nights out to gain study time, for example, your marks won't improve in a week. Changing a habit is a process; trust that the rewards are somewhere down the road.

Look at the positive and negative effects of your habits to decide which you want to keep and which you need to change or improve. Take the following steps to evaluate a habit and, if necessary, make a change (if the habit has more negative effects than positive ones). Don't try to change more than one habit at a time—trying to reach perfection in everything all at once can overwhelm you.

1. *Define and evaluate the habit.* Name your habit and look at the negative and positive effects. If there are more negatives than positives, it is most likely a habit worth changing.

2. *Decide to keep or change the habit.* Until you are convinced that you will receive a benefit, efforts to change will not get you far. Commit to a change if you see too many negative effects.

3. *Start today—and keep it up.* Don't put it off until after this week, after the family reunion, or after the semester. Each day gained is a day you can benefit from a new lifestyle. To have the best chance at changing a habit, be consistent for at least three weeks so that you become accustomed to the new habit.

4. *Reward positive steps.* Choose a reward that encourages you to stay on target. If you earn a good grade, for example, treat yourself to one night out instead of slacking off on studying for all of the following week.

Finally, don't get too discouraged if the process seems difficult. Rarely does someone make the decision to change and do so without a setback or two. Take it one step at a time; when you lose steam, reflect on what you stand to gain. With persistence and positive thinking, you can reach your goal.

Be responsible

In your post-secondary career, you are in charge of your life in a way that you may never have been before. Even if you have lived on your own and held a job, helped raise a family, or both, post-secondary education adds greatly to that responsibility. You are responsible for making decisions that keep you in motion and avoiding choices that stall you in your tracks. You are your own manager.

Taking responsibility is all about living up to your obligations, both those that are imposed on you and those that you impose on yourself. Through action, you prove that you are responsible—think of it as "response-able": able to respond. When something has to be done, a responsible person does it—as efficiently as possible and to the best of his or her ability.

Responsibility means action. Taking responsibility is taking action—and doing it reliably. In college or university, responsible people can be trusted to live up to obligations like these:

- Attending class and participating in activities and discussions
- Completing reading and assignments on time
- Communicating with instructors and fellow students

These actions may sound mundane to you, everyday requirements that don't have much bearing on the greater goals in your life. However, they are the building blocks of responsibility that get you where you want to go. Here's why:

- **Everyday responsibilities get you in the action habit.** As with any other habit, the more you do something, the more it becomes second nature. The more often you complete and turn in assignments on time, for example, the more likely you are to stay on top of your job tasks down the road when you are on a tight deadline.

- **The small accomplishments make a big impression.** When you show up to class, pay attention, contribute, and work hard, you send a message. An instructor who observes these behaviours is more likely to trust and respect you. People who trust you may give you increasing power and opportunities for growth because you have shown that you are capable of making the best of both.

- **Fulfilling day-to-day responsibilities gives you freedom.** The more responsible you are, and the more responsibilities you take on, the more those around you will give you the freedom to handle situations and problems on your own. You will be perceived as a fully functioning team member who can be counted on to pull his or her share of the load, no matter what the circumstances.

INITIATIVE

The power to begin or to follow through energetically with a plan or task; determination.

Responsibility means initiative. When you show **initiative**, you push yourself to take that first, often difficult, step. Initiative is the spark plug of responsibility—it jump-starts you into action. By taking initiative, you respond quickly and continually to changes that occur.

Initiative means that you make a move on your own instead of waiting for people, rules, requirements, or circumstances to push you. You show initiative when you go to a counsellor for help with a problem, make an appointment with an instructor to discuss an assignment, talk to a friend about a conflict, speak up in class, find a better way to do a task at work, vote in an election, or start an exercise program. Once you take that first step, it is often easier to keep your momentum going and continue to act responsibly.

Responsibility can take enormous effort. Remember that you gain self-respect when you prove that you can live up to your promises.

Face your fears

Everyone experiences fear. Anything unknown—new people, experiences, challenges, situations—can be frightening. The changes involved in pursuing an education, for example, can inspire fear. You may wonder if you can handle the work, if you have chosen the right school or program, or if your education will prepare you to find a job that you like and that pays well.

If your fears become overwhelming, they can derail your motivation. Some people give in to fear because they feel safer with the familiar, even if it doesn't make them happy. Ultimately, though, giving in to fear by giving up on your motivation may keep you from living the life you have envisioned.

The challenges you face as you work toward your goals demand a willingness to face your fears and push your limits. The following steps will help you work through fear with courage:

1. *Acknowledge fears.* The act of naming your fear begins to lessen its hold on you. Be specific. Knowing that you fear taking a biology course may not inspire you to action, whereas focusing on your fear of working with live mice in biology lab gives you something tangible to deal with.

2. *Examine fears.* Sometimes one fear hides a larger one. If you fear a test, determine whether you fear the test itself or the fact that if you pass it, you will have to take a tougher class next. If you fear the test, take steps to prepare for it. If you fear the next class, you might talk with your instructor about it.

3. *Develop a plan of attack.* Evaluate what will help you overcome your fear. For example, if you are scared of reading Shakespeare, help yourself by asking your instructor for advice, going over assigned plays with a study group, and watching a Shakespearean movie.

4. *Move ahead with your plan.* Courage is the key to moving ahead. Take the steps that help you to confront and move beyond your fears.

As you work through your fears, talk about them with people you trust. Everyone has fears, and when people share strategies, everyone benefits.

Build self-esteem

When people believe in their value and capabilities, their **self-esteem** fuels their motivation to succeed. Belief, though, is only half the game. The other half is the action and effort that help you feel that you have earned your self-esteem. Rick Pitino, a highly successful basketball coach, discusses developing self-esteem in his book *Success Is a Choice*: "Self-esteem is directly linked to deserving success. If you have established a great work ethic and have begun the discipline that is inherent with that, you will automatically begin to feel better about yourself. It's all interrelated. You must deserve victory to feel good about yourself."[10]

Building self-esteem, therefore, involves both *thinking positively* and *taking action.* Together, they help you generate the belief in yourself that keeps you motivated.

Think positively. Attitudes influence your choices and affect how you perceive and relate to others. A positive attitude can open your mind to learning experiences and inspire you to action. If, for example, you keep an open mind in a course that at first seems like a waste of time, you might discover that the course teaches you something valuable. You have the power to create your own reality, and with a positive attitude you can make that reality a positive one.

One way to create a positive attitude is through **positive self-talk.** When you hear negative thoughts in your mind ("I'm not very smart"), replace them with positive ones ("It won't be easy, but I'm smart enough

SELF-ESTEEM
A strong and deeply felt belief that you as a person have value in the world.

POSITIVE SELF-TALK
Supportive and positive thoughts and ideas that a person communicates to himself or herself.

to figure it out"). You would probably never criticize a good friend in the same way that you sometimes criticize yourself. These hints will help you put positive self-talk into action:

- **Stop negative talk in its tracks.** If you catch yourself thinking, "I can never write a decent paper," stop and say to yourself, "I can write better than that and next time I will." Then think about some specific steps you can take to improve your writing.

- **Pay yourself a compliment.** Note your successes. Be specific: "I have really improved my spelling and proofreading." Some people keep a list of positive statements about themselves in a notebook or use calendars with daily affirmations. These are great reminders of positive self-talk.

- **Replace words of obligation with words of personal intent.**

  | I should | *becomes* | I choose to. |
  | I'll try | *becomes* | I will. |

Words of intent give you power and control because they imply a personal decision to act. For example, when you say, "I have to be in class by nine o'clock," you're saying that someone else has power over you and has handed you a required obligation. When you say, "I want to be in class by nine o'clock because I don't want to miss anything I need to learn," you're saying that the choice is yours.

It can sometimes be difficult to think positively. If you have a deep-rooted feeling of unworthiness, you may want to see a counsellor. Many people have benefited from skilled professional advice.

Take action. Although thinking positively sets the tone for success, it cannot get you there by itself. You have to take action. Without action, positive thoughts become empty statements or even lies.

Consider, for example, a student in a first year English writing class. This student thinks every possible positive thought: "I am a great student. I know how to write well. I can get a B in this class. I will succeed in school." And so on. She even writes her thoughts down on notes and posts them where she can see them. Then, during the semester, she misses about one-third of the class meetings, turns in some of her papers late, and completely forgets a couple of assignments. She doesn't make use of opportunities to work with her study partner. At the end of the course, when she barely passes, she wonders how things went so wrong when she had such a positive attitude.

This student did not succeed because she did not earn her belief in herself through action and effort. By the end of a semester like this, positive thoughts look like lies. "If I can get a B, why did I get a D? If I am such a great student, why did I barely make it through this course?" Eventually, with nothing to support them, the positive thoughts disappear, and with neither positive thoughts nor action, a student will have a hard time achieving any level of success.

Following are some ways to get moving in a positive direction:

- **Build your own code of discipline.** Develop general guidelines to follow, based on what actions are important to your success. Perhaps your top priorities are personal relationships and achievement in school. Construct each day's goals and actions so that they help you achieve your larger objectives.

- **Make action plans and follow through.** Figure out how you plan to take action for any situation, so that, for example, "I am a great student" is backed up by specific actions to ensure success. When you have a plan, just do it. Only after taking action can you reap the benefit.

- **Acknowledge every step.** Even the smallest action is worth your attention because every action reinforces a positive thought and builds self-esteem. First you believe that you are a good student, then you work hard in class, then you do well on a test, then you believe more emphatically that you are a good student, then you complete a successful group project, then you feel even better about yourself, and so on.

The process of building and maintaining self-esteem involves many successes and disappointments. Only by having a true sense of self-esteem, though, can you achieve your dreams. You are in control of your self-esteem because you alone are ultimately responsible for your thoughts and actions. Do what it takes to both believe in yourself and take the action that anchors and inspires that belief.

Believing in yourself helps you make good choices. When your self-esteem is strong, you are more likely to choose actions that you can be proud of.

How can *what you learn now* help you succeed in school, work, and life?

In his book *TechnoTrends—24 Technologies That Will Revolutionize Our Lives*, futurist Daniel Burns describes a tomorrow that is linked to continuing education: "The future belongs to those who are capable of being retrained again and again," he says. "Think of it as periodically upgrading your human assets throughout your career. . . . Humans are infinitely upgradeable, but it does require an investment" in lifelong learning.[11] In *Boom, Bust & Echo 2000*, David Foot and Daniel Stoffman claim that jobs for Canadians without college or university education will continue to disappear.[12] Colleges and universities are the ideal training grounds for learning skills that will serve you throughout your life.

Education prepares you to learn from failure and celebrate success

Every life has problems to be solved and difficult decisions to be made. Even the most successful people and organizations make mistakes and experience failures. There is a lot to be gained from failing. In fact, failure is one of the greatest teachers. Failure is an opportunity to realize what you didn't know so that you can learn and improve. What you learn from a failure will most likely stay with you more intensely and guide you more effectively than many other things you learn.

Post-secondary education brings new challenges, and with them come situations in which you may fail. When you face difficult obstacles, let yourself down or disappoint others, or make mistakes, what is important is how you deal with the situation. Although it's human to pretend a failure didn't happen, to blame yourself or blame someone else, choices like these can deny you valuable lessons. If you can accept failure as part of life, forgive yourself, and learn from it, you will be able to pick yourself up and keep improving.

Learning from failure. Learning from your failures and mistakes involves careful thinking. One useful course of action is to first look at what happened, make any improvements that you can, and finally decide how to change your action or approach in the future. For example, imagine that, after a long night of studying for a test, you forgot that you had a deadline for a five-page paper the next day.

Look at what happened. Your exhaustion and concern about the test caused you to forget to check your planner to see what else was on your plate. Now you may face a lower mark on your paper if you turn it in late, plus you may be inclined to rush it and quickly turn in a paper that isn't as good as it could be.

Make any possible improvements on the situation. You could visit your instructor during office hours or send an email, explain the situation, and ask if you can have a brief extension on the paper.

Make changes for the future. You can set a goal to note deadlines in a bright colour and to check your planner more often. You can also try to arrange your study schedule so that you will be less exhausted.

Facing failure can be hard. Here are some ways to boost your outlook when failure gets you down:

- **Stay aware of the fact that you are a capable, valuable person.** Focus your energy on your best abilities and know that you have the strength to try again.
- **Share your thoughts and disappointment with others.** Exchange creative energy that can help you learn from failures rather than having a mutual gripe session.
- **Look on the bright side.** At worst, you flunk the test or paper. At best, you have learned a lesson that will help you avoid similar situations in the future. There might even be other positive results.

Finally, remember that your value as a human being does not diminish when you make a mistake. Expect that you always will do the best that you can, knowing that just getting through another day as a student, employee, or parent is a success. In addition, because failure is a frequent result of risk taking, people who can manage failure show that they have the courage to take risks and learn. Employers often value risk takers who sometimes fail more than they value people who avoid failure by never going beyond the status quo.

Assess Yourself as a Creative Thinker

For each statement, circle the number that feels right to you, from 1 for "not at all true for me" to 5 for "very true for me."

1. I tend to question rules and regulations. 1 2 3 4 5

2. I see myself as "unique," "full of ideas," "innovative." 1 2 3 4 5

3. When working on a problem in a group setting, I generate a lot of ideas. 1 2 3 4 5

4. I am energized when I have a brand-new experience. 1 2 3 4 5

5. If you say something is too risky, I'm ready to give it a shot. 1 2 3 4 5

6. I often wonder if there is a different way to do or see something. 1 2 3 4 5

7. Too much routine in my work or schedule drains my energy. 1 2 3 4 5

8. I tend to see connections among ideas that others do not. 1 2 3 4 5

9. I feel comfortable allowing myself to make mistakes as I test out ideas. 1 2 3 4 5

10. I'm willing to champion an idea even when others disagree with me. 1 2 3 4 5

Total your answers here: _____

If your total ranges from 38–50, you consider your creative thinking skills to be *strong*.

If your total ranges from 24–37, you consider your creative thinking skills to be *average*.

If your total ranges from 10–23, you consider your creative thinking skills to be *weak*.

Remember that you can improve your creative thinking skills with focus and practice.

Celebrating success. Success is being who you want to be and doing what you want to do. You may not feel successful until you reach an important goal you have set for yourself. However, success is a process. Each step along the way to improvement and growth, no matter how small, is a success worth acknowledging. If you received a C on a paper and then earned a B on the next one, for example, your advancement is successful. When you are trying to drop a harmful habit, each day you stay on course is a victory.

Education builds a foundation for learning throughout life

As a student just beginning a post-secondary career, you may have so much on your plate that you can't imagine thinking past next month, never mind what you need to learn throughout life. However, you are investing time, money, and energy in your education—and you should know that the learning skills you are developing now will bring you success far beyond graduation.

The importance of being a lifelong learner is linked to the enormous changes taking place in the world. Changes such as the following demand continued learning in the years ahead.

- **Knowledge in nearly every field is changing every two to three years.** That means that if you stop learning for even a few years, your knowledge base will be inadequate to keep up with the changes in your career.

- **Technology is changing how you live and work.** The internet and technology will continue to shape communications and improve knowledge and productivity during the next 20 years—and will require continual learning.

- **The global economy is moving from a product and service base to a knowledge and talent base.** Jobs of the past are being replaced by knowledge-based jobs that ask workers to think critically to come up with solutions. Statistics Canada says that the 2001 Census echoes this finding: They maintain that "average annual earnings surpassed $30,000 for the first time in 2000, as working Canadians began reaping the benefits of globalization and the knowledge based economy."[13] They also report that "Canada is better educated than ever. In the years between 1991 and 2001 the number of adults 25 and over with trade, college or university credentials increased by 2.7 million, an increase of 39%."[14]

- **Workers are changing jobs and careers more frequently.** The average employee changes jobs every three to four years, and it is estimated that a 22-year-old graduate will have an average of eight employers in his or her first ten years in the workplace.[15] Every time you decide to start a new career, you need new knowledge and skills. Coming back to school is a good place to learn new skills and to evaluate the employability skills you already have.

All of these signs point to the need to become a lifelong learner—an individual who continues to build knowledge and intelligence as a mechanism for improving life and career. Through successful intelligence, you will maintain the kind of flexibility that will enable you to adapt to the demands of the twenty-first century. If you analyze what is happening,

Assess Yourself as a Practical Thinker

For each statement, circle the number that feels right to you, from 1 for "not at all true for me" to 5 for "very true for me."

1. I can find a way around any obstacle. 1 2 3 4 5

2. I see myself as a "doer," the "go-to" person; I "make things happen." 1 2 3 4 5

3. When working on a problem in a group setting, I like to figure out who will do what and when it should be done. 1 2 3 4 5

4. Because I learn well from experience, I don't tend to repeat a mistake. 1 2 3 4 5

5. I finish what I start and don't leave loose ends hanging. 1 2 3 4 5

6. I pay attention to my emotions in academic and social situations to see if they help or hurt me as I move toward a goal. 1 2 3 4 5

7. I can sense how people feel, and can use that knowledge to interact with others effectively in order to achieve a goal. 1 2 3 4 5

8. I manage my time effectively. 1 2 3 4 5

9. I find ways to adjust to the teaching styles of my instructors and the communication styles of my peers. 1 2 3 4 5

10. When involved in a problem-solving process, I can shift gears as needed. 1 2 3 4 5

Total your answers here: _____

If your total ranges from 38–50, you consider your practical thinking skills to be *strong*.

If your total ranges from 24–37, you consider your practical thinking skills to be *average*.

If your total ranges from 10–23, you consider your practical thinking skills to be *weak*.

Remember that you can improve your practical thinking skills with focus and practice.

STRESSBUSTER

ALEJANDRA GONZALEZ   Seneca College, Toronto, Ontario

Different students face different challenges when they begin their post-secondary education. What challenges do you face? How do you intend to overcome these challenges in a constructive way?

As a mature student, I'm confronted with many stressful situations daily such as driving to work, maintaining my job, and paying for tuition. I live about 40 to 50 km away from school, so taking the bus is not an option. I also work every day when I'm not in school, so commuting takes up much of my day. Driving to school and work is followed by the responsibility of paying for my car, gas, and insurance, as well as maintaining my car. I also pay for my own tuition and books, which can be very costly. On top of everything, I am striving to do very well in school and reach all the goals that I have set for myself.

It's definitely fair to say that money and time are the two major issues that I have to overcome in order to be successful in my school studies. There are many ways of dealing with the money situation, such as school bursaries and/or loans. Time management is very critical. Without time management it would be very difficult to be organized and keep up with school and workload. Procrastination is definitely not an option!

The only way that I can stay organized without falling behind is by keeping a weekly schedule, as opposed to a monthly or yearly one. It can be very overwhelming to look at the amount of work that needs to be done in a month. A weekly planner helps me accomplish many tasks without feeling overwhelmed. Procrastinating and being disorganized can make it even harder to cope with schoolwork, which often leads to failing marks or just dropping out because of stress. I feel that managing my time and staying organized will be the key to my success at Seneca College.

come up with creative approaches for handling it, and make a practical plan to put your ideas into motion, you can stay on track toward your goals. Or, you may decide to shift direction toward a new goal that never occurred to you before the change.

Facing change means taking risks. When you enter college, you accept certain challenges and risks as necessary hurdles on the path toward success. As a successfully intelligent lifelong learner, you will find ways to continue to learn and strive toward what you want. Welcome to the beginning of the road to your dreams.

Successful Intelligence Wrap-Up

You have the power to engage your successful intelligence to pursue goals that are most important to you. Although college presents challenges and risks to everyone, persistent and motivated learners can manage them effectively. Here's how you have built skills in Chapter 1:

Analytical

By completing the three self-assessments, you analyzed where you are now in analytical, creative, and practical intelligence. At the beginning and end of the chapter, you explored how learning—in college and throughout life—can promote success. In learning about the theory of successful intelligence, you considered how successful intelligence can enable you to reach important goals.

Creative

Reading about the global marketplace may have inspired new ideas of what you want out of college. Thinking about the three parts of successful intelligence helped to provide a new perspective of your potential as a student. Exploring strategies about learning from failure, working with others in a team, and facing fears may have helped you see connections among these topics that you didn't see before.

Practical

You examined specific practical actions that are the building blocks of college success: fulfill day-to-day academic responsibilities, stay motivated, and learn from failure. Finally, you considered specific, practical actions to take when working in a project team or study group.

Egyszer volt budán kutyavásár

(edge-zehr volt bu-darn ku-tcho-vah-shahr)

This unusual Hungarian phrase, translated literally, means "There was a dog-market in Buda only once." In modern English, you would interpret this to be a favourable opportunity that comes along only once—something that you should grasp with both hands, lest you regret not taking advantage of it later.[16]

For you, this opportunity has arrived. Make the most of all that your university or college has to offer, and gather learning skills that you will use throughout your life. By taking the initiative to use your time well, you can build the successful intelligence that will help you realize your dreams.

"There is no elevator to success. You have to take the stairs."

UNKNOWN

Building World-Class Skills
for Post-secondary, Career and Life Success

SUCCESSFUL INTELLIGENCE
Think, Create, Apply

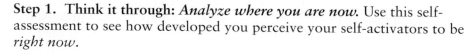

Activate yourself. Robert Sternberg found that successfully intelligent people, despite differences in thinking and personal goals, have 20 particular characteristics in common. He calls these characteristics *self-activators*—things that get you moving and keep you going.[17]

Step 1. Think it through: *Analyze where you are now.* Use this self-assessment to see how developed you perceive your self-activators to be *right now*.

1	2	3	4	5
Not at all like me	Somewhat unlike me	Not sure	Somewhat like me	Definitely like me

Please circle the number that best represents your answer:

1. I motivate myself well.   1 2 3 4 5
2. I can control my impulses.   1 2 3 4 5
3. I know when to persevere and when to change gears.   1 2 3 4 5
4. I make the most of what I do well.   1 2 3 4 5
5. I can successfully translate my ideas into action.   1 2 3 4 5
6. I can focus effectively on my goal.   1 2 3 4 5
7. I complete tasks and have good follow-through.   1 2 3 4 5
8. I initiate action—I move people and projects ahead.   1 2 3 4 5
9. I have the courage to risk failure.   1 2 3 4 5
10. I avoid procrastination.   1 2 3 4 5
11. I accept responsibility when I make a mistake.   1 2 3 4 5
12. I don't waste time feeling sorry for myself.   1 2 3 4 5

13. I independently take responsibility for tasks.	1 2 3 4 5
14. I work hard to overcome personal difficulties.	1 2 3 4 5
15. I create an environment that helps me to concentrate on my goals.	1 2 3 4 5
16. I don't take on too much work or too little.	1 2 3 4 5
17. I can delay gratification in order to receive the benefits.	1 2 3 4 5
18. I can see both the big picture and the details in a situation.	1 2 3 4 5
19. I am able to maintain confidence in myself.	1 2 3 4 5
20. I can balance my analytical, creative, and practical thinking skills.	1 2 3 4 5

Step 2. Think out of the box: *Brainstorm over time.* Looking at the self-assessment, choose five self-activators that you most want to develop throughout the term. Then, pretend you are an instructor recommending yourself for a scholarship or a job. Write yourself a short email about how strong you are in the areas of those five self-activators. Save the email as a reminder of what you would like such a person to be able to truly say about you.

Step 3. Make it happen: *Prepare yourself for action.* Let this self-assessment direct your decisions about how you approach the material in this course. If you wish to procrastinate less, for example, pay special attention to the time-management information in Chapter 2. To jump-start your focus, look at the self-assessment again and circle or highlight the five self-activators that you most want to concentrate on at this point. In the last chapter of this book you will revisit this self-assessment and get more specific about actions you have taken, and plan to take, to promote personal growth.

TEAMWORK

Create Solutions Together

Motivators. Gather in a group of three to five. Together, brainstorm *motivation blockers*—situations or things that most often kill your motivation to succeed in school. When you have listed as many problems as you have group members, each person should choose one problem and write it at the top of a blank sheet of paper. Look at the motivation blocker on your page. Under it, write one practical idea you have about how to overcome it. When everyone is finished, pass the pages to the person on the left. Then write an idea about the new blocker at the top of the page you've received. If you can't think of anything, pass the page as is. Continue this way until your page comes back to you. Then discuss the ideas as a group, analyzing which ideas might work better than others. Add other ideas to the lists if you think of them.

The last step: On your own, keeping in mind your group discussion, list three specific actions that you commit to taking in order to keep motivation high when the going gets rough.

1. _____

2. _____

3. _____

WRITING

Journal and Put Skills to Work

Record your thoughts on a separate piece of paper, in a journal, or on a computer file.

Journal entry: *Reasons for college.* Think about why you are here. Why did you decide to attend college, and what do you want out of the experience? What sacrifices—in terms of time, hard work, finances—are you willing to make in your quest for success?

Real-life writing: *Initial impressions.* Although you have not been in school for long, you already have some sense of your instructors, their style, and how classes are likely to proceed. Compare and contrast your initial impressions of two of your instructors and the courses they teach. Discuss teaching style, course expectations, degree of difficulty, how the classroom is run, and any other factor that is significant to you. Finally, note any changes you think you should make—in your in-class or study approach—based on these impressions.

PERSONAL PORTFOLIO

Prepare for Career Success

This is the first of 12 portfolio assignments you will complete, one for each chapter. By the end of the term, you will have built skills that promote success in pursuing any career as you compile a portfolio of documents that will help you achieve career goals.

Type your work and store the documents electronically in one file folder. Use loose paper for assignments that ask you to draw or make collages.

Setting career goals. Whether you have a current career, have held a few different jobs, or have not yet entered the workplace, college is an ideal time to take stock of your career goals. The earlier in your college education that you consider career goals, the more that you can take advantage of how college can help prepare you for work, in both job-specific and general ways. Having a strong vision of where you wish to go will also be a powerful motivator as you face some of the inevitable challenges of the next few years.

Take some time to think about your working life. Spend 15 minutes brainstorming everything that you wish you could be, do, have, or experience in your career 10 years from now—the skills you want to have, money you want to earn, benefits, experiences, travel, anything you can think of. List your wishes, draw them, depict them using cut-outs from magazines, or combine these ideas—whatever you like best.

Now, look at your list. To discover how your wishes relate to one another, group them in order of priority. Label three computer pages or three pieces of paper as Priority 1, Priority 2, and Priority 3. Write each wish where it fits, with Priority 1 being the most important, Priority 2 the second most important, and Priority 3 the third.

Look at your priority lists. What do they tell you about what is most important to you? What wishes are you ready to work toward right now? Circle or highlight the three highest-priority wishes (they will most likely appear on your Priority 1 page). Write down the trade-offs you may have to make today to make these wishes come true. Don't let yourself off the hook—be realistic and direct. You may want to look back at these materials at the end of the term to see what changes may have taken place in your priorities.

SUGGESTED READINGS

Evers, Frederick T., James Cameron Rush, and Iris Berdow. *The Bases of Competence: Skills for Lifelong Learning and Employability*. San Francisco, CA: Jossey-Bass, 1998.

Foot, David, and Daniel Stoffman. *Boom, Bust & Echo 2000*. Toronto: McFarlane, Walter and Ross, 1998.

Friedman, Thomas L. *The World Is Flat: A Brief History of the Twenty-first Century*. New York: Farrar, Straus & Giroux, 2006.

Jeffers, Susan. *Feel the Fear . . . And Beyond: Mastering the Techniques for Doing It Anyway*. New York: Ballantine, 1998.

Kadar, Andrew. *College Life 102: The No-Bull Guide to a Great Freshman Year*. Lincoln, NE: iUniverse, 2006.

Lombardo, Alison. *Navigating Your Freshman Year*. New York: Natavi Guides, 2003.

Newport, Cal. *How to Win at College: Surprising Secrets for Success from the Country's Top Students*. New York: Broadway Books, 2005.

Simon, Linda. *New Beginnings: A Reference Guide for Adult Learners*, 3rd ed. Upper Saddle River, NJ: Prentice Hall, 2005.

Sternberg, Robert. *Successful Intelligence: How Practical and Creative Intelligence Determine Success in Life*. New York: Plume, 1997.

Students Helping Students. *Navigating Your Freshman Year: How to Make the Leap to College Life*. New York: Penguin, 2005.

Tyler, Suzette. *Been There, Should've Done That II: More Tips for Making the Most of College*. Lansing, MI: Front Porch Press, 2001.

Weinberg, Carol. *The Complete Handbook for College Women: Making the Most of Your College Experience*. New York: New York University Press, 1994.

INTERNET RESOURCES

Association of Canadian Community Colleges:
www.accc.ca

Association of Universities and Colleges of Canada:
www.aucc.ca

Campus Access, an online guide to everything you ever wanted to know about college and university life in Canada:
www.campusaccess.com

Career Prospects, an online guide to career planning for everyone:
www.canadaprospects.com

The Conference Board of Canada:
www.conferenceboard.ca

Motivation on the Run podcasts:
www.larryhendrick.com/motivate

National Public Radio, "For Workers, 'The World Is Flat'": April 14, 2005, broadcast of *Fresh Air from WHYY*:
www.npr.org/templates/story/story.php?storyId=4600258

1. Thomas Friedman, *The World Is Flat* (New York: Farrar, Straus & Giroux, 2006), 8.

2. Statistics Canada, *Census of Population: Earnings, Levels of Schooling, Field of Study and School Attendance*, March 11, 2003, http://www.statcan.ca/daily.

3. Conference Board of Canada, *Employability Skills 2000+*, http://www.conferenceboard.ca/education/learning-tools/pdfs/esp2000.pdf.

4. Robert J. Sternberg, *Successful Intelligence* (New York: Plume, 1997), 11.

5. Lawrence F. Lowery, *The Biological Basis of Thinking and Learning*, Full Option Science System, University of California at Berkeley, 1998, http://lhsfoss.org/newsletters/archive/pdfs/FOSS_BBTL.pdf.

6. Carol Dweck, *Mindset: The New Psychology of Success* (New York: Random House, 2006), 22.

7. Sternberg, *Successful Intelligence,* 12.

8. Ibid, 127.

9. Ibid, 127–128.

10. Rick Pitino, *Success Is a Choice* (New York: Broadway Books, 1997), 40.

11. Cited in Colin Rise and Malcolm J. Nicholl, *Accelerated Learning for the 21st Century* (New York: Dell, 1997), 5–6.

12. David K. Foot and Daniel Stoffman, *Boom, Bust & Echo 2000: Profiting from the Demographic Shift in the New Millennium* (Toronto: MacFarlane, Walter and Ross, 1998).

13. Statistics Canada, *Census of Population: Earnings, Levels of Schooling, Field of Study and School Attendance*, March 11, 2003, http://www.statcan.ca/daily.

14. Ibid.

15. Jay Palmer, "Marry Me a Little," *Barron's*, July 24, 2000, 25.

16. Christopher J. Moore, *In Other Words: A Language Lover's Guide to the Most Intriguing Words around the World* (New York: Walker, 2004), 43.

17. List and descriptions based on Sternberg, *Successful Intelligence*, 251–269.

VALUES, GOALS, TIME, AND STRESS
Managing yourself

2

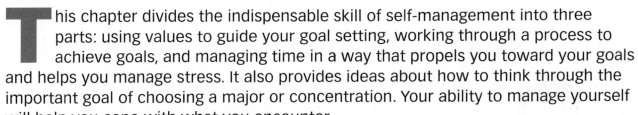

"Successfully intelligent people are well aware of the penalties for procrastination. They schedule their time so that the important things get done—and done well."

ROBERT J. STERNBERG

This chapter divides the indispensable skill of self-management into three parts: using values to guide your goal setting, working through a process to achieve goals, and managing time in a way that propels you toward your goals and helps you manage stress. It also provides ideas about how to think through the important goal of choosing a major or concentration. Your ability to manage yourself will help you cope with what you encounter, achieve your goals, and build skills that fuel your success now and in the future. Goal setting and time management are just two ways to take responsibility for your life and actions and are two keys to success listed in the Conference Board of Canada's *Employability Skills 2000+* profile (see Key 1.2).

In this chapter you will explore answers to the following questions:

- Why is it important to know what you value? 34

- How do you set and achieve goals? 39

- How can you effectively manage your time? 43

- How do you cope with the stress of post-secondary life? 53

- Successful Intelligence Wrap-Up 57

Analytical	Creative	Practical
• Examining values • Analyzing how you manage time • Considering what goals are most important to you	• Developing ideas for how to reach a goal • Creating ways to avoid procrastination • Brainstorming what majors interest you	• How to set effective goals • How to achieve a goal • How to manage a schedule

VALUES

Principles or qualities that one considers important.

Why is it important to know *what you value?*

You make life choices—what to do, what to believe, what to buy, how to act—based on your personal **values.** Your choice to pursue a degree, for example, reflects that you value the personal and professional growth that comes from a college education. Being on time for your classes shows that you value punctuality. Paying bills regularly and on time shows that you value financial stability.

Values play a key role in your drive to achieve important goals, because they help you to:

- **Understand what you want out of life.** Your most meaningful goals should reflect what you value most.

- **Build "rules for life."** Your values form the foundation for your decisions. You will return repeatedly to them for guidance, especially when you find yourself in unfamiliar territory.

- **Find people who inspire you.** Spending time with people who share similar values will help you to clarify how you want to live and to find support as you work toward what's important to you.

Now that you have an idea of how you can use values, focus on how to identify yours.

Identifying and evaluating values

Ask yourself questions: What do you focus on in a given day? What do you consider important to be, to do, or to have? What do you wish to accomplish in your life? Answers to questions like these will point you toward your values. The Get Analytical exercise on page 36 will help you think through your values in more detail.

After you determine your values, evaluate them to see if they make sense for you. Many forces affect your values—family, friends, culture, media, school, work, neighbourhood, religious beliefs, world events. No matter how powerful these external influences may be, whether a value feels right should be your primary consideration in deciding to adopt it.

Answering the following questions about a value will help you decide if it "feels right."

- Where did the value come from?
- What other different values could I consider?
- What might happen as a result of adopting this value?
- Have I made a personal commitment to this choice? Have I told others about it?
- Do my life goals and day-to-day actions reflect this value?

Even the most solid set of values needs a re-evaluation from time to time. Why? Because values often change. Life experience and education give you new perspectives that may alter what you consider important. For example, a fun-loving student who is seriously injured in an auto accident may place greater value on friends and family after the accident than he or she did before. If you let your values shift to fit you as you grow, you will always have a base on which to build achievable goals and wise decisions.

How values affect your educational experience

Well-considered values can lead to smart choices while you are in school. Your values will help you:

- **Keep going when the going gets tough.** Translate your value of education into specific actions. Remember that success takes hard work and dedication. If you have trouble in one particular course, set aside some extra time to work on it.
- Choose your major or program of study and a career direction. If you've always been an environmentalist, then you may choose to major in environmental science. If you feel fulfilled when you help people, then you might consider a career in social work.
- Choose friends and activities that enrich your life. Having friends who share your desire to succeed in school will increase your motivation and reduce your stress. Joining organizations whose activities support your values will broaden your educational experience.
- Choose what you want out of school and how hard you want to work. What kinds of skills and knowledge do you wish to build? Do you want to focus on coursework that will lead to career success? Do you want to learn about Egyptian archaeology simply because it interests you? Do you want to read every novel Margaret Atwood ever wrote? Decide also how hard you are willing to work to achieve your goals. Going above and beyond will build your drive to succeed and hone your work habits—two items that will be useful in a competitive job market.

Explore Your Values

Rate each of the values in the list on a scale from 1 to 5, with 1 being least important to you and 5 being most important.

___ Knowing yourself	___ Leadership and teamwork skills	___ Good relationships with family
___ Being liked by others	___ Staying fit through exercise	___ Community involvement
___ Reading	___ Competing and winning	___ Creative/artistic pursuits
___ Self-improvement	___ Getting a good job	___ Helping others
___ Taking risks	___ Pursuing an education	___ Keeping up with the news
___ Time to yourself	___ Spiritual/religious life	___ Being organized
___ Improving physical/mental health	___ Making a lot of money	___ Financial stability
___ Time for fun/relaxation		___ Other (write below)
___ Lifelong learning		

Write your top three values here:

1. _____

2. _____

3. _____

Now connect your values to educational goals. (*Example*: A student who values helping others chooses to study nursing.) Choose one top value that is a factor in an educational choice you have made. Explain the choice and how the value is involved:

_____

_____

_____

_____

Name an area of study that you think would help you live according to this value:

_____

Finally, your values affect your success at school and beyond, because the more ethical a student you are, the more likely you are to stay in school and to build lasting knowledge and skills.

Academic integrity: How ethical values promote success at school

Having **academic integrity** promotes learning and ensures a quality education based on ethics and hard work. Read your school's academic integrity policy in your student handbook. When you enrolled, you agreed to abide by it.

Defining academic integrity

The Center for Academic Integrity, part of the Kenan Institute for Ethics at Duke University, defines academic integrity as a commitment to five fundamental values: honesty, trust, fairness, respect, and responsibility.[1] These values are the positive actions that define academic integrity.

- **Honesty.** Honesty defines the pursuit of knowledge and implies a search for truth in your class work, papers and lab reports, and teamwork with other students.
- **Trust.** Mutual trust—between instructor and student, as well as among students—makes possible the free exchange of ideas that is fundamental to learning. Trust means being true to your word.
- **Fairness.** Instructors must create a fair academic environment in which students are judged against clear standards and in which procedures are well defined.
- **Respect.** In a respectful academic environment, both students and instructors accept and honour a wide range of opinions, even if the opinions are contrary to core beliefs.
- **Responsibility.** You are responsible for making choices that will provide you with the best education—choices that reflect fairness and honesty.

Unfortunately, the principles of academic integrity are frequently violated on college campuses. In a recent survey, three out of four college students admitted to cheating at least once during their undergraduate careers.[2] Violations of academic integrity—turning in previously submitted work, using unauthorized devices during an exam, providing unethical aid to another student, or getting unauthorized help with a project—constitute a sacrifice of ethics that isn't worth the price.

Students who are discovered violating school policies experience a variety of consequences. In most cases, students are brought before a chair, dean, or committee of instructors to determine whether the offence has occurred. Consequences vary from school to school and include participation in academic integrity seminars, grade reduction, course failure, suspension, or expulsion.

ACADEMIC INTEGRITY

Following a code of moral values, prizing honesty and fairness in all aspects of academic life—classes, assignments, tests, papers, projects, and relationships with students and faculty.

Why academic integrity is worth it

Choosing to act with integrity has the following positive consequences:

- **Increased self-esteem.** Self-esteem is tied to action. The more you act in respectful and honourable ways, the better you feel about yourself, and the more likely you are to succeed.
- **Acquired knowledge.** If you cheat you might pass a test—and a course—but chances are you won't retain the knowledge and skills you need for success. Honest work is more likely to result in knowledge that lasts—and that you can use to accomplish career and life goals.
- **Effective behavioural patterns.** When you condition yourself to play fair now, you set a pattern for your behaviour at work and with friends and family.
- **Mutual respect.** Respecting the work of others will lead others to respect your work.

The last two bullet points reflect the positive effect that integrity has on your relationships. This is only one way in which values help you to successfully relate to, work with, and understand the people around you. Here's another way: Being open to different values, often linked with different cultures, can enhance your understanding of cultural diversity.

Values and cultural diversity

At college, you may meet people who seem different in ways that you may not expect. Many of these differences stem from attitudes and behaviours that are unfamiliar to you. These attitudes and behaviours are rooted in the values that people acquire from their **culture**, either from the continuing influence of family and community here in Canada or from their homeland.

CULTURE

A set of values, behaviours, tastes, knowledge, attitudes, and habits shared by a group of people.

Cultural competence

In a multicultural country like Canada, the ability to understand and appreciate differences, and to respond to people of all cultures in a way that values their worth, means respecting their beliefs and practices as well as building communication and relationships.

Cultural misunderstandings can interfere with the relationships and friendships you form in school, career, and life. As someone who accepts and appreciates diversity, you have a goal to develop the cultural competence to understand and appreciate these differences so that they enhance—rather than hinder—communication.[3]

A simple model to help you avoid communication problems with people from other cultures was developed by Edward Hall, an anthropologist and an authority on cross-cultural communication. Hall linked communication styles to what he called high-context and low-context cultures:[4]

- People from *high-context* cultures rely heavily on context and situation in their communication, as well as on body language and eye contact. Time (past, present, and future), fate, personal relationships and status, gender roles, trust, gestures, and sense of self and space are just some of the factors that influence communication in these cultures. High-context countries span the world and include China, Japan, Brazil, Saudi Arabia, Italy, and France.

- In contrast, people from *low-context* cultures focus on what is explicitly said or written and pay little attention to context and nonverbal cues. Countries with low-context cultures include Canada, the United States, England, Australia, Germany, and the Scandinavian countries.

As you continue to read *Keys to Success*, look for examples of how cultural diversity impacts everything, from teamwork and relationships to listening, questioning, and more. Then think of the words of Canada's Governor General, Michaëlle Jean, whom you will read about in Chapter 3. She sees Canada as a place where people value tolerance, respect, and sharing. In many ways, this echoes the wisdom of cultural diversity consultant Helen Turnbull on turning differences into strengths:

We must suspend our judgment. We should not judge others negatively because they are indirect, or their accents aren't clear, or their tone of voice is tentative, or they avoid eye contact. We must learn patience and suspend judgment long enough to realize these differences don't make one of us right and the other wrong. They simply mean that we approach communication from a different frame of reference and, many times, a different value system.[5]

Although clarifying your values will help you choose your educational path, goal-setting and goal-achievement skills will help you travel that path to the end. Goals turn values into tools and put them to practical use.

How do you set and *achieve goals*?

When you identify something that you want, you set a **goal**. Actually *getting* what you want—from college, career, or life— demands working to *achieve* your goals. Achieving goals, whether they are short-term or long-term, involves following a goal-achievement plan. Think of the plan you are about to read as a map; with its helping you to establish each segment of the trip, you will be able to define your route and follow it successfully.

GOAL
An end toward which effort is directed; an aim or intention.

Set long-term goals

Start by establishing the goals that have the largest scope, the *long-term goals* that you aim to attain over a period of six months, a year, or more. When you are a student, your long-term goals include attending school and earning a degree or certificate. Getting an education is a significant goal that often takes years to reach.

Some long-term goals have an open-ended time frame. (For example, if your goal is to become a better musician, you may work at it over a lifetime.) These goals also invite more creative thinking; you have more time and freedom to consider all sorts of paths to your goal. Other goals, such as completing all the courses in your major, have a shorter scope, a more definite end, and often fewer options for how to get from A to Z.

The following long-term goal statement, written by Carol Carter, a *Keys to Success* author, may take years to complete:

> My goal is to build my own business in which I create opportunities for students to maximize their talents. In this business, I will reach thousands of students and teachers through books, the internet, teacher seminars, and student-oriented programs.

Carol also has long-term goals that she hopes to accomplish in no more than a year:

> Develop and publish one book. Design three seminars for teachers with accompanying PowerPoints and other materials. Create internet-based materials that encourage student success and use them in student seminars.

Just as Carol's goals are tailored to her personality, abilities, and interests, your goals should reflect your uniqueness. To determine your long-term goals, think about what you want to accomplish while you are in school and after you graduate. Think of ways you can link your personal values and professional aims, as in the following examples:

- **Values:** Health and fitness, helping others
- **Goal:** To become a physical therapist
- **Values:** Independence, financial success
- **Goal:** To obtain a degree in business and start a company

Basing your long-term goals on values increases your motivation. The more your goals focus on what is most important to you, the greater your drive to reach them.

Set short-term goals

Short-term goals are smaller steps that move you toward a long-term goal. Lasting as little as a few hours or as long as a few months, these goals help you manage your broader aspirations as they narrow your focus and encourage progress. If you had a long-term goal of graduating with a degree in nursing, for example, you may want to accomplish the following short-term goals in the next six months:

- I will learn the names, locations, and functions of every human bone and muscle.
- I will work with a study group to understand the musculoskeletal system.

© VisualField—Fotolia.com

These same goals can be broken down into even smaller parts, such as the following one-month goals:

- I will work with onscreen tutorials of the musculoskeletal system until I understand and memorize the material.
- I will spend three hours a week with my study partners.

In addition to monthly goals, you may have short-term goals that extend for a week, a day, or even a couple of hours in a given day. To support your month-long goal of regularly meeting with your study partners, you may wish to set the following short-term goals:

- By the end of today: Call study partners to ask them about when they might be able to meet.
- One week from now: Have scheduled each of our weekly meetings this month.
- Two weeks from now: Have had our first meeting.
- Three weeks from now: Type up and send around notes from the first meeting; have the second meeting.

Try to pay special attention to goals that are intermediate in length—for example, one-month or one-semester goals on the way to a year-long goal. Why?—Because your motivation is at its peak when you begin to move toward a goal and when you are about to achieve that goal. If you work hard to stay motivated in the middle, you will have a more successful journey and a better result.

As you consider your long- and short-term goals, notice how all of your goals are linked to one another. As Key 2.1 shows, your long-term

Goals reinforce one another.

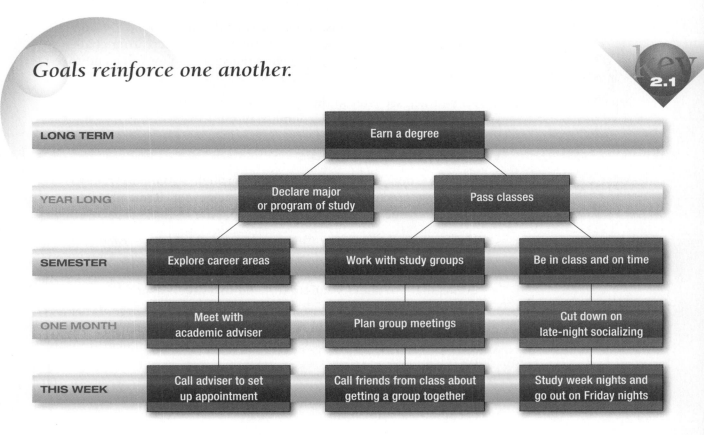

LONG TERM	Earn a degree		
YEAR LONG	Declare major or program of study	Pass classes	
SEMESTER	Explore career areas	Work with study groups	Be in class and on time
ONE MONTH	Meet with academic adviser	Plan group meetings	Cut down on late-night socializing
THIS WEEK	Call adviser to set up appointment	Call friends from class about getting a group together	Study week nights and go out on Friday nights

Reviewing animal physiology while caring for her son is just part of how this single parent and pre-med student juggles responsibilities on a daily basis.

PRIORITIZE
To arrange or deal with in order of importance.

goals establish a context for the short-term goals. In turn, your short-term goals make the long-term goals seem clearer and more reachable.

At any given time, you will be working toward goals of varying importance. Setting priorities helps you decide where and when to focus your energy and time.

Prioritize goals

When you **prioritize**, you evaluate everything you are working toward, decide which goals are most important, and focus your time and energy on them. What should you consider as you evaluate?

- **Your values.** Thinking about what you value will help you establish the goals that take top priority—for example, graduating in the top 25 percent of your class or developing a strong network of personal contacts.

- **Your personal situation.** Are you going to school and working part-time? Are you a parent with young children who need your attention? Are you an athlete on a sports team? Are you a student with identified special needs? Every individual situation requires unique priorities and scheduling.

- **Your time commitments.** Hours of your day may already be committed to class, team practices, a part-time job, or sleep. Your challenge is to make sure these commitments reflect what you value and to establish priorities for the remaining hours.

As you will see later in the chapter, setting clear priorities will help you manage your time and accomplish more.

Work to achieve goals

When you've done all the work to think through a goal you want to achieve, these practical steps will help you achieve it. Remember, the more specific your plans, the more likely you are to fulfill them.

- **Define your goal-setting strategy:** *How do you plan to reach your goal?* Brainstorm different paths that might get you there. Choose one; then map out its steps and strategies. Focus on specific behaviours and events that are under your control and that are measurable.

- **Set a timetable:** *When do you want to accomplish your goal?* Set a realistic timeline that includes specific deadlines for each step and strategy you have defined. Charting your progress will help you stay on track.

- **Be accountable for your progress:** *What safeguards will keep you on track?* Define a personal reporting or buddy system that makes accountability a priority.

Map Out a Personal Goal

Working backwards can help you find an interesting path toward an important goal.

Name one important personal goal you have for this year:

_____

Now imagine that you have achieved your goal and an impressed friend asks you to describe how you did it. Write three important steps you took first:

1. _____
2. _____
3. _____

Briefly describe how you followed the rest of the plan:

_____

_____

_____

Finally, tell your friend what positive results have come from achieving your goal:

_____

_____

You just created a potential plan. Consider putting it—or a plan similar to it—to work. As you begin, let the image of the success you created in this exercise motivate and inspire you.

- **Get unstuck:** *What will you do if you hit a roadblock?* Define two ways to get help with your efforts if you run into trouble. Be ready to pursue more creative ideas if those don't work.

Through this process, you will continually be thinking about how well you are using your time. In fact, goal achievement is directly linked to effective time management.

How can you effectively *manage your time*?

Time is a universal resource; everyone has the same 24 hours in a day, every day. Depending on what's happening in your life, however, your sense of time may change. On some days you feel like you have hours to spare, while on others the clock becomes your worst enemy.

Your challenge is to turn time into a goal-achievement tool by making smart choices about how to use it. Think of each day as a jigsaw puzzle: You have all of the pieces in a pile, and your task is to form a picture of how you want your day to look. Successful time management starts with identifying your time-related needs and preferences. This self-knowledge sets the stage for building and managing your schedule, avoiding procrastination, and being flexible in the face of change.

Identify your time-related needs and preferences

Body rhythms and habits affect how each person deals with time. Some people are night owls; others are at their best in the morning. Some people are chronically late; others get everything done with time to spare. Individual tendencies become clear as people build up "records" of behaviour.

A mismatch between your habits and your schedule causes stress and drains energy. For example, a person who loses steam in the mid-afternoon may struggle in classes that meet between 3:00 and 5:00 p.m. However, an awareness of your needs and preferences will help you create a schedule that maximizes your strengths and cuts down on stress. If you are a morning person, for example, look for sections of required courses that meet early in the day. If you work best at night, schedule most of your study time at a library that stays open late.

Take the following steps to identify your time-related needs and preferences:

Create a personal time "profile." Ask yourself these questions: At what time of day do I have the most energy? The least energy? Do I tend to be early, on time, or late? Do I focus well for long stretches or need regular breaks? Your answers will help you find the schedule set-up that works best for you.

Evaluate the effects of your profile. Which of your time-related habits and preferences will have a positive impact on your success at school? Which are likely to cause problems?

Successful Intelligence Connections Online

Listen to author Sarah Kravits describe how to use analytical, creative, and practical intelligence to define your personal time profile.

Go to the *Keys to Success* Companion Website at www.pearsoned. ca/carter to listen or download as a podcast.

Establish what schedule preferences suit your profile best. Make a list of these preferences—or even map out an ideal schedule as a way of illustrating them. For example, one student's preference list might read: "Classes bunched together on Mondays, Wednesdays, and Fridays. Tuesdays and Thursdays free for studying and research. Study time primarily during the day."

Next, it's time to build the schedule that takes all of this information into account, helping you maximize your strengths and compensate for your weaker time-management areas.

Build a schedule

You've set up your "goal map," with all of the steps that you need to accomplish to reach your destination. With a schedule you place each step in time and, by doing so, commit to making it happen. Schedules help you gain control of your life in two ways: They provide segments of time for tasks related to the fulfillment of your goals, and they remind you of tasks, events, due dates, responsibilities, and deadlines.

Use a planner

A planner is the ideal practical tool for managing your time. With it, you can keep track of events and commitments, schedule goal-related tasks, and rank tasks according to priority. Time-management expert Paul Timm says that "rule number one in a thoughtful planning process is: Use some form of a planner where you can write things down."[6]

There are two main types of planners. One is a book or notebook in which to note commitments. If you write detailed daily plans, look for the kind that devotes a page to each day. If you prefer to see more days at a glance, try the kind that shows a week's schedule on a two-page spread. Some planners contain sections for monthly and yearly goals.

© Iryna Petrenko—Fotolia.com

STRESSBUSTER

KEVIN FORSETH   Sprott-Shaw Community College, Duncan, British Columbia

Time management can be the source of a lot of stress. Having too much to do and too little time is a common student experience. What techniques do you use to reduce schedule overloads and thereby reduce stress? How do you deal with stress when your schedule becomes too full?

Stress plays a major factor in the way you live and the way you plan your life. I am the father of four children. I work full-time and go to school full-time, so I have my fair share of stress. I have had to learn how to schedule my time and my finances. Being able to accommodate school and work while trying to spend quality time with my family gives me a feeling of victory. When I started out,

however, if someone had asked me if I could handle it, I would have laughed and said, "Not in your lifetime!"

I have purchased a daily planner that helps me to keep on top of things. With so much on the go all the time, it's hard to keep everything in your head. You have to remember appointments, assignments, and bills, and you can't forget to plan some quality time with your family.

If I could give you one word of advice, it would be this: If stress gets the better of you, sit down, relax, and make a schedule. It will make your life more enjoyable during the tough times instead of having to live through the complete agony of stress.

The other option is an electronic planner or personal digital assistant (PDA). Basic PDA functions allow you to schedule days and weeks, note due dates, make to-do lists, perform mathematical calculations, and create and store an address book. You can enter information with an onscreen or attachable keyboard or hand write with a stylus. You can also transfer information to and from a computer.

Though electronic planners are handy and have a large data capacity, they cost more than the paper versions, and their small size means they can be easy to lose. Analyze your preferences and options, and decide which tool you are most likely to use every day. A simple notebook will work as well as a top-of-the-line PDA as long as you use it conscientiously.

Keep track of events and commitments

Your planner is designed to help you schedule and remember events and commitments. A quick look at your notations will remind you when items are approaching.

Putting your schedule in writing will help you anticipate and prepare for crunch times. For example, if you see that you have three tests and a presentation coming up all in one week, you may have to rearrange your schedule during the preceding week to create extra study time.

Among the events and commitments worth noting in your planner are

- test and quiz dates; due dates for papers, projects, and presentations
- details of your academic schedule, including semester and holiday breaks
- club and organizational meetings
- personal items—medical appointments, due dates for bills, birthdays, and social events
- milestones toward a goal, such as due dates for sections of a project.

Although many students don't think to do so, it's important to include class prep time—reading and studying, writing and working on assignments and projects—in the planner. According to one reasonable formula, you should schedule at least two hours of preparation for every hour of class—that is, if you take 15 credits, you should study about 30 hours a week, making your total classroom and preparation time 45 hours. Surveys have shown, however, that most students study 15 or fewer hours per week, and some study even less—often not enough to master the material.

Schedule tasks and activities that support your goals

Linking the events in your planner to your goals will give meaning to your efforts and bring order to your schedule. Planning study time for an economics test, for example, will mean more to you if you link the hours you spend studying to your goal of being accepted into business school. The simple act of relating what you do every day to what you want in your future has enormous power to move you forward.

Here is how a student might translate his goal of entering business school into action steps over a year's time:

This year: Complete enough courses to meet curriculum requirements for business school.

This semester: Complete my economics class with a B average or higher.

This month: Set up economics study group schedule to coincide with quizzes and tests.

This week: Meet with study group; go over material for Friday's test.

Today: Go over Chapter 3 in econ text.

The student can then arrange his time to move himself toward his goal. He schedules activities that support his short-term goal of doing well on the test and writes them in his planner, as shown in Key 2.2. Achieving his overarching long-term goal of doing well in a course that he needs for business school is the source of his motivation.

Before each week begins, remind yourself of your long-term goals and what you can accomplish over the next seven days to move yourself closer to them. Key 2.3 shows parts of a daily schedule and a weekly schedule.

Indicate priority levels

On any given day, the items on your schedule have varying degrees of importance. Prioritizing these items boosts scheduling success in two ways.

Schedule activities to support short-term goals.

key 2.2

Monday	Tuesday	Wednesday	Thursday	Friday	Saturday	Sunday
9 AM: Economics class Talk with study group members to schedule meeting.	3–5 PM: Study econ chapter 3.	9 AM: Economics class Drop by instructor's office hours to ask question about test	6 PM: Go over chapter 3 7–9 PM: Study group meeting.	9 AM: Economics class—Test 3:30 PM: Meet w/advisor to discuss GMAT and other business school requirements	Sleep in— schedule some down time	5 PM: Go over quiz questions with study partner

Note daily and weekly tasks.

Monday, March 14

TIME	TASKS	PRIORITY
6:00 A.M.		
7:00		
8:00	Up at 8am — finish homewo...	
9:00		
10:00	Business Administration	
11:00	Renew driver's license @ D...	
12:00 P.M.		
1:00	Lunch	
2:00	Writing Seminar (peer editi...	
3:00		
4:00	check on Ms. Schwartz's of...	
5:00	5:30 work out	
6:00	6:30	
7:00	Dinner	
8:00	Read two chapters for	
9:00	Business Admin.	
10:00		
11:00		
12:00		

Monday, March 28

8		Call: Mike Blair	1
9	BIO 212	Finanical Aid Office	2
10		EMS 262 *Paramedic	3
11	CHEM 203	role-play*	4
12			5
Evening	6pm yoga class		

Tuesday, March 29

8	Finish reading assignment!	Work @ library	1
9			2
10	ENG 112	(study for quiz)	3
11			4
12			5
Evening		until 7pm	

Wednesday, March 30

8		Meet w/advisor	1
9	BIO 212		2
10		EMS 262	3
11	CHEM 203 *Quiz		4
12		Pick up photos	5
Evening	6pm Dinner w/study group		

First, it helps you to identify your most important tasks and to focus the bulk of your energy and time on them. Second, it helps you plan when in your day to get things done. Since many top-priority items (classes, work) occur at designated times, prioritizing helps you lock in these activities and schedule less urgent items around them.

Indicate an item's level of importance by using three different categories. Identify these categories by using any code that makes sense to you. Some people use numbers, some use letters (A, B, C), and some use different-coloured pens. The three categories are as follows:

- *Priority 1* items are the most crucial. They may include attending class, completing school assignments, working at a job, picking up a child from daycare, and paying bills. Enter Priority 1 items on your planner first, before scheduling anything else.

- *Priority* 2 items are the important but more flexible parts of your routine. Examples include library study time, completing an assignment for a school club, and working out. Schedule these around Priority 1 items.
- *Priority* 3 items are least important—the "it would be nice if I could get to that" items. Examples include making a social phone call, stocking up on birthday cards, and cleaning out a closet. Many people don't enter Priority 3 tasks in their planners until they know they have time for them. Others keep a separate list of these tasks so that when they have free time they can consult it and choose what they want to accomplish.

Use scheduling techniques

The following strategies will help you turn your scheduling activities into tools that move you closer to your goals:

Plan regularly. Spending time planning your schedule will reduce stress and save you from the hours of work that might result if you forget something important. At the beginning of each week, write down specific time commitments as well as your goals and priorities. Decide where to fit activities like studying and Priority 3 items. For example, if you have a test on Thursday, you can plan study sessions on the preceding days. If you have more free time on Tuesday and Friday, you can plan workouts or other low-priority tasks. Your planner helps you only when you use it—keep it with you and check it throughout the day.

Make and use to-do lists. Use a to-do list to record the things you want to accomplish on a given day or week. Write your to-do items on a separate piece of paper so you can set priorities. Then transfer the items you plan to accomplish each day to open time periods in your planner.

To-do lists are critical time-management tools during exam week and when major projects are due. They will help you rank your responsibilities so that you get things done in order of importance.

Post monthly and yearly calendars at home. Keeping track of your major commitments on a monthly wall calendar will give you the overview you need to focus on responsibilities and upcoming events. Key 2.4 shows a monthly calendar. If you live with family or friends, create a group calendar to stay aware of each other's plans and avoid scheduling conflicts.

Avoid time traps. Try to stay away from situations that eat up time unnecessarily. Say "no" graciously if you don't have time for a project; curb excess social time that interferes with academics; delegate chores if you find yourself overloaded. Pay special attention to how much time you spend surfing the internet and chatting online, because these activities can waste hours.

Keep track of your time with a monthly calendar.

MARCH

SUNDAY	MONDAY	TUESDAY	WEDNESDAY	THURSDAY	FRIDAY	SATURDAY
	1 WORK	2 Turn in English paper topic	3 Dentist 2pm	4 WORK	5	6
7 Frank's birthday	8 Psych Test 9am WORK	9	10 6:30 pm Meeting @ Student Ctr.	11 WORK	12	13 Dinner @ Ryan's
14	15 English paper due WORK	16 Western Civ paper—Library research	17	18 Library 6 p.m. WORK	19 Western Civ makeup class	20
21	22 WORK	23 2 p.m. meeting, psych group project	20 Start running program: 3 km	25 WORK	26 Run 3 km	27
28 Run 5 km	29 WORK	30 Western Civ paper due	31 Run 3 km			

DOWNTIME

Quiet time set aside for relaxation and low-key activity.

Schedule downtime. Leisure time is more than just a nice break—it's essential to your health and success. A little **downtime** will refresh you and actually improve your productivity when you get back on task. Even half an hour per day helps. Fill the time with whatever relaxes you—reading, watching television, chatting online, playing a game or sport, walking, writing, or just doing nothing.

Fight procrastination

PROCRASTINATION

The act of putting off a task until another time.

It's human, and common for busy students, to put off difficult or undesirable tasks until later. If taken to the extreme, however, **procrastination** can develop into a habit that causes serious problems. This excerpt from the Study Skills Library at California Polytechnic State University at San Luis Obispo illustrates how procrastination can quickly turn into a destructive pattern:

> The procrastinator is often remarkably optimistic about his ability to complete a task on a tight deadline. . . . For example, he may estimate

Make a To-Do List

Reduce stress by accomplishing practical goals. Make a to-do list for what you have to do on your busiest day this week. Include all the tasks and events you know about, including attending class and studying, and the activities you would like to do (working out at the gym, watching your favourite TV show) if you have extra time. Then prioritize your list using the coding system of your choice.

Date: _____

1. _____
2. _____
3. _____
4. _____
5. _____
6. _____

7. _____
8. _____
9. _____
10. _____
11. _____
12. _____

After examining this list, record your daily schedule in your planner (if you have a busy day, you may want to list Priority 3 items separately to complete if time permits). At the end of the day, evaluate this system. Did the list help you to manage your time and tasks effectively? If you liked it, use this exercise as a guide for using to-do lists regularly.

that a paper will take only five days to write; he has fifteen days; there is plenty of time, no need to start. Lulled by a false sense of security, time passes. At some point, he crosses over an imaginary starting time and suddenly realizes, "Oh no! I am not in control! There isn't enough time!"

At this point, considerable effort is directed toward completing the task, and work progresses. This sudden spurt of energy is the source of the erroneous feeling that "I work well only under pressure." Actually, at this point you are making progress only because you haven't any choice. . . . Progress is being made, but you have lost your freedom.

Barely completed in time, the paper may actually earn a fairly good grade; whereupon the student experiences mixed feelings: pride of accomplishment (sort of), scorn for the professor who cannot recognize substandard work, and guilt for getting an undeserved grade. But the net result is reinforcement: The procrastinator is rewarded positively for his poor behavior ("Look what a decent grade I got after all!"). As a result, the counterproductive behavior is repeated time and time again.[7]

Following are some of the reasons that people procrastinate:

Perfectionism. According to Jane B. Burka and Lenora M. Yuen, authors of *Procrastination: Why You Do It and What to Do About It,* habitual procrastinators often gauge their self-worth solely by their ability to achieve. In other words, "an outstanding performance means an outstanding person; a mediocre performance means a mediocre person."[8] To the perfectionist procrastinator, not trying at all is better than an attempt that falls short of perfection.

Fear of limitations. Some people procrastinate in order to avoid the truth about what they can achieve. "As long as you procrastinate, you never have to confront the real limits of your ability, whatever those limits are,"[9] say Burka and Yuen. If you procrastinate and fail, you can blame the failure on waiting too long, not on any personal shortcoming.

Being unsure of the next step. If you get stuck and don't know what to do, sometimes it seems easier to procrastinate than to make the leap to the next level of your goal.

Facing an overwhelming task. Some projects are so big that they create immobilizing fear. If a person facing such a task fears failure, she may procrastinate in order to avoid confronting the fear.

Avoiding procrastination

Although it can bring relief in the short term, avoiding tasks almost always causes problems, such as a buildup of responsibilities and less time to complete them; work that is not up to par; the disappointment of others who are depending on your work; and stress brought on by the weight of the unfinished tasks. Particular strategies can help you avoid procrastination and the problems associated with it.

Analyze the effects of procrastinating. What may happen if you continue to put off a responsibility? Chances are you will benefit more in the long term from facing the task head-on.

Set reasonable goals. Unreasonable goals can intimidate and immobilize you. Set manageable goals and allow enough time to complete them.

Break tasks into smaller parts. If you concentrate on achieving one small step at a time, the task may become less burdensome. Setting concrete time limits for each task may help you feel more in control.

Get started whether or not you "feel like it." Review your answers to the Get Analytical exercise from earlier in the chapter for some help with identifying what values motivate you. Then, review the motivation techniques from Chapter 1. That may help you take the first steps to avoid procrastination. Once you start, you may find it easier to continue.

Ask for help. You don't have to go it alone. Once you identify what's holding you up, see who can help you face the task. Another person may come up with an innovative way that can get you moving.

Don't expect perfection. No one is perfect. Most people learn by starting at the beginning, making mistakes, and learning from those mistakes. It's better to try your best than to do nothing at all.

Reward yourself. Find ways to boost your confidence when you accomplish a particular task. Remind yourself—with a break, a movie, some kind of treat—that you are making progress.

Be flexible

No matter how well you plan your time, sudden changes can upend your plans. Any change, whether minor (a room change for a class) or major (a medical emergency), can cause stress. As your stress level rises, your sense of control dwindles.

Although you can't always choose your circumstances, you have some control over how you handle them. Your ability to evaluate situations, come up with creative options, and put practical plans to work will help you manage the changes that you will inevitably encounter. Think of change as part of life, and you will be better prepared to brainstorm solutions when dilemmas arise.

Small changes—the need to work an hour overtime at your after-school job, a meeting that runs late—can result in priority shifts that jumble your schedule. For changes that occur frequently, think through a backup plan ahead of time. For surprises, the best you can do is to keep an open mind about possibilities and rely on your internal and external resources.

When change involves serious problems—your car breaks down and you have no way to get to school; you fail a class and have to consider summer school; a family member develops a medical problem and needs you more at home—use problem-solving skills to help you through. As you will see in Chapter 4, problem solving involves identifying and analyzing the problem, brainstorming and exploring possible solutions, and choosing the solution you decide is best. Resources are available at your college to help you throughout this process. Your academic adviser, counsellor, dean, financial aid adviser, and instructors may offer ideas and assistance.

Change is one of many factors associated with stress. In fact, stress is part of the normal college experience. If you take charge of how you manage stress, then you can keep it from taking charge of you.

How do you *cope with the stress* of post-secondary life?

If you are feeling more stress in your everyday life as a student, you are not alone.[10] Stress levels among college students have increased dramatically. Today, more than 30 percent of first year students report that they frequently feel overwhelmed, almost double the rate in 1985. Stress factors for college and university students include being in a new environment; facing increased work and difficult decisions; and juggling school, work, and personal responsibilities.

Hans Selye (1907–1982), a Canadian who was a professor at McGill University in Montreal, is considered by many to be the father of stress research. He once said, "To be totally without stress is to be dead." What

Selye meant was that we won't ever be able to eliminate stress from our lives, but we can be taught to manage it effectively. Selye defined stress as our reaction to an outside stimulus. This reaction can be positive (eustress) or negative (distress).[11] Most of the time, when we think of stress we think of the negative distress. In a survey commissioned by the Canadian National Mental Health Association, 50 percent of Canadians felt "really stressed" a few times each week.[12]

Stress refers to the way in which your mind and body react to pressure. Pressure comes from situations like heavy workloads (final exam week), excitement (being a finalist for the lead in a play), change (new school, new courses), being short on time (working 20 hours a week at a job and finding time to study), or illness (having a head cold that wipes you out for a week).

The Social Readjustment Scale, developed by psychologists T. H. Holmes and R. H. Rahe, measures the intensity of people's reaction to change and the level of stress related to it (see Key 2.5). Holmes and

Use the Holmes-Rahe scale to find your "stress score."

key 2.5

To find your current "stress score," add the values of the events that you experienced in the past year. The higher the number, the greater the stress. Scoring over 300 points puts you at high risk for developing a stress-related health problem. A score between 150 and 299 reduces your risk by 30 percent, and a score under 150 means that you have only a small chance of a problem.

EVENT	VALUE	EVENT	VALUE
Death of spouse or partner	100	Son or daughter leaving home	29
Divorce	73	Trouble with in-laws	29
Marital separation	65	Outstanding personal achievement	28
Jail term	63	Spouse begins or stops work	26
Personal injury	53	Starting or finishing school	26
Marriage	50	Change in living conditions	25
Fired from work	47	Revision of personal habits	24
Marital reconciliation	45	Trouble with boss	23
Retirement	45	Change in work hours, conditions	20
Changes in family member's health	44	Change in residence	20
Pregnancy	40	Change in schools	20
Sex difficulties	39	Change in recreational habits	19
Addition to family	39	Change in religious activities	19
Business readjustment	39	Change in social activities	18
Change in financial status	38	Mortgage or loan under $10,000	17
Death of a close friend	37	Change in sleeping habits	16
Change to different line of work	36	Change in # of family gatherings	15
Change in # of marital arguments	35	Change in eating habits	15
Mortgage or loan over $10,000	31	Vacation	13
Foreclosure of mortgage or loan	30	Christmas season	12
Change in work responsibilities	29	Minor violation of the law	11

Source: Reprinted from *Journal of Psychosomatic Research,* 11(2), T. H. Holmes and R. H. Rahe, "The social readjustment rating scale," 1967, with permission from Elsevier.

Stress levels can help or hinder performance.

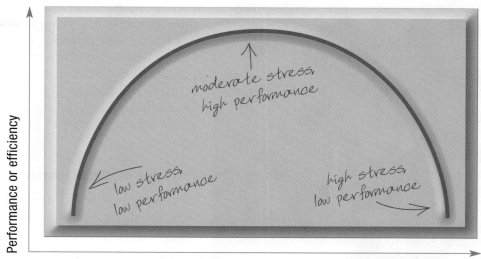

Stress or anxiety

Source: From *Your Maximum Mind* by Herbert Benson, M.D., copyright © 1987 by Random House, Inc. Used by permission of Time Books, a division of Random House, Inc.

Rahe found that people experience both positive and negative events as stressors. For example, whereas some events like the death of a relative are clearly negative, other stressors, like moving to a new house or even taking a vacation, are generally positive.

At their worst, stress reactions can make you physically ill (Chapter 10 will examine stress-related health issues—situations in which stress goes beyond normal levels, causing physical and emotional problems). But stress can also supply the heightened readiness you need to do well on tests, finish assignments on time, prepare for a class presentation, or meet new people. Your goal is to find a manageable balance. Key 2.6, based on research conducted by Drs. Robert M. Yerkes and John E. Dodson, shows that stress can be helpful or harmful, depending on how much you experience.

Successful time management and goal setting relieve stress

Dealing with the stress of college life is, and will continue to be, one of your biggest challenges. But here's a piece of good news: Every goal-achievement and time-management strategy you have read in this chapter contributes to your ability to cope with stress. Remember that stress refers to how you react to pressure. When you set up effective plans to move toward goals, you reduce pressure. When you set a schedule that works for you and stick to it, you reduce pressure. Less pressure, less stress.

Carefully analyze the relationship between stress and your time-management habits. Often, people create extra stress for themselves without realizing it. For example, say you're a night person but have

Extracurricular activities can provide relaxation and stress relief, as these students have found in their work with an a cappella singing group after class.

a habit of scheduling early classes. You are consistently stressed about waking up in time for them. What's wrong with this picture? Reduce your stress by finding practical ways to change your scheduling. Taking later classes will help, but if that isn't possible, cope in other ways. Get to bed earlier a few nights a week, nap in the afternoon, and exercise briefly before class to restore your energy. Make sure that you are not expending energy coping with stress that you can avoid with thought and planning.

Stress-management strategies

Here are some practical strategies for coping with the day-to-day stress of being a college student.

- **Eat right.** The healthier you are, the stronger you are—and the more able you will be to weather tough situations like all-nighters, illnesses, and challenging academic work. Try to eat a balanced, low-fat diet and avoid overloading on junk food. Try also to maintain a healthy weight.
- **Exercise.** Physical exercise will help you manage your stress. Find a type of exercise you like and make it a regular part of your life.
- **Get sleep.** Avoid the system-wide dysfunction that sleep deprivation can create. Figure out how much sleep you need and do your best to get it. When you pull an all-nighter, make sure you play catch-up over the next couple of days.
- **Think positively.** Try to think of the things you have to do as challenges, not problems.
- **Seek balance.** A balanced life includes time by yourself—for your thoughts, hopes, and plans—and time for relaxation, in whatever form you choose.
- **Address issues.** Try not to let things lie too long. Analyze stressful situations and use problem-solving strategies (see Chapter 4) to decide on a specific plan of action.
- **Set boundaries and learn to say no.** Try to delegate. Review obligations regularly; if you find that something has become a burden, then consider dropping it from your roster of activities.
- **Surround yourself with people who are good for you.** Focus on friends who are good listeners and who will support you when things get rough. Friendship and humour go a long way toward reducing stress.

Sometimes you'll be able to pull out the strategies that fit the situation, finding ways to cope with the stress you encounter.

Sometimes stress will make you feel frozen, not knowing where to turn to work your way out of it. At those times, remember: *Any step toward a goal is a stress-management strategy because it reduces pressure.* In that sense, this entire book is a stress-management strategy. Every useful tool, from test-taking hints to job-hunting strategies, will help you reduce the pressure and cover the distance toward your dreams.

Successful Intelligence Wrap-Up

Self-management is about making well-examined choices—and you are the manager who does the choosing. Think intelligently about what you value, what goals are important to you, and how to best manage your time. Here's how you have built skills in Chapter 2:

Analytical

In the Get Analytical exercise, you explored what you value and how your values inform educational goals. As you read the section on goals, you broke down the goal-setting process into its step-by-step parts. While exploring the topic of time management, you thought about who you are as a time manager and how that affects your scheduling and procrastination habits.

Creative

With the Get Creative exercise to motivate you, you came up with ideas about how to pursue an important personal goal. Exploring the importance of flexibility in time management showed you the key role of creativity in the face of change.

Practical

You explored the practical action of mapping out and pursuing goals step-by-step, and considered how this process applies to declaring a major or program of study. In the section on time management, you examined practical strategies for getting in control of your schedule, and created a to-do list tailored to an upcoming busy day in the Get Practical exercise. At the end of the chapter, you gathered practical, time-related techniques for managing the stress that all students encounter.

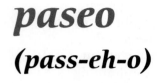

paseo

(pass-eh-o)

This Spanish word refers to an activity that traditionally takes place in Spanish towns in the time of evening after the afternoon siesta, or rest. At this late afternoon hour, families often dress up and enjoy a paseo— a walk outdoors in the town, to be seen and to socialize.[13] The relaxed pace of traditional life in many European countries holds a lesson for the overscheduled, harried student. Like many other students, you may feel like you just can't afford to take a break when there is so much to do. However, you also might not be able to afford the negative effects of the stress that results when you *don't* take a break. When you manage your time effectively, you will be able to make time for relaxation, which is critical for stress reduction. So find your version of the *paseo*—a walk on the campus, a coffee shop visit, a game of soccer— and make it part of your life.

"Goals are dreams with deadlines."

DIANA SCHARF HUNT

SUCCESSFUL INTELLIGENCE

Think, Create, Apply

Make your first term count. Campus resources, clubs, student activity groups, and other organizations can enrich your college experience. To benefit from what your school has to offer, set a goal to get involved sooner rather than later.

Step 1. Think it through: *Analyze your post-secondary self.*
Making connections with people and groups in university and college starts with understanding who you are as a student, both alone and in relation to your school's student body. On a separate sheet of paper, describe your particular circumstances, opinions, and needs in a short paragraph, using questions like these to think through your description:

- How would you describe yourself in terms of culture, ethnicity, gender, age, and lifestyle?
- How would you describe your student status—traditional or returning, full- or part-time?
- How long are you planning to be in your current college? Is it likely that you will transfer?
- What family and work obligations do you have?
- What is your current living situation?
- What do you feel are your biggest academic challenges?
- What do you like to study, and why does it interest you?

Step 2. Think out of the box: *Brainstorm your ideal extracurriculars.*
On a second piece of paper, write ideas about how you want to spend your time outside of class. To inspire creative ideas, try using one or more of the following questions as a starting point:

- If you had no fear, what horizon-broadening experience would you sign up for?
- When you were in elementary school, what were your favourite activities? Which activities might translate into current interests and pursuits?
- What kinds of organizations, activities, groups, experiences, or people make you think, "Wow, I want to do that"?

• Think about the people that bring out the best in you. What do you like to do with them? What kinds of things are they involved with?

Step 3. Make it happen: *Take practical steps toward the activities you like.* First, look in your student handbook at the resources and organizations your school offers. These may include some or all of the following:

Academic centres (reading, writing, etc.)	On-campus work opportunities
Academic organizations	Religious organizations
Adult education centre	School publications
Arts clubs (music, drama, dance, etc.)	School TV/radio stations
Fraternities/sororities	Sports clubs
International student groups	Student associations
Minority student groups	Student government
	Volunteer groups

Taking your analysis of yourself and your creative ideas into consideration, use the left-hand column on the grid that follows to list the three offices or organizations you most want to check out this term. Then—through your school publications and/or a little legwork—fill in the grid for the categories shown across the top for each item. The last column requires action—fill it in when you have made contact with each office or organization. Finally, if you wish to become more involved after your initial contact, go for it.

Office or organization	Location	Hours, or times of meetings	What it offers	Phone number or e-mail	Initial contact— date and what happened

TEAMWORK

Create Solutions Together

Multiple paths to a goal. In a group of three or four, brainstorm important academic goals that can reasonably be accomplished in the course of one year in college. Write your ideas on a piece of paper. From that list, pick out one goal to explore together.

Each group member takes two minutes alone to think about this goal in terms of the first goal-achievement step under the heading Work to Achieve Goals on page 42—defining a goal-setting strategy. In other words, answer the question "How would I do it?" Each person writes down all the paths he or she can think of.

The group then gathers and everyone shares their strategies. The group evaluates strategies and chooses one that seems effective. Finally, as a group, brainstorm the rest of the goal-achievement process on pages 42–43, based on the chosen strategy or path:

- **Set a timetable.** When do you plan to reach your goal? Discuss different time frames and how each might change the path.
- **Be accountable.** What safeguards will keep you on track? Talk about different ways to make sure you are moving ahead consistently.
- **Get unstuck.** What will you do if you hit a roadblock? Brainstorm the roadblocks that could get in the way of this particular goal. For each, come up with ways to overcome the obstacle.

At the end of the process, you should have a wealth of ideas for how to approach one particular academic goal—and an appreciation for how many paths you could take in order to get there.

WRITING

Journal and Put Skills to Work

Use the tables here to record data. Answer questions and write additional thoughts on a separate piece of paper, in a journal, or on a computer file.

Journal entry: Discover how you spend your time. In the table on the following page, estimate the total time you think you spend per week on each listed activity. Then, add the hours. If your number is over 168 (the number of hours in a week), rethink your estimates and recalculate so that the total equals 168.

Now, spend a week recording exactly how you spend your time. The chart on pages 62–63 has blocks showing half-hour increments.

Estimate time spent on activities.

Activity	Estimated Time Spent	Activity	Estimated Time Spent
Class		Chores and personal business	
Work		Friends and important relationships	
Studying		Telephone/email time	
Sleeping		Leisure/entertainment	
Eating		Spiritual life	
Family time/child care		Other	
Commuting/traveling		**ESTIMATED GRAND TOTAL**	

Monday		Tuesday		Wednesday		Thursday	
TIME	ACTIVITY	TIME	ACTIVITY	TIME	ACTIVITY	TIME	ACTIVITY
6:00 A.M.		6:00 A.M.		6:00 A.M.		6:00 A.M.	
6:30 A.M.		6:30 A.M.		6:30 A.M.		6:30 A.M.	
7:00 A.M.		7:00 A.M.		7:00 A.M.		7:00 A.M.	
7:30 A.M.		7:30 A.M.		7:30 A.M.		7:30 A.M.	
8:00 A.M.		8:00 A.M.		8:00 A.M.		8:00 A.M.	
8:30 A.M.		8:30 A.M.		8:30 A.M.		8:30 A.M.	
9:00 A.M.		9:00 A.M.		9:00 A.M.		9:00 A.M.	
9:30 A.M.		9:30 A.M.		9:30 A.M.		9:30 A.M.	
10:00 A.M.		10:00 A.M.		10:00 A.M.		10:00 A.M.	
10:30 A.M.		10:30 A.M.		10:30 A.M.		10:30 A.M.	
11:00 A.M.		11:00 A.M.		11:00 A.M.		11:00 A.M.	
11:30 A.M.		11:30 A.M.		11:30 A.M.		11:30 A.M.	
12:00 P.M.		12:00 P.M.		12:00 P.M.		12:00 P.M.	
12:30 P.M.		12:30 P.M.		12:30 P.M.		12:30 P.M.	
1:00 P.M.		1:00 P.M.		1:00 P.M.		1:00 P.M.	
1:30 P.M.		1:30 P.M.		1:30 P.M.		1:30 P.M.	
2:00 P.M.		2:00 P.M.		2:00 P.M.		2:00 P.M.	
2:30 P.M.		2:30 P.M.		2:30 P.M.		2:30 P.M.	
3:00 P.M.		3:00 P.M.		3:00 P.M.		3:00 P.M.	
3:30 P.M.		3:30 P.M.		3:30 P.M.		3:30 P.M.	
4:00 P.M.		4:00 P.M.		4:00 P.M.		4:00 P.M.	
4:30 P.M.		4:30 P.M.		4:30 P.M.		4:30 P.M.	
5:00 P.M.		5:00 P.M.		5:00 P.M.		5:00 P.M.	
5:30 P.M.		5:30 P.M.		5:30 P.M.		5:30 P.M.	
6:00 P.M.		6:00 P.M.		6:00 P.M.		6:00 P.M.	
6:30 P.M.		6:30 P.M.		6:30 P.M.		6:30 P.M.	
7:00 P.M.		7:00 P.M.		7:00 P.M.		7:00 P.M.	
7:30 P.M.		7:30 P.M.		7:30 P.M.		7:30 P.M.	
8:00 P.M.		8:00 P.M.		8:00 P.M.		8:00 P.M.	
8:30 P.M.		8:30 P.M.		8:30 P.M.		8:30 P.M.	
9:00 P.M.		9:00 P.M.		9:00 P.M.		9:00 P.M.	
9:30 P.M.		9:30 P.M.		9:30 P.M.		9:30 P.M.	
10:00 P.M.		10:00 P.M.		10:00 P.M.		10:00 P.M.	
10:30 P.M.		10:30 P.M.		10:30 P.M.		10:30 P.M.	
11:00 P.M.		11:00 P.M.		11:00 P.M.		11:00 P.M.	
11:30 P.M.		11:30 P.M.		11:30 P.M.		11:30 P.M.	
12–6 A.M.		12–6 A.M.		12–6 A.M.		12–6 A.M.	

Friday		Saturday		Sunday		Notes
TIME	ACTIVITY	TIME	ACTIVITY	TIME	ACTIVITY	
6:00 A.M.		6:00 A.M.		6:00 A.M.		
6:30 A.M.		6:30 A.M.		6:30 A.M.		
7:00 A.M.		7:00 A.M.		7:00 A.M.		
7:30 A.M.		7:30 A.M.		7:30 A.M.		
8:00 A.M.		8:00 A.M.		8:00 A.M.		
8:30 A.M.		8:30 A.M.		8:30 A.M.		
9:00 A.M.		9:00 A.M.		9:00 A.M.		
9:30 A.M.		9:30 A.M.		9:30 A.M.		
10:00 A.M.		10:00 A.M.		10:00 A.M.		
10:30 A.M.		10:30 A.M.		10:30 A.M.		
11:00 A.M.		11:00 A.M.		11:00 A.M.		
11:30 A.M.		11:30 A.M.		11:30 A.M.		
12:00 P.M.		12:00 P.M.		12:00 P.M.		
12:30 P.M.		12:30 P.M.		12:30 P.M.		
1:00 P.M.		1:00 P.M.		1:00 P.M.		
1:30 P.M.		1:30 P.M.		1:30 P.M.		
2:00 P.M.		2:00 P.M.		2:00 P.M.		
2:30 P.M.		2:30 P.M.		2:30 P.M.		
3:00 P.M.		3:00 P.M.		3:00 P.M.		
3:30 P.M.		3:30 P.M.		3:30 P.M.		
4:00 P.M.		4:00 P.M.		4:00 P.M.		
4:30 P.M.		4:30 P.M.		4:30 P.M.		
5:00 P.M.		5:00 P.M.		5:00 P.M.		
5:30 P.M.		5:30 P.M.		5:30 P.M.		
6:00 P.M.		6:00 P.M.		6:00 P.M.		
6:30 P.M.		6:30 P.M.		6:30 P.M.		
7:00 P.M.		7:00 P.M.		7:00 P.M.		
7:30 P.M.		7:30 P.M.		7:30 P.M.		
8:00 P.M.		8:00 P.M.		8:00 P.M.		
8:30 P.M.		8:30 P.M.		8:30 P.M.		
9:00 P.M.		9:00 P.M.		9:00 P.M.		
9:30 P.M.		9:30 P.M.		9:30 P.M.		
10:00 P.M.		10:00 P.M.		10:00 P.M.		
10:30 P.M.		10:30 P.M.		10:30 P.M.		
11:00 P.M.		11:00 P.M.		11:00 P.M.		
11:30 P.M.		11:30 P.M.		11:30 P.M.		
12–6 A.M.		12–6 A.M.		12–6 A.M.		

As you go through the week, write in what you do each hour, indicating when you started and when you stopped. Don't forget activities that don't feel like "activities"—such as sleeping, relaxing, or watching TV. Finally, be sure to record your *actual* activities instead of how you want to spend or think you should have spent your time. There are no wrong answers.

After a week, go through your filled-in chart and add up how many hours you spent on the activities for which you previously estimated your hours by tallying the hours in the second column in the table below. Use straight tally marks—round off to half hours and use a short tally mark for each half hour. In the third column, total the hours for each activity. Leave the "Ideal Time in Hours" column blank for now.

Add up actual time spent on activities.

Activity	Time Tallied Over One-Week Period	Total Time in Hours	Ideal Time in Hours
Example: Class	IIII IIII IIII II	16.5	
Class			
Work			
Studying			
Sleeping			
Eating			
Family time/child care			
Commuting/traveling			
Chores and personal business			
Friends and important relationships			
Telephone/email time			
Leisure/entertainment			
Spiritual life			
Other			
ACTUAL GRAND TOTAL			

Add the totals in the third column to find your actual grand total. Compare your actual grand total to your estimated grand total; then for each category, compare your actual time spent in hours to your "Estimated Time Spent" totals (from the chart on page 61). Use a separate sheet of paper to answer the following questions:

- What matches and what doesn't? Describe the most interesting similarities and differences.
- Where do you waste the most time? What do you think that is costing you?

Now evaluate what kinds of changes might improve your ability to achieve goals. Analyze what you do daily, weekly, and monthly. Go back to the table on page 64 and fill in the "Ideal Time in Hours" column. Consider the difference between actual hours and ideal hours. Ask yourself questions:

- On what activities do you think you should spend more or less time?
- What are you willing to do to change, and why?

Finally, write a short paragraph describing two key time-management changes in detail. Describe what goal you are aiming for, and map out how you plan to put the changes into action.

Real-life writing. Examine two areas of academic specialty. Use your course catalogue to identify two academic areas that look interesting. Write a short report comparing and contrasting the majors or concentrations in these areas, being sure to note GPA requirements, number of courses, relevance to career areas, campus locations of departments, "feel" of the departments, other requirements, and any other relevant characteristics. Conclude your report with observations about how this comparison and evaluation process has refined your thinking.

PERSONAL PORTFOLIO

Prepare for Career Success

Complete the following in your electronic portfolio or on separate sheets of paper.

Knowledge, skills, and attitudes. No matter what career goals you ultimately pursue, certain knowledge, skills, and attitudes are useful in any career area. Consider this list of what employers look for in people they hire:

Acceptance	Continual learning
Critical thinking	Goal setting
Leadership	Teamwork
Communication	Creativity
Flexibility	Integrity
Positive attitude	

Choose and circle three of these that you want to focus on developing this year. Map out a plan for your progress by indicating a series of smaller goals that will lead you toward developing these skills. For example:

Skill: Teamwork

Long-term goal: To be comfortable and effective working with others

Short-term goal: I will join, or form, a study group for my economics class.

Short-term goal: I will participate in a short-term volunteering opportunity for which I am required to work in a team with others.

Short-term goal: When looking into courses with my adviser, I will consider teamwork opportunities (small group work, small seminar courses) as one of my criteria.

SUGGESTED READINGS

Allen, David. *Getting Things Done: The Art of Stress-Free Productivity.* New York: Penguin Books, 2003.

Burka, Jane B., Ph.D., and Lenora M. Yuen, Ph.D. *Procrastination.* Reading, MA: Perseus Books, 1983.

Covey, Stephen. *The Seven Habits of Highly Effective People.* New York: Simon & Schuster, 1995.

Emmett, Rita. *The Procrastinator's Handbook: Mastering the Art of Doing It Now.* New York: Walker & Co., 2000.

Gleeson, Kerry. *The Personal Efficiency Program: How to Get Organized to Do More Work in Less Time,* 2nd ed. New York: John Wiley & Sons, 2000.

Lakein, Alan. *How to Get Control of Your Time and Your Life.* New York: New American Library, 1996.

Leyden-Rubenstein, Lori. *The Stress Management Handbook.* New York: McGraw-Hill, 1999.

Sapadin, Linda, and Jack Maguire. *Beat Procrastination and Make the Grade: The Six Styles of Procrastination and How Students Can Overcome Them.* New York: Penguin USA, 1999.

Timm, Paul R. *Successful Self-Management: A Psychologically Sound Approach to Personal Effectiveness.* Los Altos, CA: Crisp Publications, 1996.

INTERNET RESOURCES

Jim Blakley, a counsellor for Loyalist College in Belleville, Ontario, offers students many tips on time management:
www.loyalistc.on.ca/services/counsel/time.html

Top Achievement—goal-setting and self-improvement resources are available at
www.topachievement.com

The University of Waterloo offers a useful online exercise to help you identify your values:
www.cdm.uwaterloo.ca/step1_3.asp

The University of Toronto offers this online material for their students. It includes tips on stress at university and on time management:
www.calss.utoronto.ca/Publications/coping.htm and www.calss.utoronto.ca/Publications/tm.htm

1. *A Report from the Center for Academic Integrity,* Center for Academic Integrity, Kenan Institute for Ethics, Duke University, October 1999, http://www.academicintegrity.org (accessed March 2001).

2. Ibid.

3. Background information on cultural diversity from Afsaneh Nahavandi and Ali Malekzadeh, *Organizational Behavior: The Person-Organization Fit* (Upper Saddle River, NJ: Prentice Hall, 1999).

4. Louis E. Boone, David L. Kurtz, and Judy R. Block, *Contemporary Business Communication,* 2nd ed. (Upper Saddle River, NJ: Prentice Hall, 1997), 68–72.

5. Louis E. Boone and David L. Kurtz, *Contemporary Business Communication* (Englewood Cliffs, NJ: Prentice Hall, 1994), 643.

6. Paul Timm, *Successful Self-Management: A Psychologically Sound Approach to Personal Effectiveness* (Los Altos, CA: Crisp Publications, 1987), 22–41.

7. William E. Sydnor, "Procrastination," from the California Polytechnic State University Study Skills Library [online]. Based on *Overcoming Procrastination* by Albert Ellis, May 2003, http://www.sas.calpoly.edu/asc/ssl/procrastination.html. Used with permission.

8. Jane B. Burka, Ph.D., and Lenora M. Yuen, Ph.D., *Procrastination* (Reading, MA: Perseus Books, 1983), 21–22.

9. Ibid.

10. The following articles were used as sources in this section: Glenn C. Altschuler, "Adapting to College Life in an Era of Heightened Stress," *New York Times,* Education Life, Section 4A, August 6, 2000, 12; Carol Hymowitz and Rachel Emma Silverman, "Can Workplace Stress Get Worse?" *Wall Street Journal,* January 16, 2001, B1; Robert M. Sapolsky, "Best Ways to Reduce Everyday Levels of Stress . . . Bad Ol' Stress," *Bottom Line Personal,* January 15, 2000, 13; Kate Slaboch, "Stress and the College Student: A Debate," April 4, 2001, http://www.jour.unr.edu/outpost/voices/voi.slaboch.stress.html; University of South Florida, The Counseling Center for Human Development, "Coping with Stress in College," April 4, 2001 http://usfweb.usf.edu/counsel/self-hlp/stress.htm; Jodi Wilgoren, "Survey Shows High Stress Levels in College Freshmen," *New York Times,* January 23, 2000.

11. Hans Selye, *The Stress of Life* (New York: McGraw-Hill, 1976).

12. Patricia Chisholm, "Coping with Stress," *Maclean's,* January 8, 1996, 33–36.

13. Christopher J. Moore, *In Other Words: A Language Lover's Guide to the Most Intriguing Words around the World* (New York: Walker, 2004), 36–37.

LEARNING HOW YOU LEARN
Making the most of your abilities

3

"Successfully intelligent people figure out their strengths and their weaknesses, and then find ways to capitalize on their strengths—make the most of what they do well—and to correct for or remedy their weaknesses—find ways around what they don't do well, or make themselves good enough to get by."

ROBERT J. STERNBERG

As a post-secondary student, you are investing valuable resources—time, effort, and money—in your education. Learning is the return on your investment. How well you learn, and therefore how good a return you receive, depends in part on knowing yourself in two ways: knowing *how* you learn and knowing what you want to *do* with what you learn.

This chapter focuses first on helping you identify your learning styles, because when you understand how you learn, you will be a more effective student. Then you will read about majors, programs of study, and careers, because knowing where you want your education to take you will motivate you toward a goal.

Learning is not something you do just in college or university. In its report entitled *Employability Skills 2000+* (see Key 1.2), the Conference Board of Canada recognizes the need for employees to "learn and grow continuously." It also stresses the importance of assessing one's own strengths and weaknesses as well as setting goals for learning on your own terms. In other words, it is important in the "real world" to know what your learning style is.

In this chapter you will explore answers to the following questions:

- Why explore who you are as a learner? 70

- What tools can help you assess how you learn and interact with others? 72

- How can you use your self-knowledge? 80

- How can you choose a major or program of study? 83

- How can multiple intelligences help you explore majors/programs of study and careers? 86

- How can you identify and manage learning disabilities? 89

- *Successful Intelligence Wrap-Up* 91

Analytical	Creative	Practical
• Analyzing your eight multiple intelligences	• Creating new ways to develop your abilities	• How to choose and use your best study strategies
• Investigating how you relate to others	• Envisioning career ideas based on how you learn	• How to adjust to an instructor's teaching style
• Evaluating how useful you find particular strategies	• Developing a new vision of yourself as a learner	• How to manage a learning disability

Why explore *who you are* as a learner?

People have particular ideas about themselves that often come from family members, friends, and experiences. Maybe your mother thinks you are "the funny one," or "the quiet one." School experiences may have resulted in a label of "thinker," "slacker," "go-getter," or "shy." However, you probably have *not* thought about yourself as a learner. Most students, even those who do well in the areas traditionally valued by schools (verbal and mathematical skills), conclude that "this high (or low) GPA is who I am. I am intelligent (or not)." More often than not, decisions stretching throughout a lifetime are made based on that self-assessment.

Your unique intelligence can change and develop

Each person in the world is unique, with an individual blend of characteristics that define everything from how you look, to your health, to your ability to take on physical and mental challenges. Each person also has a particular way in which the mind receives and processes information. However, even when instructors are aware of these learning differences, it is impossible for them to tailor a classroom presentation to 15, 40, or 300 unique learners. Everyone is also born with particular levels of ability and potential in different areas. For example, there are "natural" musicians who can play anything they hear, and champion chess players who can anticipate an opponent's moves. Those natural abilities, plus effort and environmental influences, combine to create a recipe for the achievement level a person can attain.

Picture a bag of a variety of rubber bands. Some are thick, some are thin; some are long, some are short. *But all of them can stretch.* A small rubber band, stretched out, can reach the length of a larger one that lies unstretched. In other words, with effort and focus, you can grow to some extent whatever raw material you have at the start. *To reach your individual potential is your most worthy goal, and the most you can ask of yourself.*

When people adhere to the idea of unchangeable intelligence, they tend to lock themselves into a level of performance consistent with the labels pinned on them, as Sternberg did in his early education. If you believe that no matter what you do, you can never learn to write well, why try to write? If, however, you believe you can become a strong writer with effort and practice, you are likely to strive to improve. Studies of the brain, showing that humans of any age are able to build new neuropathways and thereby learn new ideas and skills, support Sternberg's theory that intelligence can change over time.[1] Set aside the notion that your intelligence has a "fixed" level as you continue through this chapter, through college, and into your life after college. Work instead to understand your strengths—to define the characteristics of your rubber band and stretch it to the limit. And, as you work with others, work to see them in terms of their potential, doing what you can to help them see and stretch their own rubber bands.

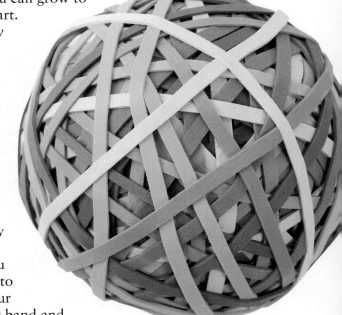

© Jaimie Duplass—Fotolia.com

Assessments can help you learn about yourself

Whereas a test seeks to identify a level of performance, an assessment—as professor and psychologist Howard Gardner puts it—is "the obtaining of information about a person's skills and **potentials** . . . providing useful feedback to the person."[2] You can think of an assessment as an exploration that, if honest, will reliably produce interesting and helpful information.

With the information you gain from the two assessments you will take in this chapter—*Multiple Pathways to Learning* and the *Personality Spectrum*—you will learn more about what your strengths and weaknesses are, leading you to the ability to maximize those strengths and compensate for those weaknesses as a successfully intelligent learner. For example, if math gives you trouble, you can draw diagrams of math problems if you have strength in visual–spatial intelligence or talk out problems with a study partner if you have strength in interpersonal intelligence. (You will learn about these **intelligences** and other characteristics later in the chapter.)

Understanding yourself as a learner will also help you to see and appreciate how people differ. In a study group or classroom, each person is taking in the material in a unique way. You can use what you know about how others approach learning to improve communication and teamwork.

Self-knowledge is an important, lifelong goal

Self-knowledge is a key to personal power. There is much about yourself, your surroundings, and your experiences that you cannot control. However, with self-knowledge, you *can* work toward controlling how you respond to circumstances as you and your environment change, making adjustments that will help you cope and grow. Because you and

POTENTIALS
Abilities that may be developed.

INTELLIGENCE
As defined by H. Gardner, an ability to solve problems or fashion products that are useful in a particular cultural setting or community.

your circumstances will change throughout your life, self-knowledge is a lifelong quest.

What role do assessments play in this quest for self-knowledge? Any assessment is simply a snapshot, a look at who you are at a given moment. There are no "right" answers, no "best" set of scores. Use these assessments to help you look at the present—and plan for the future—by asking questions: "Who am I right now?" "How does this compare with who I want to be?"

As you continue through the chapter and complete the assessments, beware of seeing them as definitive answers to the question of who you are. Compare the process of responding to the assessment questions to the experience of trying on new eyeglasses to correct blurred vision. The glasses will not create new paths and possibilities, but they will help you see more clearly the ones that exist today.

What tools can help you assess *how you learn and interact* with others?

This chapter presents two assessments that help you discover your style of learning and personality traits. View these as two equally important halves that help you form a whole picture of who you are as a learner.

The first assessment, which focuses on learning preferences, is called Multiple Pathways to Learning. It is based on the Multiple Intelligences Theory developed by Howard Gardner.

The second assessment is geared toward personality analysis and is based on the Myers-Briggs Type Inventory® (MBTI). The assessment is called Personality Spectrum and helps you evaluate how you react to people and situations.

Multiple intelligences

There is a saying, "It is not how smart you are, but how you are smart." In 1983, Howard Gardner, a Harvard University professor, changed the way people perceive intelligence and learning with his theory of Multiple Intelligences. This theory holds that there are at least eight distinct intelligences possessed by all people, and that every person has developed some intelligences more fully than others. According to the Multiple Intelligences Theory, when you find a task or subject easy, you are probably using a more fully developed intelligence; when you have more trouble, you may be using a less developed intelligence.[3]

Gardner believes that the way you learn is a unique blend of intelligences that result from your distinctive abilities, challenges, experiences, and training. In addition, how you learn isn't necessarily set in stone—particular levels of ability in the intelligences may develop or recede based on changes in your life. Traditionally, the notion of intelligence has been linked to tests such as the Stanford-Binet IQ test and others like it that rely on mathematical, logical, and verbal measurements.

Gardner, however, thinks that this doesn't accurately reflect the entire spectrum of human ability:

I believe that we should . . . look . . . at more naturalistic sources of information about how peoples around the world develop skills important to their way of life. Think, for example, of sailors in the South Seas, who find their way around hundreds, or even thousands, of islands by looking at the constellations of stars in the sky, feeling the way a boat passes over the water, and noticing a few scattered landmarks. A word for intelligence in a society of these sailors would probably refer to that kind of navigational ability.[4]

Key 3.1 offers brief descriptions of the focus of each of the intelligences. You can find information on related skills and study techniques in Key 3.2 on page 78. The Multiple Pathways to Learning assessment helps you determine the levels to which your intelligences are developed.

Each intelligence is linked to specific abilities.

key 3.1

INTELLIGENCE	DESCRIPTION	HIGH-ACHIEVING EXAMPLE
Verbal–Linguistic	Ability to communicate through language; listening, reading, writing, speaking	Playwright William Shakespeare
Logical–Mathematical	Ability to understand logical reasoning and problem solving; math, science, patterns, sequences	Microsoft founder Bill Gates
Bodily–Kinesthetic	Ability to use the physical body skilfully and to take in knowledge through bodily sensation; coordination, working with hands	Canadian Olympic Gold Medal–winning rower Adam van Koeverden
Visual–Spatial	Ability to understand spatial relationships and to perceive and create images; visual art, graphic design, charts and maps	Architect Frank Gehry
Interpersonal	Ability to relate to others, noticing their moods, motivations, and feelings; social activity, co-operative learning, teamwork	Telejournalist George Stroumboulopoulos
Intrapersonal	Ability to understand one's own behaviour and feelings; self-awareness, independence, time spent alone	The Dalai Lama
Musical	Ability to comprehend and create meaningful sound; sensitivity to music and musical patterns	Canadian Singer and musician Jann Arden
Naturalist	Ability to identify, distinguish, categorize, and classify species or items, often incorporating high interest in elements of the natural environment	Conservationist David Suzuki

Personality spectrum

Personality assessments indicate how you respond to both internal and external situations—in other words, how you react to information, thoughts, and feelings, as well as to people and events. Employers may give such assessments to employees and use the results to set up and evaluate teams.

The Myers-Briggs Type Inventory is one of the most widely used personality inventories in both psychology and business, and was one of the first instruments to measure psychological types. Katharine Briggs and her daughter, Isabel Briggs Myers, together designed the MBTI. Later, David Keirsey and Marilyn Bates combined the 16 Myers-Briggs types into four temperaments and developed an assessment called the Keirsey Temperament Sorter based on those temperaments.

Derived in part from the Myers-Briggs and Keirsey theories, the *Personality Spectrum* assessment adapts and simplifies their material into four personality types—Thinker, Organizer, Giver, and Adventurer—and was developed by Dr. Joyce Bishop in 1997. The Personality Spectrum gives you a personality perspective on how you can maximize your functioning at school and work. For each personality type, you'll see techniques that improve work and school performance, learning strategies, and ways of relating to others. Page 76 gives you more details about each type.

Scoring the assessments

The assessments follow this section of text. As you complete them, try to answer the questions objectively—in other words, answer the questions to best indicate who you are, not who you want to be (or who your parents or instructors want you to be). Then, enter your scores on page 75. Don't be concerned if some of your scores are low—that is true for almost everyone.

Following each assessment is information about the typical traits of, and appropriate study strategies for, each intelligence (Key 3.2) or spectrum (Key 3.3) dimension. You have abilities in all areas, though some are more developed than others. Therefore, you may encounter useful suggestions under any of the headings. During this course, try a large number of new study techniques and keep what works for you.

IMPORTANT NOTE   *about scoring...*

The two assessments that follow are scored *differently.* For Multiple Pathways to Learning, each intelligence has a set of numbered statements, and you consider each numbered statement on its own, giving it the number you feel best suits your response to it. You will, therefore, have any combination of numbers for each intelligence, from all 4s to all 1s or anywhere in between.

For Personality Spectrum, you rank the four items that complete each statement, giving a 4 to the one most like you, a 3 to the one next most like you, a 2 to the next, and a 1 to the one least like you. You will, therefore, have a 4, 3, 2, and 1 for each of the eight numbered questions.

MULTIPLE PATHWAYS TO LEARNING

Directions: Rate each statement as follows. Write the number of your response (1–4) on the line next to the statement and total each set of six questions.

rarely	sometimes	usually	always
1	2	3	4

1. _____ I enjoy physical activities.
2. _____ I am uncomfortable sitting still.
3. _____ I prefer to learn through doing.
4. _____ When sitting, I move my legs or hands.
5. _____ I enjoy working with my hands.
6. _____ I like to pace when I'm thinking or studying.

_____ TOTAL for BODILY–KINESTHETIC

1. _____ I enjoy telling stories.
2. _____ I like to write.
3. _____ I like to read.
4. _____ I express myself clearly.
5. _____ I am good at negotiating.
6. _____ I like to discuss topics that interest me.

_____ TOTAL for VERBAL–LINGUISTIC

1. _____ I use maps easily.
2. _____ I draw pictures/diagrams when explaining ideas.
3. _____ I can assemble items easily from diagrams.
4. _____ I enjoy drawing or photography.
5. _____ I do not like to read long paragraphs.
6. _____ I prefer a drawn map over written directions.

_____ TOTAL for VISUAL–SPATIAL

1. _____ I like math.
2. _____ I like science.
3. _____ I problem-solve well.
4. _____ I question how things work.
5. _____ I enjoy planning or designing something new.
6. _____ I am able to fix things.

_____ TOTAL for LOGICAL–MATHEMATICAL

1. _____ I listen to music.
2. _____ I move my fingers or feet when I hear music.
3. _____ I have good rhythm.
4. _____ I like to sing along with music.
5. _____ People have said I have musical talent.
6. _____ I like to express my ideas through music.

_____ TOTAL for MUSICAL

1. _____ I need quiet time to think.
2. _____ I think about issues before I want to talk.
3. _____ I am interested in self-improvement.
4. _____ I understand my thoughts and feelings.
5. _____ I know what I want out of life.
6. _____ I prefer to work on projects alone.

_____ TOTAL for INTRAPERSONAL

1. _____ I like doing a project with other people.
2. _____ People come to me to help settle conflicts.
3. _____ I like to spend time with friends.
4. _____ I am good at understanding people.
5. _____ I am good at making people feel comfortable.
6. _____ I enjoy helping others.

_____ TOTAL for INTERPERSONAL

1. _____ I enjoy nature whenever possible.
2. _____ I think about having a career involving nature.
3. _____ I enjoy studying plants, animals, or oceans.
4. _____ I avoid being indoors except when I sleep.
5. _____ As a child I played with bugs and leaves.
6. _____ When I feel stressed I want to be out in nature.

_____ TOTAL for NATURALISTIC

PERSONALITY SPECTRUM

STEP 1. Rank order all four responses to each question from most like you (4) to least like you (1). Use the circles next to the responses to indicate your rankings.

4 most like me   **3** more like me   **2** less like me   **1** least like me

1. I like instructors who

   a. ☐ tell me exactly what is expected of me.
   b. ☐ make learning active and exciting.
   c. ☐ maintain a safe and supportive classroom.
   d. ☐ challenge me to think at higher levels.

2. I learn best when the material is

   a. ☐ well organized.
   b. ☐ something I can do hands-on.
   c. ☐ about understanding and improving the human condition.
   d. ☐ intellectually challenging.

3. A high priority in my life is to

   a. ☐ keep my commitments.
   b. ☐ experience as much of life as possible.
   c. ☐ make a difference in the lives of others.
   d. ☐ understand how things work.

4. Other people think of me as

   a. ☐ dependable and loyal.
   b. ☐ dynamic and creative.
   c. ☐ caring and honest.
   d. ☐ intelligent and inventive.

5. When I experience stress I would most likely

   a. ☐ do something to help me feel more in control of my life.
   b. ☐ do something physical and daring.
   c. ☐ talk with a friend.
   d. ☐ go off by myself and think about my situation.

6. I would probably not be a close friend with someone who is

   a. ☐ irresponsible.
   b. ☐ unwilling to try new things.
   c. ☐ selfish and unkind to others.
   d. ☐ an illogical thinker.

7. My vacations could be described as

   a. ☐ traditional.
   b. ☐ adventuresome.
   c. ☐ pleasing to others.
   d. ☐ a new learning experience.

8. One word that best describes me is

   a. ☐ sensible.
   b. ☐ spontaneous.
   c. ☐ giving.
   d. ☐ analytical.

STEP 2. Add up the total points for each letter.

TOTAL FOR   **a.** ☐ Organizer   **b.** ☐ Adventurer   **c.** ☐ Giver   **d.** ☐ Thinker

STEP 3. Plot these numbers on the brain diagram on page 77.

Name: _____   Date: _____

Personality Spectrum: Place a dot on the appropriate number line in the brain diagram for each of your four scores from p. 76; connect the dots; then shade each section using a different colour. Write your scores in the four circles just outside the diagram. See information regarding scores below.

Multiple Pathways to Learning: In the vertical bars below the brain diagram, indicate your scores from p. 75 by shading from the bottom going up until you reach the number corresponding to your score for that intelligence. See information regarding scores below.

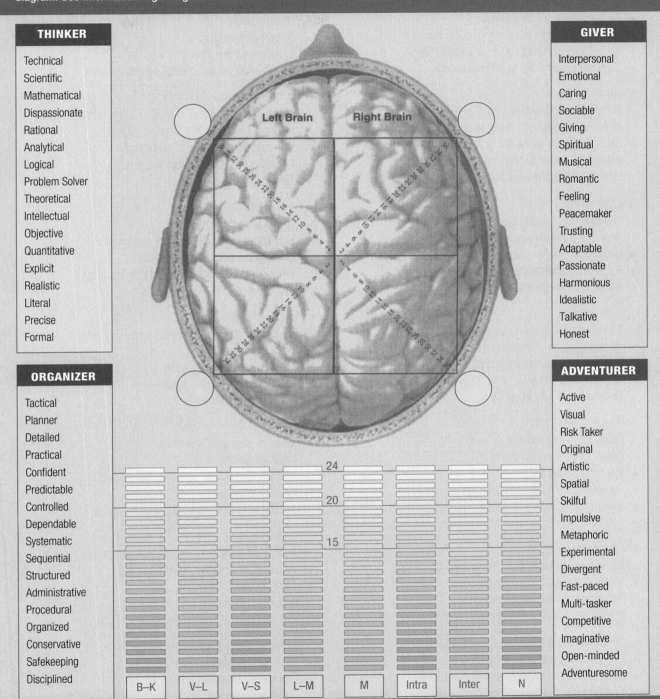

THINKER

Technical
Scientific
Mathematical
Dispassionate
Rational
Analytical
Logical
Problem Solver
Theoretical
Intellectual
Objective
Quantitative
Explicit
Realistic
Literal
Precise
Formal

GIVER

Interpersonal
Emotional
Caring
Sociable
Giving
Spiritual
Musical
Romantic
Feeling
Peacemaker
Trusting
Adaptable
Passionate
Harmonious
Idealistic
Talkative
Honest

ORGANIZER

Tactical
Planner
Detailed
Practical
Confident
Predictable
Controlled
Dependable
Systematic
Sequential
Structured
Administrative
Procedural
Organized
Conservative
Safekeeping
Disciplined

ADVENTURER

Active
Visual
Risk Taker
Original
Artistic
Spatial
Skilful
Impulsive
Metaphoric
Experimental
Divergent
Fast-paced
Multi-tasker
Competitive
Imaginative
Open-minded
Adventuresome

Left Brain   Right Brain

24
20
15

B–K   V–L   V–S   L–M   M   Intra   Inter   N

For the Personality Spectrum, 26–36 indicates a strong tendency in that dimension, 14–25 a moderate tendency, and below 14 a minimal tendency.

For Multiple Pathways to Learning, 21–24 indicates a high level of development in that particular type of intelligence, 15–20 a moderate level, and below 15 an underdeveloped intelligence.

Source for brain diagram: *Understanding Psychology*, 3rd ed., by Morris, © 1996. Adapted by permission of Prentice Hall, Inc., Upper Saddle River, NJ.

How to put your Multiple Intelligences to work for you.

ABILITIES AND SKILLS ASSOCIATED WITH EACH INTELLIGENCE

Verbal–Linguistic
- Analyzing own use of language
- Remembering terms easily
- Explaining, teaching, learning, using humour
- Understanding syntax and meaning of words
- Convincing someone to do something

Musical–Rhythmic
- Sensing tonal qualities
- Creating or enjoying melodies and rhythms
- Being sensitive to sounds and rhythms
- Using "schemas" to hear music
- Understanding the structure of music

Logical–Mathematical
- Recognizing abstract patterns
- Reasoning inductively and deductively
- Discerning relationships and connections
- Performing complex calculations
- Reasoning scientifically

Visual–Spatial
- Perceiving and forming objects accurately
- Recognizing relationships between objects
- Representing something graphically
- Manipulating images
- Finding one's way in space

Bodily–Kinesthetic
- Connecting mind and body
- Controlling movement
- Improving body functions
- Expanding body awareness to all senses
- Coordinating body movement

Intrapersonal
- Evaluating own thinking
- Being aware of and expressing feelings
- Understanding self in relationship to others
- Thinking and reasoning on higher levels

Interpersonal
- Seeing things from others' perspectives
- Co-operating within a group
- Communicating verbally and non-verbally
- Creating and maintaining relationships

Naturalist
- Deep understanding of nature
- Appreciation of the delicate balance in nature

STUDY TECHNIQUES TO MAXIMIZE EACH INTELLIGENCE

Verbal–Linguistic
- Read text and highlight no more than ten percent
- Rewrite notes
- Outline chapters
- Teach someone else
- Recite information or write scripts/debates

Musical–Rhythmic
- Create rhythms out of words
- Beat out rhythms with hand or stick
- Play instrumental music, write raps
- Put new material to songs you already know
- Take music breaks

Logical–Mathematical
- Organize material logically
- Explain material sequentially to someone
- Develop systems and find patterns
- Write outlines and develop charts and graphs
- Analyze information

Visual–Spatial
- Develop graphic organizers for new material
- Draw mind maps
- Develop charts and graphs
- Use colour in notes to organize
- Visualize material

Bodily–Kinesthetic
- Move or rap while you learn
- Pace and recite
- Move fingers under words while reading
- Create "living sculptures"
- Act out scripts of material, design games

Intrapersonal
- Reflect on personal meaning of information
- Visualize information, keep a journal
- Study in quiet settings
- Imagine experiments

Interpersonal
- Study in a group
- Discuss information
- Use flash cards with others
- Teach someone else

Naturalist
- Connect with nature whenever possible
- Form study groups of people with like interests

Adapted by Dr. Joyce Bishop from David Lazear, *Seven Pathways of Learning*, Zephyr Press, 1994.

How to put your Personality Spectrum to work for you.

CHARACTERISTICS OF EACH PERSONALITY TYPE

Thinker

- Solving problems
- Developing models and systems
- Analytical and abstract thinking
- Exploring ideas and potentials
- Ingenuity
- Going beyond established boundaries
- Global thinking—seeking universal truth

Organizer

- Responsibility, reliability
- Operating successfully within social structures
- Sense of history, culture, and dignity
- Neatness and organization
- Loyalty
- Orientation to detail
- Comprehensive follow-through on tasks
- Efficiency

Giver

- Honesty, authenticity
- Successful, close relationships
- Making a difference in the world
- Cultivating your own potential and that of others
- Negotiation; promoting peace
- Communicating with others
- Openness
- Helping others

Adventurer

- High ability in a variety of fields
- Courage and daring
- Approaching problem solving in a hands-on fashion
- Living in the present
- Spontaneity and action
- Ability to negotiate
- Non-traditional style
- Flexibility
- Zest for life

STUDY TECHNIQUES TO MAXIMIZE PERSONALITY TYPES

Thinker

- Find time to reflect independently on new information
- Learn through problem solving
- Design new ways of approaching issues
- Convert material into logical charts and graphs
- Try to minimize repetitive tasks
- Look for opportunities where you have the freedom to work independently

Organizer

- Try to have tasks defined in clear, concrete terms so that you know what is required
- Look for a well-structured, stable environment
- Request feedback
- Use a planner to schedule tasks and dates
- Organize material by rewriting and organizing class or text notes, making flash cards, or carefully highlighting

Giver

- Study with others
- Teach material to others
- Seek out tasks, groups, and subjects that involve helping people
- Find ways to express thoughts and feelings clearly and honestly
- Put energy into your most important relationships

Adventurer

- Look for environments that encourage non-traditional approaches
- Find hands-on ways to learn
- Seek people whom you find stimulating
- Use or develop games and puzzles to help memorize terms
- Fight boredom by asking if you can do something extra or perform a task in a more active way

Joyce Bishop, *Keys to Success*, © 2001.

Remember also that knowing your learning style is not only about guiding your life toward your strongest abilities, it is also about using other strategies when you face challenges. No one goes through life always able to find situations where strengths are in demand and weaknesses are uninvolved. Use the strategies for your weaker areas when what is required of you involves tasks and academic areas that you find difficult. For example, if you are not characteristically strong in logical–mathematical intelligence and have to take a required math or science course, the suggestions geared toward logical–mathematical learners may help you build what skill you have.

How can you *use your self-knowledge?*

 he knowledge you have gained by taking the assessments in this chapter can guide you to smart choices that will bring success in your studies, the classroom, and the workplace.

Study benefits

Knowing how you learn helps you choose study techniques that capitalize on your strengths. For example, if you learn successfully from a linear, logical presentation, you can look for order (for example, a chronology or a problem–solution structure) as you review notes. If you are a strong inter-personal learner, you can try to work in study groups whenever possible.

Learning style also points you toward strategies that help with tasks and topics that don't come so easily. An adventurer who does *not* respond well to linear information, for example, has two choices when faced with logical presentations. She can apply her strengths to the material—for example, she might find a hands-on approach. Or she can work on her ability to handle the material by developing study skills that work well for linear learners.

When you study with others, an understanding of diverse learning styles will help you assign tasks effectively and learn more comprehensively. An interpersonal learner might take the lead in teaching material to others; an organizer might be the schedule coordinator for the group; a musical learner might present information in a new way that helps to solidify concepts.

Successful Intelligence Connections Online

Listen to author Sarah Kravits discuss analytical, creative, and practical ideas for how to choose your best setting for successful studying.

Go to the *Keys to Success* Companion Website at www.pearsoned.ca/carter to listen or download as a podcast.

Classroom benefits

Knowing your learning style can help you make the most of the teaching styles of your instructors (an instructor's teaching style often reflects his or her learning style). Your particular learning style may work well with the way some instructors teach—and yet be a mismatch with other instructors. Occasionally, you may be able to choose an instructor who teaches in a way that maximizes how you learn. Class schedules, however, usually don't make such choices possible.

After several class meetings, you should be able to assess the instructor's teaching styles (it's common for

Maximize Your Classroom Experience

Consider first what you know about yourself as a learner. Then reflect on your instructors' teaching styles this term. Analyze which instructors mesh well with how you learn, and which don't. Make notes here about the situation that you think is the most challenging.

Course: _____ Instructor style: _____

Your analysis of the problem: _____

_____

Next, brainstorm at least three ideas about actions you can take to improve the situation:

1. _____

2. _____

3. _____

Finally, choose one action and put it to practical use. Briefly note what happened: Were there improvements as a result? _____

_____

instructors to have more than one style). Key 3.4 sets forth some common styles. If your style doesn't match up well with that of your instructor, you have a number of options.

Bring extra focus to your weaker areas. Working on your weaker points helps you break new ground in your learning. For example, if you're a verbal person in a math- and logic-oriented class, increase your focus and concentration during class so that you get as much as you can from the presentation. Then spend extra study time on the material, ask others from your class to help you, and search for additional supplemental materials and exercises to reinforce your knowledge.

Ask your instructor for additional help. For example, a visual person might ask an instructor to recommend visuals that help to illustrate the points made in class. Take advantage of your instructor's office hours to talk one-on-one about what's giving you trouble—in a large lecture, your instructor won't know what's going on with you unless you speak up.

"Convert" class material during study time. For example, an interpersonal learner takes a class with an instructor who presents big-picture information in lecture format. This student might organize study groups

Lecture	Instructor speaks to the class for the entire period; little to no class interaction.
Group discussion	Instructor presents material but encourages class discussion throughout.
Small groups	Instructor presents material and then breaks class into small groups for discussion or project work.
Visual focus	Instructor uses visual elements such as diagrams, photographs, drawings, and transparencies.
Verbal focus	Instructor relies primarily on words, either spoken or written on the board or overhead projector.
Logical presentation	Instructor organizes material in a logical sequence, such as by time or importance.
Random presentation	Instructor tackles topics in no particular order, changes topics a lot, or digresses.

and talk through concepts with other group members while filling in the factual gaps. Likewise, a visual student might rewrite notes in different colours to add a visual element—for example, using one colour for central ideas, another for supporting examples.

Instructors are as unique as students, and no instructor can fulfill the particular needs of a whole classroom of individuals. You often have to shift elements of your habitual learning approach to better mesh with how your instructor presents material. Being flexible in this way benefits you throughout life. Just as you can't hand-pick your instructors, in the workplace you are rarely, if ever, able to choose your boss or change his or her style.

Workplace benefits

Because different careers require different abilities, there is no one "best" learning style for the workplace. As the Conference Board of Canada suggests in its document *Employability Skills 2000+* (see Key 1.2), knowing how you learn brings you the following key benefits on the job:

- **Better performance.** Because so much of what you do at school (e.g., interacting with others, reading, taking notes) is what you do on the job, it follows that your learning style is essentially the same as your working style. If you know how you learn, you can look for a career, position, and environment that suit you best. You can perform at the top of your ability if you work at a job in which you feel competent and happy.

- **Better teamwork.** Teamwork is a primary feature of the modern workplace. The better your awareness of your abilities and personality traits, the better you are able to communicate with others and identify what tasks you can best perform in a team situation.

- **Better self-awareness.** Knowing how you learn helps you pinpoint roadblocks. This helps you to work on difficult areas; plus, when a task requires a skill that is tough for you, you can either take special care with it or suggest someone else whose style may be better suited to it.

STRESSBUSTER

MICHAEL MURRAY   University of British Columbia

What techniques have you adopted to focus on your learning strengths and to address your weaknesses as a student? How has this reduced stress in your everyday life, and in your studies?

In order to complete my degree in geography, I need to balance a course load that includes both humanities and science classes. My learning style is more verbal–linguistic, and when I first started my degree, I studied for each course in the same way: I rewrote my notes, highlighted text, and drafted chapter outlines. I found this approach to be really effective for me.

Unfortunately, this study method didn't work as well for my science credits. No matter how hard I studied, I kept having the same problems with courses requiring complex calculations and analyses. I was stressed out and convinced that I would fail and never get my degree.

It wasn't until I changed my study techniques to suit the logical–mathematical skills these courses required, that things finally turned around. I used graphic organizers, charts, and maps to assist with my studying, and it made a big difference.

Knowing my learning style and understanding how to adapt to take on those tougher courses helped to alleviate a lot of my stress. I now know the kinds of courses that I am better suited for and understand when certain science courses require more time and different study techniques.

How can you *choose a major or program of study?*

Taking a practical approach to declaring a **major/program of study** can help you avoid becoming overwhelmed by the task. Think of it as a long-term goal made up of multiple steps (short-term goals) that begin with knowing your learning styles, interests, and talents; exploring academic options; and establishing your academic schedule. You will be wise to start the process now, even though you probably don't need to decide right away—and even if, as is true of many students, you don't yet know what you want to study.

> MAJOR/PROGRAM OF STUDY
>
> An academic subject chosen as a field of specialization, requiring a specific course of study.

Short-term goal #1: Use learning styles assessments to identify interests and talents

Considering what you like and what you do well can lead to a fulfilling area of study. When you identify your interests and talents and choose a major that focuses on them, you are likely to have a positive attitude and perform at your highest level.

To pinpoint the areas that spark your interest, use your Multiple Intelligences and Personality Spectrum assessment results from earlier in this chapter to answer the following questions:

- What courses have I enjoyed the most in post-secondary education and high school? What do these courses have in common?
- What subjects am I drawn to in my personal reading?
- What activities do I look forward to most?
- In what skills or academic areas do I perform best? Am I a "natural" in any area?
- What do people say I do well?
- What are my dominant learning styles?

Short-term goal #2: Explore academic options

Next, find out about the academic choices available at your school. Plan to achieve the following mini-goals in order to reach this short-term goal.

Learn what's possible. Consult your school's undergraduate calendar for guidelines on declaring (and changing) your major. Find answers to these questions:

- When do I have to declare a major/choose my program of study?
- What majors/programs of study are offered at my school?

If a major looks interesting, explore it further by answering these questions:

- What are the minimum requirements?
- What overall average must I maintain in the courses included in the major?
- What preparatory courses (prerequisites) are required? Will I need to upgrade any high-school courses?
- What courses will I be required to take, and in what sequence? How many credits do I need to graduate in the major/program of study?
- Will I have to write a thesis or complete a co-op to graduate?

Work closely with your adviser. Early on, begin discussing your major/program of study with your adviser; he or she can help you evaluate different options.

Visit the department. When considering a major/program of study, analyze your comfort with the academic department as well as with the material. To learn more about the department, ask at the department office for information. Then sit in on several classes to get a feel for the instructors and the work. Consider asking an instructor for an appointment to discuss the program.

Speak to people with experience in the major/program of study. Ask students who are a year or two ahead of you to describe their experiences with the courses, the workload, and the instructors.

Consider creative options for majoring/choosing a program of study. Think beyond the traditional majoring path or program of study, and investigate the possibilities at your school. One or more of the following may be open to you:

- **Double majors.** If, for example, you want to major in English and philosophy, ask your academic adviser if it is possible to meet the requirements for both departments.

- **Interdisciplinary majors.** If your preferred major isn't in the undergraduate calendar, consult your adviser. Some schools allow students to design majors with guidance from advisers and instructors.

- **Minors.** A minor involves a concentration of departmental courses but has fewer requirements than a major. Many students choose a minor that is suited for a career.

- **Majors involving courses outside your school.** Some schools may offer study-abroad programs (in which students spend a semester or a year at an affiliated college in a different country) or opportunities to take courses at nearby schools. Such courses might apply to a major/program of study that interests you.

Short-term goal #3: Establish your academic schedule

Effective time management will enable you to fulfill the requirements of your major and complete all additional credits.

Look at your time frame. How many years do you plan to study? Do you plan to continue your education once you've graduated? If so, do you plan to go there directly after graduation or to take time off?

Set timing for short-term goals. Within your time frame, pinpoint when to accomplish the important short-term goals that will lead to graduation. What are the deadlines for completing core requirements, declaring a major/program of study, completing your co-op, or writing a thesis? Although you won't need to plan out your entire college or university course load at the beginning of your first semester, drafting a tentative curriculum—both within and outside your major/program of study—can help clarify where you are heading.

Identify dates connected to your goal fulfillment. Pay attention to academic dates (you will find an academic calendar in each year's college catalogue and on the college's website). Such dates include registration dates, final date to declare a major/program of study, final date to drop a course, and so forth. Plan ahead so you don't miss a deadline.

Be flexible as you come to a decision

As with any serious challenge that involves defining your path, flexibility is essential. Many students change their minds as they consider majors/programs of study; some declare a major/program of study and then change it one or more times before finding a good fit. Just act on any change right away—once you have

© Dimitrije Tanaskovic—Fotolia.com

considered it carefully—by informing your adviser, completing any required paperwork, and redesigning your schedule to reflect your new choices.

How can multiple intelligences help you *explore majors/programs of study and careers?*

A ll that you have learned in this chapter about your learning styles and strengths has practical application as you begin thinking about your future at school and in the workplace. A strength in one or more intelligences may lead you to a major, an internship, and even a lifelong career.

Key 3.5 lists some possibilities for the eight intelligence types. This list is by no means complete. Rather, it represents only a fraction of the available opportunities. Use what you see here to inspire thought and spur investigation.

Career exploration strategies

Whatever your major, you will benefit from starting to think about careers early on. Use the following strategies to explore what's out there (later in the text, we will examine the topic of career exploration in depth).

Keep what you value in mind. Ask yourself what careers support the principles that guide your life. How important to you are service to others, financial security, a broad-based education, and time for family?

Follow your passion. Find something you love doing more than anything else in the world, and then find a way to make money doing it. If you are sure of what you love to do but cannot pinpoint a career niche, open yourself to your instructors' advice.

Use career resources. Visit your school's career centre to read current media, take an assessment, or explore the career areas that currently have good prospects. Check out careers, industries, and companies on the internet. Talk with people who have jobs that interest you.

Explore educational requirements of careers. How much your choice of a major/program of study matters may depend on the career. For example, pursuing a career in medicine usually requires majoring in the biological sciences. In contrast, aiming for a career in law gives you more flexibility (political science, philosophy, and English are just a few possibilities for pre-law students).

Try hands-on exploration. Extracurricular activities and volunteering opportunities might provide experiences that help you decide. For example, a student interested in teaching may volunteer as a camp counsellor or an after-school tutor.

Multiple intelligences may open doors to majors/programs of study, internships, and careers.

MULTIPLE INTELLIGENCE	CONSIDER MAJORING IN . . .	THINK ABOUT AN INTERNSHIP AT A . . .	LOOK INTO A CAREER AS A . . .
Bodily–Kinesthetic	Massage Therapy Physical Therapy Kinesiology Construction Engineering Chiropractics Sports Medicine Anatomy Dance Theatre	Sports Physician s Office Athletic Club Physical Therapy Centre Chiropractor's Office Construction Company Surveying Company Dance Studio Athletic Club Drafting Firm Theatre Company	Carpenter Draftsman Recreational Therapist Physical Therapist Mechanical Engineer Massage Therapist Dancer or Acrobat Exercise Physiologist Actor
Intrapersonal	Psychology Sociology English Finance Liberal Arts Biology Computer Science Economics	Research and Development Firm Accounting Firm Computer Company Publishing House Pharmaceutical Company Engineering Firm Biology Lab	Research Scientist Motivational Speaker Engineer Physicist Sociologist Computer Scientist Economist Author Psychologist
Interpersonal	Psychology Sociology Education Real Estate Public Relations Nursing Business Hotel/Restaurant Management Rhetoric/Communications	Hotel or Restaurant Travel Agency Real Estate Agency Public Relations Firm Human Resources Customer Service Teaching Assistant Marketing/Sales Office Group Counselling Social Service	Social Worker PR Rep/Media Liaison Human Resources Officer Travel Agent Sociologist Anthropologist Counsellor Therapist Teacher Nurse
Naturalistic	Forestry Astronomy Geology Biology Zoology Atmospheric Sciences Oceanography Agriculture Animal Husbandry Environmental Law Physics	Museum National Park Oil Company Botanical Gardens Environmental Law Firm Outward Bound Adventure Travel Agency Zoo Camp Biological Research Firm	Forest Ranger Botanist or Herbalist Geologist Ecologist Marine Biologist Archaeologist Astronomer Adventure Travel Agent Wildlife Tour Guide Landscape Architect

(continued)

MULTIPLE INTELLIGENCE	CONSIDER MAJORING IN . . .	THINK ABOUT AN INTERNSHIP AT A . . .	LOOK INTO A CAREER AS A . . .
Musical	Music Musical History Musical Theory Performing Arts Composition Voice Liberal Arts Entertainment Law	Performance Hall Radio Station Record Label Ballet or Theatre Company Recording Studio Children's Music Camp Orchestra or Opera Company Musical Talent Agency Entertainment Law Firm	Lyricist or Composer Singer or Musician Voice Coach Music Teacher or Critic Record Executive Conductor Radio DJ Sound Engineer Entertainment Lawyer
Logical–Mathematical	Math Accounting Physics Economics Medicine Banking/Finance Astronomy Computer Science Systems Theory Law Chemistry Engineering	Law Firm Health Care Office Real Estate Brokerage Accounting Firm Animal Hospital Science Lab Consulting Firm Pharmaceutical Firm Bank	Doctor, Dentist, or Veterinarian Accountant Pharmacist Chemist Physicist Systems Analyst Investment Banker Financial Analyst Computer Scientist
Verbal–Linguistic	Communications Marketing English/Literature Journalism Foreign Languages Linguistic Theory Political Science Advertising/PR	Newspaper/Magazine Network TV Affiliate Publishing House Law Firm PR/Marketing Firm Speech Therapist Ad Agency Training Company Human Resources Customer Service	Author Playwright Journalist TV/Radio Producer Literature Teacher Speech Pathologist Business Executive Copywriter or Editor
Visual–Spatial	Visual Arts Architecture Interior Design Multimedia Design Film Theory Photography Art History	Art Gallery Museum Photography Studio Design Firm Advertising Agency Theatrical Set Design Multimedia Firm Architecture Firm Film Studio	Graphic Artist Photographer Architect Cinematographer Art Therapist Designer Cartoonist/Illustrator Art Museum Curator Art Teacher

How can you *identify and manage* learning disabilities?

Although almost everyone faces challenges during their post-secondary career, people with diagnosed learning disabilities have unique challenges that may interfere with university or college success. Focused assistance can help students who are learning disabled to manage their conditions and excel in school.

Some learning disabilities cause reading problems, some create difficulties in math, and some make it difficult for students to process the language they hear. The following will help you understand learning disabilities and, should you be diagnosed with one, give you the tools to manage your disability successfully.

Identifying a learning disability

The National Center for Learning Disabilities (NCLD) defines learning disabilities in terms of what they are and what they are not:[6]

- They are neurological disorders that interfere with one's ability to store, process, and produce information.
- They do *not* include mental retardation, autism, behavioural disorders, impaired vision, hearing loss, or other physical disabilities.
- They do *not* include attention deficit disorder and attention deficit hyperactivity disorder (disorders involving consistent and problematic inattention, hyperactivity, and/or impulsivity), although these problems may accompany learning disabilities.[7]
- They often run in families and are lifelong, although learning-disabled people can use specific strategies to manage and even overcome areas of weakness.
- They must be diagnosed by professionals in order for the disabled person to receive federally funded aid.

How can you determine if you should be evaluated for a learning disability? According to the NCLD, persistent problems in any of the following areas may indicate a learning disability:[8]

- reading or reading comprehension
- math calculations, understanding language and concepts
- social skills or interpreting social cues
- following a schedule, being on time, meeting deadlines
- reading or following maps
- balancing a chequebook
- following directions, especially on multi-step tasks
- writing, sentence structure, spelling, and organizing written work

Details on specific learning disabilities appear in Key 3.6. For an evaluation, contact your school's learning centre or student health centre for a referral to a licensed professional.

What different learning disabilities are and how to recognize them.

DISABILITY/CONDITION	WHAT ARE THE SIGNS?
Dyslexia and related reading disorders	Problems with reading (including spelling, word sequencing, and comprehension) and processing (translating written language to thought or thought to written language)
Dyscalculia (developmental arithmetic disorders)	Difficulties in recognizing numbers and symbols, memorizing facts, aligning numbers, understanding abstract concepts like fractions, and applying math to life skills (time management, gauging distance, handling money, etc.)
Developmental writing disorders	Difficulties in composing complete sentences, organizing a writing assignment, or translating thoughts coherently to the page
Handwriting disorders (dysgraphia)	Disorder characterized by writing disabilities, including writing that is distorted or incorrect; sufferers have poor handwriting that is difficult to read because of inappropriately sized and spaced letters; the use of wrong or misspelled words is also common
Speech and language disorders	Problems with producing speech sounds, using spoken language to communicate, and/or understanding what others say
LD-related social issues	Problems in recognizing facial or vocal cues from others, controlling verbal and physical impulsivity, and respecting others' personal space
LD-related organizational issues	Difficulties in scheduling and in organizing personal, academic, and work-related materials

Source: LD Online: Learning Disabilities Information and Resources, www.ldonline.org (accessed March 17, 2004). © 2001 WETA.

Managing a learning disability

If you are diagnosed with a learning disability, focused action will help you manage it and maximize your ability to learn and succeed:

Be informed about your disability. Search the library and the internet—try The Learning Disabilities Association of Canada at www.ldac-taac.ca, the NCLD at www.ncld.org or LD Online at www.ldonline.org (other websites are listed at the end of the chapter). Seek assistance from your school. Speak with your adviser about specific accommodations that will help you learn. Services mandated by law for students who are learning disabled include:

- extended time on tests
- note-taking assistance (for example, having a fellow student take notes for you)
- assistive technology devices (tape recorders or laptop computers)
- modified assignments
- alternative assessments and test formats

Other services are tutoring, study skills assistance, and counselling.

Be a dedicated student. Be on time and attend class. Read assignments before class. Sit where you can avoid distractions. Review notes soon after class. Spend extra time on assignments. Ask for help.

Build a positive attitude. See your accomplishments in light of how far you have come. Rely on people who support you. Know that the help you receive will give you the best possible chance to learn and grow.

Successful Intelligence Wrap-Up

Think back to Chapter 1, and to Robert Sternberg's definition of successful intelligence—"the kind of intelligence used to achieve important goals." Knowing who you are and how you learn are keys to determining what will work best for you as you pursue goals that are important to you. Here's how you have built skills in Chapter 3:

Analytical

With the Multiple Pathways to Learning self-assessment, you analyzed your levels of ability in the Multiple Intelligences. With the Personality Spectrum self-assessment, you examined how you relate to people and the world around you. In the Get Analytical, Creative, Practical exercise, you examined how your instructors' teaching styles relate to how you learn.

Creative

As you read about Multiple Intelligences and the Personality Spectrum, you may have developed new ideas about your abilities and talents and how you relate to others. In the Get Analytical, Creative, Practical exercise, you brainstormed ideas about how to improve a situation where how you learn doesn't match up well with how an instructor teaches. Reading Key 3.5 about how intelligences relate to majors/programs of study and internships may have inspired thoughts about your major and job plans.

Practical

In the Get Analytical, Creative, Practical exercise, you put an action to practical use in trying to improve your experience in a classroom where you have trouble with the teaching style. Reading Keys 3.2 and 3.3 gave you practical study strategies relating to each Multiple Intelligence and Personality Spectrum dimension. Reading the material on learning disabilities offered practical ways to address and manage any learning disability that you have.

Oruko lonro ni

(o-roo-ko lon-ro nee)

In the language of the Yoruba, an ethnic group living primarily in Nigeria and other West African countries, *oruko lonro ni* translates as "names affect behaviour." This belief, common among the Yoruba people, refers to the idea that people live up to the names given to them by others or even chosen by themselves.[9] As Robert Sternberg learned when he found himself living up to his "lackluster" label as an elementary school student, names and labels have enormous power.

As you think about how you learn, use this idea to understand, and rise above, the confines of the names and labels that you give yourself or that others give you. Use the Multiple Intelligences Theory and the Personality Spectrum dimensions as tools to learn more, not boxes into which to fit yourself. Work to clearly see your unique learning strengths and challenges and to understand your potential for change.

"... no two selves, no two consciousnesses, no two minds are exactly alike. Each of us is therefore situated to make a unique contribution to the world."

HOWARD GARDNER, PSYCHOLOGIST AND EDUCATOR

PERSONAL TRIUMPH

MICHAËLLE JEAN,   Canada's Governor General

Former journalist Michaëlle Jean was installed as the 27th Governor General of Canada on September 27, 2005. She succeeded Adrienne Clarkson. She is the third woman to hold the position and the first black person to be appointed to the position. Prime Minister Paul Martin referred to Jean as "a woman of talent and achievement. Her personal story is nothing short of extraordinary. And extraordinary is precisely what we seek in a Governor General—who must after all represent all of Canada to all Canadians and to the rest of the world as well." Read this account of her life's journey; then use a separate piece of paper to answer the questions on page 94.

Rideau Hall in Ottawa is a long way from Port-au-Prince, Haiti, but that's where Michaëlle Jean's destiny led her.

Born on September 6, 1957, Michaëlle Jean and her family fled Haiti in 1968. Her father, a philosopher, was tortured by government officials under the rule of François "Baby Doc" Duvalier. While Canada was certainly a welcome destination for Jean's family, it wasn't without problems. She and her family experienced racism here in Canada. As a child, she was the target of racial slurs. When she was young, she remembers her classmates touching her black skin to see if it was real.

Despite the adversity she faced as a child, Jean worked to overcome these obstacles. At her swearing-in ceremony, Jean said "The story of that little girl, who watched her parents, her family, and her friends grappling with the horrors of a ruthless dictatorship, who became the woman standing before you today, is a lesson in learning to be free."

On the Personality Spectrum introduced earlier in this chapter, Jean is certainly an Adventurer and a Giver. It was that side of her personality that helped shape who she became. Her academic adventures have taken her to the University of Florence and The Catholic University of Milan. She is fluent in five languages: English, French, Haitian-Creole, Spanish, and Italian. While working on her Master's Degree in Comparative Literature at the University of Montreal, Jean was also making a difference in the community by helping those in need become free from abuse, violence, and harm. Between 1979 and 1987, she worked at shelters for battered women and with immigrant aid organizations. In 1987, she helped coordinate a landmark study into abusive and violent relationships. She hopes to have given hope to those in need. "Hope has been a beacon for me since childhood and into my adult years. It is embodied in this country with its unlimited possibilities—this country that we sometimes take for granted."

She took her passion for social issues and put them on the national media agenda. For 18 years, Jean was a broadcast journalist on CBC Radio-Canada in Quebec. English-speaking Canadians recognize her as the host of CBC Newsworld's documentary programs *The Passionate Eye* and *Rough Cuts*. She is also a social activist filmmaker. Her husband, Jean-Daniel Lafond, is a critically-acclaimed documentary filmmaker. Their films *L'heure de Cuba* (*Cuba's Hour*) and *Haïti dans tous nos rêves* (*Haiti In All Our Dreams*) have won critical acclaim around the world. Jean herself has won many awards for journalism, including the Amnesty International Journalism Award.

Despite some controversy when her appointment was announced, Jean summed up her philosophy on life and Canada in her inaugural speech, "I am determined that the position I occupy as of today will be more than ever a place where citizens' words will be heard, where the values of respect, tolerance and sharing that are essential to me and to all Canadians, will prevail. Those values, which are paramount to me, are linked inextricably with the Canada I love. We must eliminate the spectre of all solitudes and promote solidarity among all the citizens who make up the Canada of today."

SUCCESSFUL INTELLIGENCE

Think, Create, Apply

Learn from the experiences of others. Look back to Michaëlle Jean's Personal Triumph on page 93. After you've read her story, relate her experience to your own life by completing the following:

Step 1. Think it through: *Analyze your learning style or location on the Personality Spectrum.* What is a passion for you as a student? As a person? How might this be explained by your learning style or personality type?

Step 2. Think out of the box: *Imagine ways of advising.* You are an adviser to a student identical to yourself. Be a harsh adviser—how would you criticize your performance as a student? Then be a wise adviser, focused on tapping into learning styles and personality types information—how would you identify challenges and suggest ways to handle them?

Step 3. Make it happen: *Head off your own challenges with practical strategies.* You have identified your learning style and type of personality—and you have imagined what you would say as your own adviser. Now identify steps that will help you face your challenge (choosing particular courses, meeting with an adviser or instructor who can give you ideas, approaching work in particular ways, brainstorming some ways to apply your particular style and gifts).

TEAMWORK

Create Solutions Together

Ideas about personality types. Divide into groups according to the four types of the Personality Spectrum— Thinker-dominant students in one group, Organizer-dominant students in another, Giver-dominant students in a third, and Adventurer-dominant students in a fourth. If you have scored the same in more than one of these types, join whatever group is smaller. With your group, brainstorm the following lists for your type:

1. the strengths of this type
2. the struggles it brings

3. the stressors (things that cause stress) for this type
4. career areas that tend to suit this type
5. career areas that are a challenge for this type
6. people who annoy this type the most (often because they are strong in areas where this type needs to grow)

If there is time, each group can present this information to the entire class; this will boost understanding and acceptance of diverse ways of relating to information and people.

WRITING

Journal and Put Skills To Work

Record your thoughts on a separate piece of paper or in a journal.

Journal entry: Strengths and weaknesses. What have the personal assessments in this chapter taught you about your strengths? Choose what you consider your greatest strength and discuss how you plan to use it to your advantage this semester. What areas of weakness did the assessments highlight? Choose a weakness that has given you difficulty in school and brainstorm ways to compensate for it this semester. Finally, brainstorm ideas for how you will deal this semester with the kinds of people who challenge you the most.

PERSONAL PORTFOLIO

Prepare for Career Success

Complete the following. Use a separate sheet of paper or, if you can, use a graphics program.

Self-portrait. Because self-knowledge helps you to make the best choices about your future, a self-portrait is an important step in your career exploration. Use this exercise to synthesize everything you have been exploring about yourself into one comprehensive "self-portrait." Design your portrait in "think link" style, using words and visual shapes to describe your dominant Multiple Intelligences and Personality Spectrum dimensions, values, abilities, career interests, and anything else that is an important part of who you are.

A "think link" is a visual construction of related ideas, similar to a map or web, that represents your thought process. Ideas are written inside geometric shapes, often boxes or circles, and related ideas and facts are attached to those ideas by lines that connect the shapes. See the note-taking section in Chapter 6 for more about think links.

Use the style shown in the example in Key 3.7 or create your own. For example, in this exercise you may want to create a "wheel" of ideas coming off your central shape, entitled "Me." Then, spreading out from each of those ideas (interests, learning style, etc.), draw lines connecting all of the thoughts that go along with that idea. Connected to "Interests," for example, might be "singing," "stock market," and "history."

You don't have to use the wheel image. You might want to design a treelike think link or a line of boxes with connecting thoughts written below the boxes, or anything else you like. Let your design reflect who you are, just as what you write does.

One example of a self-portrait.

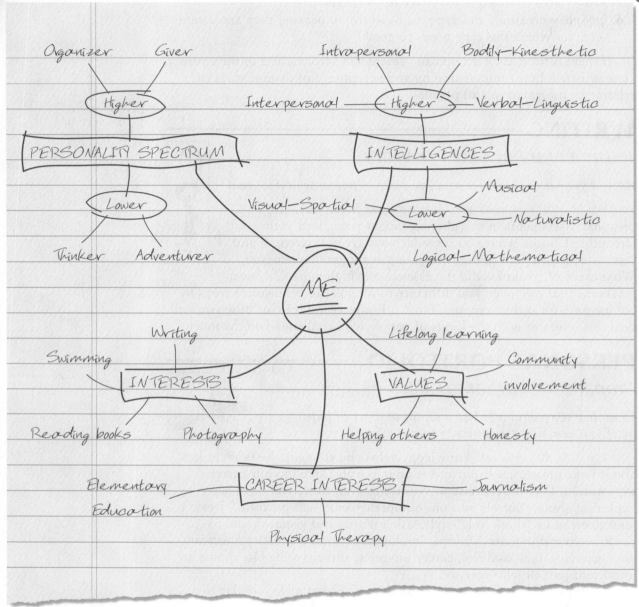

SUGGESTED READINGS

Cobb, Joyanne. *Learning How to Learn: A Guide for Getting into College with a Learning Disability, Staying in, and Staying Sane.* Washington, DC: Child Welfare League of America, 2001.

College Board, ed. *The College Board Index of Majors and Graduate Degrees 2001.* New York: College Entrance Examination Board, 2000.

Gardner, Howard. *Intelligence Reframed: Multiple Intelligences for the 21st Century.* New York: Basic Books, 2000.

Gardner, Howard. *Multiple Intelligences: New Horizons.* New York: Perseus Books, 2006.

Fogg, Neeta, et al. *The College Majors Handbook with Real Career Paths and Payoffs: The Actual Jobs,*

Earnings, and Trends for Graduates of 60 College Majors. Indianapolis, IN: Jist Works, 2004.

Keirsey, David. *Please Understand Me II: Temperament, Character, Intelligence.* Del Mar, CA: Prometheus Nemesis Book Company, 1998.

Levine, Mel. *A Mind at a Time.* New York: Simon & Schuster, 2003.

Mooney, Jonathan, and David Cole. *Learning Outside the Lines: Two Ivy League Students with Learning Disabilities and ADHD Give You the Tools.* New York: Fireside, 2000.

Pearman, Roger R., and Sarah C. Albritton. *I'm Not Crazy, I'm Just Not You: The Real Meaning of the 16 Personality Types.* Palo Alto, CA: Consulting Psychologists Press, 1997.

Phifer, Paul. *College Majors and Careers: A Resource Guide for Effective Life Planning*, 4th ed. Chicago: Ferguson Publishing, 1999.

Sclafani, Annette. *College Guide for Students with Learning Disabilities.* New York: Laurel Publications, 2003.

Smilstein, Rita. *We're Born to Learn: Using the Brain's Natural Learning Process to Create New Curriculum.* Thousand Oaks, CA: Corwin Press, 2005.

INTERNET RESOURCES

All Kinds of Minds (learning strategies for all types of learners):
www.allkindsofminds.org

Attention Deficit Disorder Association:
www.add.org

Canadian Learning Disabilities Resource Community:
www.ldrc.ca

Children and Adults with Attention Deficit/Hyperactivity Disorder:
www.chadd.org

Howard Gardner, Multiple Intelligences, and Education:
www.infed.org/thinkers/gardner.htm

International Dyslexia Association:
www.interdys.org

Internet Archive (podcast on Multiple Intelligences):
www.archive.org/details/dcampdaraabrams

Keirsey Temperament Sorter and other Myers-Briggs information:
www.keirsey.com

The Learning Disabilities Association of Canada:
www.ldac-taac.ca

Learning Disabilities Online:
www.ldonline.org

New Horizons for Learning—Multiple Intelligences:
www.newhorizons.org/strategies/mi/front_mi.htm

PodcastDirectory.com (overview of learning disabilities):
www.podcastdirectory.com/podshows/407721

ENDNOTES

1. One such study is K. Warner Schaie, "The Seattle Longitudinal Studies of Adult Intelligence," in *Essential Papers on the Psychology of Aging*, ed. M. Powell Lawton and Timothy A. Salthouse (New York: New York University Press, 1998), 263–271. Also available online at http://www.memory-key.com/seniors/longitudinal.htm.

2. Howard Gardner, *Multiple Intelligence: New Horizons* (New York: Basic Books, 2006), 180.

3. Howard Gardner, *Multiple Intelligences: The Theory in Practice* (New York: HarperCollins, 1993), 5–49.

4. Ibid, 7.

5. Developed by Joyce Bishop, Ph.D., Golden West College, Huntington Beach, CA. Based on Howard Gardner, *Frames of Mind: The Theory of Multiple Intelligences* (New York: HarperCollins, 1993).

6. National Center for Learning Disabilities, "LD at a Glance" [online], http://www.ncld.org/LDInfoZone/InfoZone_FactSheet_LD.cfm (accessed May 2003).

7. National Center for Learning Disabilities, "Adult Learning Disabilities: A Learning Disability Isn't Something You Outgrow. It's Something You Learn to Master" [pamphlet] (New York: National Center for Learning Disabilities).

8. National Center for Learning Disabilities, "LD Advocates Guide" [online], http://www.ld.org/Advocacy/tutorial_talking_about.cfm (accessed May 2003).

9. Christopher J. Moore, *In Other Words: A Language Lover's Guide to the Most Intriguing Words around the World* (New York: Walker, 2004), 78.

ANALYTICAL, CREATIVE, AND PRACTICAL THINKING

Solving problems and making decisions

4

"Successfully intelligent people define problems correctly and thereby solve those problems that really confront them, rather than extraneous ones. . . . [They] carefully formulate strategies for problem solving. In particular, they focus on long-range planning rather than rushing in and then later having to rethink their strategies."

ROBERT J. STERNBERG

To serve you successfully, your education must do more than fill your head with facts and figures: It must also give you the tools to work through problems and decisions. These tools take the form of analytical, creative, and practical thinking skills and are at the heart of *successful intelligence*.

This chapter will help you build your ability to analyze information, come up with creative ideas, and put a practical plan into action. This ability is emphasized by the Conference Board of Canada's Employability Skills 2000+ report (see Key 1.2) in which employers underline the significance of being able to "assess situations, identify problems and then evaluate and implement solutions."

In this chapter you will explore answers to the following questions:

- What does it mean to think with successful intelligence? 100

- How can you improve your analytical thinking skills? 102

- How can you improve your creative thinking skills? 108

- How can you improve your practical thinking skills? 113

- How can you use successful intelligence to solve problems and make decisions? 118

- Successful Intelligence Wrap-Up 124

Chapter 4's Successful Intelligence Skills

Analytical

- Evaluating facts, opinions, assumptions, and perspectives
- Analyzing whether examples support ideas
- Evaluating potential and actual solutions and choices

Creative

- Brainstorming
- Taking risks and promoting a creative environment
- Developing potential solutions and choices

Practical

- How to identify problems and decisions
- How to use a plan to work through problems and decisions
- How to adapt to your environment and learn from experience

What does it mean to think with successful intelligence?

Some tasks primarily engage one thinking skill at a time. You might use analytical thinking (also known as *critical thinking*) to complete a quiz, creative thinking to write a poem, or practical thinking to get errands done on a busy day. However, when you need to solve a problem or make a decision, combining your analytical, creative, and practical thinking skills gives you the greatest chance of moving forward successfully.[1] These three skills give you any number of ways to connect to material in school and out (Key 4.1).

Successfully intelligent thinking means asking and answering questions

What is thinking? According to experts, it is what happens when you ask questions and move toward the answers.[2] "To think through or rethink anything," says Dr. Richard Paul, director of research at the Center for Critical Thinking and Moral Critique, "one must ask questions that stimulate our thought. Questions define tasks, express problems and delineate issues. . . . [O]nly students who have questions are really thinking and learning."[3]

As you answer questions, you transform raw data into information that you can use. A *Wall Street Journal* article entitled "The Best Innovations Are Those That Come from Smart Questions" relates the

DISCIPLINE	ANALYTICAL THINKING	CREATIVE THINKING	PRACTICAL THINKING
Behavioural Science	Comparing one theory of child development with another	Devising a new theory of child development	Applying child development theories to help parents and teachers understand and deal with children more effectively
Literature	Analyzing the development of the main character in a novel	Writing alternative endings to the novel	Using the experience of the main character to better understand and manage one's own life situations
History	Considering similarities and differences between WWI and WWII	Imagining yourself as a German citizen, dealing with economic depression after WWI	Deciding which WWI and WWII lessons can be applied to current Middle East conflicts
Sports	Analyzing the opposing team's strategy on the soccer field	Coming up with innovative ways to move the ball downfield	Using tactics to hide your strategy from an opposing team—or a competing company

Source: Adapted from Robert J. Sternberg, *Successful Intelligence*. Plume: New York, 1997, p. 149.

story of a cell biology student, William Hunter, whose professor told him that "the difference between good science and great science is the quality of the questions posed." Later, as a doctor and the president and CEO of a pharmaceutical company, Dr. Hunter asked questions about new ways to use drugs. His questions led to the development of a revolutionary product—a drug-coated coronary stent that prevents scar tissue from forming. Through seeking answers to probing questions, Dr. Hunter reached a significant goal.[4]

You use questions in order to analyze ("How bad is my money situation?"), come up with creative ideas ("How could I earn money?"), and apply practical solutions ("How can I get a job on campus?"). Later in the chapter, in the sections on analytical, creative, and practical thinking, you will find examples of the kinds of questions that drive each skill.

Like any aspect of thinking, questioning is not often a straightforward process. Sometimes the answer doesn't come right away. Often the answer leads to more—and more specific—questions.

Successfully intelligent thinking requires purpose and drive

To ask useful questions, you need to know *why* you are questioning. A general question can be your starting point for defining your purpose: "What am I trying to accomplish, and why?" As you continue your thought process, you will find more specific purposes that help you generate questions along the way.

Knowing your purpose helps you with one of the most important tools you need in order to activate your thinking powers: The *drive* to think. "Critical-thinking skills are different from critical-thinking dispositions, or a willingness to deploy these skills," says cognitive psychologist D. Alan Bensley of Frostburg State University in Maryland. In other words, having the skills isn't enough—you also have to want to use them. Skilled thinkers not motivated to use their thinking skills are likely to make decisions in ways similar to those who don't have the thinking skills to use.[5]

The bottom line is that the three skills, or aspects, of successful intelligence are useful to you only if you activate them. As Sternberg says, "It is more important to know when and how to use these aspects of successful intelligence than just to have them."[6] If you know and understand your purpose, you are more likely to be willing to use your skills. Begin by exploring the analytical thinking skills that you'll need to solve problems and make decisions effectively.

How can you improve your *analytical thinking* skills?

Analytical thinking—also known as critical thinking—is the process of gathering information, analyzing it in different ways, and evaluating it for the purposes of gaining understanding, solving a problem, or making a decision. The first step in analytical thinking, as with all aspects of successful intelligence, is to define your purpose. What do you want to analyze, and why? Perhaps you need to analyze the plot of a novel in order to determine its structure; maybe you want to analyze your schedule in order to figure out whether you are arranging your time and responsibilities effectively.

Once you define your purpose, the rest of the analytical process involves gathering the necessary information, analyzing and clarifying the ideas, and evaluating what you've found.

Gather information

Information is the raw material for thinking. Choosing what to gather requires a careful analysis of how much information you need, how much time you will spend gathering it, and whether the information is relevant. Say, for instance, that your assignment is to write a paper on rock 'n' roll music in Canada. If you gathered every available resource on the topic, it might be next semester before you got to the writing stage.

Here's how you might use analysis to effectively gather information for that paper:

- Reviewing the assignment, you learn that the paper should be 10 pages and cover at least three influential Canadian musicians.

- At the library and online, you find a lot of what appears to be relevant information.

- You choose Neil Young, Randy Bachman, and Joni Mitchell, and then select three in-depth sources on each of the three musicians and how they influenced the development of rock music in Canada.

In this way you achieve a sub-goal—a selection of useful materials—on the way to your larger goal of writing a well-crafted paper.

Analyze and clarify information

Once you've gathered the information, the next step is to analyze it to determine whether the information is reliable and useful in helping you answer your questions.

Break information into parts

When analyzing information, you break information into parts and examine the parts so that you can see how they relate to each other and to information you already know. The following strategies help you break information down into pieces and set aside what is unclear, unrelated, or unimportant, resulting in a deeper and more reliable understanding.

Separate the ideas. If you are reading about Neil Young, you might want to break down his career and significant contributions to music into those as a solo artist and those as a member of The Mynah Birds, Buffalo Springfield, and Crosby, Stills, Nash, and Young. You might also want to separate his contributions as a performer and as a songwriter.

Compare and contrast. Look at how things are similar to, or different from, each other. You might explore how these three musicians are similar in style. You might look at how they differ in what they want to communicate with their music.

Examine cause and effect. Look at the possible reasons why something happened (possible causes) and its consequences (effects, both positive and negative). You might also wish to examine which contemporary Canadian musicians were influenced by Neil Young or how the grunge movement of the 1990s was inspired by Young.

Look for themes, patterns, and categories. Note connections that arise out of how bits of information relate to one another. You may choose to write about the theme of social and political consciousness in the lyrics of Neil Young. What category would Neil Young's music best fit into: rock or folk?

Once the ideas are broken down, you can examine whether examples support ideas, separate fact from opinion, consider perspective, and investigate hidden assumptions.

Examine whether examples support ideas

When you encounter an idea or claim, examine how it is supported with examples or evidence (facts, expert opinion, research findings, personal experience, and so on). Ideas that aren't backed up with solid evidence or made concrete with examples are not useful. Be critical of the information you gather; don't take it at face value.

For example, a blog written by a 12-year-old may make statements about what kids do on the internet. The word of one person, who may or may not be telling the truth, is not adequate support. On the other hand, a report on children and internet safety published by the National Crime Prevention Centre of Justice Canada may be more reliable.

Whenever you see an **argument** in written materials, you use questioning to judge the quality of the evidence, whether it supports the central idea, and whether examples and ideas connect logically.

Distinguish fact from opinion

Finding credible, reliable information with which to answer questions and come up with ideas enables you to separate fact from opinion.

A *statement of fact* is information presented as objectively real and verifiable ("It's raining outside right now"). In contrast, a *statement of opinion* is a belief, conclusion, or judgment that is inherently difficult—and sometimes impossible—to verify ("This is the most miserable rainstorm ever"). Key 4.2 defines important characteristics

ARGUMENT
A set of connected ideas, supported by examples, made by a writer to prove or disprove a point.

Examine how fact and opinion differ.

key
4.2

OPINIONS INCLUDE STATEMENTS THAT . . .	FACTS INCLUDE STATEMENTS THAT . . .
. . . *show evaluation.* Any statement of value indicates an opinion. Words such as *bad, good, pointless,* and *beneficial* indicate value judgments. Example: "Bob Geldof is the most socially consious rock star ever."	. . . *deal with actual people, places, objects, or events.* Example: "In 1985, Bob Geldof organized Live Aid, which raised money and awareness for famine relief in Africa. In 2005, LIVE 8 helped push the G8 Summit agenda into the mainstream."
. . . *use abstract words.* Words that are complicated to define, like *misery* or *success,* usually indicate a personal opinion. Example: "The charity event was a smashing success."	. . . *use concrete words or measurable statistics.* Example: "The charity event raised $5,862."
. . . *predict future events.* Statements that examine future occurrences are often opinions. Example: "Mr. Maurin's course is going to set a new enrolment record this year."	. . . *describe current events in exact terms.* Example: "Mr. Maurin's course has set a new enrolment record this semester."
. . . *use emotional words.* Emotions are by nature unverifiable. Attending chances are that statements using such words as *delightful* or *miserable* express an opinion. Example: "Attending that class is a miserable experience."	. . . *avoid emotional words and focus on the verifiable.* Example: "Citing dissatisfaction with the instruction, 7 out of the 25 students in that class withdrew in September."
. . . *use absolutes.* Absolute qualifiers, such as *all, none, never,* and *always,* often point to an opinion. Example: "All students need to have a job while in school."	. . . *avoid absolutes.* Example: "Some students need to have a job while in school."

Source: Adapted from Ben E. Johnson, *Stirring Up Thinking.* New York: Houghton Mifflin, 1998, pp. 268–270.

of fact and opinion. Even though facts may seem more solid, you can also make use of opinions if you determine that they are backed up with facts. However, it is important to examine opinions for their underlying perspectives and assumptions.

Examine perspectives and assumptions

Perspective is a characteristic way of thinking about people, situations, events, and ideas. Perspectives can be broad, such as a generally optimistic or pessimistic view of life. Or they can be more focused, such as an attitude about whether students should commute or live on campus.

Perspectives are associated with *assumptions*—judgments, generalizations, or biases influenced by experience and values. For example, the perspective that there are many different successful ways to be a family leads to assumptions such as "Single-parent homes can provide nurturing environments" and "Same-sex couples can rear well-adjusted children." Having a particular experience with single-parent homes or same-sex couples can build or reinforce a perspective.

Shifting your perspective helps you accept and understand different ways of living and interacting. Two students communicate via sign language on campus.

Assumptions often hide within questions and statements, blocking you from considering information in different ways. Take this classic puzzler as an example: "Which came first, the chicken or the egg?" Thinking about this question, most people assume that the egg is a chicken egg. If you think past that assumption and come up with a new idea—such as, the egg is a dinosaur egg—then the obvious answer is that the egg came first!

Examining perspectives and assumptions is important for two reasons. First, they often affect your perception of the validity of materials you read and research. Second, your own perspectives and assumptions can cloud your interpretation of the information you encounter.

Perspectives and assumptions in information. Being able to determine the perspectives that underlie materials will help you separate **biased** from unbiased information. For example, the conclusions in two articles on federal versus provincial government control of education may differ radically if one appears in a politically conservative publication and one appears in a liberal publication. Comparing those articles will require that you understand and take into account the conservative and liberal perspectives on government's role in education.

Assumptions often affect the validity of materials you read and research. A historical document that originated online in a conservative

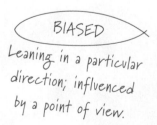

BIASED

Leaning in a particular direction; influenced by a point of view.

blog may assume that liberal policies on health care are flawed, but may also leave out information to the contrary. Clearly understanding such a document means separating the assumptions from the facts.

Personal perspectives and assumptions. Your own preferences, values, and prejudices—which influence your perspective—can affect how accurately you view information. Students who think that the death penalty is wrong, for example, may have a hard time analyzing the facts and arguments in an article that supports it. Or in a research situation, they might use only materials that agree with their perspective.

Consider the perspectives and assumptions that might follow from your values. Then when you have to analyze information, try to set them aside. "Anticipate your reactions and prejudices and then consciously resist their influence," says Colby Glass, professor of information research and philosophy.[7]

In addition to helping you analyze accurately, opening yourself to new perspectives will help you build knowledge. The more you know, the more information you have to work with as you move through life and encounter new problems and decisions. Come to school ready to hear and read about new ideas, think about their merits, and make informed decisions about what you believe. Says Sternberg, "We need to . . . see issues from a variety of viewpoints and, especially, to see how other people and other cultures view issues and problems facing the world."[8]

Evaluate information

You've gathered and analyzed your information. You have examined its components, its evidence, its validity, its perspective, and any underlying assumptions. Now, based on an examination of evidence and careful analysis, you *evaluate* whether an idea or piece of information is good or bad, important or unimportant, right or wrong. You then set aside what is not useful and use the rest to form an opinion, possible solution, or decision.

For example, you're working on a group presentation on the effects of television-watching on young children. You've gathered information that relates to your topic, come up with an idea, and analyzed whether the information supports this idea. Now you evaluate all of the evidence and present what's useful in an organized, persuasive way. Another example: In creating a résumé, you decide which information to include that will generate the most interest from potential employers and present you in the best light possible.

See Key 4.3 for some questions you can ask to build and use analytical thinking skills.

Analytical thinking is only part of the picture. Pursuing your goals in school and in the workplace requires not just analyzing information but also thinking creatively about how to use it.

Ask questions like these in order to analyze.

To gather information, ask:	• What requirements does my goal have?
	• What kinds of information do I need to meet my goal?
	• What information is available?
	• Where and when is it available? Where and when can I access it?
	• Of the sources I found, which ones will best help me achieve my goal?

To analyze, ask:	• What are the parts of this information?
	• What is similar to this information? What is different?
	• What are the reasons for this? Why did this happen?
	• What ideas or themes emerge from this material?
	• How would you categorize this information?
	• What conclusions can you make about this information?

To see if examples support an idea, ask:	• What examples, or evidence, support the idea?
	• Does the evidence make sense?
	• Does the evidence support the idea/claim?
	• Is this evidence key information that I need to answer my question?
	• Are there examples that might disprove the idea/claim?

To distinguish fact from opinion, ask:	• Do the words in this information signal fact or opinion? (see Key 4.2)
	• What is the source of this information? Is the source reliable?
	• How does this information compare to other facts or opinions?
	• If this is an opinion, is it supported by facts?
	• How can I use this fact or opinion?

To examine perspectives and assumptions, ask:	• Who is the author? What perspectives might this person have?
	• What might be emphasized or left out as a result of the perspective?
	• How could I consider this information from a different perspective?
	• What assumptions might lie behind this statement or material?
	• How could I prove or disprove an assumption?
	• What contradictory assumptions might be equally valid?
	• How might a personal perspective or assumption affect the way I see this material?

To evaluate, ask:	• Do I agree with this information?
	• Does this information fit what I'm trying to prove or accomplish?
	• Is this information true or false, and why?
	• How important is this information?
	• Which ideas or pieces of information would I choose to focus on?

Adapted from www.ed.fnal.gov/trc/tutorial/taxonomy.html (Richard Paul, *Critical Thinking: How to Prepare Students for a Rapidly Changing World,* 1993) and from www.kcmetro.edu/longview/ctac/blooms.htm, Barbara Fowler, Longview Community College "Bloom's Taxonomy and Critical Thinking."

GET ANALYTICAL!

Analyze a Statement

Consider this statement; then analyze it by answering the questions that follow.

"The internet is the best place to find information about any topic."

Is this statement fact or opinion? Why?

_____

_____

What examples can you think of that support or negate this statement?

_____

_____

What perspectives are guiding this statement?

_____

_____

What assumptions underlie the statement? Pose a problem: What negative effects might result from accepting these assumptions and therefore agreeing with the statement?

_____

_____

As a result of your critical thinking, what is your evaluation of this statement?

_____

_____

How can you improve your *creative thinking* skills?

hat is creativity?

- Some researchers define creativity as combining existing elements in an innovative way to create a new purpose or result (using a weak adhesive to mark pages in a book, a 3M scientist created Post-it® Notes).

- Others see creativity as the art of generating ideas from taking a fresh look at how things are related (noting what ladybugs eat inspired organic farmers to bring them in to consume crop-destroying aphids).

- Still others, including Sternberg, define it as the ability to make unusual connections—to view information in quirky ways that bring about unique results

Creativity connects analytical and practical information.

Creativity is not limited to inventions. For example, when she was in her first year of college, Meghan E. Taugher used her creative mind in two ways. First, she and her study group, as part of their class on electrical circuits, devised a solar-powered battery for a laptop computer. "We took the professor's laptop, put all the parts together, and sat outside watching it with a little device to see how much power it was saving. When it fully charged the battery, it was one of those times I felt that what I was learning was true, because I was putting it to use in real life."[9] Second, her experience led her to generate an idea for a new major and career plan—engineering.

Where does creativity come from? Some people, through luck or natural inclination, seem to come up with inspired ideas more often than others. However, creative thinking, like analytical thinking, is a skill that can be developed. Creativity expert Roger von Oech says that mental flexibility is essential. "Like race-car drivers who shift in and out of different gears depending on where they are on the course," he says, you can enhance your creativity by learning to "shift in and out of different types of thinking depending on the needs of the situation at hand."[10]

The following actions will help you make those shifts and build your ability to think creatively. Note that, because creative ideas often pop up at random, writing them down as they arise will help you remember them. Keep a pen and paper by your bed, your BlackBerry or your Palm Pilot in your pocket, and a notepad in your car so that you can grab ideas before they fade from your mind.

Brainstorm

Brainstorming is also referred to as *divergent thinking*: You start with a question and then let your mind diverge—go in many different directions—in search of solutions. Think of brainstorming as *deliberate* creative thinking—you go into it fully aware that you are attempting to create new ideas. When you brainstorm, generate ideas without thinking about how useful they are; evaluate their quality later. Brainstorming works well in groups because group members can become inspired by, and make creative use of, one another's ideas.[11]

BRAINSTORMING
Letting your mind free-associate to come up with different ideas or answers.

ANALOGY

A comparison based on a resemblance of things that are otherwise unalike.

One way to inspire ideas when brainstorming is to think of similar situations—in other words, to make analogies. For example, the discovery of Velcro is a product of **analogy**: When imagining how two pieces of fabric could stick to each other, the inventor thought of the similar situation of a burr sticking to clothing.

When you are brainstorming ideas, don't get hooked on finding the one right answer. Questions may have many "right answers"—or many answers that have degrees of usefulness. The more possibilities you generate, the better your chance of finding the best one. Also, don't stop the process when you think you have the best answer—keep going until you are out of steam. You never know what may come up in those last gasps of creative energy.[12]

Take a new and different look

Just because everyone believes something doesn't make it so; just because something "has always been that way" doesn't make it good. Changing how you look at a situation or problem can inspire creative ideas. Here are some ways to do it:

Challenge assumptions. In the late 1960s, conventional wisdom said that school provided education and that television provided entertainment. Jim Henson, a pioneer in children's television, asked, "Why can't we use TV to educate young children?" From that question, the characters of *Sesame Street*—and a host of other educational programs—were born.

Shift your perspective. Try on new perspectives by asking others for their views, reading about new ways to approach situations, or deliberately going with the opposite of your first instinct.[13] Then use those perspectives to inspire creativity. For your English Lit course, analyze a novel from the point of view of one of the main characters. For Political Science, craft a position paper for a local MP or MPP candidate. Perception puzzles are a fun way to experience how looking at something in a new way can bring a totally different idea (see Key 4.5).

Try these perception puzzles.

key 4.5

Is this a face or a musician?

lines or a letter?

a duck or a bunny?

Face puzzle: "Sara Nadar" illustration from *Mind Sights* by Roger Shepard. Copyright © 1990 by Roger Shepard. Reprinted by permission of Henry Holt & Company.

Ask "what if" questions. Set up hypothetical environments in which new ideas can grow: "What if I knew I couldn't fail?" "What if I had unlimited money or time?" Ideas will emerge from your "what if" questions. For example, the founders of Seeds of Peace, faced with generations of conflict in the Middle East, asked: What if Israeli and Palestinian teens met at a summer camp so that the next generation has greater understanding and respect than the last? And what if follow-up programs and reunions are set up to cement friendships so that relationships change the politics of the Middle East? Based on the ideas that came up, they created an organization to prepare teenagers from the Middle East with the leadership skills needed to coexist peacefully.

Set the stage for creativity

Use these strategies to give yourself the best possible chance at generating creative ideas.

Choose—or create—environments that free your mind. Find places that energize you. Play music that moves you. Paint your study walls your favourite colour. Seek out people who inspire you. Sternberg agrees: "Find the environment that rewards what you have to offer," he says, "and then make the most of your creativity and of yourself in that environment."[14]

Be curious. Try something you consider new and different—take a course that is completely unlike your major, try a new sport or game, listen to a new genre of music, read a magazine or book that you've never seen before. Seeking out new experiences and ideas will broaden your knowledge, giving you more raw materials with which to build creative ideas.[15]

Give yourself time to "sit" with a question. Our society values speed—so much so that to say someone is "quick" is to say that person is intelligent.[16] Equating speed with intelligence can stifle creativity because many creative ideas come when you allow time for thoughts to percolate. Take breaks when figuring out a problem. Take the pressure off by getting some exercise, napping, talking with a friend, working on something else, doing something fun. Creative ideas often come when you give your brain permission to "leave the job" for a while.[17]

Take risks

Creative breakthroughs can come from sensible risk taking.

Fly in the face of convention. Entrepreneur Michael Dell turned tradition on its ear when he took a "tell me what you want and I will build it for you" approach to computer marketing instead of a "build it and they will buy it" approach. The possibility of failure did not stop him from risking money, time, energy, and reputation to achieve a truly unique and creative goal.

Successful Intelligence Connections Online

Listen to author Sarah Kravits discuss some additional ways to boost your creativity.

Go to the *Keys to Success* Companion Website at www.pearsoned.ca/carter to listen or download as a podcast.

Let mistakes be okay. Open yourself to the learning that comes from not being afraid to mess up. When Dr. Hunter—successful inventor of the drug-coated coronary stent—and his company failed to develop a particular treatment for multiple sclerosis, he said, "You have to celebrate the failures. If you send the message that the only road to career success is experiments that work, people won't ask risky questions, or get any dramatically new answers."[18]

As with analytical thinking, asking questions powers creative thinking. See Key 4.6 for examples of the kinds of questions you can ask to get your creative juices flowing.

Ask questions like these to jump-start creativity.

key 4.6

To brainstorm, ask:	• What do I want to accomplish?
	• What are the craziest ideas I can think of?
	• What are 10 ways that I can reach my goal?
	• What ideas or strategies have worked before and how can I apply them?
	• How else can this be done?
To take a new and different look, ask:	• How has this always been done—and what would be a different way?
	• What is another way to look at this situation?
	• How can I approach this task from a completely new angle?
	• How would others do this? How would they view this?
	• What if . . . ?
To set the stage for creativity, ask:	• Where and with whom do I feel relaxed and inspired?
	• What music helps me think out of the box?
	• When in the day or night am I most likely to experience a flow of creative ideas?
	• What do I think would be new and interesting to try, to see, to read?
	• What is the most outrageous outcome of a situation that I can imagine?
To take risks, ask:	• What is the conventional way of doing this? What would be a totally different way?
	• What would be a risky approach to this problem or question?
	• What choice would people caution me about and why?
	• What is the worst that can happen if I take this risk? What is the best?
	• What have I learned from this mistake?

Activate Your Creative Powers

get creative!

First, think about the past month; then, list three creative acts you performed.

1. In order to study, I _____

2. In my personal life, I _____

3. At work or in the classroom, I _____

Now think of a problem or situation that is on your mind. Brainstorm one new idea for how to deal with it.

_____

_____

Write down a second idea—but focus on the risk-taking aspect of creativity. What would be a risky way to handle the situation? How do you hope it would pay off?

_____

_____

Finally, sit with the question—then write down one more idea *only* after you have been away from this page for at least 24 hours.

_____

_____

Keep these in mind. You may want to use one soon!

How can you improve your *practical thinking* skills?

Practical thinking—also called "common sense" or "street smarts"—refers to how you adapt to your environment, or shape or change your environment to adapt to you, in order to pursue important goals. Think again about the successfully intelligent boy in the story in Chapter 1: He quickly sized up his environment (bear and slower boy) and adapted (got ready to run) in order to pursue his goal (to escape becoming the bear's dinner).

Here is another example: Your goal is to pass your required first year communication course. You are a visual learner. To achieve your goal, you can use the instructor's electronic slide presentations or other visual media to enhance your learning (adapt to your environment) or enrol in an internet course that is primarily visual (change your environment to adapt to you)—or both.

Why practical thinking is important

Although the traditional classroom tends to focus on analytical thinking, real-world problems and decisions require you to move beyond analysis alone. Your success in a sociology class, for example, usually is not just a product of your academic work—it may depend in part on adapting to your instructor's style or personality as well. Similarly, how you solve a personal financial dilemma has a more significant impact on your life than how you work through a problem in an accounting course.

Furthermore, academic knowledge on its own isn't enough to bring you success in the workplace. You need to be able to actively apply what you know to problems and decisions that come up periodically. For example, while students majoring in elementary education may successfully quote facts about child development on an exam, it won't mean much to their career success unless they can adapt to the classroom by evaluating and addressing real children's needs. Successfully solving real-world problems demands a practical approach.[19]

Through experience you acquire emotional and social intelligence

You gain much of your ability to think practically—your common sense—from personal experience, rather than from formal lessons. This knowledge is an important tool in achieving goals.[20]

What you learn from experience answers "how" questions—how to talk, how to behave, how to proceed.[21] For example, after completing a few papers for a particular course, you may pick up cues about how to impress that instructor. Following a couple of conflicts with a partner, you may learn how to avoid sore spots when the conversation heats up. See Key 4.7 for ways in which this kind of knowledge can be shown in "if–then" statements.

There are two keys to making practical knowledge work for you. First, make an active choice to learn from experience—to pay attention to how things work at school, in personal relationships, and at work. Second, make sure you apply what you learn, thereby assuring that you will not have to learn the same lessons over and over again. As Sternberg says, "What matters most is not how much experience you have had but rather how much you have profited from it—in other words, how well you apply what you have learned."[22]

The emotional intelligence connection

Part of what you learn from experience involves *emotional intelligence*. Based on the work of psychologist Daniel Goleman, your emotional intelligence quotient (EQ) is the set of personal and social competencies that involve knowing yourself, mastering your feelings, and developing social skills.[23] *Social competence*—involving skills such as sensing other people's feelings and needs, getting your message across to others, managing conflict, leading and bonding with people—usually is built through experience rather than by reading theory or a how-to manual.

Emotional intelligence has a significant effect on your ability to communicate and manoeuvre in a social environment in a way that helps you achieve your goals. It will be examined in greater detail in the section on communication and diversity in Chapter 9.

One way to map out what you learn from experience.

Goal: You want to talk to the soccer coach about your status on the team.

IF the team has had a good practice and IF you've played well during the scrimmage and IF the coach isn't rushing off somewhere, THEN grab a moment with him right after practice ends.

IF the team is having a tough time and IF you've been sidelined and IF the coach is in a rush and stressed, THEN drop in on his office hours tomorrow.

Practical thinking means action

Learning different ways to take action and stay in motion builds your practical thinking ability. Strategies you learn throughout this course will keep you moving toward your goals:[24]

- **Stay motivated.** Use techniques from Chapter 1 to persevere when you face a problem. Get started on achieving results instead of dwelling on exactly how to start. Translate thoughts into concrete actions instead of getting bogged down in "analysis paralysis."

- **Make the most of your personal strengths.** What you've learned in Chapter 2 will help you see what you do best—and use those strengths as you apply practical solutions.

- **When things go wrong, accept responsibility and reject self-pity.** You know from Chapter 1 that failure is an excellent teacher. Learn from what happened, act on what you have learned, and don't let self-pity stall your momentum.

- **Focus on the goal and avoid distractions.** Keep your eye on the big picture and complete what you've planned, rather than getting lost in the details. Don't let personal problems or other distractions take you off the track.

- **Manage time and tasks effectively.** Use what you know from Chapter 2 to plan your time in a way that promotes goal accomplishment. Avoid the pitfalls of procrastination. Accurately gauge what you can handle—don't take on too many projects, or too few.

- **Believe in yourself.** Have faith in your ability to achieve what you set out to do.

See Key 4.8 for some questions you can ask in order to apply practical thinking to your problems and decisions.

To learn from experience, ask:	• What worked well, or not so well, about my approach? My timing? My tone? My wording?
	• What did others like or not like about what I did?
	• What did I learn from that experience, conversation, event?
	• How would I change things if I had to do it over again?
	• What do I know I would do again?
To apply what you learn, ask:	• What have I learned that would work here?
	• What have I seen others do, or heard about from them, that would be helpful here?
	• What does this situation have in common with past situations I've been involved in?
	• What has worked in similar situations in the past?
To boost your ability to take action, ask:	• How can I get motivated and remove limitations?
	• How can I, in this situation, make the most of what I do well?
	• If I fail, what can I learn from it?
	• What steps will get me to my goal, and what trade-offs are involved?
	• How can I manage my time more effectively?

get practical!

Take a Practical Approach to Building Successful Intelligence Skills

Use the wheel on the facing page to get a big-picture look at how you perceive your skills in all three aspects of successful intelligence. In the appropriate sections of the circle, write your self-assessment scores from the Get Analytical (page 12), Get Creative (page 21), and Get Practical (page 23) features in Chapter 1. Then, in each of the three areas of the wheel, draw a curved line approximately at the level of the number of your score and fill in the wedge below that line (see the sample wheel). Look at what the wheel says about how balanced you perceive your three aspects of successful intelligence to be. If it were a real wheel, would it roll?

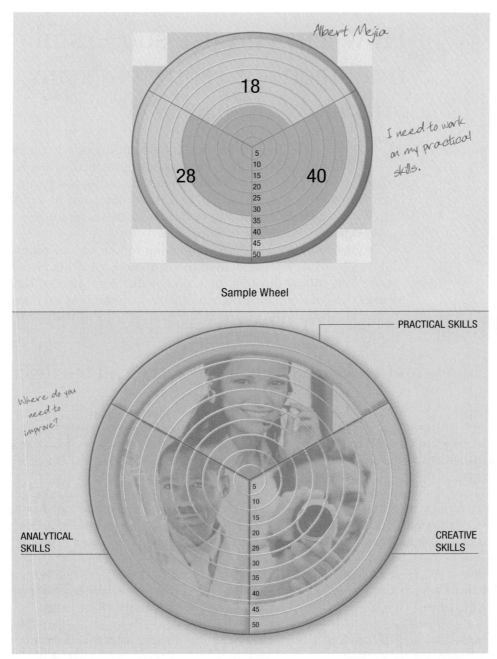

Albert Mejia

18

28   40

I need to work on my practical skills.

5
10
15
20
25
30
35
40
45
50

Sample Wheel

PRACTICAL SKILLS

Where do you need to improve?

5
10
15
20
25
30
35
40
45
50

ANALYTICAL
SKILLS

CREATIVE
SKILLS

Source: Based on "The Wheel of Life" model developed by the Coaches Training Institute. © Co-Active Space 2000.

Based on looking at your wheel, in which area do you most want to build strength?

_____

Write down two practical actions you can take that will improve your skills in that area. For example, someone who wants to be more creative could take a course focused on creativity; someone who wants to be more practical could work on paying attention to social cues; someone who wants to be more analytical could decide to analyze one newspaper article every week

_____

_____

How can you use successful intelligence to *solve problems* and *make decisions*?

You have developed your understanding of what it means to think analytically, creatively, and practically. You have explored your perception of where your strengths and weaknesses lie. Now you will see how to put analytical, creative, and practical thinking together to solve problems and make decisions successfully—at school, in the workplace, or in your personal life.

Problem solving and decision making follow similar paths. Both require you to identify and analyze a situation, generate possibilities, choose one, follow through on it, and evaluate its success. Key 4.9 gives an overview of the paths, indicating how you think at each step.

Solve problems and make decisions using successful intelligence.

key 4.9

PROBLEM SOLVING	THINKING SKILL	DECISION MAKING
Define the problem—recognize that something needs to change, identify what's happening, look for true causes	**STEP 1** DEFINE	Define the decision—identify your goal (your need) and then construct a decision that will help you get it
Analyze the problem—gather information, break it down into pieces, verify facts, look at perspectives and assumptions, evaluate information	**STEP 2** ANALYZE	Examine needs and motives—consider the layers of needs carefully, and be honest about what you really want
Generate possible solutions—use creative strategies to think of ways you could address the causes of this problem	**STEP 3** CREATE	Name and/or generate different options—use creative questions to come up with choices that would fulfill your needs
Evaluate solutions—look carefully at potential pros and cons of each, and choose what seems best	**STEP 4** ANALYZE (EVALUATE)	Evaluate options—look carefully at potential pros and cons of each, and choose what seems best
Put the solution to work—persevere, focus on results, and believe in yourself as you go for your goal	**STEP 5** TAKE PRACTICAL ACTION	Act on your decision—go down the path and use practical strategies to stay on target
Evaluate how well the solution worked—look at the effects of what you did	**STEP 6** ANALYZE (RE-EVALUATE)	Evaluate the success of your decision—look at whether it accomplished what you had hoped
In the future, apply what you've learned—use this solution, or a better one, when a similar situation comes up again	**STEP 7** TAKE PRACTICAL ACTION	In the future, apply what you've learned—make this choice, or a better one, when a similar decision comes up again

Examine how problems and decisions differ.

SITUATION	YOU HAVE A PROBLEM IF . . .	YOU NEED TO MAKE A DECISION IF . . .
Planning summer activities	Your low GPA means you need to attend summer school—and you've already accepted a summer job.	You've been accepted into two summer-abroad internship programs.
Declaring a major/program of study	It's time to declare, but you don't have all the prerequisites for the major/program of study that you want.	There are three majors/programs of study that appeal to you, and you qualify for them all.
Handling relationships with instructors	You are having trouble following the lecture style of a particular instructor.	Your psychology survey course has seven sections taught by different instructors; you have to choose one.

How do you choose which path to follow? Understanding the differences will help. First of all, problem solving generally requires more focus on coming up with possible solutions; when you face a decision, your choices are often determined. Second, problem solving aims to remove or counteract negative effects; decision making aims to fulfill a need. See Key 4.10 for some examples. Remember too that, whereas all problem solving requires you to make a decision—when you decide on a solution—only some decision making requires you to solve a problem.

What approach may best help you to overcome barriers and achieve your goal? Talk to people who are where you want to be—professionally or personally—and ask them what you should anticipate.

Solving a problem

A problem exists when a situation has negative effects. Recognizing that there is a problem—being aware of those effects—is essential before you can begin to solve it. In other words, your first move is to go from the effects—"I'm unhappy/uneasy/angry"—to determining why: "My schedule is overwhelming me." "I'm over my head in this course." "My credit card debt is out of control." Then you begin the problem-solving process in earnest.

What happens if you *don't* act in a successfully intelligent way? Take, for example, a student having an issue with an instructor. He may get into an argument with the instructor during class time. He may stop showing up to class. He may not make an effort with assignments. All of these choices will most likely have negative consequences for him.

Now look at how this student might work through this problem using his analytical, creative, and practical thinking skills. Key 4.11 shows how his effort can pay off.

As you go through the problem-solving process, keep these tips in mind.

Use probing questions to define problems. Focus on causes. If you are not happy in a class, for example, you could ask questions like these:

- What do I think about when I feel unhappy?
- Do my feelings involve my instructor? My classmates?
- Is the subject matter difficult? The volume of work too much?

Working through a problem . . . relating to an instructor.

DEFINE PROBLEM HERE:	ANALYZE THE PROBLEM
I don't like my Composition instructor	We have different views and personality types— I don't feel respected or heard. I'm not interested in being there and my grades are suffering from my lack of motivation.

Use boxes below to list possible solutions:

POTENTIAL POSITIVE EFFECTS	SOLUTION #1	POTENTIAL NEGATIVE EFFECTS
List for each solution: Don't have to deal with that instructor Less stress	Drop the course	*List for each solution:* Grade gets entered on my transcript I'll have to take the course eventually; it's required for my major
Getting credit for the course Feeling like I've honoured a commitment	**SOLUTION #2** Put up with it until the end of the semester	Stress every time I'm there Lowered motivation Probably not such a good final grade
A chance to express myself Could get good advice An opportunity to ask direct questions of the instructor	**SOLUTION #3** Schedule meetings with adviser and instructor	Have to face instructor one-on-one Might just make things worse

Now choose the solution you think is best—circle it and make it happen.

ACTUAL POSITIVE EFFECTS	PRACTICAL ACTION	ACTUAL NEGATIVE EFFECTS
List for chosen solution: Got some helpful advice from adviser Talking in person with the instructor actually promoted a fairly honest discussion I won't have to take the course again	I scheduled and attended meetings with both adviser and instructor, and opted to stick with the course.	*List for chosen solution:* The discussion was difficult and sometimes tense I still don't know how much learning I'll retain from this course

FINAL EVALUATION: Was it a good or bad solution?

The solution has improved things. I'll finish the course, and even though the instructor and I aren't the best of friends, we have a mutual understanding now. I feel more respected and more willing to put my time into the course.

Chances are that how you answer one or more of these questions may lead to a clear definition—and ultimately to the right solution.

Analyze carefully. Gather all the information you can, so that you can consider the situation comprehensively. Consider what you can learn from how the problem is similar to or different from other problems. Clarify facts. Note your own perspective, and ask others for theirs. Make sure you are not looking at the problem through the lens of an assumption.

Generate possible solutions based on causes, not effects. Addressing a cause provides a lasting solution, whereas "fixing" an effect cannot. Say your shoulder hurts when you use your computer. Getting a friend to massage it is a nice but temporary solution, because the pain returns whenever you go back to work. Changing the height of your keyboard and mouse is a better idea, because it eliminates the cause of your pain.

STRESSBUSTER

GABRIEL SCHROEDTER **Red River College, Winnipeg, Manitoba**

Was there ever a time when you felt so stressed out that you just didn't know what to do? How did you get back on track?

Late last year I was running into a potential catastrophe. I had presentations and supporting material to work on, final exams, as well as writing and layout for five pages of a magazine project. My truck was leaking gas constantly, making any driving a stress that I didn't need. I felt like I was stuck between an immovable object, in the form of a mountain of work, and an unstoppable force, deadlines rushing towards me at the speed of light.

The problem was that I wasn't taking any time to get my bearings, and was just flailing about trying to grab hold of something. I felt like I needed something to clear my mind for at least an hour. Just one hour and then I'd be okay.

I thought video games might work. They didn't; neither did going out and partying. That kind of stuff doesn't clear your mind as much as cloud it up so you can't see the problems for a bit.

What I had to do was something that I had never thought of doing before, something so different from my routine that I'd use a totally different part of my brain. It's the novelty that relaxes you; learning becomes fun again. The best part for students is that they are good at learning.

What I came up with was Tai Chi, but it could be different things for different people. It could be learning to play an instrument, taking a cooking class, or something like that.

If you can't think of something, don't worry; you could still be on the right track. Watch a couple of movies and wait until you see something that makes you say, "Wow, I'd like to do that. I think I will."

Yes, I know how it sounds, but think about it next time you feel stress start to creep in. You don't even really have to go so far as to take a class. Just do something that surprises you, and you'll feel like you've created a little more distance between your unstoppable force and your immovable object.

Making a decision

Psychologists who have studied decision making have learned that many random factors influence the choices people make. For example, you may choose a major/program of study not because you love the subject but because you think your parents will approve of it. The goal is to make considered decisions despite factors that may derail your thinking.

What happens when you make important decisions quickly, without using your analytical, creative, and practical thinking skills? Consider a student trying to work on a budget. Right now, she won't have enough money to continue in school next semester. If she drops out, that would mean she would lose her year and the time/money spent on her education. Does she drop down to part-time? That might mean graduating at a later date. Now look at how this student might make a successfully intelligent decision. Key 4.12 shows how she worked through the analytical, creative, and practical parts of the process.

As you use the steps in Key 4.12 to make a decision, remember these hints.

Look at the given options—then try to think of more. Some decisions have a given set of options. For example, your school may allow you to major, double major, or major and minor. However, when you are making your decision, you may be able to brainstorm with an adviser to come up with more options—such as an interdisciplinary major you create on your own.

Think about how your decision affects others. For example, students thinking about a transfer consider the impact on friends and family. What they conclude about that impact may influence when they transfer and even the school they choose.

Gather perspectives. Talk with others who have made similar decisions. There are more ways of doing things than one brain can possibly imagine on its own.

After you've made the decision, look at the long-term effects. For important decisions, do a short-term evaluation and another evaluation after a period of time. See whether your decision has sent you down a path that has continued to bring positive effects.

Keeping your balance

No one has equal strengths in analytical, creative, and practical thinking. Adjusting your expectations to match what you can accomplish is a key principle of successful intelligence. It requires that you

- use what you've learned in this chapter and the rest of the text to maximize your analytical, creative, and practical abilities.
- reflect on what you do well, and focus on strengthening weaker skills.
- combine all three thinking skills to accomplish your goals, knowing when and how to apply your analytical, creative, and practical abilities.
- believe in your skills as a thinker.

Working through a problem . . . financing course work.

DEFINE PROBLEM HERE:	ANALYZE THE PROBLEM
I don't have enough money to cover tuition next semester	Lost financial aid due to slipping grades
	Part-time job doesn't bring in much money
	Need to find money from a different source
	Might be unable to continue school right now

Use boxes below to list possible solutions:

POTENTIAL POSITIVE EFFECTS	SOLUTION #1	POTENTIAL NEGATIVE EFFECTS
List for each solution:	Find new source of financial aid	*List for each solution:*
Ability to stay on planned school schedule		Money might not be renewable like current grant
Ability to stay in school		Time and effort spent to find and qualify for new aid

POTENTIAL POSITIVE EFFECTS	SOLUTION #2	POTENTIAL NEGATIVE EFFECTS
More money to pay for school	Find full-time, better-paying job	Less time for school
More on-the-job experience		May have to take classes part-time, graduate later

POTENTIAL POSITIVE EFFECTS	SOLUTION #3	POTENTIAL NEGATIVE EFFECTS
More time to study	Take classes part-time next semester	Extends how long I'll be in school
More ability to focus		Could make me ineligible for certain kinds of aid

Now choose the solution you think is best—circle it and make it happen.

ACTUAL POSITIVE EFFECTS	PRACTICAL ACTION	ACTUAL NEGATIVE EFFECTS
List for chosen solution:	For next semester, take classes part-time and work full-time	*List for chosen solution:*
More money earned		Had to put off planned graduation date
More study time and ability to focus resulted in better grades		Ineligible this semester for most aid, had to use my own money for tuition

FINAL EVALUATION: Was it a good or bad solution?

It was tough but it worked out well. Even though I had to pay for courses myself, the full-time job and fewer classes allowed me to do that. Then, with better focus, I was able to raise my average back up so that next semester I'll requalify for aid and can go back to being a full-time student.

"Successfully intelligent people," says Sternberg, "defy negative expectations, even when these expectations arise from low scores on IQ or similar tests. They do not let other people's assessments stop them from achieving their goals. They find their path and then pursue it, realizing that there will be obstacles along the way and that surmounting these obstacles is part of the challenge."[25] Let the obstacles come, as they will for everyone in all aspects of life. You can face and overcome them with the power of your successfully intelligent thinking.

Successful Intelligence Wrap Up

With the power of successful intelligence, you can identify your most significant goals, devise ways to pursue them, and, most importantly, take concrete actions to attain them. In addition, you can move beyond a fixed view of your intelligence. Here's how you have built skills in Chapter 4:

Analytical

You explored the steps and parts of analytical thinking in the section on analytical thinking skills, including crucial topics such as fact vs. opinion, perspective, and how examples support an idea. In the Get Analytical exercise, you honed your skills by analyzing a statement. At the end of the chapter, you considered how to use your analytical skills to evaluate potential ideas and choices in the problem-solving and decision-making processes.

Creative

You developed a detailed understanding of creative thinking as you read the section on creative thinking skills. You learned of some creativity-boosting strategies and probably thought of more. In the Get Creative exercise, you brainstormed creative acts as well as new ideas about how to deal with a problem. In the section on problem solving and decision making, you explored ways to brainstorm solutions and choices.

Practical

You broadened your concept of practical thinking as you read the section on practical thinking skills, including developing more specific ideas of how to apply your emotional and social intelligence. In the Get Practical exercise, you built a picture of how you see your successful intelligence and generated practical ideas about how to improve. When reading about problem solving and decision making, you explored practical ways to put solutions and choices to work.

kunnskaping
(kun-skahp-ping)

This Norwegian word is a creative combination of *kunnskap* (meaning "knowledge") and *verdiskaping* (meaning "value creation"). It translates loosely as "knowledging," which can be read as developing knowledge and meaning that are of use in school and work.[26] In the global marketplace described by Thomas Friedman (see Chapter 1), knowledge as a tool and product is more important than ever before.

Think of this concept as you use your analytical, creative, and practical thinking skills to solve problems, make decisions, innovate, and question. Successful intelligence enables you to put knowledge to work as you strive toward your goals. It also empowers you to be creative, in much the same way that some clever Norwegian was when he or she coined *kunnskaping* and made it part of the language.

"I am enough of an artist to draw freely upon my imagination. Imagination is more important than knowledge. Knowledge is limited. Imagination encircles the world."

ALBERT EINSTEIN, MATHEMATICIAN AND SCIENTIST

SUCCESSFUL INTELLIGENCE

Think, Create, Apply

Make an important decision. Put the decision-making process to work on something that matters to you. You will apply your analytical, creative, and practical thinking skills. Use a separate sheet of paper for Steps 2 and 3.

Step 1. Analyze: *Define the decision.* Write an important long-term goal that you have, and define the decision that will help you fulfill it. Example: "My goal is to become a nurse. My decision: What to specialize in."

Step 2. Analyze: *Examine needs and concerns.* What do you want? What are your needs, and how do your values come into play? What needs of others will you need to take into account? What roadblocks might be involved? List everything you come up with. For example, the prospective nurse might list needs like: "I need to feel that I'm helping people. I intend to help with the nursing shortage. I need to make a good living."

Step 3. Create: *Generate options.* Ask questions to imagine what's possible. Where might you work? What might be the schedule and pace? Who might work with you? What would you see, smell, and hear on your job? What would you do every day? List, too, all of the options you can think of. The prospective nurse, for example, might list emergency room, pediatrics, surgery, oncology, geriatrics, and so on. Brainstorm other options that might not seem so obvious.

Step 4. Analyze: *Evaluate options.* Think about how well your options will fulfill your needs. For two of your options, write potential positive and negative effects (pros and cons) of each.

Option 1:

_____

Potential pros:

_____

Potential cons:

_____

Option 2:

_____

Potential pros:

_____

Potential cons:

_____

Step 5. Get practical: *Imagine acting on your decision.* Describe one practical course of action, based on your thinking so far, that you might follow. List the specific steps you would take. For example, the prospective nurse might list actions that help him or her determine what type of nursing suits him or her best, such as interning, summer jobs, academic goals, and talking to working nurses.

Finally, over time, plan to put your decision into action. Eventually you will need to complete the two final steps of the process. **Step 6** is to evaluate the decision: How did it work out? Analyze whether you and others got what you needed. **Step 7** is to practically apply what you've learned from the decision to other decisions you make in the future.

TEAMWORK

Create Solutions Together

Powerful group problem solving. On an index card or a plain sheet of paper, each student in the class writes a school-related problem—this could be a fear, a challenge, a sticky situation, or a roadblock. Students hand these in without names. The instructor writes the list on the board.

Divide into groups of two to four. Each group chooses one problem to work on (try not to have two groups working on the same problem). Use the blank problem-solving flow chart (Key 4.13) on p. 128 to fill in your work.

Step 1. Analyze: *Define the problem.* As a group, look at the negative effects and state your problem specifically. Then explore and write down the causes.

Step 2. Analyze: *Examine the problem.* Pick it apart to see what's happening. Gather information from all group members, verify facts, go beyond assumptions.

Step 3. Create: *Generate possible solutions.* From the most likely causes of the problem, derive possible solutions. Record all the ideas that group members offer. After 10 minutes or so, each group member should choose one possible solution to evaluate independently.

Step 4. Analyze: *Evaluate each solution.* In thinking independently through the assigned solution, each group member should (a) weigh the positive and negative effects, (b) consider similar problems, and (c) describe how the solution affects the causes of the problem. Evaluate your assigned solution. Is it a good one? Will it work?

Step 5. Get practical: *Choose a solution.* Group members come together, share observations and recommendations, and then take a vote: Which solution is the best? You may have a tie or may want to combine two different solutions. Try to find the solution that works for most of the group. Then, together, come up with a plan for how you would put your solution to work.

Step 6. Analyze: *Evaluate your solution.* As a group, share and discuss what you had individually imagined the positive and negative effects of this solution would be. Try to come to an agreement on how you think the solution would work out.

Work through a problem using this flow chart.

DEFINE PROBLEM HERE:	ANALYZE THE PROBLEM

Use boxes below to list possible solutions:

POTENTIAL POSITIVE EFFECTS	SOLUTION #1	POTENTIAL NEGATIVE EFFECTS
List for each solution:		*List for each solution:*

SOLUTION #2

SOLUTION #3

Now choose the solution you think is best—circle it and make it happen.

ACTUAL POSITIVE EFFECTS	PRACTICAL ACTION	ACTUAL NEGATIVE EFFECTS
List for chosen solution:		*List for chosen solution:*

FINAL EVALUATION: Was it a good or bad solution?

Source: Based on heuristic created by Frank T. Lyman Jr. and George Eley, 1985.

Step 7 is to practically apply what you've learned from solving the problem to other problems you encounter in the future.

WRITING
Journal and Put Skills to Work

Record your thoughts on a separate piece of paper or in a journal.

Journal entry: Wiser choices. Think about a choice you made that, looking back, you wish you had handled differently. First, describe what the decision was, what option you chose, and what the consequences were. Then write about what you would do if you could make the decision again. What did you learn from your experience that you can apply to other decisions? How could being analytical, creative, and practical have helped you reach a more effective outcome?

PERSONAL PORTFOLIO
Prepare for Career Success

Generating ideas for your co-op or work term. People often put more time and effort into deciding what cellphone to buy than they do with life-altering decisions like how to prepare for career success. Pursuing a co-op or work term is part of a comprehensive career decision-making process. It's a practical way to get experience, learn what you like and don't like, and make valuable connections.

Fill in the following:

Career areas that I'm considering. Why?

1. _____ Because: _____

2. _____ Because: _____

3. _____ Because: _____

People whom I want to interview about their fields/professions. Why?

1. _____ Because: _____

2. _____ Because: _____

3. _____ Because: _____

Next, take practical steps to investigate. Talk to the people you listed. Contact companies you would like to work for and see what co-op or work term opportunities are available. Talk with someone in your school's career office. If a company doesn't yet offer co-ops or work terms, ask them if you might be a pioneer for the program.

Finally, after you have gathered some useful information, use a separate sheet of paper to creatively envision your ideal experience. Describe it: What would it look like? What would you do each day? Each week? Where would you go? With whom would you work? What would you contribute with your gifts and talents? Make it happen with your successful intelligence.

SUGGESTED READINGS

Cameron, Julia, with Mark Bryan. *The Artist's Way: A Spiritual Path to Higher Creativity,* 10th ed. New York: G. P. Putnam's Sons, 2002.

de Bono, Edward. *Lateral Thinking: Creativity Step by Step.* New York: Perennial Library, 1990.

Goleman, Daniel. *Emotional Intelligence: Why It Can Matter More Than IQ.* New York: Bantam, 1995.

Moscovich, Ivan. *1000 Playthinks.* New York: Workman Publishing, 2001.

Noone, Donald J., Ph.D. *Creative Problem Solving.* New York: Barron's, 1998.

SARK. *Make Your Creative Dreams Real: A Plan for Procrastinators, Perfectionists, Busy People, and People Who Would Rather Sleep All Day.* New York: Fireside Press, 2004.

von Oech, Roger. *A Kick in the Seat of the Pants.* New York: Harper & Row Publishers, 1986.

von Oech, Roger. *A Whack on the Side of the Head.* New York: Warner Books, 1998.

INTERNET RESOURCES

Creativity at Work (resources for workplace creativity):
www.creativityatwork.com

Creativity for Life (tips and strategies for creativity):
www.creativityforlife.com

Learn more about critical thinking from the University of Victoria's Counselling Services:
www.coun.uvic.ca/learning/critical-thinking/index.html

Reasonably appreciate the importance of critical thinking with Reason!Able software:
www.goreason.com

Roger von Oech's Creative Think website:
http://creativethink.com

ENDNOTES

1. Robert J. Sternberg, *Successful Intelligence* (New York: Plume, 1997), 12.
2. Vincent Ruggiero, *The Art of Thinking*, 2001, quoted in "Critical Thinking," Oregon State University, http://success.oregonstate.edu/template/criticalthinking.html (accessed April, 2004).
3. Richard Paul, "The Role of Questions in Thinking, Teaching, and Learning," The Critical Thinking Community, http://www.criticalthinking.org/resources/articles/the-role-of-questions.shtml (accessed April, 2004).
4. "The Best Innovations Are Those That Come from Smart Questions," *Wall Street Journal*, April 12, 2004, B1.
5. Quoted in Sharon Begley, "Critical Thinking: Part Skill, Part Mindset and Totally up to You," *Wall Street Journal*, October 20, 2006, B1.
6. Sternberg, *Successful*, 128.
7. Colby Glass, "Strategies for Critical Thinking," 2005, http://www.criticalthink.info/Phil1301/ctstrategies.htm (accessed August, 2008).
8. Sternberg, *Successful*, 49.
9. Elizabeth F. Farrell, "Engineering a Warmer Welcome for Female Students: The Discipline Tries to Stress its Social Relevance, an Important Factor for Many Women," *The Chronicle of Higher Education*, February 22, 2002, http://chronicle.com/weekly/v48/i24/24a03101.htm [subscription-based] (accessed March, 2004).
10. Roger von Oech, *A Kick in the Seat of the Pants* (New York: Harper & Row Publishers, 1986), 5–21.
11. Dennis Coon, *Introduction to Psychology: Exploration and Application*, 6th ed (St. Paul: West Publishing Company, 1992), 295.
12. Roger von Oech, *A Whack on the Side of the Head* (New York: Warner Books, 1990), 11–168.
13. J. R. Hayes, *Cognitive Psychology: Thinking and Creating* (Homewood, IL: Dorsey, 1978).
14. Sternberg, *Successful*, 219.
15. Adapted from T. Z. Tardif and R. J. Sternberg, "What Do We Know about Creativity?" in *The Nature of Creativity*, ed. R. J. Sternberg (London: Cambridge University Press, 1988).
16. Sternberg, *Successful*, 212.
17. Hayes, *Cognitive Psychology*.
18. "The Best Innovations Are Those That Come from Smart Questions," *Wall Street Journal*, April 12, 2004, B1.
19. Sternberg, *Successful*, 229–230.
20. Sternberg, *Successful*, 236.
21. Robert J. Sternberg and Elena L. Grigorenko, "Practical Intelligence and the Principal," Yale University, Publication Series no. 2 (2001): 5.
22. Sternberg, *Successful*, 241.
23. Daniel Goleman, *Emotional Intelligence: Why It Can Matter More Than IQ* (New York: Bantam, 1995).
24. Sternberg, *Successful*, 251–269.
25. Sternberg, *Successful*, 19.
26. Christopher J. Moore, *In Other Words: A Language Lover's Guide to the Most Intriguing Words around the World* (New York: Walker, 2004), 61.

STUDY BREAK: GET READY FOR EXAMS

Because some instructors may schedule exams early and often in the semester, begin right away to develop strategies for test success. Starting off on the right foot will boost your confidence and motivate you to work even harder. The saying that "success breeds more success" couldn't be more true as you begin college.

The material in this Study Break is designed to help you organize yourself as you prepare for exams. As you learn to create a pre-test study plan and schedule, you will also build your ability to use your time efficiently.

When you reach Chapter 7, "Test Taking," you will study test taking in depth, including test preparation, test anxiety, general test-taking strategies, strategies for handling different types of test questions, and learning from test mistakes.

Decide on a study plan

Start your test preparation by deciding what you will study. Go through your notes, texts, related primary sources, and handouts, and set aside materials you don't need. Then prioritize the remaining materials. Your goal is to focus on information that is most likely to be on the exam. Use the test preparation tips in Chapter 7 and the material on studying your text in Chapter 5 to boost your effectiveness as you prepare.

Create a study schedule and checklist

Next, use the time-management and goal-setting skills from Chapter 2 to prepare a schedule. Consider all of the relevant factors—your study materials, the number of days until the test, and the time you can study each day. If you establish your schedule ahead of time and write it in a planner, you are more likely to follow it.

A checklist like the one on the following page will help you organize and stay on track as you prepare. Use a checklist to assign specific tasks to particular study times and sessions. That way, not only do you know when you have time to study, but you also have defined goals for each study session. Make extra copies of the checklist so that you can fill out a new one each time you have an exam.

Course: _____ Instructor: _____

Date, time, and place of test: _____

Type of test (is it a midterm or a minor quiz?): _____

What the instructor said about the test, including the types of test questions, test length, and how much the test counts toward your final grade:

_____

_____

Topics to be covered on the test, in order of importance (information should also come from your instructor):

1. _____

2. _____

3. _____

4. _____

5. _____

Study schedule, including materials you plan to study (texts, class notes, homework problems, and so forth) and dates you plan to complete each:

MATERIAL   DATE OF COMPLETION

1. _____   _____

2. _____   _____

3. _____   _____

4. _____   _____

5. _____   _____

Materials you are expected to bring to the test (textbook, sourcebook, calculator, etc.):

_____

_____

Special study arrangements (for example, plan study group meetings, ask the instructor for special help, get outside tutoring):

_____

_____

Life-management issues (such as rearranging work hours):

_____

_____

Source: Adapted from Ron Fry, "*Ace" Any Test*, 3rd ed. Franklin Lakes, NJ: Career Press, 1996, pp. 123–24.

Decide how well these techniques work for you

After you've used these studying and scheduling techniques to prepare for a few exams, answer the following questions:

- How did this approach help you organize your time before an exam?

- How did this approach help you organize your study material so that you remembered to cover every topic?

- Can you think of ways to change the checklist to improve your test-preparation efficiency? If you can, list the ways here and incorporate them into the checklist.

SELF-STUDY QUIZ

MULTIPLE-CHOICE QUESTIONS

Circle or highlight the answer that seems to fit best.

1. A *motivator* is

   A. the ability to achieve a goal.

   B. progress toward a goal.

   C. a decision to take action.

   D. a want or need that moves a person to action.

2. The direct benefits of responsibility include

   A. earning the trust of others at school, work, and home.

   B. getting motivated to achieve study goals.

   C. improved ability to plan strategically.

   D. moving up at work.

3. A *learning style* is

   A. the best way to learn when attending classes.

   B. a particular way of being intelligent.

   C. an affinity for a particular job choice or career area.

   D. a way in which the mind receives and processes information.

4. The best way to use learning-style assessments is to see them as

   A. a reference point rather than a label; a tool with which to see yourself more clearly.

   B. a road map for your life; a message that shows the paths you must take in order to be successful.

   C. a lesson about group learning; a way to find the group of learners with whom you work best.

   D. a definitive label for your working style; a clear-cut category where you fit.

5. When choosing and evaluating your values, it is important to

   A. set goals according to what your friends and family value.

   B. keep your values steady over time.

   C. re-evaluate values periodically as you experience change.

   D. set aside values that no one else seems to think are good for you.

6. It is important to link daily and weekly goals with long-term goals because

   A. the process will help you focus on the things that are most important to you.

   B. short-term goals have no meaning if they are not placed in a longer time frame.

   C. the process will help you eliminate frivolous activities.

   D. others expect you to know how everything you do relates to what you want to accomplish in life.

Complete the following sentences with the appropriate word(s) or phrase(s) that best reflect what you learned in the chapters. Choose from the items that follow each sentence.

1. When you make a(n) _____, you do what you say you will do. (initiative, motivation, commitment)

2. Showing _____ helps you to take that first step toward a goal and respond to changes in your life. (motivation, initiative, integrity)

3. One way to look at learning style is to divide it into two equally important aspects: _____ and _____. (learning preferences/personality traits, verbal/visual, interests/abilities)

4. The best careers and majors/programs for you are ones that take into consideration your _____ and _____. (references/contacts, learning style/abilities, interests/abilities)

5. Your _____ is a philosophy outlining what you want to be, what you want to do, and the principles by which you want to live. (responsibility, mission, integrity)

6. Being _____ helps you cope with day-to-day changes and life changes. (organized, flexible, on time)

The following essay questions will help you organize and communicate your ideas in writing, just as you must do on an essay test. Before you begin answering a question, spend a few minutes planning (brainstorm possible approaches, write a thesis statement, jot down main thoughts in outline or think link form [see Chapters 3 and 6 for more about think links]). To prepare yourself for actual test conditions, limit writing time to no more than 30 minutes per question.

1. Discuss habits, both good and bad. What are the effects of each? Describe a useful plan for changing a habit that is having negative effects.

2. Define *values* and *value system*. How do values develop and what effect do they have on personal choices? How are values connected to goal setting? Give an example from your life of how values have influenced a personal goal.

READING AND STUDYING
Focusing on content

5

"Successful intelligence is most effective when it balances all three of its analytical, creative, and practical aspects. It is more important to know when and how to use these aspects of successful intelligence than just to have them."

ROBERT J. STERNBERG

Your ability to read—and to understand, analyze, and use what you read—is the cornerstone of post-secondary learning. Taking a step-by-step approach to reading linked to analytical, creative, and practical thinking techniques will help you master content, whether you are getting ahead of the game with a stack of summer reading or staying up late studying for finals. This chapter introduces strategies to increase your efficiency and depth of understanding so that every hour you spend reading will be more valuable. The Conference Board of Canada considers the ability to read to be a fundamental employability skill.

In this chapter you will explore answers to the following questions:

- What will improve your reading comprehension? 138

- How can SQ3R help you master content? 148

- How can you respond critically to what you read? 154

- How can you customize your text with highlighting and notes? 156

- Successful Intelligence Wrap-Up 160

Analytical

- Identifying steps to improve comprehension
- Mastering SQ3R
- Building vocabulary by mastering roots, prefixes, and suffixes
- Critically evaluating reading passages

Creative

- Creating an environment that encourages concentration
- Adapting SQ3R to your unique studying needs
- Using colours and notations to highlight text and take text notes

Practical

- How to study word parts to build vocabulary
- How to make SQ3R a personal tool
- How to put highlighting and note-taking systems into action

What will improve your reading comprehension?

Reading is an analytical process that requires you, the reader, to make meaning from written words. You do this by connecting what you know to what you read. Your understanding is affected by your familiarity with a subject, your cultural background and life experiences, and the way you interpret words and phrases.

Because these factors are different for every person, your reading experiences are uniquely your own. If, for example, your family owns a hardware store where you worked during summers, you will read a retailing chapter in a business text from the perspective of your work in the store. While you are comparing text concepts to your family's business practices, your classmates may be reading for basic ideas and vocabulary.

Improving your reading comprehension is especially important in college or university compared to high school because assignments are generally longer, more difficult, and require more independent work. In addition, what you learn from introductory-level texts is the foundation for your understanding in advanced courses. When you struggle through and master concepts that you considered impossible the first time you read them, you'll be proud of your ability to overcome obstacles instead of giving up. This pride will motivate you every time you read.

See the Movie— Read the Book

Movies from *Gone with the Wind* to *The Devil Wears Prada* are based on popular books. The Mid-Continent Public Library (www.mcpl.lib.mo.us/readers/movies/year.cfm) compiles a yearly list of movies made from books. Search this list, choose a movie you would like to see (or see again), and then watch it on video. List the name of the movie here:

_____

On a separate sheet or computer file, jot down your thoughts about the plot and characters and describe your reaction. Hold onto these thoughts for later.

During a school break, when you have time to read for pleasure, *read the book* on which the movie is based and write a similar page of reflections.

Then compare what you thought of the movie version to what you thought of the book. List three major differences here:

1. _____
2. _____
3. _____

Describe what you gained from reading the book that you *did not* get from watching the movie.

_____

_____

Based on this experience, are you likely to make the movie–book connection again? Why or why not?

_____

_____

How might you use another work as a starting point for your own creative effort?

_____

_____

_____

Set your expectations

On any given day during your post-secondary career, you may be faced with reading assignments like these:

- A textbook chapter on the contributions made by Aboriginal Peoples (Canadian history)
- An original research study on the relationship between sleep deprivation and the development of memory problems (psychology)

- A review of *Late Nights on Air*, by Elizabeth Hay, winner of the Canadian 2007 Giller Prize (Canadian literature)
- A technical manual on the design of computer anti-spam programs (computer science—software design)

This material is rigorous by anyone's standards. You can help yourself handle it by setting higher expectations—*know at the start that you will need to read more than you ever did in high school*—and challenging yourself to handle more complex texts.

Take an active approach to difficult texts

Because texts are often written to challenge the intellect, even well-written, useful texts may be difficult to read. Some textbook authors may not explain information in the most user-friendly manner for non-experts. And, as every student knows, some textbooks are poorly written and organized.

Generally, the further you advance in your education, the more complex is your required reading. You may encounter new concepts, words, and terms that seem like a foreign language. Assignments can also be difficult when the required reading is from *primary sources*—original documents rather than another writer's interpretation of these documents—or from academic journal articles and scientific studies that don't define basic terms or supply a wealth of examples. Primary sources include

- historical documents
- works of literature (e.g., novels, poems, and plays)
- scientific studies, including lab reports and accounts of experiments
- journal articles about research studies

The following strategies will help you take an active, positive approach to reading difficult material:

Think positively. Instead of telling yourself that you cannot understand, think positively. Tell yourself: "I can learn this material. I am a good reader. I can succeed."

Have an open mind. Be careful not to prejudge assignments as impossible or boring or a waste of time and energy.

Look for order and meaning in seemingly chaotic reading materials. Use a study technique known as SQ3R (*Survey, Question, Read, Recite, Review*) and the critical reading strategies introduced later in this chapter to discover patterns and connections.

Don't expect to master material on the first pass. Instead, create a multi-step plan: On your first reading, your goal is to gain an overview of key concepts and interrelationships. On subsequent readings, you grasp ideas and relate them to what you already know. By your last reading, you master concepts and details and can apply the material to problems.

Know that some texts require extra work and concentration. If new material doesn't click, scan background material—including the text you used last term—for information that will help you understand. Set a goal to make your way through the material, whatever it takes. *If you want to learn, you will.*

Define unclear concepts and words. Use your practical intelligence as you consult resources—instructors, study group partners, tutors, and reference materials—for help. Build a library of texts in your major and minor areas of study and refer to them when needed, and bookmark helpful websites.

Choose the right setting

Finding a place and time that minimize distractions helps you achieve the focus and discipline that your reading requires. Here are some suggestions.

Select the right company (or no company at all). If you prefer to read alone, establish a relatively interruption-proof place and time such as an out-of-the-way spot at the library or an after-class hour in an empty classroom. Even if you don't mind activity nearby, try to minimize distraction.

Select the right location. Many students study at a library desk. Others prefer an easy chair at the library or at home, or even the floor. Choose a spot that's comfortable but not so cushy that you fall asleep. Make sure that you have adequate lighting and aren't too hot or cold. You may also want to avoid the distraction of studying in a room where people are talking or a television is on.

Select the right time. Choose a time when you feel alert and focused. Try reading just before or after the class for which the reading is assigned, if you can. Eventually, you will associate preferred places and times with focused reading.

Deal with internal distractions. Although a noisy environment can get in the way of your work, so can internal distractions—for example, personal worries, anticipation of an event, or even hunger. Different strategies may help. You may want to take a break and tend to one of the issues that worry you. Physical exercise may relax and refocus you. For some people, studying while listening to music quiets a busy mind. For others, silence may do the trick. If you're hungry, take a snack break and come back to your work.

Students with families have an additional factor involved when deciding when, where, and how to read. Key 5.1 explores some ways that parents or others caring for children may be able to maximize their study efforts. These techniques will also help after graduation if you choose to telecommute—work from home through an internet-linked computer—while your children are still at home under your care.

Define your purpose for reading

When you define your purpose, you ask yourself *why* you are reading a particular piece of material. One way to do this is by completing this sentence: "In reading this material, I intend to define/learn/answer/ achieve . . ." With a clear purpose in mind, you can decide how much time and what kind of effort to expend on various reading assignments.

Achieving your reading purpose requires adapting to different types of reading materials. Being a flexible reader—adjusting your reading strategies and pace—helps you to adapt successfully.

Keep them up to date on your schedule.

Let them know when you have a big test or project due and when you are under less pressure, and what they can expect of you in each case.

Explain what your education entails.

Tell them how it will improve your life and theirs. This applies, of course, to older children who can understand the situation and compare it with their own schooling.

Find help.

Ask a relative or friend to watch your children or arrange for a child to visit a friend. Consider trading babysitting hours with another parent, hiring a sitter to come to your home, or using a daycare centre.

Keep them active while you study.

Give them games, books, or toys. If there are special activities that you like to limit, such as watching videos or TV, save them for your study time.

Offset study time with family time and rewards.

Children may let you get your work done if they have something to look forward to, such as a movie night or a trip for ice cream.

Study on the phone.

You might be able to have a study session with a fellow student over the phone while your child is sleeping or playing quietly.

SPECIAL NOTES FOR INFANTS

Study at night if your baby goes to sleep early, or in the morning if your baby sleeps late.

Study during nap times if you aren't too tired yourself.

Lay your notes out and recite information to the baby. The baby will appreciate the attention, and you will get work done.

Put baby in a safe and fun place while you study, such as a playpen, motorized swing, or jumping seat.

Purpose determines reading strategy

With purpose comes direction; with direction comes a strategy. Following are four reading purposes. You may have one or more for any "reading event."

Purpose 1: Read for understanding. In college and university, studying means reading to comprehend the material. The two main components of comprehension are *general ideas* and *specific facts or examples.* Facts and examples help to explain or support ideas, and ideas provide a framework for details.

Purpose 2: Read to evaluate analytically. Analytical evaluation involves understanding. It means approaching the material with an open mind, examining causes and effects, evaluating ideas, and asking questions that test the writer's argument and search for assumptions. Critical reading brings an understanding of the material that goes beyond basic information recall (see the section "How can you respond critically to what you read?" on page 154 for more on critical reading).

Purpose 3: Read for practical application. A third purpose for reading is to gather usable information that you can apply toward a specific goal. When you read a computer manual or an instruction sheet for assembling a gas barbecue, your goal is to learn how to do something. Reading and action usually go hand in hand.

Purpose 4: Read for pleasure. Some materials you read for entertainment, such as *Rolling Stone* or the latest Stephen King thriller.

Use your class syllabus to help define your purpose for each assignment. If, for example, you know that the topic of inflation will be discussed in your next economics class, read the assigned chapter, targeting what your instructor will expect you to know about and do with the material. He may expect you to master definitions, economic models, causes and consequences, government intervention strategies, and historical examples—and to be able to apply your knowledge to economic problems. In this case, depending on what your instructor expects, you may have three reading purposes—understanding, critical evaluation, and practical application. If you are confused about your purpose, email your instructor for clarification. He is likely to be impressed with your motivation to stay on top of your assignments.

You'll need more than good intentions to finish reading assignments on schedule. You'll have to put in hours of work every day. One formula for success is this: *For every hour you spend in the classroom each week, spend at least two hours preparing for the class.* For example, if you are carrying a course load of 15 credit hours, you should spend 30 hours a week studying outside of class. Students who fall far short of this goal are likely to have trouble keeping up.

Use special strategies with math and science texts

Math and science readings present unique challenges to many students. Try some of the following analytical, creative, and practical thinking techniques to succeed:

- **Interact with the material critically as you go.** Math and science texts are problem-and-solution based. Keep a pad nearby to solve problems and take notes. Draw sketches to help visualize material. Try not to move on until you understand the example and how it relates to the central ideas. Write down questions for your instructor or classmates.

- **Note formulas.** Make sure you understand the principle behind every formula—why it works—before memorizing it.

- **Use memory techniques.** Science textbooks are packed with specialized vocabulary. To learn these new words, use mnemonic devices, flash cards, and rehearsing aloud or silently (for more on memory techniques, see Chapter 6). Selective highlighting and summarizing your readings in table format will also help.

Develop strategies to manage learning disabilities

Students with reading-related learning disabilities may need to engage their practical thinking skills and emotional and social intelligence to manage reading assignments. Roxanne Ruzic of the Center for Applied Special Technology explored the strategies used by two LD students:[1]

- Danielle received an A in her art history survey course, in part because she chose some courses with heavy reading requirements and some with light requirements. This allowed her to complete all her assignments on time. In addition, she frequently sought instructors' advice about what they wanted her to learn from assigned texts and used tutors whenever she needed extra help.

- Chloe received an A in her course Introduction to Psychology, in part because she met twice weekly with a tutor who helped her prioritize reading assignments and keep on top of her work. She also learned to tailor the amount of time she spent on different text sections to the importance of the material on upcoming tests. Finally, when she felt comfortable with text concepts, she read them quickly or skipped them entirely, but when she had trouble with the material, she did extra reading or sought help.

If you have a learning disability, think of these two students as you investigate the services your college or university offers through counselling departments and tutoring programs. Remember: *The ability to succeed is often linked to the willingness to ask for help.*

Build reading speed

Many students balance heavy academic loads with other important responsibilities. It's difficult to make time to study at all, let alone handle all of your reading assignments. If you can increase your reading speed, you will save valuable time and effort—as long as you don't sacrifice comprehension. Greater comprehension is the primary goal and actually promotes faster reading.

The average adult reads between 150 and 350 words per minute, and faster readers can be capable of speeds up to 1000 words per minute.[2] However, the human eye can only move so fast; reading speeds in excess of 350 words per minute involve "skimming" and "scanning" (see page 148). The following suggestions will help increase your reading speed:

- Try to read groups of words rather than single words.
- Avoid pointing your finger to guide your reading; use an index card to move quickly down the page.
- When reading narrow columns, focus your eyes in the middle of the column. With practice, you'll be able to read the entire column width as you read down the page.
- Avoid *vocalization*—speaking the words or moving your lips—when reading.

The key to building reading speed is practice and more practice, says reading expert Steve Moidel. To achieve your goal of reading between 500 and 1000 words per minute, Moidel suggests that you start practising at three times the rate you want to achieve, a rate that is much faster than you can comprehend.[3] For example, if your goal is 500 words per minute, increase

MULTIPLE INTELLIGENCE STRATEGIES FOR

Reading

Use selected reading techniques in Multiple Intelligence areas to strengthen your ability to read for meaning and retention.

INTELLIGENCE	SUGGESTED STRATEGIES	WHAT WORKS FOR YOU? WRITE NEW IDEAS HERE
Verbal–Linguistic	• Mark up your text with marginal notes while you read. • When tackling a chapter, use every stage of SQ3R, taking advantage of each writing opportunity (writing Q-stage questions, writing summaries, and so on).	
Logical–Mathematical	• Read material in sequence. • Think about the logical connections between what you are reading and the world at large; consider similarities, differences, and cause-and-effect relationships.	
Bodily–Kinesthetic	• Take physical breaks during reading sessions—walk, stretch, exercise. • Pace while reciting important ideas.	
Visual–Spatial	• As you read, take particular note of photos, tables, figures, and other visual aids. • Make charts, diagrams, or think links illustrating difficult concepts you encounter in your reading.	
Interpersonal	• With a friend, have a joint reading session. One should read a section silently and then summarize aloud the important concepts for the other. Reverse the order of summarizer and listener for each section. • Discuss reading material and clarify important concepts in a study group.	
Intrapersonal	• Read in a solitary setting and allow time for reflection. • Think about how a particular reading assignment makes you feel, and evaluate your reaction by considering the material in light of what you already know.	
Musical	• Play music while you read. • Recite important concepts in your reading to rhythms or write a song to depict those concepts.	
Naturalistic	• Read and study in a natural environment. • Before reading indoors, imagine your favourite place in nature in order to create a relaxed frame of mind.	

your speed up to 1500 words per minute. Reading at such an accelerated rate pushes your eyes and mind to adjust to the faster pace. When you slow down to 500 words per minute—the pace at which you can read and comprehend—your reading rate will feel comfortable even though it is much faster than your original speed. You may even want to check into self-paced computer software that helps you improve reading speed.

Expand your vocabulary

As your reading materials at school and at work become more complex, how much you comprehend—and how readily you do it—depends on your vocabulary. A strong vocabulary increases reading speed and comprehension; when you understand the words in your reading material, you don't have to stop as often to think about what they mean.

The best way to build your vocabulary is to commit yourself to learning new and unfamiliar words as you encounter them. This involves certain steps.

ROOT

The central part or basis of a word, around which prefixes and suffixes can be added to produce different words.

Analyze word parts. Often, if you understand part of a word, you can figure out what the entire word means. This is true because many English words are made up of a combination of Greek and Latin prefixes, **roots**, and suffixes. *Prefixes* are word parts that are added to the beginning of a root. *Suffixes* are added to the end of a root. Key 5.2 contains just a few of the prefixes, roots, and suffixes you will encounter as you read. Knowing these verbal building blocks dramatically increases your vocabulary. Key 5.3 shows how one root can be the stem of many different words.

Using prefixes, roots, and suffixes, you can piece together the meaning of many new words you encounter. To use a simple example, the word *prologue* is made up of the prefix *pro* (before) and the root *logue* (to speak). Thus, *prologue* refers to words spoken or written before the main text.

Use words in context. Most people learn words best when they read and use them in written or spoken language. Although a definition tells you what a word means, it may not include a context. Using a word in context after defining it helps to anchor the information so that you can remember it and continue to build on it. Here are some strategies for using context to solidify new vocabulary words.

- Use new words in a sentence or two right away. Do this immediately after reading their definitions while everything is still fresh in your mind.

- Reread the sentence where you originally saw the word. Go over it a few times to make sure that you understand how the word is used.

- Use the word over the next few days whenever it may apply. Try it while talking with friends, writing letters or notes, or thinking your own thoughts.

- Consider where you may have seen or heard the word before. When you learn a word, going back to sentences you previously didn't "get" may solidify your understanding.

- Seek knowledgeable advice. If after looking up a word you still have trouble with its meaning, ask an instructor or friend to help you figure it out.

Common prefixes, roots, and suffixes.

PREFIX	PRIMARY MEANING	EXAMPLE
a-, ab-	from	avert, abstain
con-, cor-, com-i-	with, together	convene, correlate, compare
il-	not	illegal, illegible
sub-, sup-	under	subordinate, suppose

ROOT	PRIMARY MEANING	EXAMPLE
-chron-	time	synchronize
-ann-	year	biannual
-sper-	hope	desperate
-voc-	speak, talk	convocation

SUFFIX	PRIMARY MEANING	EXAMPLE
-able	able	recyclable
-meter	measure	thermometer
-ness	state of	carelessness
-y	inclined to	sleepy

Building words from a single root.

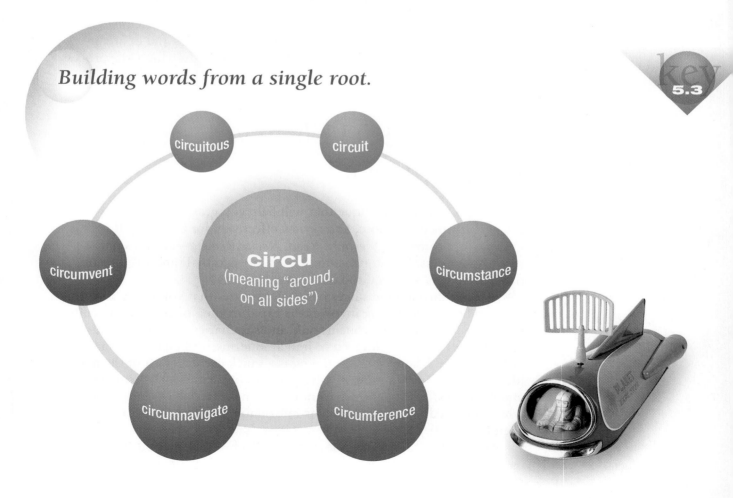

circuitous

circuit

circumvent

circu
(meaning "around, on all sides")

circumstance

circumnavigate

circumference

Use a dictionary. Standard dictionaries provide broad information such as word origin, pronunciation, part of speech, and multiple meanings. Using a dictionary whenever you read increases your comprehension. Buy a standard dictionary, keep it nearby, and consult it for help in understanding passages that contain unfamiliar words. Some textbooks also have a text-specific "dictionary" called a *glossary* that defines terms found in the text. Such definitions are often limited to the meaning of the term as used in that particular textbook.

You may not always have time to use the following suggestions, but when you can use them, they will help you make the most of your dictionary.

- **Read every meaning of a word, not just the first.** Think critically about which meaning suits the context of the word in question, and choose the one that makes the most sense to you.

- **Substitute a word or phrase from the definition for the word.** Use the definition you have chosen. Imagine, for example, that you read the following sentence and do not know the word *indoctrinated*:

The cult indoctrinated its members to reject society's values.

In the dictionary, you find several definitions, including *brainwashed* and *instructed*. You decide that the one closest to the correct meaning is *brainwashed*. With this term, the sentence reads as follows:

The cult brainwashed its members to reject society's values.

So far, this chapter has focused on reading as a deliberate, purposeful process of meaning construction. Recognizing obstacles and defining reading purposes lays the groundwork for effective studying—the process of mastering the concepts and skills contained in your texts.

How can SQ3R *help you master content?*

SQ3R is a technique that will help you grasp ideas quickly, remember more, and review effectively for tests. SQ3R stands for *Survey, Question, Read, Recite, Review*—all steps in the studying process. Developed almost 70 years ago by Francis Robinson, the technique is still used today because it works.[4]

Moving through the stages of SQ3R requires that you know how to skim and scan. **Skimming** involves the rapid reading of chapter elements, including introductions, conclusions, and summaries; the first and last lines of paragraphs; boldfaced or italicized terms; and pictures, charts, and diagrams. The goal of skimming is a quick construction of the main ideas. In contrast, **scanning** involves the careful search for specific facts and examples. You might use scanning during the review phase of SQ3R when you need to locate particular information (such a formula in a chemistry text).

Approach SQ3R as a framework on which you build your house, not as a tower of stone. In other words, instead of following each step by rote, bring your personal learning styles and study preferences to the

SKIMMING

Rapid, superficial reading of material that involves glancing through to determine central ideas and main elements.

SCANNING

Reading material in an investigative way, searching for specific information.

system. For example, you and another classmate may focus on elements in a different order when you survey, write different types of questions, or favour different sets of review strategies. Explore the strategies, evaluate what works, and then make the system your own. (Note that SQ3R is not appropriate for literature)

Survey

Surveying refers to the process of previewing, or pre-reading, a book before you actually study it. Compare it to looking at a map before you drive somewhere—those few minutes spent taking a look at your surroundings and where you intend to go will save you a lot of time and trouble once you are on the road.

Most textbooks include devices that give students an overview of the whole text as well as of the contents of individual chapters. When you survey, pay attention to the following elements.

The front matter. Before you even get to page 1, most textbooks have a table of contents, a preface, and other materials. The table of contents gives you an overview with clues about coverage, topic order, and features. The preface, in particular, can point out the book's unique approach.

The chapter elements. Generally, each chapter has devices that help you make meaning out of the material. Among these are

- the chapter title, which establishes the topic and perhaps author perspective;
- the chapter introduction, outline, list of objectives, or list of key topics;
- within the chapter, headings, tables and figures, quotes, marginal notes, and photographs that help you perceive structure and important concepts;
- special chapter features, often presented in boxes set off from the main text, that point you to ideas connected to themes that run through the text;
- particular styles or arrangements of type (**boldface**, *italics*, <u>underline</u>, larger fonts, bullet points, boxed text) that call your attention to new words or important concepts.

At the end of a chapter, a summary may help you tie concepts together. Review questions and exercises help you review and think critically about the material. Skimming these *before* reading the chapter gives you clues about what's important.

The back matter. Some texts include a glossary in the back matter. You may also find an index to help you locate individual topics and a bibliography that lists additional reading on particular topics covered in the text.

Question

Your next step is to examine the chapter headings and, on a separate piece of paper or in the margins, to write *questions* linked to them. If your reading material has no headings, develop questions as you read. These questions focus your attention and increase your interest, helping

GET ANALYTICAL!

Survey a Text

Practice will improve your surveying skills. So start now with this text or another you are currently using.

- Skim the front matter, including the table of contents and preface. What does this material tell you about the theme? About the book s approach and point of view?

  _____

  _____

- Are any unexpected topics listed in the table of contents? Are any topics missing that you expected to see?

  _____

  _____

- Now look at a typical chapter. List the devices that organize the structure and content of the material.

  _____

  _____

- After skimming the chapter, what do you know about the material? What elements helped you skim quickly?

  _____

  _____

- Finally, skim the back matter. What elements can you identify?

  _____

  _____

- How do you plan to use each of the elements you identified in your text survey when you begin studying?

  _____

  _____

you build comprehension and relate new ideas to what you already know. You can take questions from the textbook or from your lecture notes, or come up with them on your own when you survey, based on what ideas you think are most important.

Use Bloom's Taxonomy to Formulate Questions

Educational psychologist Benjamin Bloom developed Bloom's taxonomy because he believed that not all questions are created equal and that the

Use Bloom's taxonomy to formulate questions at different cognitive levels.

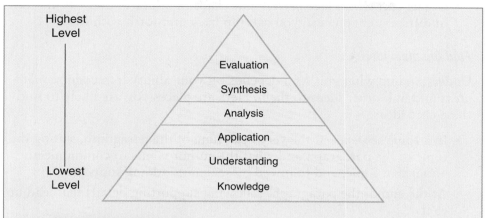

Verbs That Indicate Each Level

1. **Knowledge:** average, define, duplicate, label, list, memorize, name, order, recognize, relate, recall, repeat, reproduce, state.
2. **Understanding:** classify, describe, discuss, explain, express, identify, indicate, locate, recognize, report, restate, review, select, translate.
3. **Application:** apply, choose, demonstrate, dramatize, employ, illustrate, interpret, operate, practise, schedule, sketch, solve, use, write.
4. **Analysis:** analyze, appraise, calculate, categorize, compare, contrast, criticize, differentiate, discriminate, distinguish, examine, experiment, question, test.
5. **Synthesis:** arrange, assemble, collect, compose, construct, create, design, develop, formulate, manage, organize, plan, prepare, propose, set up, write.
6. **Evaluation:** appraise, argue, assess, attach, choose, compare, defend, estimate, judge, predict, rate, score, select, support, value, evaluate.

greatest learning results from rigorous inquiry.[5] While some questions ask for a simple recall, said Bloom, others ask for higher levels of thinking. Key 5.4 shows the six levels of questions identified by Bloom: knowledge, understanding, application, analysis, synthesis, and evaluation. It also identifies verbs that are associated with each level. As you read, using these verbs to formulate specific questions will help you learn. Recognizing these verbs on essay tests will help you answer effectively.

Read

Your text survey and questions give you a starting point for *reading*, the first R in SQ3R. Retaining what you read requires an active approach, as follows:

- Focus on the key points of your survey. Pay special attention to points raised in headings, in italics and boldface type, in chapter objectives, and in the summary.

- Focus on your Q-stage questions. Read the material with the purpose of answering each question. Write down or highlight ideas and examples that relate to your questions.

- **Mark up your text and take text notes.** Write notes in the margins or on separate paper, circle critical ideas, or highlight key points to focus on what's important. These cues will help you study for exams. Text-marking and note-taking techniques will be examined later in the chapter.
- **Create text tabs.** Place plastic index tabs or adhesive notes at the start of different chapters so you can flip back and forth with ease.

Find the main idea

Understanding what you read depends on your ability to recognize *main ideas* and link other ideas to them. Here are places you are likely to find these core ideas:

- In a *topic sentence* at the very beginning of the paragraph, stating the topic of the paragraph and what the author wants to communicate about that topic, and followed by sentences adding support.
- At the end of the paragraph, following supporting details that lead up to it.
- Buried in the middle of the paragraph, sandwiched between supporting details.
- In a compilation of ideas from various sentences, each of which contains a critical element. It is up to the reader to piece these elements together to create the essence of meaning.
- Never explicitly stated, but implied by the information presented in the paragraph.

How, then, do you decide just what the main idea is? Ophelia H. Hancock, a specialist in improving reading skills for post-secondary students, takes a three-step approach:[6]

1. *Search for the topic of the paragraph.* The topic of the paragraph is not the same as the main idea. Rather, it is the broad subject being discussed—for example, Apple CEO Steve Jobs, hate crimes on campus, or binge drinking on campus.
2. *Identify the aspect of the topic that is the paragraph's focus.* If the general topic is Steve Jobs, the author may focus on any of thousands of aspects of that topic, such as his co-founding of Apple Computer in 1976, his role in the Pixar computer animation company, or his role in the development of the iPod portable music player.
3. *Find what the author wants you to know about that specific aspect; this is the main idea.* The main idea of a paragraph dealing with Jobs' role in the development of the iPod may be this: In his role as CEO of Apple Computer, Steve Jobs oversaw the creation of the iPod portable music player, which changed the way the world listens to and purchases music.

Recite

Once you finish reading a topic, stop and answer the questions you raised in the Q-stage of SQ3R. You may decide to *recite* each answer aloud, silently speak the answers to yourself, tell or teach the answers to another person, or write your ideas and answers in brief notes. Writing is often the most effective way to solidify what you have read because writing from memory checks your understanding.

Keep your learning styles (Chapter 3) in mind when you explore different strategies. For example, an intrapersonal learner may prefer writing, while an interpersonal learner might want to recite answers aloud to a classmate. A logical–mathematical learner may benefit from organizing material into detailed outlines, while a musical learner might want to chant information aloud to a rhythm.

After you finish one section, read the next. Repeat the question–read–recite cycle until you complete the entire chapter. If you find yourself fumbling for thoughts, you may not yet "own" the ideas. Reread the section that's giving you trouble until you master its contents. Understanding each section as you go is crucial because the material in one section often forms a foundation for the next.

When do you stop to recite? Waiting for the end of a chapter is too late; stopping at the end of a paragraph is too soon. The best plan is to recite at the end of each text section, right before a new text heading. Repeat the question–read–recite cycle until you complete the chapter. If you find yourself fumbling for thoughts, you have not mastered the ideas. Reread the section that's giving you trouble until you know it cold.

Review

Reviewing, both immediately and periodically in the days and weeks after you read, is the step that solidifies your understanding. Chances are good that if you close the book after you read, much of your focused reading work will slip away from memory. Here are some techniques for reviewing—try many and use what works best for you.

- Reread your notes. Then summarize them from memory.
- Review and summarize in writing the text sections you highlighted or bracketed. Try to condense the material so that you can focus on key ideas.
- Answer the end-of-chapter review, discussion, and application questions.
- Reread the preface, headings, tables, and summary.
- Recite important concepts to yourself, or record and play them back on a tape recorder.
- Listen to audio recordings of your text and other reading materials on your MP3 player.
- Make flash cards with a word or concept on one side and a definition, examples, or other related information on the other. Test yourself.
- Quiz yourself, using the questions you raised in the Q stage. If you can't answer a question, scan the text for the answer.
- Discuss the concepts with a classmate or in a study group. Use each other's Q-stage questions to help one another learn.
- Finally, ask your instructor for help with difficult material. Define exactly what you want to discuss and then schedule a meeting during office hours or email your questions.

Refreshing your knowledge is easier and faster than learning it the first time. Set up regular review sessions; for example, once a week. Reviewing in as many different ways as possible increases the likelihood of retention. Critical reading may be the most important of these ways. Key 5.5 summarizes how SQ3R turns you into an active reader.

STAGE OF SQ3R	DESCRIPTION
Survey	*Pre-reading a book before studying it.* Involves skimming and scanning as you examine the front matter, chapter elements, and back matter for clues about text content and organization.
Question	*Developing questions linked to chapter headings and to what you already know about the topic.* Questioning engages your critical thinking skills.
Read	*Reading the material to answer the questions formulated in the Q stage and to find main ideas.* You can take notes as you read or highlight key ideas and information in your text.
Recite	*Recitation involves answering—perhaps for a second time—your Q-stage questions.* You may decide to recite the answers aloud or silently to yourself, teach them to a study partner, or record them in writing.
Review	*Using various techniques to learn the material before an exam.* Become actively involved with the material through summarizing notes, answering study questions, writing outlines or think links, reciting concepts, using flash cards, thinking critically, and so on.

How can you *respond* critically to what you read?

The fundamental purpose of all college or university reading is understanding. Think of your reading process as an archaeological dig. The first step is to excavate a site and uncover the artifacts—that's your initial survey and reading of the material. As important as the excavation is, the process is incomplete if you stop there. The second step is to investigate each item, evaluate what they all mean, and derive knowledge from what you discover. Critical reading allows you to complete that crucial second step.

Like critical thinking, critical reading is a part of analytical thinking (see Chapter 4). Instead of simply accepting what you read, seek understanding by questioning the material as you move from idea to idea. The best critical readers question every statement for accuracy, relevance, and logic. They also extend critical analysis to all media.

Use knowledge of fact and opinion to evaluate arguments

Critical readers evaluate arguments to determine whether they are accurate and logical. In this context, *argument* refers to a persuasive case—a set of connected ideas supported by examples—that a writer makes to prove or disprove a point.

It's easy—and common—to accept or reject an argument outright, according to whether it fits with your point of view. If you ask questions,

STRESSBUSTER

CLAIRE DOUGLAS   York University, Toronto, Ontario

Do you sometimes find it difficult to find the time or proper setting to study? What sorts of distractions do you face? How do you cope with these distractions and reduce the stress associated with them?

We all occasionally have trouble finding the time to study. There always seems to be something else that needs to be done. I find the greatest distractions are assignments and readings from other courses I am taking. If I have many things due around the same time, I sometimes get overwhelmed with figuring out how I am going to get everything done on time.

I have learned over the years that I am most effective if I am calm and if I can focus on one task at a time. When I start to feel overwhelmed I take time to prioritize my assignments, my studying, and my reading and to come up with a general timeline for each project.

Once I have the time laid out, I choose a setting where I can study without external distractions. I know that I often get distracted by the television, email, and telephone. I am probably like most people in that I can get quite bored with the repetition of studying. It always seems like a great idea to pick up the phone so I can have a "quick study break," but it usually isn't very quick. Study breaks should be times that you can control. I find that a quick walk around the block to get some exercise is really refreshing and allows me to focus more on studying. When it is really cold out I drink a cup of peppermint tea to refresh my mind.

Finally, I try to remember that I can only do so much studying. Instead of worrying about the mark I might get on an exam, I focus on being prepared for the exam and on doing the best I can.

however, you can determine the argument's validity and understand it in greater depth. Evaluating an argument involves

- evaluating the quality of the evidence.
- evaluating whether the support fits the concept.
- evaluating the logical connections.

When quality evidence combines with appropriate support and tight logic, the argument is solid.

What is the quality of the evidence? Ask the following questions to evaluate the evidence:

- What is the source?
- Is the source reliable and free of bias?
- Who wrote this and with what intent?
- What assumptions underlie this material?
- Is the argument based on opinion?
- How does the evidence compare with evidence from other sources?

Successful Intelligence Connections Online

Listen to author Sarah Kravits describe how to use analytical, creative, and practical intelligence to customize your text with highlighting and notes.

Go to the *Keys to Success* Companion Website at www.pearsoned.ca/carter to listen or download as a podcast.

How well does the evidence support the idea? Ask these questions to determine whether the evidence fits the concept:

- Is there enough evidence to support the central idea?
- Do examples and ideas logically connect to one another?
- Is the evidence convincing? Do the examples build a strong case?
- What different and perhaps opposing arguments seem just as valid?

Approach every argument with healthy skepticism. Have an open mind in order to assess whether you are convinced or have serious questions. Use critical thinking to make an informed decision.

How can you customize your text with highlighting and notes?

Textbooks are designed and written with students in mind, but they are not customized to meet your unique reading and studying needs. It is up to you to do that for yourself through text highlighting and notes. Your goal is to transform your texts into very personal study tools.

Highlight the text effectively

Highlighting involves the use of special markers or regular pens or pencils to flag important passages. When used correctly, highlighting is an essential study technique. The following techniques will help you make highlighting a learning tool:

- **Develop a highlighting system and stick to it.** For example, use your creative intelligence to decide if you will use different coloured markers for different elements, brackets for long passages, or pencil underlining. Make a key that identifies each notation.
- **Consider using a regular pencil or pen instead of a highlighter pen.** The copy will be cleaner and look more like a textbook than a colouring book.
- **Read an entire paragraph before you begin to highlight, and don't start until you have a sense of what is important.** Only then put pencil or highlighter to paper as you pick out key terms, phrases, and ideas.
- **Avoid overmarking.** A phrase or two in any paragraph is usually enough. Enclose long passages with brackets rather than marking every line. Avoid underlining entire sentences, when possible. The less colour the better. As a general rule, you should not be highlighting more than 10 percent of your textbook. If you are, you may be confusing highlighting with learning.
- **Highlight supporting evidence.** Mark examples that explain important ideas.

Although these techniques will help you highlight effectively, they won't help you learn the material. Ironically, they may actually obstruct learning as you diligently add colour to the page. Experts agree that you will not learn what you highlight unless you *interact* with the material through surveying, questioning, reading, reciting, and reviewing. Without this interaction, all you are doing is marking your book.

Take text notes as reminders

When you combine highlighting with marginal notes or text flags, you remind yourself what a particular passage is about and why you consider it important. This combination customizes your text, which helps you study for exams. Going a step further by taking a full set of text notes is an excellent way to commit material to memory.

As you will also see in Chapter 6, note taking on texts and in class is critical because material is cumulative—that is, what you learn today builds on what you learned yesterday and on all the days since the beginning of the term.

Making marginal notes

Here are some tips for making marginal notes right on the pages of your text:

- Use pencil so you can erase comments or questions that are answered as you read.
- Write your Q questions from SQ3R in the margins right next to text headings.
- Mark critical sections with marginal notations such as "def." for definition, "e.g." for helpful example, or "concept" for an important concept.
- Write notes at the bottom of the page connecting the text to what you learned in class or in research. You can also attach adhesive notes with your comments.

Key 5.6 shows how to underline effectively and make marginal notes in an introduction to business textbook that introduces the concept of target marketing and market segmentation.

Your customized text will be uniquely yours; no one else will highlight or take text notes as you do because no one else has your knowledge, learning style, or study techniques. Because text customization is so important to learning, you may find it hard to use previously owned texts that are heavily highlighted or filled with marginal notations. Even if the prior owner was a good student, he or she is not you—and that fact alone will affect your ability to master content.

Creating full-text summaries

Taking a full set of notes on assigned readings helps you learn as you summarize main ideas in your own words. Taking notes makes you an active participant as you think about (1) how material fits into what you already know and (2) how to capture key points.

To construct a summary, focus on the main ideas and examples that support them. Don't include your own ideas or evaluations at this point.

Underlining and taking marginal notes help you master content.

5.6

Chapter 10: Understanding Marketing Processes and Consumer Behavior **297**

How does target marketing and market segmentation help companies sell product?

■ TARGET MARKETING AND MARKET SEGMENTATION

Marketers have long known that products cannot be all things to all people. Buyers have different tastes, goals, lifestyles, and so on. The emergence of the marketing concept and the recognition of consumer needs and wants led marketers to think in terms of **target markets**—groups of people with similar wants and needs. <u>Selecting target markets is usually the first step in the marketing strategy.</u>

Target marketing requires **market segmentation**—dividing a market into categories of customer types or "segments." <u>Once they have identified segments, companies may adopt a variety of strategies. Some <u>firms market products to more</u> than one segment.</u> General Motors *(www.gm.com)*, for example, offers compact cars, vans, trucks, luxury cars, and sports cars with various features and at various price levels. GM's strategy is to provide an automobile for nearly every segment of the market.

In contrast, <u>some businesses offer a narrower range of products</u>, each aimed toward a specific segment. Note that segmentation is a strategy for analyzing consumers, not products. The process of fixing, adapting, and communicating the nature of the product itself is called *product positioning.*

How do companies identify market segments?

Identifying Market Segments

By definition, <u>members of a market segment</u> must <u>share some common traits that affect</u> their <u>purchasing decisions.</u> In identifying segments, researchers look at several different influences on consumer behavior. Three of the most important are *geographic, demographic,* and *psychographic variables.*

What effect does geography have on segmentation strategies?
Geographic Variables Many buying decisions are affected by the places people call home. The heavy rainfall in Washington State, for instance, means that people there buy more umbrellas than people in the Sun Belt. Urban residents don't need agricultural equipment, and sailboats sell better along the coasts than on the Great Plains. **Geographic variables** are the geographical units, from countries to neighborhoods, that may be considered in a segmentation strategy.

<u>These patterns affect decisions about marketing mixes for a huge range of products.</u> For example, consider a plan to market down-filled parkas in rural Minnesota. Demand will be high and price competition intense. Local newspaper ads may be

Definitions

target market
Group of people that has similar wants and needs and that can be expected to show interest in the same products

← *GM eg*

market segmentation
Process of dividing a market into categories of customer types

GM makes cars for diff. market segments

Buying decisions influenced by where people live

geographic variables
Geographical units that may be considered in developing a segmentation strategy

*— good eg —
selling parkas in Minnesota*

Thought
Geographical variables change with the seasons

Source: Business Essentials, 5th ed., by Ebert/Griffin, © 2005. Reprinted by permission of Pearson/Prentice Hall, Upper Saddle River, NJ.

Your summary should simply condense the material, making it easier to focus on concepts and interrelationships when you review. Here are suggestions for creating effective full-text summaries:

- Try to use your own words, because repeating the author's words may mean parroting concepts you do not understand. However, when studying a technical subject with precise definitions, you may have little choice but to use text wording.

Mark Up a Page
to Learn a Page

Below, the text material in Key 5.6 continues. Put your own pencil to paper as you highlight concepts and take marginal notes. Compare your efforts to those of your classmates to see how each of you approached the task and what you can learn from their methods.

Part IV: Understanding Principles of Marketing

effective, and the best retail location may be one that is easily reached from several small towns.

Although the marketability of some products is geographically sensitive, others enjoy nearly universal acceptance. Coke, for example, gets more than 70 percent of its sales from international markets. It is the market leader in Great Britain, China, Germany, Japan, Brazil, and Spain. Pepsi's international sales are about 15 percent of Coke's. In fact, Coke's chief competitor in most countries is some local soft drink, not Pepsi, which earns 78 percent of its income at home.

demographic variables
Characteristics of populations that may be considered in developing a segmentation strategy

Demographic Variables Demographic variables describe populations by identifying such traits as age, income, gender, ethnic background, marital status, race, religion, and social class. For example, several general consumption characteristics can be attributed to certain age groups (18–25, 26–35, 36–45, and so on). A marketer can, thus, divide markets into age groups. Table 10.1 lists some possible demographic breakdowns. Depending on the marketer's purpose, a segment can be a single classification (*aged* 20–34) or a combination of categories (*aged* 20–34, *married with children, earning* $25,000–$34,999). Foreign competitors, for example, are gaining market share in U.S. auto sales by appealing to young buyers (under age 30) with limited incomes (under $30,000). Whereas companies such as Hyundai (*www.hyundai.net*), Kia (*www.kia.com*), and Daewoo (*www.daewoous.com*) are winning entry-level customers with high quality and generous warranties, Volkswagen (*www.vw.com*) targets under-35 buyers with its entertainment-styled VW Jetta.[4]

psychographic variables
Consumer characteristics, such as lifestyles, opinions, interests, and attitudes, that may be considered in developing a segmentation strategy

Psychographic Variables Markets can also be segmented according to such **psychographic variables** as lifestyles, interests, and attitudes. Take, for example, Burberry (*www.burberry.com*), whose raincoats have been a symbol of British tradition since 1856. Burberry has repositioned itself as a global luxury brand, like Gucci (*www.gucci.com*) and Louis Vuitton (*www.vuitton.com*). The strategy, which recently resulted in a 31-percent sales increase, calls for attracting a different type of customer—the top-of-the-line, fashion-conscious individual—who shops at such stores as Neiman Marcus and Bergdorf Goodman.[5]

Psychographics are particularly important to marketers because, unlike demographics and geographics, they can be changed by marketing efforts. For example, Polish companies have overcome consumer resistance by promoting the safety and desirability of using credit rather than depending solely on cash. One product of changing attitudes is a booming economy and the emergence of a robust middle class.

TABLE 10.1

Demographic Variables

Age	Under 5, 5–11, 12–19, 20–34, 35–49, 50–64, 65+
Education	Grade school or less, some high school, graduated high school, some college, college degree, advanced degree
Family life cycle	Young single, young married without children, young married with children, older married with children under 18, older married without children under 18, older single, other
Family size	1, 2–3, 4–5, 6+
Income	Under $9,000, $9,000–$14,999, $15,000–$24,999, $25,000–$34,999, $35,000–$45,000, over $45,000
Nationality	African, American, Asian, British, Eastern European, French, German, Irish, Italian, Latin American, Middle Eastern, Scandinavian
Race	Native American, Asian, Black, White
Religion	Buddhist, Catholic, Hindu, Jewish, Muslim, Protestant
Sex	Male, female

- Try to make your notes, simple, clear, and brief. Include what you need to understand about the topic, while eliminating less important details.
- Consider creating an outline of the text content so you can see how ideas relate to one another.
- Before you write, identify the main idea of a passage.
- Once that idea ends and another begins, begin taking notes from memory, using your own words. Go back into the text, as needed, to cull information that you didn't get on first reading.
- Take notes on tables, charts, photographs, and captions; these visual presentations may contain information presented nowhere else in the text.
- Use shorthand symbols to write quickly (see Chapter 6).
- Create notes in visual form:
  - Construct your own charts, tables, and diagrams to depict written concepts
  - Devise a colour-coding system to indicate level of importance of different ideas, and then mark up your notes with these colours.
  - Devise symbols and numbers and use them consistently to indicate the level of importance of different ideas. Write these in different coloured pens.

Successful Intelligence Wrap-Up

Reading and studying are the tools you will use over and over again to acquire information in your personal and community life and career. After college or university, you will be figuring out almost everything on your own—your RRSP, a new office-wide computer system, or even the fine print in a cellphone contract. Your reading success may depend on your ability to use successful intelligence. Here's how you have built skills in Chapter 5:

Analytical

You explored an analytical approach to reading comprehension, taking a close look at reading environment, reading purpose, and vocabulary. In the Get Analytical exercise, you used surveying skills to analyze the front matter and one chapter of a textbook. Within the section on critical reading, you examined how to consider fact and opinion, how arguments are supported, and perspectives in your approach to reading materials.

Creative

In the Get Creative exercise, you generated ideas from reading a book and then seeing a movie made from the same story. Reading about concentration may have inspired ideas about how to create a reading environment that suits you best. When exploring the SQ3R reading method, you may have adopted different ideas about how to implement it into a blend that is uniquely your own.

Practical

You discovered practical actions that can build your knowledge of roots, prefixes, and suffixes. You explored how emotional involvement can deepen your reading experience. You saw examples of how to put the practical steps of the SQ3R reading system into action. In the Get Practical exercise, you applied your knowledge of how to highlight and mark up text to a specific textbook page, solidifying your understanding of which strategies work best for you.

yokomeshi
(yo-ko-meh-shi)

Reading your textbooks may feel at times like what this Japanese word literally means: "eating a meal sideways" (*meshi* means "boiled rice" and *yoko* means "horizontal"). The Japanese use this word to describe how difficult it is to learn a foreign language, since Japanese characters are vertical while most other world languages are horizontal. When the Japanese use this word to describe a difficult intellectual task, they force themselves to laugh at the image, which decompresses the stress. If you feel overwhelmed by the new concepts and specialized vocabulary in your readings, just think of the challenge of eating a meal sideways. Then take heart in the certainty that you are not alone in trying to figure out what things mean. You will succeed by taking as many deep breaths as you need, by keeping your sense of humour, and by committing yourself to using the strategies suggested in this chapter to meet new reading challenges.[7]

"Somewhere, something incredible is waiting to be known."

CARL SAGAN, ASTRONOMER

SUCCESSFUL INTELLIGENCE

Think, Create, Apply

Studying a text page. The following page is from the chapter "Understanding Entrepreneurship, Small Business and New Venture Creation," in the Sixth Canadian Edition of *Business* by Griffin, Ebert and Starke. Apply SQ3R as you read the excerpt. Using what you learned in this chapter about study techniques, complete the questions that follow (some questions ask you to mark the page itself).

Step 1. Think it through: *Gather information and analyze it.* First gather: Skim the excerpt. Identify the headings on the page and the relationships among them. Mark primary (first-level) headings with #1, secondary (second-level) headings with #2, and tertiary (third-level) headings with #3. Then analyze:

Which heading serves as an umbrella for the rest?

_____

What do the headings tell you about the content of the page?

_____

What are three concepts that seem important to remember?

1. _____

2. _____

3. _____

THE LINKS AMONG SMALL BUSINESS, NEW VENTURE CREATION, AND ENTREPRENEURSHIP

Every day, approximately 380 businesses are started in Canada.[1] New firms create the most jobs,[2] are noted for their entrepreneurship, and are typically small. But does this mean that most small businesses are entrepreneurial? Not necessarily.

The terms *small business*, *new venture*, and *entrepreneurship* are closely linked terms, but each idea is distinct. In the following paragraphs we will explain these terms to help you understand these topics and how they are interrelated.

Small Business

1 Explain the meaning of and inter-relationship among the terms *small business*, *new venture creation*, and *entrepreneurship*.

Defining a "small" business can be a bit tricky. Various measures might be used, including the number of people the business employs, the company's sales revenue, the size of the investment required, or the type of ownership structure the business has. Some of the difficulties in defining a small business can be understood by considering the way the Canadian government collects and reports information on small businesses.

Industry Canada is the main federal government agency responsible for small business. In reporting Canadian small business statistics, the government relies on two distinct sources of information, both provided by Statistics Canada: the Business Register (which tracks businesses), and the Labour Force Survey (which tracks individuals). To be included in the register, a business must have at least one paid employee, annual sales revenues of $30 000 or more, or be incorporated (we describe incorporation later in the chapter). A goods-producing business in the register is considered small if it has fewer than 100 employees, while a service-producing business is considered small if it has fewer than 50 employees.

The Labour Force Survey uses information from *individuals* to make estimates of employment and unemployment levels. Individuals are classified as self-employed if they are working owners of a business that is either incorporated or unincorporated, if they work for themselves but do not have a business (some musicians, for example, would fall into this category), or if they work without pay in a family business.[3]

In its publication *Key Small Business Statistics* (www.strategis.gc.ca/epic/internet/insbrp-rppe.nsf/en/rd00760e.html), Industry Canada reports that there are 2.2 million "business establishments" in Canada and about 2.5 million people who are "self-employed."[4] There is no way of identifying how much overlap there is in these two categories, but we do know that an unincorporated business operated by a self-employed person (with no employees) would *not* be counted among the 2.2 million *businesses* in the register. This is an important point because the majority of businesses in Canada have no employees (just the owner), nor are they incorporated.

These facts need to be kept in mind when considering statistics or research that excludes these firms. When either of these indicators is used to find businesses to study, the number of new firms will be underestimated. A study by the Panel Study of Entrepreneurial Dynamics (PSED), conducted by members of the Entrepreneurship Research Consortium (ERC), tracked a sample of Canadian **nascent entrepreneurs**—people who were trying to start a business—over four years. Only 15 percent of those who reported establishing an operating business had incorporated their firm.[5]

nascent entrepreneurs People who are trying to start a business from scratch.

Step 2. Think out of the box: *Create useful study questions.* Based on the three concepts you pulled out, write three study questions that you can review with an instructor, a teaching assistant, or a fellow student.

1. _____

2. _____

3. _____

Step 3. Make it happen: *Read and remember.* Read the excerpt, putting SQ3R to work. Using a marker pen, highlight key phrases and sentences. Write short marginal notes to help you review the material later. After reading the excerpt thoroughly, write a short summary paragraph.

TEAMWORK

Create Solutions Together

Organizing a study group. Organize a study group with three or four members of your class. At the group's first meeting:

- **Set a specific goal for the group.** The goal might be to prepare for an upcoming test or project, for example. Create a weekly schedule. Write everything down and make sure everyone has a copy.

- **Talk about the specific ways you will work together.** Discuss which of the following methods you want to try in the group: pooling your notes, teaching each other difficult concepts; creating, administering, and grading quizzes for each other; creating study flash cards; using SQ3R to review required readings. Set specific guidelines for how group members will be held accountable.

As an initial group exercise, try the following:

- **Review the study questions that you wrote for the *Business* excerpt.** Each person should select one question to focus on while reading (no two people should have the same question). Group members should then reread the excerpt individually, thinking about their questions as they read, and answering them in writing.

- **When you finish reading critically, gather as a group.** Each person should take a turn presenting the question, the response or answer that was derived through critical reading, and any other ideas that came up while reading. The other members of the group may then present any other ideas to add to the discussion. Continue until all group members have had a chance to present their concepts.

Over several weeks, try the group study methods you have chosen. Then evaluate the methods as a group, singling out the methods that most effectively helped group members master the course material. Finally, revise the group's methods if necessary, to focus on the most useful methods.

WRITING

Journal and Put Skills to Work

Record your thoughts on a separate piece of paper or in a journal.

Reading challenges. What course this semester presents your most difficult reading challenge? What makes it tough—the type of material you have to read, the amount, the level of difficulty? Thinking about the strategies in this chapter, create and describe a plan that addresses this challenge. What techniques might help, and how will you use them? What positive effects do you think they'll have?

PERSONAL PORTFOLIO

Prepare for Career Success

Complete the following in your electronic portfolio or on separate sheets of paper.

Reading skills on the job. Excellent reading skills are a requirement for almost every twenty-first-century job. Employers expect that you will read independently to master new skills and keep up with change. "Literacy is no longer defined merely as a basic threshold of reading ability, but rather as the ability to understand and use printed information in daily activities at home, at work, and in the community."[8] This is echoed by the Conference Board of Canada, which says that the power to "read and understand information presented in a variety of forms" is a fundamental employability skill.[9]

For each of the following skill areas listed, indicate all of the ways in which you use that skill on the job or know you will need to use it in your future career. Then for each skill, rate your ability on a scale from 1 to 10, with 10 being highest. Finally, on the same document or sheet of paper, highlight or circle the two skills that you think will be most important for your career as well as for your success as a learner in college or university.

- ability to define your reading purpose
- reading speed
- reading comprehension
- vocabulary building
- identification and use of text-surveying devices
- using analytical thinking skills when reading
- evaluating reading material with others
- ability to understand and use visual aids

For the two skill areas in which you rated yourself lowest, think about how you can improve your abilities. Make a problem-solving plan for each (you may want to use a flow chart like Key 4.13). Check your progress in one month and at the end of the semester.

SUGGESTED READINGS

Armstrong, William H., and M. Willard Lampe II. *Barron's Pocket Guide to Study Tips: How to Study Effectively and Get Better Grades*. New York: Barron's Educational Series, 2004.

Chesla, Elizabeth. *Reading Comprehension Success: In 20 Minutes a Day*, 2nd ed. Florence, KY: Thomson Delmar Learning, 2002.

Cutler, Wade E. *Triple Your Reading Speed*, 4th ed. New York: Pocket Books, 2003.

Frank, Steven. *The Everything Study Book*. Holbrook, MA: Adams Media, 1997.

Labunski, Richard E. *The Educated Student: Getting the Most out of Your College Years*. Versailles, KY: Marley and Beck, 2003.

Luckie, William R., Wood Smethurst, and Sarah Beth Huntley. *Study Power Workbook: Exercises in Study Skills to Improve Your Learning and Your Grades*. Cambridge, MA: Brookline Books, 1999.

Olsen, Amy E. *Active Vocabulary: General and Academic Words*, 3rd ed. New York: Longman, 2006.

Silver, Theodore. *The Princeton Review Study Smart: Hands-on, Nuts and Bolts Techniques for Earning Higher Grades*. New York: Villard Books, 1996.

INTERNET RESOURCES

Academictips.org (study tips and links):
www.academictips.org

College Tutor Study Guide:
www.amelox.com/study.htm

HowToStudy.com (study advice with valuable links):
www.howtostudy.com

Improve Your Study Skills (tips from SoYouWanna.com):
www.soyouwanna.com/site/syws/studyskills/studyskills.html

Lesson Tutor—Good Study Habits:
www.lessontutor.com/studygeneralhome.html

Merriam-Webster's Word of the Day (free word of the day in audio form available on the internet or as podcasts):
www.merriam-webster.com/cgi-bin/mwwod.pl

Princeton Review Vocab Minute (free vocabulary-building podcasts using songs to help you remember):
www.learnoutloud.com/Podcast-Directory/Languages/Vocabulary-Building/Princeton-Review-Vocabulary-Minute-Podcast/18871#plink

Study Guides and Strategies:
www.studygs.net

Taking College Courses:
www.math.usf.edu/~mccolm/Aclasses.html

Prentice Hall Student Success Supersite:
www.prenhall.com/success

1. Roxanne Ruzic, "Lessons for Everyone: How Students with Reading-Related Learning Disabilities Survive and Excel in College Courses with Heavy Reading Requirements," paper presented at the Annual Meeting of the American Educational Research Association, Seattle, April 13, 2001, http://iod.unh.edu/EE/articles/lessons_for_everyone.html.

2. Steve Moidel, *Speed Reading* (Hauppauge, NY: Barron's Educational Series, 1994), 18.

3. Ibid.

4. Francis P. Robinson, *Effective Behaviour* (New York: Harper &Row, 1941).

5. Benjamin S. Bloom, *Taxonomy of Educational Objectives, Handbook I: The Cognitive Domain* (New York: McKay, 1956).

6. Ophelia H. Hancock, *Reading Skills for College Students*, 5th ed. (Upper Saddle River, NJ: Prentice Hall, 2001), 54–59.

7. Christopher J. Moore, *In Other Words: A Language Lover's Guide to the Most Intriguing Words around the World* (New York: Walker, 2004), 87.

8. U.S. Department of Education, National Center for Education Statistics, *The Condition of Education, 1996*, NCES 96-304, by Thomas M. Smith (Washington, DC: U.S. Government Printing Office, 1996), 84.

9. Conference Board of Canada, Employability Skills 2000+, http://www.conferenceboard.ca/education/learning-tools/pdfs/esp2000.pdf.

LISTENING, NOTE TAKING, AND MEMORY

Taking in, recording, and retaining information

6

"Successfully intelligent people find their path and then pursue it, realizing that there will be obstacles along the way and that surmounting these obstacles is part of their challenge."

ROBERT J. STERNBERG

P ost-secondary education exposes you daily to all kinds of information—and your job as a student is to take it in, write it down, and keep what is important. As the Conference Board of Canada points out, the ability to "listen and ask questions" is an important employability skill.[1] This chapter shows you how to accomplish this by building your skills in the areas of listening (taking in information), note taking (recording what's important), and memory (retaining information). Each process engages your analytical, creative, and practical abilities and helps you build knowledge you can use.

Chapter 6's
Successful Intelligence Skills

Analytical

- Understanding the listening process and the challenge of good listening
- Evaluating the importance of class notes and different note-taking systems
- Analyzing the nature of memory and why memory strategies work

Creative

- Constructing active listening strategies that help you learn
- Personalizing note-taking systems and strategies
- Thinking of and using mnemonic devices to boost recall

Practical

- How to overcome distractions to listen actively
- How to use note-taking systems and shorthand and craft a master note set
- How to use mnemonics to learn

How can you become a better listener?

LISTENING

A process that involves sensing, interpreting, evaluating, and reacting to spoken messages.

The act of hearing isn't quite the same as the act of **listening**. While *hearing* refers to sensing spoken messages from their source, *listening* involves a complex process of communication. Successful listening occurs when the speaker's intended message reaches the listener. In school and at home, poor listening may cause communication breakdowns and mistakes. Skilled listening, however, promotes progress and success. Listening is a teachable—and learnable—skill.

Ralph G. Nichols, a pioneer in listening research, studied 200 students over a nine-month period. His findings demonstrate that effective listening depends as much on a positive attitude as on specific skills.[2] Just as understanding the steps involved in critical thinking helps you work out problems, understanding the listening process helps you become a better listener.

Know the stages of listening

Listening is made up of four stages that build on one another: sensing, interpreting, evaluating, and reacting. These stages take the message from the speaker to the listener and back to the speaker (see Key 6.1).

- During the *sensation* stage (also known as hearing), your ears pick up sound waves and transmit them to the brain. For example, you are sitting in class and hear your instructor say, "The only opportunity to make up last week's test is Tuesday at 5:00 p.m."

Stages of listening.

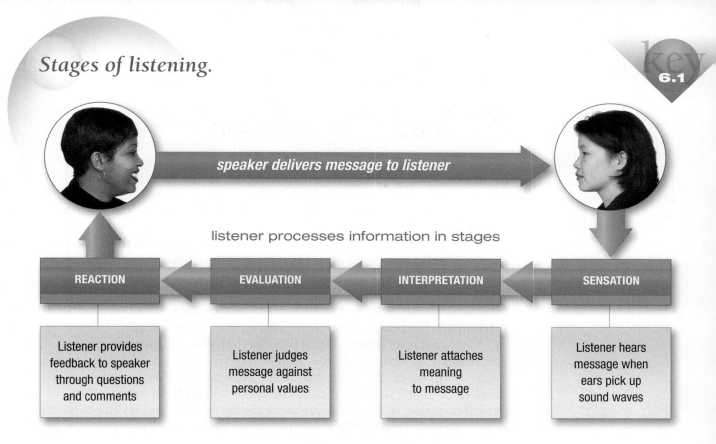

speaker delivers message to listener

listener processes information in stages

| REACTION | EVALUATION | INTERPRETATION | SENSATION |

| Listener provides feedback to speaker through questions and comments | Listener judges message against personal values | Listener attaches meaning to message | Listener hears message when ears pick up sound waves |

- In the *interpretation* stage, listeners attach meaning to a message. This involves understanding what is being said and relating it to what you already know. For example, you relate this message to your knowledge of the test, whether you need to make it up, and what you are doing on Tuesday at 5:00 p.m.

- In the *evaluation* stage of listening, you decide what you think or how you feel about the message—whether, for example, you like it or agree with it. This involves considering the message as it relates to your needs and values. In this example, if you do need to make up the test but have to work Tuesday at 5:00 p.m., you may evaluate the message as less than satisfactory.

- The final stage of listening involves a *reaction* to the message in the form of direct feedback. Your reaction, in this example, may be to ask the instructor for an alternative to the scheduled makeup test time.

Improving your listening skills involves two primary actions: managing listening challenges and becoming an active listener. Although becoming a better listener will help in every class, it is especially important in subjects that are challenging for you.

Manage listening challenges

Communication barriers can interfere with listening at every stage. In fact, classic studies have shown that immediately after listening, students are likely to recall only half of what was said. This is partly due to particular listening challenges such as divided attention and distractions, the tendency to shut out the message, the inclination to rush to judgment, and partial hearing loss or learning disabilities.[3]

To help create a positive listening environment in both your mind and your surroundings, explore how to manage these challenges.

Divided attention and distractions. Imagine you are talking with a co-worker in the company cafeteria when you hear your name mentioned across the room. You strain to hear what someone might be saying about you and, in the process, hear neither your friend nor the person across the room very well. This situation illustrates the consequences of divided attention. Although you are capable of listening to more than one message at the same time, you may not completely hear or understand any of them.

Internal and external distractions often divide your attention. *Internal distractions* include anything from hunger to headache to personal worries. Something the speaker says may also trigger a recollection that causes your mind to drift. In contrast, *external distractions* include noises (e.g., whispering or sirens) and excessive heat or cold. It can be hard to listen in an overheated room in which you are falling asleep.

Your goal is to reduce distractions so that you can focus on what you're hearing. Sitting near the front where you can clearly see and hear helps you to listen. To avoid distracting activity, you may want to sit away from people who might chat or make noise. Dress comfortably, paying attention to the temperature of the classroom, and try not to go to class hungry or thirsty. Work to concentrate on class when you're in class and worry about personal problems later.

Shutting out the message. Instead of paying attention to everything the speaker says, many students fall into the trap of focusing on specific points and shutting out the rest of the message. If you perceive that a subject is too difficult or uninteresting, you may tune out. Shutting out the message makes listening harder from that point on because the information you miss may be the foundation for future class discussions.

Creating a positive listening environment includes accepting responsibility for listening. Although the instructor is responsible for communicating information to you, he or she cannot force you to listen. You are responsible for taking in that information. Instructors often cover material from outside the textbook during class and then test on that material. If you work to take in the whole message in class, you can read over your notes later and think critically about what is most important.

The rush to judgment. People tend to stop listening when they hear something they don't like. If you rush to judge what you've heard, making a quick uncritical assumption about it, your focus turns to your personal reaction rather than the content of the message. Judgments also involve reactions to the speakers themselves. If you do not like your instructors or if you have preconceived notions about their ideas or background, you may assume that their words have little value.

Work to recognize and control your judgments by listening first without jumping to conclusions. Ask critical-thinking questions about assumptions. Stay aware of what you tend to judge so that you can avoid rejecting messages that clash with your opinions. Consider education as a continuing search for evidence, regardless of whether that evidence supports or negates your perspective.

Partial hearing loss and learning disabilities. Good listening techniques don't solve every listening problem. If you have some level of hearing loss, seek out special services that can help you listen in class. For example, you may be able to record the lecture and play it back at a louder-than-normal volume after class, have special tutoring, or arrange for a classmate to take notes for you. In addition, you may be able to arrange to meet with your instructor outside of class to clarify your notes.

Other disabilities, such as attention deficit disorder (ADD) or a problem with processing spoken language, can make it hard to focus on and understand oral messages. If you have one of these disabilities, don't blame yourself for your difficulty. Visit your school's counselling or student health centre, or talk with your adviser or instructors about getting the help you need to meet your challenges.

Successful Intelligence Connections Online

Listen to author Sarah Kravits describe how to use analytical, creative, and practical intelligence to improve your listening skills.

Go to the *Keys to Success* Companion Website at www.pearsoned.ca/ carter to listen or download as a podcast.

Become an active listener

On the surface, listening seems like a passive activity: you sit back and listen as someone else speaks. Effective listening, however, is really an active process that involves the following factors:

Be there. Being an active listener requires that you show up on time— preferably a few minutes before class begins. Instructors often make important announcements in the first few minutes and may also summa ize the last lecture.

Set purposes for listening. Before every class, use your analytical intelligence to establish what you want to achieve, such as understanding difficult concepts or mastering a task. Many instructors start a lecture with a statement of purpose, so listen carefully to their introductory words. Then write them at the top of your notes to help you focus.

Accomplishing your purpose requires that you read assignments before class and review your notes from the previous class. This preparation will set the stage for you to follow the lecture and will help you tell the difference between important and unimportant material. Without it, you may find yourself scrambling to take down every word.

Making your purpose for listening *personal* will motivate you to listen closely. As you prepare for class, ask yourself how the material relates to your academic goals. With the mindset that what you hear will help *you*, you will be more able to make listening a top priority in class.

Pay attention to verbal signposts. You can identify important facts and ideas and predict test questions by paying attention to the speaker's specific choice of words. **Verbal signposts** often involve transition words and phrases that help organize information, connect ideas, and indicate what is and is not important. Let phrases like those in Key 6.2 direct your attention to the material that follows them.

Ask questions. Successful listening is closely linked to asking questions. A willingness to ask questions shows a desire to learn and is the mark of a critical thinker. Asking questions has two benefits. First of all, it helps you to deepen your understanding of what you hear. This happens when

VERBAL SIGNPOSTS

Spoken words or phrases that call your attention to the information that follows.

SIGNALS POINTING TO KEY CONCEPTS	SIGNALS OF SUPPORT
There are two reasons for this...	For example,...
A critical point in the process involves...	Specifically,...
Most importantly,...	For instance,...
The result is...	Similarly,...

SIGNALS POINTING TO DIFFERENCES	SIGNALS THAT SUMMARIZE
On the contrary,...	Finally,...
On the other hand,...	Recapping this idea,...
In contrast,...	In conclusion,...
However,...	As a result,...

you ask either informational or clarifying questions. *Informational* questions, such as any questions beginning with "Can you explain . . . ," seek information that you haven't yet heard or acquired. *Clarifying* questions ask if your understanding of something you just heard is correct, such as "So some learning disabilities can be improved with treatment?" Second of all, questions help to solidify your memory of what you are hearing. As you think of the question, raise your hand, speak, and listen to the answer, brain activity and physical activity combine to reinforce the information you are taking in.

Effective listening skills prepare you to take effective notes—a necessary and powerful study tool.

How can you make the most of class notes?

Taking notes makes you an active class participant—even when you don't say a word—and provides you with study materials. Class notes have two primary purposes: to serve as a record of what happened in class and to use for studying, alone and in combination with your text notes. Because it is virtually impossible to take notes on everything you hear, note taking encourages you to use your analytical intelligence to critically evaluate what is worth remembering. Remember that what's on the line here is nothing short of your academic success.

Choose a note-taking system

There is more than one way to take good notes. You benefit most from the system that feels most comfortable to you and makes the most sense for the course content. For example, you might take notes in a different style for a history class than for a foreign language class. The most common note-taking systems include outlines, the Cornell system, and think links.

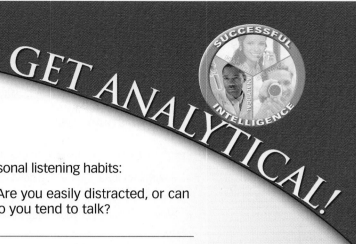

Discover Yourself as a Listener

Complete the following as you focus on your personal listening habits:

- Analyze how present you are as a listener. Are you easily distracted, or can you focus well? Do you prefer to listen or do you tend to talk?

  _____

  _____

- When you are listening, what tends to distract you?

  _____

  _____

- What happens to your listening skills when you become confused?

  _____

  _____

- How do you react when you strongly disagree with something your instructor says—when you are convinced that you are "right" and your instructor is "wrong"?

  _____

  _____

- Thinking about your answers and about your listening challenges, list two strategies from the chapter that will help you improve your listening skills:

  1. _____

  2. _____

As you consider each system, remember your learning styles from Chapter 3. In each class, choose a system that takes both your learning styles and the class material into account. For example, a visual learner may take notes in think link style most of the time, but may find that only the Cornell style works well for a particular chemistry course. Experiment to discover what works best in any situation.

Taking notes in outline form

Outlines use a standard structure to show how ideas interrelate. *Formal outlines* indicate idea dominance and subordination with Roman numerals, uppercase and lowercase letters, and numbers. In contrast, *informal outlines* show the same associations but replace the formality with a system of consistent indenting and dashes. See the formal and informal outline structure in Key 6.3. Many students find informal outlines easier for in-class note taking. Key 6.4 shows how the structure

Note Taking

Note taking is a critical learning tool. The tips below will help you retain information for both the short and long term.

INTELLIGENCE	SUGGESTED STRATEGIES	WHAT WORKS FOR YOU? WRITE NEW IDEAS HERE
Verbal–Linguistic	• Rewrite important ideas and concepts in class notes from memory. • Write summaries of your notes in your own words.	
Logical–Mathematical	• Organize the main points of a lecture or reading using outline form. • Make charts and diagrams to clarify ideas and examples.	
Bodily–Kinesthetic	• Make note taking as physical as possible—use large pieces of paper and different coloured pens. • When in class, choose a comfortable spot where you have room to spread out your materials and shift body position when you need to.	
Visual–Spatial	• Take notes using coloured markers. • Rewrite lecture notes in think link format, focusing on the most important and difficult points from the lecture.	
Interpersonal	• Whenever possible, schedule a study group right after a lecture to discuss class notes. • Review class notes with a study buddy. See what you wrote that he or she missed and vice versa.	
Intrapersonal	• Schedule some quiet time as soon as possible after a lecture to reread and think about your notes. If no class is meeting in the same room after yours and you have free time, stay in the room and review there.	
Musical	• Play music while you read your notes. • Write a song that incorporates material from one class period's notes or one particular topic. Use the refrain to emphasize the most important concepts.	
Naturalistic	• Read or rewrite your notes outside. • Review notes while listening to a nature CD—running water, rain, forest sounds.	

Outlines show levels of importance as they link details to main ideas.

FORMAL OUTLINE	INFORMAL OUTLINE
TOPIC	**TOPIC**
I. First Main Idea	First Main Idea
A. Major supporting fact	—Major supporting fact
B. Major supporting fact	—Major supporting fact
1. First reason or example	—First reason or example
2. Second reason or example	—Second reason or example
a. First supporting fact	—First supporting fact
b. Second supporting fact	—Second supporting fact
II. Second Main Idea	Second Main Idea
A. Major supporting fact	—Major supporting fact
1. First reason or example	—First reason or example
2. Second reason or example	—Second reason or example
B. Major supporting fact	—Major supporting fact

An informal outline is excellent for taking class notes.[4]

Tropical Rain Forests

—What are tropical rain forests?
  —Areas in South America and Africa, along the equator
  —Average temperatures between 25° and 30° C (77°–86° F)
  —Average annual rainfalls range between 250 to 400 centimeters (100 to 160 inches)
  —Conditions combine to create the Earth's richest, most biodiverse ecosystem.
    —A biodiverse ecosystem has a great number of organisms co-existing within a defined area
    —Examples of rain forest biodiversity
      —2½ acres in the Amazon rain forest has 283 species of trees
      —a 3-square-mile section of a Peruvian rain forest has more than 1,300 butterfly species and 600 bird species.
      —Compare this biodiversity to what is found in the entire U.S.
        —only 400 butterfly species and 700 bird species
—How are humans changing the rain forest?
  —Humans have already destroyed about 40% of all rain forests.
    —They are cutting down trees for lumber or clearing the land for ranching or agriculture.
  —Biologist Edwin O. Wilson estimates that this destruction may lead to the extinction of 27,000 species.
  —Rain forest removal is also linked to the increase in atmospheric carbon dioxide, which worsens the greenhouse effect.
    —The greenhouse effect refers to process in which gases such as carbon dioxide trap the sun's energy in the Earth's atmosphere as heat, resulting in global warming.
  —Recognition of the crisis is growing as are conservation efforts.

of an informal outline helps a student take notes on the topic of tropical rain forests. The Multiple Intelligence Strategies table in this chapter (see page 176) is designed to help harness different learning approaches for note-taking. From time to time, an instructor may give you a guide, usually in outline form, to help you take notes in class. This outline, known as *guided notes*, may be on the board, on an overhead projector, or on a handout that you receive at the beginning of class. Because guided notes are usually general and sketchy, they require that you fill in the details.

Using the Cornell note-taking system

The Cornell note-taking system, also known as the T-note system, was developed more than 45 years ago by Walter Pauk at Cornell University.[5] The system is successful because it is simple—and because it works. It consists of three sections on ordinary notepaper:

- Section 1, the largest section, is on the right. Record your notes here in informal outline form.
- Section 2, to the left of your notes, is the *cue column*. Leave it blank while you read or listen; then fill it in later as you review. You might fill it with comments that highlight main ideas, clarify meaning, suggest examples, or link ideas and examples. You can even draw diagrams.
- Section 3, at the bottom of the page, is the *summary area*. Here you use a sentence or two to summarize the notes on the page. When you review, use this section to reinforce concepts and provide an overview.

When you use the Cornell system, create the note-taking structure before class begins. Picture an upside-down letter T and use Key 6.5 as your guide.

- Start with a sheet of standard loose-leaf paper. Label it with the date and title of the lecture.
- To create the cue column, draw a vertical line about 6 centimetres from the left side of the paper. End the line about 5 centimetres from the bottom of the sheet.
- To create the summary area, start at the point where the vertical line ends (about 5 centimetres from the bottom of the page) and draw a horizontal line that spans the entire paper.

Key 6.5 shows how a student used the Cornell system to take notes in an introductory business course.

Creating a think link

A *think link*, also known as a mind map, is a visual form of note taking. When you draw a think link, you diagram ideas by using shapes and lines that link ideas and supporting details and examples. The visual design makes the connections easy to see, and the use of shapes and pictures extends the material beyond just words. Many learners respond well to the power of **visualization**. You can use think links to brainstorm ideas for paper topics as well.

One way to create a think link is to start by writing your topic in the middle of a sheet of paper and putting a circle or square around it. Next, draw a line from the central topic and write the name of one major idea at

VISUALIZATION

The interpretation of verbal ideas through the use of mental visual images.

Sample Cornell system notes.

October 3, 200X, p. 1

UNDERSTANDING EMPLOYEE MOTIVATION

Why do some workers have a better attitude toward their work than others?	Purpose of motivational theories — To explain role of human relations in motivating employee performance — Theories translate into how managers actually treat workers
Some managers view workers as lazy; others view them as motivated and productive.	2 specific theories — Human resources model, developed by Douglas McGregor, shows that managers have radically different beliefs about motivation. — Theory X holds that people are naturally irresponsible and uncooperative — Theory Y holds that people are naturally responsible and self-motivated
Maslow's Hierarchy	— Maslow's Hierarchy of Needs says that people have needs in 5 different areas, which they attempt to satisfy in their work.

Maslow's Hierarchy

self-actualization needs (challenging job)

esteem needs (job title)

social needs (friends at work)

security needs (health plan)

physiological needs (pay)

— Physiological need: need for survival, including food and shelter

— Security need: need for stability and protection

— Social need: need for friendship and companionship

— Esteem need: need for status and recognition

— Self-actualization need: need for self-fulfillment

Needs at lower levels must be met before a person tries to satisfy needs at higher levels.

— Developed by psychologist Abraham Maslow

Two motivational theories try to explain worker motivation. The human resources model includes Theory X and Theory Y. Maslow's Hierarchy of Needs suggests that people have needs in 5 different areas: physiological, security, social, esteem, and self-actualization.

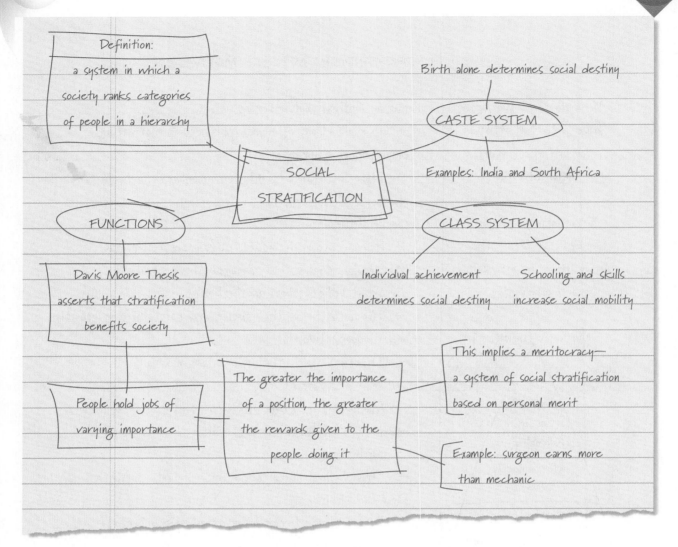

the end of the line. Circle that idea also. Then jot down specific facts related to the idea, linking them to the idea with lines. Continue the process, connecting thoughts to one another by using circles, lines, and words. Key 6.6 shows a think link on a sociology concept called social stratification.

This is only one of many think link styles; other examples include stair steps (showing connecting ideas that build to a conclusion) and a tree shape (roots as causes and branches as effects). You can design any think link that makes sense to you.

A think link may be tough to construct in class, especially if your instructor talks quickly. In this case, use another note-taking system during class. Then make a think link as you review your notes.

Using other visual note-taking strategies

Several other note-taking strategies help you organize your information and are especially useful to visual learners. These strategies may be too involved to complete quickly during class, so you may want to use them when taking notes on a text chapter or when rewriting your notes for review.

Timelines. A timeline can help you organize information—such as the dates Canadian prime ministers took office or eras of different psychology practices—into chronological order. Draw a vertical or horizontal line on the page and connect each item to the line, in order, noting the dates.

Tables. There are tables throughout this text that show information in vertical or horizontal columns. Use tables to arrange information according to particular categories.

Hierarchy charts. These charts can help you understand information in terms of how each piece fits into the **hierarchy**. A hierarchy chart could show levels of government, for example, or levels of the scientific classification of animals and plants. One version of a hierarchy is called a *matrix*—a table that has categories listed across the top and along the left side. Each box inside shows information that relates to the categories above and beside it. Key 10.4 on page 324 is an example of a matrix.

Once you choose a note-taking system, your success depends on how well you use it. Personal shorthand (discussed later in this chapter) will help you make the most of whatever system you choose.

HIERARCHY
A graded or ranked series.

Perform note taking as a three-step process

Taking good class notes requires practice—practice preparing, practice doing, and practice reviewing. Involved are a number of analytical and practical strategies.

1. Prepare

Showing up for class on time with pad and pen in hand is only the beginning of the preparation stage.

Preview your reading material. More than anything else you can do, reading assigned materials before class will give you the background to take effective notes. Check your class syllabi daily to see when assignments are due, and then plan your reading time with these deadlines in mind.

Review what you know. Taking 15 minutes before class to review your notes from the previous class and your reading assignment notes for that day will enable you to follow the lecture from the start. Without this preparation, you may find yourself flipping back in your notebook instead of listening to new information.

Gather your supplies. Use a separate notebook for each course, and start a new page for each class. If you use a three-ring binder, punch holes in handouts and insert them right after your notes for that day. If you use a laptop, open the file containing your class notes right away.

Location, location, location. Find a comfortable seat that is away from friends to minimize distractions. Be ready to write as soon as the instructor begins speaking.

Choose the best note-taking system. Use your emotional and social intelligence to select a system that will work best in each class. Take these factors into account when making your choices:

- The instructor's style. This will be clear after a few classes. In the same term, you may have one instructor who is organized and speaks slowly, another who jumps around and talks rapidly, and a third who digresses in response to questions. Be flexible enough to adapt your note taking to each situation.
- The course material. You may decide that an informal outline works best for a highly structured lecture and that a think link is right for a looser presentation. Try one note-taking system for several classes, then adjust if necessary.
- Your learning style. Choose strategies that make the most of your strengths and compensate for weaknesses. A visual–spatial learner might prefer think links or the Cornell system; a thinker type might be comfortable with outlines; an interpersonal learner might use the Cornell system and fill in the cue column in a study group. You might even find that one system is best in class and another in review sessions.

Gather support. In each class, set up a support system with one or two students so you can look at their notes after an absence.

2. Record information effectively during class

The following practical suggestions will help you record what is important in a format that you can review later:

- Date and identify each page. When you take several pages of notes, add an identifying letter or number to the date to keep track of page order: 11/27A, 11/27B, for example, or 11/27—1 of 2, 11/27—2 of 2. Indicate the lecture topic at the top so you can gather all your notes on that topic.
- If your instructor jumps from topic to topic during a single class, it may help to start a new page for each new topic.
- Record whatever your instructor emphasizes by paying attention to verbal and non-verbal cues (see Key 6.7).
- Write down all key terms and definitions.
- Try to capture explanations of difficult concepts by noting relevant examples, applications, and links to other material.
- Write down every question your instructor raises, since these questions may be on a test.
- Be organized, but not fussy. Remember that you can always improve your notes later.
- Write quickly but legibly, using shorthand and short phrases instead of full sentences.

3. Review and revise

By their very nature, class notes require revision. They may be incomplete in some places, confusing in others, and illegible in still others. That is why it is critical that you review and revise your notes as soon as possible after

Pick up on instructors' verbal and non-verbal cues.

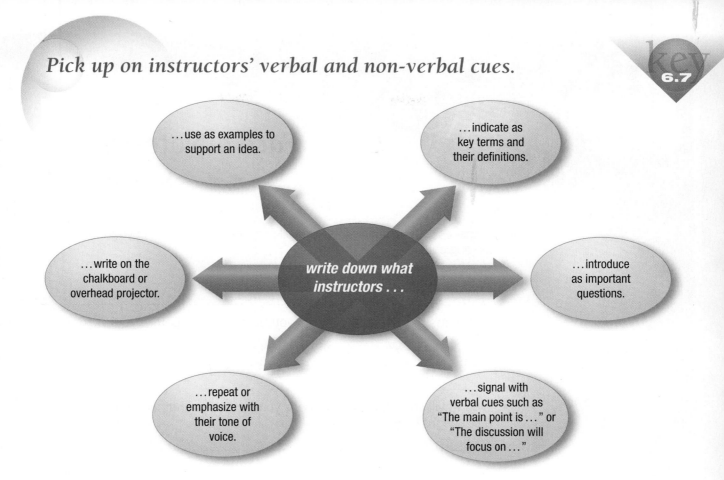

…use as examples to support an idea.

…indicate as key terms and their definitions.

…write on the chalkboard or overhead projector.

write down what instructors . . .

…introduce as important questions.

…repeat or emphasize with their tone of voice.

…signal with verbal cues such as "The main point is . . ." or "The discussion will focus on . . ."

class. This will enable you to fill in gaps while the material is fresh, to clarify sloppy handwriting, or to raise questions. Reviewing and revising your class notes prepares you for the vital step of combining class and reading notes.

Combine class and reading notes into a master set

Studying from either text or class notes alone is not enough, because your instructor may present material in class that is not in your text or may gloss over topics that your text covers in depth. The process of combining class and text notes enables you to see patterns and relationships among ideas, find examples for difficult concepts, and much more. Follow these steps to combine your class and text notes into a **master note set**:

Step 1: Act quickly. Combine your class and reading notes into a logical, comprehensive presentation while the material is fresh in your mind.

Step 2: Focus on what's important by condensing to the essence. Now, reduce your combined notes so they contain only key terms and concepts. (You are likely to find repetition in your notes, which will make it easy to reduce the material.) Tightening and summarizing force you to critically evaluate which ideas are most important and to rewrite your notes with only this material. As you begin to study, move back and forth between the full set and the reduced set.

MASTER NOTE SET

The complete, integrated note set that contains both class and text notes.

Face a Note-Taking Challenge

In the spaces below, record how you will prepare to take notes in your most challenging course.

- Course name and date of class:

  _____

- List all the reading assignments you have to finish before your next class:

  _____

  _____

- Where will you sit in class to focus your attention and minimize distractions?

  _____

  _____

- Which note-taking system is best suited for the class and why?

  _____

  _____

- Write the phone numbers or email addresses of two students whose notes you can look at if you miss a class:

  _____

  _____

Step 3: Recite what you know. As you approach exam time, use the terms in your bare-bones notes as cues for reciting what you know about a topic. Many students assume that they know concepts simply because they understand what they read. What they are actually demonstrating is a passive understanding that doesn't necessarily mean that they can re-create the material on an exam or apply it to problems. Make the process more active by reciting out loud during study sessions, writing your responses on paper, making flash cards, or working with a partner.

Step 4: Use critical thinking. Now toss around ideas in the following ways as you reflect on your combined notes—both the comprehensive and reduced sets:

- Brainstorm examples from other sources that illustrate central ideas. Write down new ideas or questions that come up as you review.

- Think of ideas from your readings or from class that support or clarify your notes.
- Consider what in your class notes differed from your reading notes and why.
- Apply concepts to problems at the end of textbook chapters, to problems posed in class, or to real-world situations.

Step 5: Review and review again. To ensure learning and prepare for exams, review your key word summary and critical thinking questions until you know every topic.

Try to vary your review methods, focusing on active involvement. Recite the material to yourself, have a Q&A session with a study partner, take a practice test. Another helpful technique is to summarize your notes in writing from memory after you review them. This will tell you whether you'll be able to recall the information on a test. You may even want to summarize as you read, then summarize from memory, and compare the two summaries.

How can you take notes faster?

When taking notes, many students feel that they can't keep up with the instructor. Using some personal **shorthand** (not standard secretarial shorthand) can help you push your pen faster. Shorthand is writing that shortens words or replaces them with symbols. Because you are the only intended reader, you can misspell and abbreviate words in ways that only you understand.

The only danger with shorthand is that you might forget what your writing means. To avoid this problem, review your shorthand notes while your abbreviations and symbols are fresh in your mind. If there is any confusion, spell out words as you review.

Here are some suggestions that will help you master this important skill:

SHORTHAND

A system of rapid handwriting that employs symbols, abbreviations, and shortened words to represent words, phrases, and letters.

1. Use standard abbreviations (shown in Key 6.8) in place of complete words.
2. Shorten words by removing vowels from the middle of words:

    prps = purpose

    Crvtte = Corvette (as on a vanity licence plate for a car)

    cmptr = computer

3. Substitute word beginnings for entire words:

    assoc = associate; association

    info = information

    subj = subject

4. Form plurals by adding *s*:

    prblms = problems

    prntrs = printers

    envlps = envelopes

Use standard abbreviations in place of complete words.

w/	with		cf	compare, in comparison to
w/o	without		ff	following
→	means; resulting in		Q	question
←	as a result of		p.	page
↑	increasing		*	most importantly
↓	decreasing		<	less than
∴	therefore		>	more than
∵ or b/c	because		=	equals
≈	approximately		%	percent
+ or &	and		△	change
—	minus; negative		2	to; two; too
NO. or #	number		vs	versus; against
i.e.	that is,		e.g.	for example
etc.	and so forth		c/o	care of
ng	no good		lb	pound

5. Make up your own symbols and use them consistently:

   b/4   =   before

   4tn   =   fortune

   2thake =   toothache

6. Use key phrases instead of complete sentences ("German—nouns capped" instead of "In German, all nouns are capitalized").

   Finally, throughout your note taking, remember that the primary goal is for you to generate materials that help you learn and remember information. No matter how sensible any note-taking strategy, abbreviation, or system might be, it won't do you any good if it doesn't help you reach that goal. Keep a close eye on what works for you and stick to it.

   If you find that your notes aren't comprehensive, legible, or focused enough, think critically about how you might improve them. Can't read your notes? You might have been too sleepy, or you might have a handwriting issue. Confusing gaps in the information? You might be distracted in class, have an instructor who skips around, or have a lack of understanding of the course material. Put your problem-solving skills to work and brainstorm solutions from the variety of strategies in this chapter. With a little time and effort, your notes will truly become a helpful learning tool in school and beyond.

Once you have figured out how to effectively record what you hear, your next task is to remember it so that you can use it. The following information about memory will help you remember what you learn so that you can put it to use.

How can you improve memory?

Your accounting instructor is giving a test tomorrow on the double-entry accounting system. You feel confident because you spent hours last week memorizing your notes. Unfortunately, by the time you take the test, you remember very little. This is not surprising, since most forgetting occurs within minutes after memorization.

In a classic study conducted in 1885, researcher Herman Ebbinghaus memorized a list of meaningless three-letter words such as CEF and LAZ. He then examined how quickly he forgot them. Within one hour he forgot more than 50 percent of what he had learned; after two days, he knew fewer than 30 percent of the material. Although Ebbinghaus's recall of the nonsense syllables remained fairly stable after that, his experiment shows how fragile memory can be—even when you take the time and expend the energy to memorize information.[6]

How your brain remembers: Short-term and long-term memory

Memories are stored in three different "storage banks" in your brain. The first, called sensory memory, is an exact copy of what you see and hear and lasts for a second or less. Certain information is then selected from sensory memory and moved into short-term memory, a temporary information storehouse that lasts no more than 10 to 20 seconds. You are consciously aware of material in short-term memory. Unimportant information is quickly dumped. Important information is transferred to long-term memory—the mind's more permanent storehouse.

Although all three stages are important, targeting long-term memory will solidify learning the most. "Short-term—or working—memory is useful when we want to remember a phone number until we can dial," says biologist James Zull. "We use short-term memory for these momentary challenges, all the time, every day, but it is limited in capacity, tenacity, and time."[7] Zull explains that short-term memory can hold only small amounts of information for brief periods. In addition, it is unstable—a distraction can easily dislodge information.

How you can use memory strategies to improve recall

The following practical and analytical strategies will help improve your recall.

Have purpose and intention. Why can you remember the lyrics to dozens of popular songs but not the functions of the pancreas? Perhaps this is because you want to remember the lyrics or you have an emotional tie to

STRESSBUSTER

ANNA GRIFFIN   Algonquin College, Ottawa, Ontario

Do you ever have trouble following a lecture? Do you find it difficult to keep track of everything you are supposed to remember? What have you done to overcome these challenges?

Starting a new day can be extremely overwhelming. Knowing that school will take up all of a normal working day and knowing that you have to go to a job right afterwards is enough to make you want to quit. School is a full-time job, and it feels like the rest of the world has no idea what you're going through. When you do get to class, you can't take good notes or concentrate on what the professor is saying because all you can think about is the long day ahead.

The way that I've come to terms with this is to wake up in the morning and meet the day ahead of me straight on. You've got a challenge for me . . . bring it on! I start by doing something as simple as listening to my favourite music on the way to school, which always brightens my day. If I don't understand a question when I'm sitting in class, I ask. If *you* don't get it, you can almost guarantee that at least 50 percent of the people around you are lost too. That might sound obvious, but you will only take good notes and remember things that you understand. Asking questions takes a huge weight off your shoulders, and with it goes a lot of the stress you were carrying.

Also, be sure to have something that you enjoy outside of school and work. It could be music, photography, or friends—as long as it isn't school-related. Tension just melts away when you don't make school your entire world. When you have other hobbies, you will see the change in your attitude towards school . . . you will begin to enjoy it even more.

them. To strengthen your intention to remember academic information, focus on why the information is important and how you can use it.

Understand what you memorize. The best way to guarantee that concepts become part of your long-term memory is to use your analytical ability to understand them inside and out. With a depth of learning comes the framework on which to place related concepts. Thus, if you are having trouble remembering something new, think about how the idea fits into what you already know. A simple example: If a new vocabulary word puzzles you, try to identify the word's root, prefix, or suffix. Knowing that the root *bellum* means "war" and the prefix *ante* means "before" will help you recognize and remember that *antebellum* means "before the war."

Use critical thinking. Critical thinking encourages you to associate new information with what you already know. Imagine that you have to remember information about the signing of the Treaty of Versailles, the agreement that ended World War I. You might use critical thinking—combined with some quick internet research—in the following ways:

- Recall everything that you know about the topic.
- Think about how this event is similar to other events in history.

- Consider what is different and unique about this treaty in comparison with other treaties.
- Explore the causes that led up to this event, and look at the event's effects.
- From the general idea of treaties that ended wars, explore other examples of such treaties.

Critical exploration of this kind will make it easier for you to remember specific facts and overarching concepts.

Recite, rehearse, and write. When you *recite* material, you repeat key concepts aloud, in your own words, to help you memorize them. *Rehearsing* is similar to reciting but is done silently. It is the process of mentally repeating, summarizing, and associating information with other information. *Writing* is reciting on paper. Organizational tools, such as an outline or a think link, will help you record material in ways that show the logical connections within its structure.

Study during short, frequent sessions. Research has shown that you can improve your chances of remembering material if you learn it more than once. To get the most out of study sessions, spread them over time and rest in between. You may feel as though you accomplish a lot by studying for an hour without a break; however, you'll probably remember more from three 20-minute sessions.

Sleep can actually aid memory because it reduces interference from new information. Since you can't always go to sleep immediately after studying for an exam, try postponing the study of other subjects until your exam is over. When studying for several tests at once, avoid studying two similar subjects back to back. Your memory is likely to be more accurate when you study history right after biology rather than, for example, chemistry after biology.

Limit and organize material. This involves two key activities:

- **Separate main points from unimportant details.** Ask yourself: What is the most important information? Highlight only the key points in your texts, and write notes in the margins about central ideas. See the example in Key 5.6 on page 158.
- **Divide material into manageable sections.** Generally, when material is short and easy to understand, studying it from start to finish improves recall. With longer material, however, you may benefit from dividing it into logical sections, mastering each section, putting all the sections together, and then testing your memory of all the material. Actors take this approach when learning the lines of a play, and it can work just as well for students trying to learn new concepts.

Practise the middle. When you are trying to learn something, you usually study some material first, attack other material in the middle of the session, and approach still other topics at the end. The weak link in your recall is likely to be the material you study midway. It pays to give this material special attention.

Create groupings. When items do not have to be remembered in any particular order, the act of grouping can help you recall them better.

Flash cards help you memorize important facts.

THEORY
- Definition: Explanation for a phenomenon based on careful and precise observations
- Part of the scientific method
- Leads to hypotheses

HYPOTHESIS
- Prediction about future behaviour that is derived from observations and theories
- Methods for testing hypotheses: case studies, naturalistic observations, and experiments

Say, for example, that you have to memorize these four 10-digit numbers:

9806875087 9876535703 7636983561 6724472879

It may look impossible. If you group the numbers to look like telephone numbers, however, the job may become more manageable:

(980) 687–5087 (987) 653–5703 (763) 698–3561 (672) 447–2879

In general, try to limit groups to 10 items or fewer. It's hard to memorize more at one time.

Use flash cards. Flash cards are a great visual memory tool. They give you short, repeated review sessions that provide immediate feedback, and they are portable, which gives you the flexibility to use them wherever you go. Use the front of an index card to write a word, idea, or phrase you want to remember. Use the back for a definition, an explanation, and other key facts. Key 6.9 shows two flash cards used to study for a psychology exam.

Here are some suggestions for making the most of your flash cards:

- Carry the cards with you and review them frequently.
- Shuffle the cards and learn the information in various orders.
- Test yourself in both directions. First, look at the terms and provide the definitions or explanations. Then turn the cards over and reverse the process.

Use an audio recorder and MP3 player. Use a tape or digital recorder as an immediate feedback "audio flash card." Record short-answer study questions on tape, leave 10 to 15 seconds between questions to answer out loud, then record the correct answer after each pause. For example, a question for a writing class might be, "What are the three elements of effective writing? . . . (10–15 second pause) . . . topic, audience, and purpose."

Use mnemonic devices

Certain performers entertain their audiences by remembering the names of 100 strangers or flawlessly repeating 30 ten-digit phone numbers.

Although these performers probably have superior memories, they also rely on memory techniques, known as **mnemonic devices** (pronounced neh-MAHN-ick), for assistance.

Mnemonic devices depend on vivid associations (relating new information to other information). Instead of learning new facts by rote (repetitive practice), associations give you a "hook" on which to hang these facts and retrieve them later. Mnemonic devices make information familiar and meaningful through unusual, unforgettable mental associations and visual pictures. Forming mnemonics depends on activating your creative ability.

There are different kinds of mnemonic devices, including visual images and associations, acronyms, and songs and rhymes. Study how these devices work, then use your creative thinking skills to apply them to your own memory challenges.

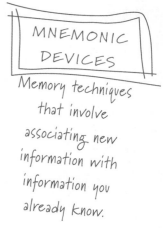

MNEMONIC DEVICES
Memory techniques that involve associating new information with information you already know.

Create visual images and associations. You are more likely to remember a piece of information if you link it to a visual image. The best mental images often involve bright colours, three dimensions, action scenes, inanimate objects with human traits, ridiculousness, and humour.

Turning information into mental pictures helps improve memory, especially for visual learners. To remember that the Spanish artist Picasso painted *The Three Women*, you might imagine the women in a circle dancing to a Spanish song with a pig and a donkey (pig-asso). The more outlandish the image the better, since these images are the most memorable.

Use the mental walk strategy to remember items in a list. Using the mental walk strategy, you imagine that you store new ideas in familiar locations. Say, for example, that for biology you have to remember the major endocrine glands. To do this, you can think of the route you take to the library. You pass the college theatre, the science centre, the bookstore, the cafeteria, the athletic centre, and the social science building before reaching the library. At each spot along the route, you "place" the idea or concept you wish to learn. You then link the concept with a similar-sounding word that brings to mind a vivid image:

- At the campus theatre, you imagine bumping into the actor Brad Pitt, who is holding two terriers (pituitary gland).
- At the science centre, you visualize Mr. Universe with bulging thighs. When you are introduced, you learn that his name is Roy (thyroid gland).
- At the campus bookstore, you envision a second Mr. Universe with his thighs covered in mustard (thymus gland).
- In the cafeteria, you see an ad for Dean Al for president (adrenal gland).
- At the athletic centre, you visualize a student throwing a ball into a pan and creatures applauding from the bleachers (pancreas).
- At the social science building, you imagine receiving a standing ovation (ovaries).
- And at the library, you visualize sitting at a table taking a test that is easy (testes).

An acronym will help you recall the colours of the spectrum.

red

orange

yellow

green

blue

indigo

violet

R O Y G B.I V

ACRONYM

A word formed from the first letters of a series of words, created to help you remember the series.

Create acronyms. Another helpful association method involves the use of **acronyms** (see Key 6.10). For example, suppose you want to remember the names of the first six prime ministers of Canada. The first letters of their last names—Macdonald, Mackenzie, Abbott, Thompson, Bowell, and Tupper— together read MMATBT. To remember them, you might add a "y" to the end and create a short nonsense word—"mmatbty"— and remember it as the word "mmat-bity." Since there are two "t's" in your nonsense word, just remember that alphabetically, and historically, Thompson comes before Tupper. To remember their first names—John, Alexander, John, John, Mackenzie, and Charles—you might set the names to the tune of "Happy Birthday," or any other musical tune you know.

Other acronyms take the form of an entire sentence in which the first letter of each word in each sentence stands for the first letter of the memorized term. This is called a *list order acronym*. For example, when science students want to remember the list of planets in order of their distance from the sun (Mercury, Venus, Earth, Mars, Jupiter, Saturn, Uranus, and Neptune [Pluto no longer has the status of a planet]), they can learn the sentence:

My very elegant mother just served us nibblies.

Use songs or rhymes. Some of the classic mnemonic devices are rhyming poems that tend to stick in your mind. One you may have heard is the rule about the order of "i" and "e" in spelling:

I before E, except after C, or when sounded like "A" as in "neighbour" and "weigh." Four exceptions if you please: either, neither, seizure, seize.

Make up your own poems or songs, linking tunes or rhymes that are familiar to you with information you want to remember. Improving your memory requires energy, time, and work. In school, it also helps to master SQ3R, the textbook study technique that was introduced in Chapter 5. By going through the steps in SQ3R and using the specific memory techniques described in this chapter, you will be able to learn more in less time—and remember what you learn long after exams are over.

Craft Your Own Mnemonic

Create a mnemonic to help you remember some facts.

- Identify a group of connected facts that you have to memorize—for example, for political science, the names of every presidential candidate after World War II; for literature, the names of all the characters in Shakespeare's *Romeo and Juliet*. Write your choice here:

_____

_____

_____

- Now create your own mnemonic to remember the grouping using any of the devices in this chapter. Write the mnemonic here and on additional paper if necessary.

_____

_____

_____

_____

_____

Successful Intelligence Wrap Up

Achieving competence in listening, note taking, and memorizing requires more than just analytical ability. When you use all three components of successful intelligence to find your own way to listen and take in information, record information that you will need in the future, and remember what you learn, you set yourself up for future academic success. Here's how you have built skills in Chapter 6:

Analytical

Within the material about listening, you examined the listening process and the challenges you face each step along the way, getting more specific in your analysis of your own listening skills with the Get Analytical exercise. You explored note-taking systems, considering what systems may work best for your particular classroom and study situations. Near the end of the chapter, you examined the nature of memory and the importance of memory challenges.

Creative

Investigating different note-taking systems may have inspired new ideas about how to approach note taking in your courses. With what you learned about note taking, you are prepared to create self-styled methods that suit your personal preferences, the material you are working with, and your instructor's style. After you explored how mnemonic devices work, completing the Get Creative exercise gave you experience in crafting your own original mnemonic device.

Practical

You compiled practical tools for listening actively in class, getting a sense of how to manage listening challenges. You explored how to use different note-taking systems in different situations, applying your knowledge to a specific note-taking challenge in the Get Practical exercise. To your skills you added practical techniques in using personal shorthand and creating a master set of notes. You broadened your understanding of the ways in which experience solidifies memory.

Lagom
(lag-ohm)

In Swedish, the word *lagom* refers to the place between extremes, the spot that is neither too much nor too little, but just right. Many Swedish people aspire to this place in everything they do. They tend to seek stability yet remain open to what is new and different. Think of the quest for *lagom* as you challenge yourself to improve your listening, note-taking, and memory skills. With *lagom* as your guide, you will appreciate that your goal is not perfection in any of these skills, but rather the ability to hear as much as you can, to take appropriate notes that will be the foundation for your studying, and to develop just the right number of memory strategies that will help you remember what is valuable. You can never hope to take in, record, and memorize every word that your instructor speaks—and that's okay. You are aiming for "just right."[8]

"Happiness does not come from doing easy work but from the afterglow of satisfaction that comes after the achievement of a difficult task that demanded our best."

THEODORE I. RUBEN, PSYCHIATRIST AND AUTHOR

PERSONAL TRIUMPH

BLYTHE HARTLEY — Olympic Diver

As Robert Sternberg's quote at the start of this chapter suggested, the road to success isn't always straight or free of obstacles. However, people with successful intelligence always seem to find a way to reach their goals. Canadian Olympian Blythe Hartley is an exceptional athlete that overcame tremendous odds to compete for Canada at the 2008 Beijing Games.

Although her life goal in middle school was to become a veterinarian, Edmonton native Blythe Hartley found her calling high above the swimming pool. She started her diving career at the age of 12. Her talent took her to Calgary's National Sports School. After that, it was off to the University of Southern California where she received her degree in communications in 2006.

Hartley stresses the importance of setting goals as one of her keys to success. She says "in terms of developing goals, I think the best thing is to sit down, ask yourself what you want and what you're willing to do to get that goal— then stay the course. That's really what I've done through-out my career to achieve success." She also credits her family for their support over the years. "As a child, my parents encouraged participation in a variety of sports but I really liked competitive swimming and gymnastics so my parents encouraged me to combine the two and try diving."

The combination of gymnastics and swimming was a winner. As a diver, Hartley was truly gifted. In 1999, she was Canada's Junior Athlete of the Year. A year later, she competed at the Olympics in Sydney, finishing fifth in the 3-Meter Springboard. Gold medals would follow at the 2006 Commonwealth Games, the 2003 Pan-Am Games, and the 2001 FINA World Championships. She's also a 14-time Canadian National Champion. To top it all off, Blythe also won a bronze medal at the 2004 Olympics in Athens with Emilie Heymans as her partner in the 10-meter synchronized event.

Victories in the pool came often for Hartley. Then, in 2007 she received the devastating news that her brother, Dr. Strachan Hartley, had died of non-Hodgkin's lymphoma. That news, plus the fact that she was approaching 30 years of age, almost derailed Hartley's dream of compet-ing in Beijing. At times, she wasn't sure she could compete and was contemplating retiring. Shortly before the Olympic trials, Hartley said "for awhile, I wasn't sure if I was actually capable of training for the Olympics."

Faced with some hard decisions, Hartley did what she always did. She found herself setting some new goals for herself and using her family as motivation. She drew on her memories of her brother for strength. She dedicated her 2008 season, including her trip to the Olympics, to her brother. According to Hartley, "Absolutely, he's with me. I think he's with me everyday."

She also had to re-focus her goals. After Strachan's death, she found it hard to practice, often driving to prac-tice but then just turning around and going home. She says she often thought about quitting but it was the memory of her brother that eventually led Blythe to continue to train for the 2008 Olympics. Her mom believes that "the only reason she got back on the board is because Strachan would never quit and she felt that he would have wanted her to keep going. I think one of the things that impacts me the most is that's the gift Strachan left her. He left a piece of himself that will forever inspire her."

After a tough period of soul searching, Hartley decided she would compete at the Olympics. She went to Beijing focused on winning. She also had her family by her side in China to cheer her on. Plus, her brother Strachan was also there in spirit.

In the end, while her score was her best Olympic showing ever, she did not win a medal in Beijing, finishing fourth. Yet Hartley considers her experience at the Beijing Games an unqualified victory. She says "Ending my career doing my personal best at the Olympic Games, you couldn't ask for more than that. I'm walking away feeling very proud for what I've accomplished this year."

The family has also set up the Strachan Hartley Legacy Foundation. It's a group that assists under-privileged youth to get involved in sports. For more information, go to www.shlf.ca.

Compiled with files from Blythe Hartley's Tragic Inspiration (www.cbc.ca/olympics/story/2008/08/11/f-olympics-diving-hartley.html), Leap of Faith (www.canada.com/theprovince/news/story.html?id=5bfc17e4-272b-4cb4-b0e2-2b34404aaa0c), and Athlete Profile (www.talismancentre.com/about excellence hartley.cfm).

SUCCESSFUL INTELLIGENCE
Think, Create, Apply

Learn from the experiences of others. Look back to Blythe Hartley's Personal Triumph on page 195. After you've read her story, relate her experience to your own life by completing the following:

Think it through: *Analyze your experience and compare it to Blythe Hartley's.* What goal (academic or personal) are you trying to reach now that will take you a long time, and how does this relate to her experience? Why is this goal important to you? From your memory of reaching other important goals, what strategies will help you achieve it?

Think out of the box: *Let others inspire ideas.* Choose two people whom you respect. Put your listening skills to work: Spend a few minutes talking with each of them about your goal. Ask them about similar experiences they have had, and listen to the ideas that they used. From what you've heard, begin brainstorming ideas about how you will achieve your goal.

Make it happen: *Put a practical plan together.* Map out how you will achieve your goal. Create a mnemonic device that will help you remember your plan. Envision your success as you put your plan into action.

TEAMWORK
Create Solutions Together

Create a note-taking team. Although students often focus much more on taking notes in class than on taking notes while reading, reading notes are just as important to your understanding of the course material. In your most demanding course, form a study group with two other people and choose a reading assignment—a text chapter, an article, or any other assigned reading—to work on together. Agree to read it and take notes independently before your next meeting. Each student should make photocopies of his or her notes for the other group members.

When you meet again, compare your notes, focusing on the following characteristics:

- legibility (Can everyone read what is written?)

- completeness (Did you all record the same information? If not, why not?)

- organizational effectiveness (Does everyone get an idea of how ideas flow?)

- value of the notes as a study aid (Will this help everyone remember the material?)

Based on what you've discussed with your group, come up with specific ways to improve your personal note-taking skills. You can also work with your study group to compare notes taken in a particular class period and work on improving in-class note-taking techniques.

WRITING

Journal and Put Skills to Work

Record your thoughts on a separate piece of paper or in a journal.

Journal entry: How people retain information. How do you react to the following statement? "We retain 10 percent of what we read, 20 percent of what we hear, 30 percent of what we see, 50 percent of what we hear and see, 70 percent of what we say, 90 percent of what we say and do." How can you use this insight to improve your ability to retain information? What will you do differently as a result of this insight?

Real-life writing: Combining class and text notes. Create a master set of notes for one course that combines one week's classes and reading assignments. Your goal is to summarize and connect all the important information covered during the period.

PERSONAL PORTFOLIO

Prepare for Career Success

Put your listening and note-taking skills to work as you investigate your options. Choose a career area that interests you. Interview two people in that area—one from an academic setting (such as an instructor in a related subject area or an academic adviser) and one from the working world (such as a person working in that career or a career planning and placement office counsellor). Choose a setting where you can listen well and take effective notes.

Ask your interview subjects what they feel is the recipe for success in their career. You might ask specifically about curriculum (what courses are required for this area, and what courses are beneficial but not required), other preparation such as extracurricular activities and internships, qualities such as leadership and commitment, day-to-day attitudes, and anything else you are wondering about. Ask them also about the role that listening, note-taking, and memory skills play in career success. For example, if you are interviewing an account manager at an advertising agency, he might tell you that the ability to listen well, take accurate notes, and recall critical concepts is essential at client meetings. Practising and perfecting these skills while listening to your instructors will help you in your career.

When you complete your interviews, create a report that lays out the "recipe for success." Keep in mind the skills and attitudes you wish to develop as you choose next term's courses and activities.

SUGGESTED READINGS

Burley-Allen, Madelyn. *Listening: The Forgotten Skill: A Self-Teaching Guide.* New York: John Wiley & Sons, 1995.

DePorter, Bobbi, and Mike Hernacki. *Quantum Notes: Whole-Brain Approaches to Note-Taking.* Chicago: Learning Forum, 2000.

Dunkel, Patricia A., Frank Pialorsi, and Joane Kozyrez. *Advanced Listening Comprehension: Developing Aural &Note-Taking Skills,* 3rd ed. Boston: Heinle & Heinle, 2004.

Higbee, Kenneth L. *Your Memory: How It Works and How to Improve It.* New York: Marlowe & Co., 2001.

Lebauer, R. Susan. *Learn to Listen, Listen to Learn: Academic Listening and Note-Taking.* Upper Saddle River, NJ: Prentice Hall, 2000.

Levin, Leonard. *Easy Script Express: Unique Speed Writing Methods to Take Fast Notes and Dictation.* Chicago: Legend Publishing, 2000.

Lorayne, Harry. *Super Memory—Super Student: How to Raise Your Grades in 30 Days.* Boston: Little, Brown & Company, 1990.

Lorayne, Harry. *The Memory Book: The Classic Guide to Improving Your Memory at Work, at School, and at Play.* New York: Ballantine Books, 1996.

Robbins, Harvey A. *How to Speak and Listen Effectively.* New York: AMACOM, 1992.

Roberts, Billy. *Working Memory: Improving Your Memory for the Workplace.* London: Bridge Trade, 1999.

Roberts, Billy. *Educate Your Memory: Improvement Techniques for Students of All Ages.* London: Allison & Busby, 2000.

INTERNET RESOURCES

Coping.org—Tools for Coping with Life's Stressors—Improving Listening Skills:
www.coping.org/dialogue/listen.htm

Dyslexia at College—Taking Notes (tips on taking notes from books and at lectures):
www.dyslexia-college.com/notes.html

ForgetKnot (a source for mnemonic devices):
http://members.tripod.com/~ForgetKnot

Kishwaukee College Learning Skills Center (helpful advice on listening skills):
http://www.kishwaukeecollege.edu/learning_skills_center/study_skills_help/good_listener.shtml

Merriam-Webster's Word of the Day (free word of the day in audio form available on the internet or as podcasts):
www.merriam-webster.com/cgi-bin/mwwod.pl

Prentice Hall Student Success Supersite:
www.prenhall.com/success

Princeton Review Vocab Minute (free vocabulary-building podcasts using songs to help you remember):
www.learnoutloud.com/Podcast-Directory/Languages/Vocabulary-Building/Princeton-Review-Vocabulary-Minute-Podcast/18871#plink

ENDNOTES

1. Conference Board of Canada, *Employability Skills 2000+,* http://www.conferenceboard.ca/education/learning-tools/pdfs/esp2000.pdf.

2. Ralph G. Nichols, "Do We Know How to Listen? Practical Helps in a Modern Age," *Speech Teacher* (March 1961): 118–124.

3. Ibid.

4. Teresa Audesirk, Gerald Audesirk, and Bruce E. Byers, *Life on Earth*, 2nd ed. (Upper Saddle River, NJ: Prentice Hall, 2000), 660–662.

5. Walter Pauk, *How to Study in College*, 5th ed. (Boston, MA: Houghton Mifflin Company, 1993), 110–114.

6. Herman Ebbinghaus, *Memory: A Contribution to Experimental Psychology,* trans. H. A. Ruger and C. E. Bussenius (New York: New York Teacher's College, Columbia University, 1885).

7. James Zull, *The Art of Changing the Brain: Enriching Teaching by Exploring the Biology of Learning* (Sterling, VA: Stylus Publishing, 2002).

8. Christopher J. Moore, *In Other Words: A Language Lover's Guide to the Most Intriguing Words around the World* (New York: Walker, 2004), 45.

TEST TAKING
Showing what you know

7

"Successfully intelligent people seek to perform in ways that not only are competent but distinguish them from ordinary performers. They realize that the gap between competence and excellence may be small but the greatest rewards, both internal and external, are for excellence."

ROBERT J. STERNBERG

When you successfully show what you know on tests, you achieve educational goals and develop confidence. Exams also help you gauge your progress so that, when needed, you can ramp up your efforts. Most importantly, smart test preparation results in real learning that you take from course to course and into your career and life. As you will see in this chapter, test taking is about preparation, persistence, and strategy—all of which tap into your analytical, creative, and practical abilities. It is also about conquering fears, focusing on details, and learning from mistakes. Test taking prepares you to solve problems and think, two skills listed by the Conference Board of Canada as being fundamental employability skills.

Test-preparation checklist.

Course: _____ Instructor: _____

Date, time, and place of test: _____

Type of test (e.g., is it a mid-term or a minor quiz?): _____

What the instructor has told you about the test, including the types of test questions, the length of the test, and how much the test counts toward your final grade:

_____

_____

Topics to be covered on the test in order of importance:

1. _____
2. _____
3. _____
4. _____
5. _____

Study schedule, including materials you plan to study (e.g., *texts and class notes*) and dates you plan to complete each:

MATERIAL	DATE OF COMPLETION
1. _____	_____
2. _____	_____
3. _____	_____
4. _____	_____
5. _____	_____

Materials you are expected to bring to the test (e.g., *your textbook, a sourcebook, a calculator*):

_____

_____

Special study arrangements (e.g., *plan study group meetings, ask the instructor for special help, get outside tutoring*):

_____

_____

_____

Life-management issues (e.g., *rearrange work hours*):

_____

_____

_____

Source: Adapted from Ron Fry, "*Ace" Any Test*, 3rd ed. (Franklin Lakes, NJ: Career Press, 1996), 123–124.

Write Your
Own Test

Prepare for an upcoming exam using a pretest you create yourself.

Check the course outlines for the courses you are taking now, and find the test that is coming up first. Use the tips in this chapter to predict the material that will be covered on this test, the types of questions that will be asked (multiple-choice, essay, and so forth), and the nature of the questions (a broad overview of the material or specific details).

Then be creative. Your goal is to write questions that your instructor is likely to ask—interesting questions that tap what you have learned and make you think about the material in different ways. Go through the following steps:

1. On a separate sheet of paper, write the questions that you come up with.

2. Use what you created as a pretest. Set up test-like conditions—a quiet, timed environment—and see how well you do. Avoid looking at your text or notes unless the test is open book.

3. Evaluate your pretest answers against your notes and the text. How did you do?

4. Finally, after you take your instructor's exam, evaluate whether you think this exercise improved your performance on the actual exam. Would you use this technique again when you study for another exam? Why or why not?

---

study times and sessions. That way, not only do you know when you have time to study, but you also have defined goals for each study session.

Prepare through careful review

By thoroughly reviewing your materials, you will have the best shot at remembering their contents. Use the following strategies when you study.

Use SQ3R. The reading method you studied in Chapter 5 provides an excellent structure for reviewing your reading materials:

- Surveying gives you an overview of topics.
- Questioning helps you focus on important ideas and determine what the material is trying to communicate.
- Reading (or, in this case, rereading) reminds you of the ideas and supporting information.
- Reciting helps to anchor the concepts in your head.

- Review tasks, such as quizzing yourself on the Q-stage questions, summarizing sections you have highlighted, making flash cards for important concepts, and constructing a chapter outline, help you solidify your learning so that you are able to use it at test time and beyond.

Review your notes. Recall the section in Chapter 6 for making your notes a valuable after-class reference. Use the following techniques to effectively review notes:

- **Time your reviews carefully.** Review notes for the first time within a day of the lecture, if you can, and then review again closer to the test day.
- **Mark up your notes.** Reread them, filling in missing information, clarifying points, writing out abbreviations, and highlighting key ideas.
- **Organize your notes.** Consider adding headings and subheadings to your notes to clarify the structure of the information. Rewrite them using a different organizing structure—for example, an outline if you originally used a think link.
- **Summarize your notes.** Evaluate which ideas and examples are most crucial, and then rewrite your notes in shortened form, focusing on those ideas and examples. Summarize your notes in writing or with a summary think link. Try summarizing from memory as a self-test.

Think critically. Using the techniques from Chapter 4, approach test preparation as a critical thinker, working to understand the material rather than just repeat facts. As you study, try to analyze causes and effects, look at issues from different perspectives, and connect concepts that, on the surface, appear unrelated. This work will increase your understanding and probably result in a higher exam mark. Critical thinking is especially important for essay tests that ask you to develop and support a thesis.

Take a pretest

Use questions from your textbook to create your own pretest. Most textbooks include end-of-chapter questions. If your course doesn't have an assigned text, develop questions from your notes and assigned outside readings. Choose questions that are likely to be covered on the test, then answer them under test-like conditions—in quiet, with no books or notes to help you (unless your exam is open book), and with a clock telling you when to quit. (Use the information in this chapter's Get Creative feature.)

Prepare physically

Most tests ask you to work efficiently under time pressure. If your body is tired or under stress, your performance may suffer. If you can, avoid staying up all night. Get some sleep so that you can wake up rested and alert. Remember that adequate sleep can help cement memories by reducing interference from new memories (see Chapter 6).

Eating right is also important. Sugar-laden snacks bring up your energy, only to send you crashing down much too soon. Also, too much caffeine can add to your tension and make focusing difficult. Eating nothing leaves you drained, but too much food can make you sleepy. The best advice is to eat a light, well-balanced meal before a test. When time is short, grab a quick-energy snack such as a banana, orange juice, or a granola bar.

Make the most of last-minute cramming

Cramming—studying intensively, and often around the clock, right before an exam—often results in information going into your head and popping right back out shortly after the exam is over. Because study conditions aren't always ideal, nearly every student crams during their college or university career, especially when a busy schedule leaves only a few hours to prepare. Use these hints to make the most of your study time:

- **Go through your flash cards,** if you have them, one last time.
- **Focus on crucial concepts;** don't worry about the rest. Resist reviewing notes or texts page by page.
- **Create a last-minute study sheet.** On a single sheet of paper, write down key facts, definitions, formulas, and so on. Try to keep the material short and simple. If you prefer visual notes, use think links to map out ideas and supporting examples.
- **Arrive early.** Study the sheet or your flash cards until you are asked to clear your desk.
- **Jot down any useful information on scrap paper** once the text begins, and while the information is still fresh in your mind. Do this before looking at the test. Review this information as needed during the test.

After your exam, evaluate the effects cramming had on your learning. Even if you passed, you might remember very little. This low level of retention won't do you much good in the real world where you have to make use of information instead of just recalling it for a test. Think about how you can plan strategically to start earlier and improve the situation next time.

Whether you have to cram or not, you may experience anxiety on test day. The following section includes ideas for how to handle test anxiety when it strikes.

How can you work through *test anxiety?*

A certain amount of stress can be a good thing. Your body is alert, and your energy motivates you to do your best (for more on stress and stress management, see Chapter 10 and the Stressbuster boxes throughout this text). Some students, however, experience incapacitating stress levels before and during exams, especially mid-terms or finals.

Test anxiety can cause physical symptoms, such as sweating, nausea, dizziness, headaches, and fatigue, as well as psychological symptoms such as being unable to concentrate and feeling overwhelmed. You can minimize your anxiety by working on your preparation and attitude.

TEST ANXIETY
A bad case of nerves
that can make it
hard to think
or to remember.

Test Preparation

If the topic or format of a test challenges your stronger or weaker intelligences, these tips will help you make the most of your time and abilities.

INTELLIGENCE	SUGGESTED STRATEGIES	WHAT WORKS FOR YOU? WRITE NEW IDEAS HERE
Verbal–Linguistic	• Think of and write out questions your instructor may ask on a test. Answer the questions and then try rewriting them in a different format (essay, true-or-false, and so on). • Underline important words in review questions or practice questions.	
Logical–Mathematical	• Make diagrams of review or practice questions. • Outline the key steps involved in topics on which you may be tested.	
Bodily–Kinesthetic	• Use your voice to review out loud. Recite concepts, terms and definitions, important lists, dates, and so on. • Create a sculpture, model, or skit to depict a tough concept that will be on your test.	
Visual–Spatial	• Create a think link to map out an important topic and its connections to other topics in the material. Study it and redraw it from memory a day before the test. • Make drawings related to possible test topics.	
Interpersonal	• Develop a study group and encourage each other. • In your group, come up with as many possible test questions as you can. Ask each other these questions in an oral exam-type format.	
Intrapersonal	• Brainstorm test questions. Then come back to them after a break or even a day's time. On your own, take the sample "test" you developed. • Make time to review in a solitary setting.	
Musical	• Play music while you read if it does not distract you. • Study concepts by reciting them to rhythms you create or to music.	
Naturalistic	• Bring your text, lecture notes, and other pertinent information to an outdoor spot that inspires you and helps you to feel confident, and review your material there.	

Prepare and have a positive attitude

Being on top of your work from the beginning of the term is the greatest stress reliever. Similarly, creating and following a detailed study plan will build knowledge and a sense of control, as will finding out what to expect on the exam. The following strategies will help you build a positive attitude:

- **See tests as opportunities to learn.** Instead of thinking of tests as contests that you either "win" or "lose," think of them as signposts along the way to mastering material.

- **Understand that tests measure performance, not personal value.** Grades don't reflect your ability to succeed or your self-worth. Whether you get an A or an F, you are the same person.

- **Believe that instructors are on your side.** Your instructors want you to do well, even when they give challenging tests—so contact them if you need help.

- **Seek study partners who challenge you.** Find study partners who inspire you to do your best. Try to avoid people who are also anxious, because you may pick up their fears and negativity. (See Chapter 5 for more on study groups.)

- **Get tutored.** Many schools offer tutoring help at no charge. Find out what's available and then sign up for sessions.

- **Practise relaxation.** When you feel test anxiety mounting, breathe deeply and slowly, close your eyes, and visualize positive mental images such as getting a good grade. Try to ease muscle tension—stretch your neck, tighten and then release your shoulder muscles.

- **Shut out negative vibrations.** If you arrive at the testing room early for a last-minute review, pick a seat far away from others who are nervously discussing the test.

- **Practise positive self-talk.** Tell yourself that you can do well and that it is normal to feel anxious, particularly before an important exam.

- **Remind yourself of your goals.** Connecting the test to your long-term goals will help you calm down as you focus on what's important.

Math exams are a special problem for many students. Dealing with the anxieties associated with these exams will be examined in the Study Break at the end of Chapter 8 where you will find stress-management, studying, and exam-taking techniques.

Finally, a good attitude involves expecting test-taking challenges that are different from those you experienced in high school. College or university exams may ask you to critically analyze and apply material in ways that you never did before. For example, your history instructor may ask you to place a primary source in its historical context. Prepare for these challenges as you study by continually asking critical-thinking questions.

Test anxiety and the returning student

If you're returning to school after years away, you may wonder if you can compete with younger students or if your mind is still able to learn. To counteract these feelings of inadequacy, focus on the useful skills you have learned in life. For example, managing work and a family requires strong time-management, planning, and communication skills that can help you plan your study time, juggle school responsibilities, and interact with students and instructors.

In addition, life experiences give you contexts through which you can understand ideas. For example, your relationship experiences may help you understand social psychology concepts, and managing your finances may help you understand accounting. If you permit yourself to feel positive about the knowledge and skills you have acquired, you may improve your ability to achieve your goals.

Parents who have to juggle child care with study time can find the challenge especially difficult before a test. Here are some suggestions that might help:

- **Find help.** Join a babysitting co-operative, trade child care time with a neighbour, post a sign for a part-time babysitter at the local high school.
- **Plan activities.** With younger children, have a supply of games, books, and DVDs. Give young artists a box of markers and unlimited paper. Then tell them to draw scenes of their family, their home, their friends—all in brilliant colour.
- **Explain the time frame.** Tell school-aged children your study schedule and test date. Then promise them a reward for co-operating.

STRESSBUSTER

STEPHANIE JACK   Kwantlen Polytechnic University, Surrey, British Columbia

Test anxiety can have an enormous effect on your ability to succeed on mid-terms and exams. How do you avoid test anxiety? If you can't avoid it, what do you do to reduce its effect on your studying? Do you feel other stress associated with tests, e.g., finding enough time to study? How do you deal with this stress?

Writing an exam in college or university is very stressful. Often it is the only mark you have to see how you are really doing in your course, so you want to do well. Most of my instructors have not given chapter tests or quizzes like they did in high school, so I have no way of knowing how well I am prepared for a mid-term exam.

I have found that the more I study right before an exam, the more nervous I get and the less I remember.

The most important thing I can do is make sure I have some time right before to relax a little bit. The best exams I have written were first thing in the morning after I have had a good night's sleep. I know that isn't always possible so I try to give myself at least half an hour before the exam in which I have nothing to do. Even if you don't have that long, take a 5- to 10-minute walk to clear your head. Try not to think about the exam. Maybe sit and watch the clouds or the sunset. Anything that relaxes me and clears my head is a good bet right before an exam.

When I get into the exam and have been told to start, I reduce my stress by looking over every question in the exam and start with the questions I know. This reduces my stress level because it gives me the confidence I often need to answer every question on the exam.

What *general strategies* can help you succeed on tests?

Even though every test is different, some general strategies can will help you handle almost all tests, including short-answer and essay exams.

Choose the right seat

Your goal is to choose a seat that will put you in the right frame of mind and minimize distractions. Find a seat near a window, next to a wall, or in the front row so you can look into the distance. Know yourself: For many students, it's smart to avoid sitting near friends.

Successful Intelligence Connections Online

Listen to author Sarah Kravits describe how to use analytical, creative, and practical intelligence to overcome the anxiety you feel before a big test.

Go to the *Keys to Success* Companion Website at www.pearsoned.ca/carter to listen or download as a podcast.

Write down key facts

Before you even look at the test, write down key information—including formulas, rules, and definitions—that you studied recently. Use the back of the question sheet or a piece of scrap paper for your notes (be sure your instructor knows that this paper didn't come into the test room already filled in). Recording this information at the start makes forgetting less likely.

Begin with an overview

Although exam time is precious, spend a few minutes at the start of the test getting a sense of the kinds of questions you'll be answering, what type of thinking they require, the number of questions in each section, and their point values. Use this information to schedule your time. For example, if a two-hour test is divided into two sections of equal point value—an essay section with 4 questions and a short-answer section with 60 questions—you can spend an hour on the essays (15 minutes per question) and an hour on the short-answer section (1 minute per question). As you calculate, think about the level of difficulty of each section. If you think you can handle the short-answer questions in less than an hour and that you'll need more time for the essays, re-budget your time.

Read test directions

Reading test directions carefully can save you trouble. For example, although a history test of 100 true-or-false questions and 1 essay may look straightforward, the directions may tell you that you need to answer only 80 of the 100 questions or that the essay is an optional bonus. If the directions indicate that you are penalized for incorrect answers—meaning that you lose points instead of simply not gaining points—avoid guessing unless you're fairly certain. These questions may do damage, for example, if you earn two points for every correct answer and lose one point for every incorrect answer.

When you read directions, you may learn that some questions or sections are weighted more heavily than others. For example, the short-answer questions may be worth 30 points, whereas the essays are worth 70. In this case, it's smart to spend more time on the essays than on the short answers.

Mark up the questions

Mark up instructions and key words to avoid careless errors. Circle **qualifiers**, such as *always*, *never*, *all*, *none*, *sometimes*, and *every*; verbs that communicate specific instructions; and concepts that are tricky or need special attention.

QUALIFIERS
Words and phrases that can alter the meaning of a test question and that require careful attention.

Take special care on machine-scored tests

Use the right pencil (usually a number 2) on machine-scored tests, and mark your answer in the correct space, filling it completely. (Use a ruler or your pencil as a straight edge to make sure you're writing your answer on the correct line for each question.) Periodically, check the answer number against the question number to make sure they match. If you mark the answer to question 4 in the space for question 5, not only will your response to question 4 be wrong, but also your responses to all subsequent questions will be off by a line. When you plan to return to a question and leave a space blank, put a small dot next to the number on the answer sheet. Neatness counts on these tests because the computer may misread stray pencil marks or partially erased answers.

While it's tempting to rush through a test to get it over with, taking your time to think when you need to will help you be more sure of your answers and may even help you stay calm.

Work from easy to hard

Begin with the questions that seem easiest to you. You can answer these questions quickly, leaving more time for questions that require greater effort. If you like to work through questions in order, you can mark difficult questions as you reach them and return to them after you answer the questions you know. Answering easier questions first also boosts your confidence.

Master the art of intelligent guessing

When you are unsure of an answer on a short-answer test, you can leave it blank or you can guess. As long as you are not penalized for incorrect answers, guessing helps you. "Intelligent guessing," writes Steven Frank, an authority on student studying and test taking, "means taking advantage of what you do know in order to try to figure out what you don't. If you guess intelligently, you have a decent shot at getting the answer right."[1]

First, eliminate all the answers you know—or believe—are wrong. Try to narrow your choices to two possible answers; then choose the one you think is more likely to be correct. Strategies for guessing the correct answer on a multiple-choice test are discussed later in this chapter.

Take a strategic approach to questions you cannot answer

Even if you are well prepared, you may be faced with questions you do not understand or cannot answer. What do you do in this situation?

- If your instructor is proctoring the exam, ask for clarification. Sometimes a simple rewording will make you realize that you really do know the material.

- If this doesn't work, skip the question and come back to it later. Letting your subconscious mind work on the question sometimes makes a difference.

- Use what you do know about the topic to build logical connections that may lead you to the answer. Take a calculated risk by using your analytical intelligence.

- Try to remember where the material was covered in your notes and text. Creating this kind of visual picture may jog your memory about content as well.

- Start writing—even if you think you're going in the wrong direction and not answering the question that was asked. The act of writing about related material may help you recall the targeted information. You may want to do this kind of "freewriting" on a spare scrap of paper, think about what you've written, and then write your final answer on the test paper or booklet.

- If you think of an answer right before the bell, write a note on the test paper to say that you are running out of time, so you are answering in outline form. While most instructors will deduct points for this approach, they may also give partial credit because you showed that you know the material.

Maintain academic integrity

When you take a test honestly, following all the rules of the test, you strengthen the principle of trust between students and instructors, which is at the heart of academic integrity (see Chapter 2). You also receive an accurate reading on your performance, from which you can determine what you know and what you still have to learn. Finally, you reinforce the habit of honesty.

Cheating as a strategy to pass a test or get a better grade robs you of the opportunity to learn the material on which you are being tested, which, ultimately, is your loss. It also makes fair play between students impossible. When one student studies hard for an exam and another cheats and both get the same high grade, the efforts of the hard-working student are diminished. It is important to realize that cheating jeopardizes your future post-secondary education if you are caught. You may be seriously reprimanded—or even expelled—if you violate your school's code of academic integrity.

How can you master *different types* of test questions?

Every type of test question has a different way of finding out how much you know about a subject. Answering different types of questions is part science and part art. The strategy changes according to whether the question is objective or subjective. See the samples of real test questions in Key 7.2. Analyzing the types, formats, and complexity of these questions will help you gauge what to expect when you take your exams.

Real test questions from real college texts.[2]

From chapter 29, "The End of Imperialism," in *Western Civilization: A Social and Cultural History*, 2nd edition.

■ **MULTIPLE-CHOICE QUESTION**
India's first leader after independence was:
A. Gandhi   B. Bose   C. Nehru   D. Sukharno   *(answer: C)*

■ **FILL-IN-THE-BLANK QUESTION**
East Pakistan became the country of _____ in 1971.
A. Burma   B. East India   C. Sukharno   D. Bangladesh   *(answer: D)*

■ **TRUE/FALSE QUESTION**
The United States initially supported Vietnamese independence.   T   F   *(answer: false)*

■ **ESSAY QUESTION**
Answer one of the following:
1. What led to Irish independence? What conflicts continued to exist after independence?
2. How did Gandhi work to rid India of British control? What methods did he use?

From chapter 2, "Geometric Shapes and Measurement," in *College Geometry: A Problem-Solving Approach with Applications*, 2nd edition.

■ **EXERCISES/PROBLEMS**
• All squares are kites, but not all kites are squares. What additional conditions must be satisfied for a kite to be a square?
         (answer: Equiangular—all right angles)

• In the following figure, find one example of the following angles.
a. supplementary   b. complementary   c. right   d. adjacent   e. acute   f. obtuse

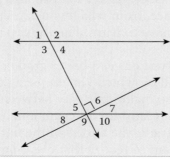

(continued)

(Geometry answers)

a. ∠1 and ∠2, ∠3 and ∠4, ∠1 and ∠3, ∠2 and ∠4, ∠6 and ∠9

b. ∠7 and ∠10, ∠5 and ∠8, ∠5 and ∠7, ∠8 and ∠10

c. ∠9 or ∠6

d. ∠1 and ∠2, ∠2 and ∠4, ∠4 and ∠3, ∠3 and ∠1, ∠5 and ∠6, ∠6 and ∠7, ∠7 and ∠10, ∠10 and ∠9, ∠9 and ∠8, ∠8 and ∠5

e. ∠1, ∠4, ∠7, ∠10, ∠8, ∠5

f. ∠2, ∠3

▨ APPLICATIONS

* The bed of a gravel truck has the shape shown next where the lateral faces are rectangles. Describes the shape as completely as possible.

(answer: right trapezoidal prism)

▨ TRUE/FALSE

* A circle is the set of all points in a plane that are the same distance from a fixed point. T F
* A parallelogram with four congruent sides is a rhombus. T F *(answers: T, T)*

From *Mosaicos: Spanish as a World Language,* 3rd edition.

▨ MATCHING QUESTIONS

You are learning new words and your teacher asks you to think of an object similar to or related to the words he says. His words are listed below. Next to each word, write a related word from the list below.

| el reloj | el cuaderno | el pupitre | una computadora |
| el televisor | la tiza | el lápiz | la mochila |

1. el escritorio _____   4. la pizarra _____

2. el bolígrafo _____   5. el libro _____

3. la videocasetera _____

(answers: 1. el pupitre; 2. el lápiz; 3. el televisor; 4. la tiza; 5. el cuaderno)

▨ ESSAY QUESTION

Your mother always worries about you and wants to know what you are doing with your time in Granada. Write a short letter to her describing your experience in Spain. In your letter, you should address the following points:

1. What classes you take   4. What you do with your time (mention three activities)

2. When and where you study   5. Where you go during your free time (mention two places)

3. How long you study every day

From chapter 13, "DNA Structure and Replication," in *Biology: A Guide to the Natural World,* 2nd edition.

▨ MULTIPLE-CHOICE QUESTION

What units are bonded together to make a strand of DNA?

A. chromatids   B. cells   C. enzymes   D. nucleotides   E. proteins   *(answer: D)*

▨ TRUE/FALSE QUESTION

Errors never occur in DNA replication, because the DNA polymerases edit out mistakes.   T   F   *(answer: false)*

▨ FILL-IN-THE-BLANK QUESTION

In a normal DNA molecule, adenine always pairs with _____ and cytosine always pairs with _____.   *(answers: thymine; guanine)*

▨ MATCHING QUESTIONS

Match the scientists and the approximate time frame (decades of their work) with their achievements.

Column 1

_____ 1. Modeled the molecular structure of DNA

_____ 2. Generated X-ray crystallography images of DNA

_____ 3. Correlated the production of one enzyme with one gene

Column 2

_____ A. George Beadle and Edward Tatum, 1930s and 1940s

_____ B. James Watson and Francis Crick, 1950s

_____ C. Rosalind Franklin and Maurice Wilkins, 1950s

(answers: 1–B; 2–C; 3–A)

OBJECTIVE
QUESTIONS
Short-answer questions
that test your ability to
recall, compare, and
contrast information and
to choose the right
answer from a limited
number of choices.

SUBJECTIVE
QUESTIONS
Essay questions that
require you to
express your answer in
terms of your own
personal knowledge
and perspective.

For **objective questions**, you choose or write a short answer you believe is correct, often making a selection from a limited number of choices. Multiple-choice, fill-in-the-blank, matching, and true-or-false questions fall into this category. **Subjective questions** demand the same information recall as objective questions, but they also require you to plan, organize, draft, and refine a written response. They may also require more extensive critical thinking and evaluation. All essay questions are subjective. Although some guidelines will help you choose the right answers to both types of questions, part of the skill is learning to "feel" your way to an answer that works.

Multiple-choice questions

Multiple-choice questions are the most popular type of question on standardized tests. The following strategies can help you answer them.

Read the directions carefully. Directions can be tricky. For example, whereas most test items ask for a single correct answer, some give you the option of marking several choices that are correct. For some tests, you might be required to answer only a certain number of questions.

Read each question thoroughly. Then, look at the choices and try to answer the question. This strategy reduces the possibility that the choices will confuse you.

Underline key words and phrases. If the question is complicated, try to break it down into small sections that are easy to understand.

Pay attention to words that could throw you off. For example, it is easy to overlook negatives in a question ("Which of the following is not . . .").

If you don't know the answer, eliminate those answers you know or suspect are wrong. Your goal is to leave yourself with two possible answers, which would give you a 50–50 chance of making the right choice. The following questions will help you eliminate choices:

- **Is the choice accurate on its own terms?** If there's an error in the choice—for example, a term that is incorrectly defined—the answer is wrong.

- **Is the choice relevant?** An answer may be accurate, but it may not relate to the essence of the question.

- **Are there any qualifiers?** Absolute qualifiers, like *always, never, all, none,* or *every,* often signal an exception that makes a choice incorrect. For example, the statement "Children always begin talking before the age of two" is untrue (most children begin talking before age two, but some start later). Analysis has shown that choices containing conservative qualifiers (e.g., *often, most, rarely,* or *may sometimes be*) are often correct.

- **Do the choices give clues?** Does a puzzling word remind you of a word you know? If you don't know a word, does any part of the word—its prefix, suffix, or root—seem familiar? (See Chapter 5 for information on the meanings of common prefixes, suffixes, and roots.)

Make an educated guess by following helpful patterns. The ideal is to know the material so well that you don't have to guess, but that isn't always possible. Test-taking experts have found patterns in multiple-choice questions that may help you. Here is their advice:

- Consider the possibility that a choice that is *more general* than the others is the right answer.
- Consider the possibility that a choice that is *longer* than the others is the right answer.
- Look for a choice that has a middle value in a range (the range can be from small to large or from old to recent). It is likely to be the right answer.
- Look for two choices that have similar meanings. One of these answers is probably correct.
- Look for answers that agree grammatically with the question. For example, a fill-in-the-blank question that has an *a* or *an* before the blank gives you a clue to the correct answer.

Make sure you read every word of every answer. Instructors have been known to include answers that are almost right, except for a single word. Focus especially on qualifying words such as *always, never, tend to, most, often,* and *frequently.*

When questions are keyed to a reading passage, read the questions first. This will help you focus on the information you need to answer the questions.

Here are some examples of the kinds of multiple-choice questions you might encounter in an Introduction to Psychology course[3] (the correct answer follows each question):

1. Arnold is at the company party and has had too much to drink. He releases all of his pent-up aggression by yelling at his boss, who promptly fires him. Arnold normally would not have yelled at his boss, but after drinking heavily he yelled because
   A. parties are places where employees are supposed to be able to "loosen up"
   B. alcohol is a stimulant
   C. alcohol makes people less concerned with the negative consequences of their behaviour
   D. alcohol inhibits brain centres that control the perception of loudness

(The correct answer is C)

2. Which of the following has not been shown to be a probable cause of or influence on the development of alcoholism in our society?
   A. intelligence   C. personality
   B. culture   D. genetic vulnerability

(The correct answer is A)

3. Blanche is a heavy coffee drinker who has become addicted to caffeine. If she completely ceases her intake of caffeine over the next few days, she is likely to experience each of the following except
   A. depression   C. insomnia
   B. lethargy   D. headaches

(The correct answer is C)

True-or-false questions

True-or-false questions test your knowledge of facts and concepts. Read them carefully to evaluate what they truly say. If you're stumped, guess (unless you will be penalized for wrong answers).

Look for qualifiers in true-or-false questions—such as *all, only*, and *always* (the absolutes that often make a statement false) and *generally, often, usually*, and *sometimes* (the conservatives that often make a statement true)—that can turn a statement that would otherwise be true into one that is false, or vice versa. For example, "The grammar rule 'I before E except after C' is always true" is *false*, whereas "The grammar rule 'I before E except after C' is usually true" is *true*. The qualifier makes the difference.

Here are some examples of the kinds of true-or-false questions you might encounter in an Introduction to Psychology course (the correct answer follows each question).

Are the following questions true or false?

1. Alcohol use is clearly related to increases in hostility, aggression, violence, and abusive behaviour. (True)

2. Marijuana is harmless. (False)

3. Simply expecting a drug to produce an effect is often enough to produce the effect. (True)

4. Alcohol is a stimulant. (False)

Matching questions

Matching questions ask you to match the terms in one list with the terms in another list, according to the directions. For example, the directions may tell you to match a communicable disease with the pathogen that usually causes it. The following strategies will help you handle these questions.

Make sure you understand the directions. The directions tell you whether each answer can be used once or more than once.

Work from the column with the longest entries. This saves time because you are looking at each long phrase only once as you scan the column with the shorter phrases for the match.

Start with the matches you know. On your first run-through, mark these matches immediately with a pencilled line, waiting to finalize your choices after you've completed all the items. Keep in mind that if you can use an answer only once, you may have to reconsider some of your original choices if later you can't find a particular match within the other answers.

Finally, tackle the matches you're not sure of. On your next run-through, focus on the more difficult matches. Look for clues and relationships you might not have thought of at first. Think back to class lectures, notes, and study sessions and try to visualize the correct response.

Fill-in-the-blank questions

Fill-in-the-blank questions, also known as sentence completion questions, ask you to supply one or more words or phrases with missing information that completes the sentence. These strategies will help you make the right choices.

Be logical. Insert your answer; then reread the sentence from beginning to end to be sure it is factually and grammatically correct and makes sense.

Note the length and number of the blanks. Use these as important clues, but not as absolute guideposts. If two blanks appear right after one another, the instructor is probably looking for a two-word answer. If a blank is longer than usual, the correct response may require additional space. However, if you are certain of an answer that doesn't fit the blanks, trust your knowledge and instincts.

Pay attention to how blanks are separated. If there is more than one blank in a sentence and the blanks are widely separated, treat each one separately.

Answering each as if it were a separate sentence-completion question increases the likelihood that you will get at least one answer correct. Here is an example:

After Preston Manning left _____ politics, he joined _____ as a lecturer.

(Answer: After Preston Manning left federal politics, he joined the University of Toronto as a lecturer.)

In this case, and in many other cases, your knowledge of one answer has little impact on your knowledge of the other answer.

Think out of the box. If you can think of more than one correct answer, put them both down. Your instructor may be impressed by your assertiveness and creativity.

Make a guess. If you are uncertain of an answer, make an educated guess. Use qualifiers like *may*, *sometimes*, and *often* to increase the chance that your answer is at least partially correct. Have faith that, after hours of studying, the correct answer is somewhere in your subconscious mind and that your guess is not completely random.

Here are examples of fill-in-the-blank questions you might encounter in an Introduction to Astronomy course[4] (correct answers follow questions):

1. A _____ is a collection of hundreds of billions of stars. (galaxy)

2. Rotation is the term used to describe the motion of a body around some _____. (axis)

3. The solar day is measured relative to the sun; the sidereal day is measured relative to the _____. (stars)

4. On December 21, known as the _____ _____, the sun is at its _____ _____. (winter solstice; southernmost point)

Essay questions

An essay question allows you to express your knowledge and views more extensively than a short-answer question. With the freedom to express your views, though, comes the challenge to exhibit knowledge and demonstrate your ability to organize and express that knowledge clearly.

Strategies for answering essay questions. The following steps will help improve your responses to essay questions. Many of these guidelines reflect methods for approaching any writing assignment. That is, you undertake an abbreviated version of the writing process as you plan, draft, revise, and edit your response (see Chapter 8). The primary differences here are that you are writing under time pressure and that you are working from memory.

1. **Start by reading the questions.** Decide which to tackle (if there's a choice) then, focus on what each question is asking. Read the directions carefully and do everything that you are asked to do. Some essay questions may contain more than one part. Knowing what you have to accomplish, budget your time accordingly. For example, if you have one hour to answer three questions, you might budget 20 minutes for each question and break that down into stages (3 minutes for planning, 15 minutes for drafting, 2 minutes for revising and editing).

2. **Watch for action verbs.** Certain verbs can help you figure out how to think. Key 7.3 explains some words commonly used in essay questions. Underline these words as you read the question, clarify what they mean, and use them to guide your writing.

3. **Plan your essay.** Brainstorm ideas and examples. Create an informal outline or think link to map your ideas and indicate the examples you plan to cite in support. (See Chapter 8 for a discussion of these organizational devices.)

4. **Draft your essay.** Start with a thesis statement that states clearly what your essay will say. Then devote one or more paragraphs to the main points in your outline. Back up the general statement that starts each paragraph with evidence in the form of examples, statistics, and so on. Use simple, clear language, and look back at your outline to make sure you cover everything. Wrap it up with a short, pointed conclusion.

5. **Revise your essay.** Make sure you have answered the question completely and have included all of your points. Look for ideas you left out, ideas you didn't support with examples, paragraphs with faulty structure, and confusing sentences. Make cuts or changes or add sentences in the margins, indicating with an arrow where they fit. Try to be as neat as possible when making last-minute changes.

6. **Edit your essay.** Check for mistakes in grammar, spelling, punctuation, and usage. No matter what your topic is, being technically correct in your writing makes your work more impressive. Keep in mind that neatness is a crucial factor in essay writing. If

Analyze—Break into parts and discuss each part separately.

Compare—Explain similarities and differences.

Contrast—Distinguish between items being compared by focusing on differences.

Criticize—Evaluate the positive and negative effects of what is being discussed.

Define—State the essential quality or meaning. Give the common idea.

Describe—Visualize and give information that paints a complete picture.

Discuss—Examine in a complete and detailed way, usually by connecting ideas to examples.

Enumerate/List/Identify—Recall and name items in the form of a list.

Evaluate—Give your opinion about the value or worth of something, usually by weighing positive and negative effects, and justify your conclusion.

Explain—Make the meaning of something clear, often by making analogies or giving examples.

Illustrate—Supply examples.

Interpret—Explain your personal view of facts and ideas and how they relate to one another.

Outline—Organize and present the main examples of an idea or sub-idea.

Prove—Use evidence and argument to show that something is true, usually by showing cause and effect or giving examples that fit the idea to be proven.

Review—Provide an overview of ideas and establish their merits and features.

State—Explain clearly, simply, and concisely, being sure that each word gives the image you want.

Summarize—Give the important ideas in brief.

Trace—Present a history of the way something developed, often by showing cause and effect.

your instructor can't read your ideas, it doesn't matter how good they are.

Key 7.4 on page 223 shows an essay that responds effectively to Question 3 in the box below.

Here are some examples of essay questions you might encounter in an Interpersonal Communication course. In each case, notice the action verbs from Key 7.3.

1. Summarize the role of the self-concept as a key to interpersonal relationships and communication.

2. Explain how internal and external noise affects the ability to listen effectively.

3. Describe three ways that body language affects interpersonal communication.

Write to the Verb

Hone your ability to read and follow essay instructions accurately.

Focusing on the action verbs in essay test instructions can mean the difference between giving instructors what they want and answering off the mark.

- Start by choosing a topic you learned about in this text—for example, the concept of successful intelligence or of internal and external barriers to listening. Write your topic here:

  _____

  _____

- Put yourself in the role of instructor. Write an essay question on this topic, using one of the action verbs in Key 7.3 to frame the question. For example, "List the three aspects of successful intelligence," or "Analyze the classroom-based challenges associated with internal barriers to listening."

  _____

  _____

- Now choose three other action verbs from Key 7.3. Use each one to rewrite your original question.

  1. _____

  2. _____

  3. _____

- Finally, analyze how each new verb changes the focus of the essay.

  1. _____

  _____

  2. _____

  _____

  3. _____

  _____

Response to an essay question.

Question: Describe three ways that body language affects interpersonal communication.

Body language plays an important role in interpersonal communication and helps shape the impression you make, especially when you meet someone for the first time. Two of the most important functions of body language are to contradict and reinforce verbal statements. When body language contradicts verbal language, the message conveyed by the body is dominant. For example, if a friend tells you that she is feeling "fine," but her posture is slumped, her eye contact minimal, and her facial expression troubled, you have every reason to wonder whether she is telling the truth. If the same friend tells you that she is feeling fine and is smiling, walking with a bounce in her step, and has direct eye contact, her body language is accurately reflecting and reinforcing her words.

The non-verbal cues that make up body language also have the power to add shades of meaning. Consider this statement: "This is the best idea I've heard all day." If you were to say this three different ways—in a loud voice while standing up; quietly while sitting with arms and legs crossed and looking away; and while maintaining eye contact and taking the receiver's hand—you might send three different messages.

Finally, the impact of non-verbal cues can be greatest when you meet someone for the first time. Although first impressions emerge from a combination of non-verbal cues, tone of voice, and choice of words, non-verbal elements (cues and tone) usually come across first and strongest. When you meet someone, you tend to make assumptions based on non-verbal behaviour such as posture, eye contact, gestures, and speed and style of movement.

In summary, non-verbal communication plays a crucial role in interpersonal relationships. It has the power to send an accurate message that may belie the speaker's words, offer shades of meaning, and set the tone of a first meeting.

How can you learn from
test mistakes?

The purpose of a test is to see how much you know, not merely to achieve a grade. Making mistakes, or even failing a test, is human. Rather than ignoring mistakes, examine them and learn from them as you learn from mistakes on the job and in relationships. Working through your mistakes helps you avoid repeating them on another test. The following strategies will help.

Try to identify patterns in your mistakes. Look for the following:

- Careless errors. In your rush to complete the exam, did you misread the question or directions, blacken the wrong box on the answer sheet, inadvertently skip a question, or write illegibly?
- Conceptual or factual errors. Did you misunderstand a concept or never learn it? Did you fail to master certain facts? Did you skip part of the text or miss classes in which ideas were covered?

If you have time, rework the questions you got wrong. Based on instructor feedback, try to rewrite an essay, recalculate a math problem from the original question, or redo questions following a reading selection. If you see patterns of careless errors, promise yourself that you'll be more careful in the future and that you'll leave enough time to double-check your work.

After reviewing your mistakes, fill in your knowledge gaps. If you made mistakes on questions because you didn't know or understand them, develop a plan to comprehensively learn the material. Solidifying your knowledge can help you on future exams and in life situations that involve the subject you're studying. You might even consider asking to retake the exam. The score might not count, but you may find that focusing on learning, rather than on grades, can improve your knowledge.

Talk to your instructors. You can learn a lot from consulting an instructor about specific mistakes you made or about subjective essays on which you were marked down. Respectfully ask the instructor for an explanation of marks or comments. In the case of a subjective test where the answers are often not clearly right or wrong, ask for specifics about what you could have done to earn a better mark. Take advantage of this opportunity to find out solid details about how you can do better next time.

If you fail a test, don't throw it away. Keep it as a reminder that many students have been in your shoes and that you have room to improve if you supply the will to succeed.

Learn from Your Mistakes

Examine what went wrong on a recent exam to build knowledge for next time.

Look at an exam on which your performance fell short of expectations. If possible, choose one that contains different types of objective and subjective questions. With the test and answer sheet in hand, use your analytical and practical thinking skills to answer the following questions:

- Identify the types of questions on which you got the most correct answers (for example, matching, essay, or multiple-choice).

  _____

- Identify the types of questions on which you made the greatest number of errors.

  _____

- Analyze your errors to identify patterns—for example, did you misread test instructions, or did you ignore qualifiers that changed the questions' meanings? What did you find?

  _____

  _____

- Finally, what are two practical actions you are committed to taking during your next exam to avoid the same problems?

  Action 1: _____

  Action 2: _____

Successful Intelligence Wrap-Up

Tests ask you to show what you know to someone who will judge your performance. However, far more important than the information a test gives to an instructor is the information it gives to you, the test taker. Tests can be your road map to subject mastery, showing you what you have learned, what you are still learning, and what stumps you. Here's how you have built skills in Chapter 7:

Analytical

You examined test-preparation techniques with an eye toward what works best for you. You investigated specific ways to maximize your chances of answering objective and subjective test questions correctly. In the Get Analytical exercise, you wrote a series of original essay questions, analyzing the effect that different action verbs had on what the questions were asking. You considered the potential positive effects from a careful analysis of test mistakes.

Creative

With the Get Creative exercise, you produced your own pretest that will help you assess if you have mastered crucial material. In reading about test anxiety, you encountered a different perspective of tests as opportunities to learn rather than contests that you win or lose. The scheduling and study techniques may have inspired you to create a personal study schedule and regimen to help you make the most of your time.

Practical

You gathered specific test-preparation techniques. You learned specific ways to calm test anxiety and to attack objective test questions. You expanded your knowledge of how to use planning tools, such as a key word outline, to help you write test essays. You deepened your understanding of how examining test mistakes helps you learn from experience. In the Get Practical exercise, you explored your mistakes on a particular test and identified steps you will take to avoid the same mistakes in the future.

hart ducha
(hahrt doo-cha)

In Polish, *hart ducha* literally means "strength of spirit" or "strength of will" to overcome life's challenges. In college, instructors challenge you on tests to demonstrate what you know and what you can do. Both before and during each test, your success depends on your *hart ducha*. With strength of will, you can commit to spending hours learning, reviewing, thinking about, and memorizing course material instead of cramming at the last minute. Think carefully about your approach because it determines far more than your exam grade. It determines what you will get out of your education.

There are no shortcuts to test success. Only old-fashioned hard work, driven by a powerful strength of will, will enable you to reach your academic potential.[5]

"The Five P's of Success: Prior preparation prevents poor performance."

JAMES A. BAKER III, FORMER SECRETARY OF STATE AND WHITE HOUSE CHIEF OF STAFF

SUCCESSFUL INTELLIGENCE

Think, Create, Apply

Prepare effectively for tests.   Take a detailed look at your performance on and preparation for a recent test.

Step 1: Think it through: *Analyze how you did.* Were you pleased or disappointed with your performance and grade? Why?

_____

_____

Thinking about your performance, look at the potential problems listed below. Circle any that you feel were a factor in this exam. Fill in the empty spaces with any key problems not listed.

- Incomplete preparation
- Fatigue
- Feeling rushed during the test
- Shaky understanding of concepts
- Poor guessing techniques
- Feeling confused about directions
- Test anxiety
- Poor essay organization or writing
- _____
- _____
- _____

If you circled any problems, think about why you made mistakes (if it was an objective exam) or why you didn't score well (if it was an essay exam).

Step 2. Think out of the box: *Be creative about test-preparation strategies.* If you had absolutely no restrictions on time or on access to materials, how would you have prepared for this test?

Describe briefly what your plan would be and how it would minimize any problems you encountered.

_____

_____

Now think back to your actual preparation for this test. Describe techniques you used and note time spent.

_____

_____

_____

How does what you would like to do differ from what you actually did?

_____

_____

Step 3. Make it happen: *Improve preparation for the future.* Think about the practical actions you will take the next time you face a similar test.

Actions I took this time, but do not intend to take next time:

_____

_____

Actions I did not take this time, but intend to take next time:

_____

_____

TEAMWORK

Create Solutions Together

Test study group. Form a study group with two or three other students. When your instructor announces the next exam, ask each study group member to record everything he or she does to prepare for the exam, including:

- learning what to expect on the test (topics and material that will be covered, types of questions that will be asked)
- examining old tests

- creating and following a study schedule and checklist
- using SQ3R to review material
- taking a pretest
- getting a good night's sleep before the exam
- doing last-minute cramming
- mastering general test-taking strategies
- mastering test-taking strategies for specific types of test questions (multiple-choice, true-or-false, matching, fill-in-the-blank, essay)

After the exam, come together to compare preparation regimens. What important differences can you identify in the routines followed by group members? How do you suspect that different routines affected test performance and outcome? On a separate piece of paper, for your own reference, write down what you learned from the test-preparation habits of your study mates that may help you as you prepare for upcoming exams.

WRITING

Journal and Put Skills to Work

Record your thoughts on a separate piece of paper or in a journal.

Test anxiety. Do you experience test anxiety? Describe how tests generally make you feel (you might include an example of a specific test situation and what happened). Identify your specific test-taking fears, and write out your plan to overcome fears and self-defeating behaviours.

PERSONAL PORTFOLIO

Prepare for Career Success

On-the-job testing. Depending on what careers you are considering, you may encounter one or more tests. Some are for entry into the field (e.g., Bar exams for lawyers); some test your proficiency on particular equipment or applications (e.g., a proficiency test on using Microsoft Word); and some move you to the next level of employment (e.g., Chartered Financial Analyst exam). Choose one career you are thinking about and investigate what tests are involved as you advance through different stages of the field. Be sure to look for tests in any of the areas described above. On a separate piece of paper, write down everything you find out about each test involved. For example:

- what it tests you on
- when you would need to take the test in the course of pursuing this career

- what preparation is necessary for the test (including coursework)
- whether the test needs to be retaken at any time (e.g., airline pilots usually need to be recertified every few years)

Finally, see if you can review any of the tests you will face if you pursue this career. For example, if your career choice requires proficiency on a specific computer program, your school's career or computer centre may have the test available.

SUGGESTED READINGS

Browning, William G., Ph.D. *Cliffs Memory Power for Exams.* Lincoln, NE: CliffsNotes Inc., 1990.

Frank, Steven. *Test Taking Secrets: Study Better, Test Smarter, and Get Great Grades.* Holbrook, MA: Adams Media Corporation, 1998.

Fry, Ron. *"Ace" Any Test,* 3rd ed. Franklin Lakes, NJ: Career Press, 1996.

Hamilton, Dawn. *Passing Exams: A Guide for Maximum Success and Minimum Stress.* Herndon, VA: Cassell Academic, 1999.

Kesselman, Judy, and Franklynn Peterson. *Test Taking Strategies.* New York: NTC/Contemporary Publishing, 1981.

Luckie, William R., and Wood Smethurst. *Study Power: Study Skills to Improve Your Learning and Your Grades.* Cambridge, MA: Brookline Books, 1997.

INTERNET RESOURCES

Concordia University offers these test-taking tips for its students:
http://cdev.concordia.ca/CnD/studentlearn/Help/Ten_Tips.html#Test

Florida State University's Centre for Assessment and Testing (list of sites offering information on tests and test-taking skills):
http://learningforlife.fsu.edu/cat/test/index.cfm

NetStudyAids.com study aids, skills, guides, and techniques—Type "study skills" into the search bar:
www.netstudyaids.com

The Ontario Ministry of Training, Education and Colleges offers this page of web links for students who want to improve their test-taking skills:
www.edu.gov.on.ca/eng/career/study-t.html

Prentice Hall Student Success Supersite (testing tips in study skills section):
www.prenhall.com/success

ENDNOTES

1. Steven Frank, *The Everything Study Book* (Holbrook, MA: Adams Media Corporation, 1996), 208.

2. Western civilization test items from Margaret L. King, *Western Civilization: A Social and Cultural History*, 2nd ed. (Upper Saddle River, NJ: Pearson Education, 2003), questions from *Instructor's Manual and Test Item File* by Dolores Davison Peterson, used with permission; Geometry exercises from Gary L. Musser, Lynn E. Trimpe, and Vikki R.

Maurer, *College Geometry: A Problem-Solving Approach with Applications*, 2nd ed. (Upper Saddle River, NJ: Pearson/Prentice Hall, 2008), 99–101, used with permission; Spanish test items from Matilde Olivella de Castells, Elizabeth Guzman, Paloma Lapuerta, and Carmen Garcia, *Mosaicos: Spanish as a World Language*, 3rd ed. (Upper Saddle River, NJ: Prentice Hall, 2002), questions from *Testing Program* by Mark Harpring, used with permission; Biology test items from David Krogh,

Biology: A Guide to the Natural World, 2nd ed. (Upper Saddle River, NJ: Prentice Hall, 2002), questions from *Test Item File* edited by Dan Wivagg, used with permission.

3. Many of the examples of objective questions used in this chapter are from Gary W. Piggrem, *Test Item File* for Charles G. Morris, *Understanding Psychology*, 3rd ed. (Upper Saddle River, NJ: Prentice Hall, 1996).

4. Questions from Eric Chaisson and Steve McMillan, *Astronomy Today*, 2nd ed. (Upper Saddle River, NJ: Prentice Hall, 1996), 27.

5. Christopher J. Moore, *In Other Words: A Language Lover's Guide to the Most Intriguing Words around the World* (New York: Walker, 2004), 45.

RESEARCHING AND WRITING
Gathering and communicating ideas

8

SUCCESSFUL

PRACTICAL   CREATIVE

ANALYTICAL

INTELLIGENCE

"When a man dies and goes to heaven, Saint Peter points to an individual, mentioning that he was a great poet. The man looks at Saint Peter, incredulous. 'Excuse me,' he says, 'but I knew that man. He was . . . a humble shoemaker. He never went to school or learned how to write.' 'Precisely so,' responds Saint Peter. Never given the chance to develop his skills, the man's . . . talent went to waste."

ROBERT J. STERNBERG

Research and writing, powerful tools that engage your successful intelligence, are at the heart of your education. Through library and internet research, you gather and analyze information from sources all over the world. Through writing, you analyze ideas, think creatively about what they mean, and communicate information and perspectives to others. The Conference Board of Canada lists being able to manage information as a key employability skill. This skill includes the capacity to "locate, gather and organize information using appropriate technology."[1] Employees must also be able to "access, analyze and apply knowledge from various disciplines."

In this chapter you will explore answers to the following questions:

• How can you make the most of your library? 234

• How can you find reliable information on the internet? 237

• What is the writing process? 243

• How can you deliver an effective oral presentation? 258

• Successful Intelligence Wrap-Up 259

Chapter 8's
Successful Intelligence Skills

Analytical

- Analyzing how to use library and internet sources
- Evaluating the reliability of internet sources
- Evaluating your writing purpose and crafting a thesis that reflects it
- Evaluating how to organize ideas and choose effective words

Creative

- Developing a personal approach to internet and library research
- Brainstorming to develop writing topics
- Using prewriting strategies to narrow topic ideas

Practical

- How to use a keyword search of library and internet sources
- How to plan, draft, revise, and edit a paper
- How to avoid plagiarism

How can you *make the most* of your library?

In this information age, when researchers have at their disposal a vast array of electronic resources, college and university libraries are more valued than ever for their role in helping you make intelligent information choices. With expanded and enhanced offerings linked to the internet and to stacks of books, journals, and other tangible resources, the library is the "brain" of your post-secondary institution. It is your challenge to use analytical, creative, and practical skills to find accurate, reliable information in every medium.

Realizing the value of library resources starts with the awareness that when you use the library's electronic databases, you will have find information more easily than if you used the internet alone. Your library subscribes to many specialized databases that link you to full-text articles, books, and other information. You won't have access to these databases without plugging into your library account.

Although most students are drawn to the internet first when researching, this chapter will give you reasons to believe that the library is the best place to begin your research. Your instructors know this and will expect to see library research citations in your work. Start here to become more familiar with what your library has to offer.

Start with a road map

Most college and university libraries are bigger than high school and community libraries, so you may feel lost on your first few visits. Make your life easier by learning how your library is organized.

Circulation desk. All publications are checked out at the circulation desk, which is usually near the library entrance.

Reference area. Here you'll find reference books, including encyclopedias, directories, dictionaries, almanacs, and atlases. You'll also find librarians and other library employees who can direct you to information. Computer terminals, containing the library's catalogue of holdings, as well as online bibliographic and full-text databases, are usually part of the reference area.

Book area. Books—and, in many libraries, magazines and journals in bound or boxed volumes—are stored in the *stacks*. In a library with "open stacks," you search for materials on your own. In a "closed-stack" system, a staff member retrieves materials for you.

Periodicals area. Here you'll find recent issues of popular and scholarly magazines, journals, and newspapers. Most libraries collect **periodicals** ranging from *Maclean's* to the *Canadian Journal of Communication* and *New England Journal of Medicine*. Because unbound periodicals are generally not circulated, you may find photocopy machines nearby where you can copy pages.

Audio/visual materials areas. Many libraries have special areas for video, art and photography, and recorded music collections.

Electronic library resources. Computer terminals, linked to college or university databases and the internet, may be scattered throughout the library or clustered in specific areas. Most schools have network systems that allow access to online library materials via personal computers. In addition, an increasing number of post-secondary institutions have wireless Wi-Fi systems that allow students to conduct research via their computer, cellphone, or PDA while sitting in a classroom or even under a tree.

Almost all college or university libraries offer orientation sessions on how to find what you need. To learn what your library offers, take a real or virtual tour and sign up for training.

Learn how to conduct an information search

Use a practical, step-by-step method that takes you from general to specific sources (see Key 8.1). At any point in your search, you can conduct a **keyword search**—a method in which you use a topic-related *keyword*, any natural-language word or phrase, as a point of reference to locate other information. To narrow your topic and reduce the number of *hits* (resources pulled up by your search), add more keywords. For example, instead of searching through the broad category "art," focus on "French art" or, more specifically, "19th century French art."

PERIODICALS
Magazines, journals, newspapers, and online publications that are published on a regular basis throughout the year.

KEYWORD SEARCH
Natural-language words and phrases that are used to search a computer data bank in order to track down specific information.

Library search strategy.

8.1

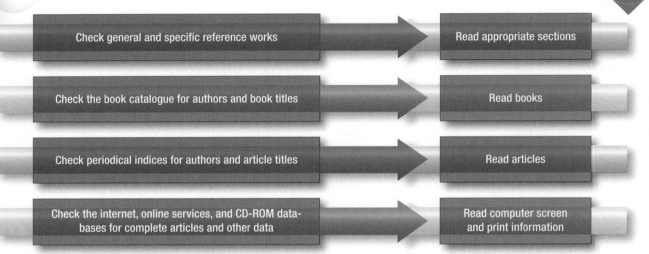

Check general and specific reference works	→	Read appropriate sections
Check the book catalogue for authors and book titles	→	Read books
Check periodical indices for authors and article titles	→	Read articles
Check the internet, online services, and CD-ROM databases for complete articles and other data	→	Read computer screen and print information

How to perform an effective keyword search.

8.2

IF YOU ARE SEARCHING FOR...	DO THIS	EXAMPLE
A word	Type the word normally	aid
A phrase	Type the phrase in its normal word order (use regular word spacing) or surround the phrase with double quotation marks	financial aid (or "financial aid")
Two or more keywords without regard to word order	Type the words in any order, surrounding the words with quotation marks (use "and" to separate the words)	"financial aid" and "scholarships"
Topic A or topic B	Type the words in any order, surrounding the words with quotation marks (use "or" to separate the words)	"financial aid" or "scholarships"
Topic A but not topic B	Type topic A first within quotation marks, and then topic B within quotation marks (use "not" to separate the words)	"financial aid" not "scholarships"

Key 8.2 provides tips for using the keyword system, including how to use "or," "and," and "not" to narrow searches with what is called *Boolean logic*.

Start with general reference works

These works cover topics in a broad, nondetailed way and are often available in print, online, or on CD-ROM. Examples of general reference works include encyclopedias (such as *The Canadian Encyclopedia Plus*), almanacs (such as the *Canadian Global Almanac*), dictionaries (such as the *Canadian Oxford Dictionary*), biographical references (such as *Canadian Who's Who*), and bibliographies (such as *Books in Print*). Scan these sources to get a topic overview and to find more specialized sources.

Search specialized reference works

Turn next to specialized reference works, including encyclopedias and dictionaries that focus on a narrow field (such as the *Canadian Journal of Communication*), for more specific facts. The short summaries in these volumes focus on critical ideas and introduce keywords you can use to conduct additional research. Bibliographies that accompany the articles point to the works of recognized experts.

Browse through books and articles on your subject

Search the computerized library catalogue by author, title, or subject to find information about where in your library to locate books and other materials on your topic. Periodicals include journals, magazines, and newspapers. **Journals** target readers with specialized knowledge (while *Newsweek* may run a general-interest article on AIDS research, for example, the *Journal of the American Medical Association* may print the original scientific study). *Periodical indexes* such as the *Readers' Guide to Periodical Literature* lead you to specific articles that are available in print, online, and on CD-ROM.

JOURNALS
Periodicals that are intended for readers with in-depth knowledge.

Ask the librarian

Librarians, also known as *media specialists* and *information technologists*, can assist you in locating unfamiliar or hard-to-find sources, navigating catalogues and databases, uncovering research shortcuts, and dealing with pesky computers and other equipment. Know what you want to accomplish before you ask a question. The more specific your inquiry, the more likely it is that the librarian will be able to help you. In addition, use your emotional and social intelligence to frame your question in a way that is likely to encourage help. Being friendly and courteous and looking the librarian in the eye when you speak will go a long way. When you can't get to the library in person, technology enables librarians at many schools to answer questions via cellphone, email, and instant-messaging.

How can you find *reliable information* on the internet?

The internet, a computer network that links organizations and people around the world, can connect you to billions of information sources. Unlike your post-secondary institution's library collection or library subscription databases—evaluated and selected for usefulness and reliability by educated librarians—internet resources are not necessarily evaluated or overseen by anyone. As a result, determining the reliability of internet research depends on your analytical judgment.

Most internet information is displayed on *websites*, cyberspace locations developed by companies, government agencies, organizations, and individuals. *Blogs* (also known as *weblogs*), interactive journal-like entries on specific topics that are created and maintained by individual users, enable readers to respond to postings and engage in cyberspace conversations with others who are interested in the topic. Currently, there are more than 100 million websites, up from just 18 000 in 1995, and 60 million blogs.[2]

Start with search engines

Search engines are tools for finding information on the internet. Using a keyword search, you gain access to websites, blogs, and other resources. With the power of the search engine to access the internet comes the potential for an enormous list of "hits" unless you carefully limit your keyword search. Among the most popular and effective search engines are Google (www.google.ca), Yahoo! (www.ca.yahoo.com), AltaVista (www.altavista.com), HotBot (www.hotbot.com), Ask (www.ask.com), Excite (www.excite.com), Go.com (www.go.com), and Lycos (www.lycos.com).

Search engines aimed at academic audiences are the Librarians' Internet Index (www.lii.org) and InfoMine (www.infomine.com). The advantage of using academic directories is that you know someone has screened the sites and listed only those that have been determined to be reliable, reputable, and regularly updated.

Meta search engines, which compare results across different search engines, include Dogpile.com, Search.com, Mamma.com, Metasearch.com, and KartOO.com.

Use a search strategy

The World Wide Web has been called "the world's greatest library, with all its books on the floor." With no librarian in sight, you need to master a practical basic **internet search strategy** that will help you evaluate the flood of online sources. Follow these steps:

1. *Think carefully about what you want to locate.* University of Michigan Prof. Eliot Soloway recommends phrasing your search in the form of a question—for example, *What vaccines are given to children before age 5?* Then, he advises identifying the important words in the question (*vaccines, children, before age 5*) as well as other related words (*chicken pox, tetanus, polio, shot, pediatrics,* and so on). This gives you a collection of terms to use in different combinations as you search.[3]

2. *Use a search directory to isolate sites under your desired topic or category.* Save the sites that look useful. (Most browsers have a "bookmark" feature for sites you want to find again.)

3. *Explore these sites to get a general idea of what's out there.* If the directory takes you where you need to go, you're in luck. More often in academic research, you need to dig deeper. Notice useful keywords and information locations in the search directory.

4. *Move on to a search engine to narrow your search.* Use your keywords in a variety of ways to uncover as many possibilities as you can.
   - Vary their order if you are using more than one keyword (e.g., search under *education, college, statistics,* and *statistics, education, college*).
   - Use *Boolean operators*—the words "and," "not," and "or"—in ways that limit your search (see Key 8.2 for techniques for using keywords for library searches).

5. *Evaluate the list of links that appear.* If there are too many, narrow your search by using more keywords or more specific keywords (*Broadway* could become *Broadway* AND *"fall season"* AND *2010*). If there are too few, broaden your search by using fewer or different keywords.

INTERNET SEARCH STRATEGY

A practical, step-by-step method that helps you locate accurate, reliable online sources.

Google (Yes, It's a Verb)

Explore ways to use Google and other search engines effectively.

Google accesses 6 billion documents and has the capacity to return 750 000 internet links in a third of a second. Despite this, Leon Botstein, president of Bard College, warns of Google's pitfalls: "In general, Google overwhelms you with too much information, much of which is hopelessly unreliable or beside the point. It's like looking for a lost ring in a vacuum bag. What you end up with mostly are bagel crumbs and dirt."[4]

With this warning in mind, use your creativity and analysis to complete the following:

- Choose a common topic—for example, apples, hockey, snowflakes. Google the topic to see how many websites you access. Write that number here. _____

    Now spend 10 minutes scanning the web listings. How many different topics did your search uncover other than the topic you intended? _____

- Pick three of the off-the-topic links you found and write a thesis statement to a paper that would require you to use these leads in your research. Be creative.

    _____

    _____

    _____

- In all likelihood, your thesis statement makes little sense. What does this tell you about the need for critical thinking when using Google and other search directories and engines in your research?

    _____

    _____

    _____

- Finally, open your mind to the creative possibilities your research uncovered. Did any of the websites spark ideas about your topic that you had never considered? Write down two ideas you never thought of before.

    1. _____

    2. _____

6. *When you think you are done, start over.* Choose another search directory or search engine and perform your search again. Why do this? Because different systems access different sites.

Use critical thinking to evaluate every source

Your internet research is only as strong as your analytical thinking. Robert Harris, professor and author of *WebQuester: A Guidebook to the Web*, has developed an easy-to-remember system for evaluating internet information called the CARS test for information quality (<u>C</u>redibility, <u>A</u>ccuracy, <u>R</u>easonableness, <u>S</u>upport). Use the information in Key 8.3 to question any source you find as you conduct research.[5]

Educational and government sites are more likely to be evaluated for accuracy and reliability than are other sites. You can identify these sites by looking at the *URL (uniform resource locator*, formerly called a *universal resource locator*)—the string of text and numbers that identifies an internet site. In American websites, look for URLs ending in *.edu* (originating at educational institutions) and *.gov* (originating at government agencies). URLs for Canadian educational institutions tend to end in *.ca*, but the name of the institution is usually within the address (e.g., Dalhousie is **www.dal.ca**; Carleton is **www.carleton.ca**). URLs for the Canadian government also end in *.ca* but include *gc* within the address (e.g., Health Canada is **www.hc-sc.gc.ca**; Canadian Heritage is **www.canadianheritage.gc.ca**); provincial governments include *gov* plus an abbreviation for the province (e.g., Ministry of Transportation in Ontario is **www.mto.gov.on.ca**, but in British Columbia it is **www.gov.bc.ca/tran**). If you are unsure of the credibility of a source, ask your instructor.

Some popular information sites sometimes have reliability problems. For example, the online encyclopedia Wikipedia, which allows all readers to create or edit articles, is plagued by incorrect information or glaring omissions. Knowing that Wikipedia's information is often written by nonexperts will raise your level of critical analysis and encourage you to cross-check the information in other places. Because of Wikipedia's problems, some colleges have banned its use in research papers.

Know when to use the library and when to use the internet

The internet is a modern reality—but it has not, as some predicted, replaced the printed word. Savvy researchers combine internet and library research to find information. As a general rule, you should consider heading to the library first in the following situations:

- When you are conducting in-depth research, requiring a historical perspective (older information is more likely to be available at the library than on the web)
- When you want to use your library's subscription databases
- When you want to verify the authenticity of what you discover on the internet
- When you need personal, face-to-face help from a librarian
- When you feel more comfortable navigating the established library system than the tangle of internet sites

Use the CARS test to determine information quality on the internet.

CREDIBILITY	ACCURACY	REASONABLENESS	SUPPORT
Examine whether a source is believable and trustworthy.	Examine whether information is correct—i.e., factual, comprehensive, detailed, and up to date (if necessary).	Examine whether material is fair, objective, moderate, and consistent.	Examine whether a source is adequately supported with citations.
What are the author's credentials? Look for education and experience; title or position of employment; membership in any known and respected organization; reliable contact information; biographical information; and reputation.	*Is it up to date, and is that important?* If you are searching for a work of literature, such as Shakespeare's play *Macbeth,* there is no "updated" version. However, if you want reviews of its latest productions in major theatres, you will need to note when that material was created. For most scientific research, you will need to rely on the most updated information you can find.	*Does the source seem fair?* Look for a balanced argument, accurate claims, and a reasoned tone that does not appeal primarily to your emotions.	*Where does the information come from?* Look at the site, the sources used by the person or group who compiled the information, and the contact information. Make sure that the cited sources seem reliable and that statistics are documented.
Is there quality control? Look for ways in which the source may have been screened. For example, materials on an organization's website have most likely been reviewed and approved by several members; information coming from an academic journal has to be screened by several people before it is published.	*Is it comprehensive?* Does the material leave out any important facts or information? Does it neglect to consider alternative views or crucial consequences? Although no one source can contain all of the available information on a topic, it should still be as comprehensive as is possible within its scope.	*Does the source seem objective?* While there is a range of objectivity in writing, you want to favour authors and organizations who can control their bias. An author with a strong political or religious agenda or an intent to sell a product may not be a source of the most truthful material.	*Is the information corroborated?* Test information by looking for other sources that confirm the facts in this information—or, if the information is opinion, sources that share that opinion and back it up with their own citations. One good strategy is to find at least three sources that corroborate each other.

(continued)

CREDIBILITY	ACCURACY	REASONABLENESS	SUPPORT
Is there any posted summary or evaluation of the source?	*For whom is the source written, and for what purpose?*	*Does the source seem moderate?*	*Is the source externally consistent?*
You may find abstracts of sources (summary), or a recommendation, rating, or review from a person or organization (evaluation). Either of these—or, ideally, both—can give you an idea of credibility before you decide to examine a source in depth.	Looking at what the author wants to accomplish will help you assess whether it has a bias. Sometimes biased information will not be useful for your purpose; sometimes your research will require that you note and evaluate bias (such as if you were to compare Civil War diaries from Union soldiers with those from Confederate soldiers).	Do claims seem possible, or does the information seem hard to believe? Does what you read make sense when compared to what you already know? While wild claims may turn out to be truthful, you are safest to check everything out.	Most material is a mix of both current and old information. External consistency refers to whether the old information agrees with what you already know. If a source contradicts something you know to be true, chances are higher that the information new to you may be inconsistent as well.
Signals of a potential lack of credibility:	*Signals of a potential lack of accuracy:*	*Signals of a potential lack of reasonableness:*	*Signals of a potential lack of support:*
Anonymous materials, negative evaluations, little or no evidence of quality control, bad grammar or misspelled words	Lack of date or old date, generalizations, one-sided views that do not acknowledge opposing arguments	Extreme or emotional language, sweeping statements, conflict of interest, inconsistencies or contradictions	Statistics without sources, lack of documentation, lack of corroboration using other reliable sources

Source: Robert Harris, "Evaluating Internet Research Sources," November 17, 1997, VirtualSalt, www.virtualsalt.com/evalu8it.htm (accessed September 3, 2008).

The limitations of internet-only research also make it smart to combine internet and library research. Search engines can't find everything, in part because not all sources are in digital format. The internet also prioritizes current information. Furthermore, some digital sources that are not part of your library's subscription offerings cost money.

Your need for solid research skills doesn't stop at graduation—especially in a workplace dominated by information and media. "Work projects may involve interviewing people, researching on the web, library research, taking a look at costs, providing input on support levels, and more . . ." says Victor Yipp of Commonwealth Edison. "These basic skills—being inquisitive and using the library, the internet, and other people to uncover information—will do well for you in school and later on in life."[6]

Library and internet research is often done as a step in writing a research paper. The success of your paper depends on the quality of your research and your ability to communicate what you know in writing.

What is the *writing process*?

The writing process for research papers and essays involves a series of steps that take you from identifying your topic to finalizing your work. The four main parts of the process are planning, drafting, revising, and editing. Analytical, creative, and practical thinking play important roles throughout.

Planning

It is during the six-step planning process that you think about how to tackle the assignment and develop writing and research strategies. Although these steps are listed in sequence, in real life they often overlap.

Pay attention to logistics

Start planning with these practical questions to determine the feasibility of different topics:

1. *How much depth does my instructor expect?* Does she want a basic introduction or a more sophisticated, high-level presentation?
2. *How much time do I have to write the paper?* Consider your other course assignments as well as personal responsibilities, such as part-time work.
3. *How long should the paper be?* Going too far above or below the number of pages your instructor specifies can count against you.
4. *What kind of research is needed?* Your topic and purpose may determine your research sources, and some sources are harder to get than others.
5. *Is it a team project or am I researching and writing alone?* If you are working with others, determine what each person will do and whether others can deliver their work on time.

Answering questions like these will help you decide on a topic and depth of coverage.

Open your mind to topic ideas through brainstorming

Start the process of choosing a paper topic with *brainstorming*—a creative technique to generate ideas without judging their worth (see Chapter 4):

- Begin by writing down anything on the assigned subject that comes to mind, in no particular order. To jump-start your thoughts, scan your text and notes, check library or internet references, or meet with your instructor to discuss ideas.
- Next, organize that list into a logical outline or think link that helps you see the possibilities more clearly.

Key 8.4 shows a portion of an outline constructed from a brainstorming list. The assignment (for an introduction to business class) is to choose an aspect of business ethics and write a short expository research paper on it. Since the student's research is only preliminary, many ideas are in question form.

The Multiple Intelligence Strategies table on page 244 is designed to help harness different learning strategies for choosing a topic and exploring related resources.

MULTIPLE INTELLIGENCE STRATEGIES FOR
Writing ◄

The techniques below allow you to access your power as a writer by uncovering valuable research sources and clearly communicating what you really want to say.

INTELLIGENCE	SUGGESTED STRATEGIES	WHAT WORKS FOR YOU? WRITE NEW IDEAS HERE
Verbal–Linguistic	• Read many resources and take comprehensive notes on them. Summarize the main points from your resources. • Interview someone about the topic and take notes.	
Logical–Mathematical	• Take notes on index cards and organize them according to topics and subtopics. • Create a detailed, sequential outline of your writing project, making sure your argument is logical if your assignment requires persuasive writing.	
Bodily–Kinesthetic	• Pay a visit to numerous sites that hold resources you need or that are related to your topic—businesses, libraries, etc. • After brainstorming ideas for an assignment, take a break involving physical activity. During the break, think about your top three ideas and see what insight occurs to you.	
Visual–Spatial	• Create full-colour charts as you read each resource or interview someone. • Use think link format or another visual organizer to map out your main topic, subtopics, and related ideas and examples. Use different colours for different subtopics.	
Interpersonal	• Discuss material with a fellow student as you gather it. • Pair up with a classmate and become each other's peer editors. Read each other's first drafts and next-to-final drafts, offering constructive feedback.	
Intrapersonal	• Take time to mull over any assigned paper topic. Think about what emotions it raises in you, and why. Let your inner instincts guide you as you begin to write. • Schedule as much research time as possible.	
Musical	• Play your favourite relaxing music while you brainstorm topics for a writing assignment.	
Naturalistic	• Pick a research topic that relates to nature. • Build confidence by envisioning your writing process as a successful climb to the top of a mountain.	

Brainstorming leads to topic ideas and sets the stage for organizing your thoughts.

Topic: <u>Business Ethics</u>

— What are business ethics?
— Recent scandals that raised ethical issues
   — Enron
   — WorldCom
— Who is responsible—the individual or the corporation?
— How do companies encourage ethical business practices?
   — Some companies have written codes of ethics
   — Codes are based on core ethical values that remain constant even as the environment changes
   — Codes of ethics only work if they are part of the corporate culture
— Why do people act unethically in business?
   — The bottom-line culture puts pressure on managers to show increasing profits every quarter.
   — Corporate cultures stress workers out to the point that they no longer ask whether actions are right or wrong.
   — People have such expensive lifestyles that they are willing to cut ethical corners to keep their jobs and earn large bonuses.

Narrow your topic through prewriting strategies

Prewriting strategies, including brainstorming, freewriting, and asking journalists' questions,[7] help you decide which possible topic you would most like to pursue. Use them to narrow your topic, focusing on the specific sub-ideas and examples from your brainstorming session.

Brainstorming. The same creative process you used to generate ideas will help you narrow your topic. Write down your thoughts about the possibilities you have chosen, do some more research, and then organize your thoughts into categories, noticing patterns that appear. See if any of the sub-ideas or examples might make good topics. Asking critical-thinking questions can spark ideas and help you focus on what to write.

Freewriting. When you *freewrite*, you jot down whatever comes to mind without censoring ideas or worrying about grammar, spelling, punctuation, or organization. Freewriting helps you think creatively and gives you an opportunity to piece together what you know about a sub-idea to see if you want to pursue it.

PREWRITING STRATEGIES

Techniques for generating ideas about a topic and finding out how much you already know before you start researching and writing.

Asking journalists' questions helps you choose a topic.

Who?	To whom do companies have an ethical responsibility? Who maintains ethical standards within corporations?
What?	What are business ethics? What is the difference between acting unethically and acting illegally, or are they the same? What is the impact of business codes of ethics on behaviour? What companies have these codes, and what impact have they had on behaviour?
When?	When is the best time for companies to address ethics problems—before or after they occur?
Where?	Do companies all over the country have ethics problems, or is the problem centered in certain geographic areas or industries?
Why?	Why do ethics problems surface? Why do companies make so many mistakes in handling ethics problems?
How?	How do companies train employees to act ethically? How do companies maintain their ethical standards in an ever-changing business environment?

Asking journalists' questions. When journalists start working on a story, they ask themselves: Who? What? When? Where? Why? How? Asking these questions about sub-ideas will help you choose a writing topic.

Prewriting helps you develop a topic that is broad enough for investigation but narrow enough to handle. Prewriting also helps you identify what you know and what you don't know. If an assignment involves more than you already know, you need to do research. Examples of how to apply journalists' questions are outlined in Key 8.5.

Conduct research and make notes

Research develops in stages as you narrow and refine your ideas. In the first brainstorming-for-ideas stage, look for an overview that can lead to a working thesis statement. In the second stage, track down information that fills in gaps. Ultimately, you will have a body of information that you can evaluate to develop and implement your final thesis.

As you research, create source notes and content notes on index cards. These help you organize your work, keep track of your sources, and avoid plagiarism.

- *Source notes* are preliminary notes, usually taken on index cards. Each should include the author's name; title of the work; edition (if any); publisher, year, and city of publication; issue and/or volume number when applicable (such as for a magazine); and page numbers consulted. Notes on internet sources should reference the website's complete name and address, including the numbers and characters that make up the URL. Include a short summary and critical evaluation for each source.

Write a working thesis statement.

Topic	Business ethics
Purpose	To inform
Audience	Instructor who assumes the position of an uninformed reader
Thesis statement	In an environment where so many executives are behaving badly and where corporate reputations are being tarnished, companies are struggling with how to set expectations of ethical behaviour. Most major corporations, including Texas Instruments and Johnson & Johnson, now believe that creating a corporate code of ethics is a critical first step in the process of sensitizing employees to how they should act under normal circumstances and during crises.

- *Content notes* written on large index cards, in a notebook, or on your computer are taken during a thorough reading and provide an in-depth look at sources. Use them to record the information you need to write your draft. To supplement your content notes, make notations—marginal notes, highlighting, and underlining—directly on photocopies of sources.

Write a working thesis statement

Next, organize your research and write a **thesis statement**—the organizing principle of your paper. Your thesis declares your specific subject and point of view and reflects your *writing purpose* (to inform or persuade) and **audience**. Key 8.6 is an example from the paper on business ethics.

Consider this to be your *working thesis*, because it may change as you continue your research and develop your draft. Be ready and willing to rework your writing—and your thesis—one or more times before you hand in your paper.

Write a working outline or think link

The final planning step is to create a working outline or think link to use as a loose structural guide. As you draft, your ideas and direction may change, so be ready to rework your thesis to reflect new material and thoughts.

Drafting

You may write many versions of the assignment until you are satisfied. Each version moves you closer to saying exactly what you want in the way you want to say it. The main challenges you face at the first-draft stage include these:

- Finalizing your thesis
- Defining an organizational structure

THESIS STATEMENT
A statement that is the central core of your paper and around which arguments will be based.

AUDIENCE
The readers of your work for whom your purpose and content must be clear.

Successful Intelligence Connections Online

Listen to author Sarah Kravits describe how to use analytical, creative, and practical intelligence to manage your time and tasks when working through a writing project.

Go to the *Keys to Success* Companion Website at www.pearsoned.ca/carter to listen or download as a podcast.

Write an effective introduction.

Open to the business section of any newspaper and you are likely to find at least one story of a corporate executive on trial and facing jail or a company paying huge fines or court settlements to the government, consumers, or investors. In the last few years, stories of alleged wrongdoing at Enron, WorldCom, Tyco International, Computer Associates, Sotheby's, and Adelphi Communications, to name just a few, have been front-page news. <u>In an environment where so many executives are behaving badly and where corporate reputations are being tarnished, companies are struggling with how to set expectations of ethical behaviour. Most major corporations, including Texas Instruments and Johnson & Johnson, now believe that creating a corporate code of ethics is a critical first step in the process of sensitizing employees to how they should act under normal circumstances and during crises.</u>

- Integrating source material into the body of your paper to fit your structure
- Finding additional sources to strengthen your presentation
- Choosing the right words, phrases, and tone
- Connecting ideas with logical transitions
- Creating an effective introduction and conclusion
- Checking for plagiarism
- Creating a list of works cited

Don't aim for perfection in a first draft. Trying to get every detail right too early in the writing process may shut the door on ideas before you even know they are there.

Freewriting your rough draft

Use everything that you developed in the planning stage as the raw material for freewriting a rough draft. For now, don't think about your introduction, conclusion, or organizational structure. Simply focus on what you want to say. Only after you have written down your thoughts should you begin to shape your work. Many people start with the introduction because it is the beginning of the paper, while others save the introduction for last to make sure it reflects the final product.

Writing an introduction

The introduction tells readers what the paper contains and includes the thesis statement. Look at the introduction for the paper on business ethics. The thesis statement is underlined at the end of the paragraph in Key 8.7.

Creating the body of a paper

The body of the paper contains your central ideas and supporting *evidence*, which underpins your thesis with facts, statistics, examples, and expert

Find the best way to organize the body of the paper.

ARRANGE IDEAS . . .	HOW TO DO IT
. . . by time	Describe events in order or in reverse order.
. . . according to importance	Start with the idea that carries the most weight and move to less important ideas. Or move from the least to the most important ideas.
. . . by problem and solution	Start with a problem and then discuss solutions.
. . . to present an argument	Present one or both sides of an issue.
. . . in list form	Group a series of items.
. . . according to cause and effect	Show how events, situations, or ideas cause subsequent events, situations, or ideas.
. . . through the use of comparisons	Compare and contrast the characteristics of events, people, situations, or ideas.
. . . by process	Go through the steps in a process; a "how-to" approach.
. . . by category	Divide topics into categories and analyze each in order.

opinions. Try to find a structure that helps you organize your ideas and evidence into a clear pattern. Several organizational options are presented in Key 8.8.

Writing the conclusion

A conclusion brings your paper to a natural ending by summarizing your main points, showing the significance of your thesis and how it relates to larger issues, calling the reader to action, or looking to the future. Let the ideas in the body of the paper speak for themselves as you wrap up.

Avoiding plagiarism: Crediting authors and sources

Using another writer's words, content, unique approach, or illustrations without crediting the author is called **plagiarism** and is illegal and unethical. The following techniques will help you properly credit sources and avoid plagiarism:

- **Make source notes as you go.** Plagiarism often begins accidentally during research. You may forget to include quotation marks around a quotation, or you may intend to cite or paraphrase a source but never do. To avoid forgetting, write detailed source and content notes as you research.

- **Learn the difference between a quotation and a paraphrase.** A *quotation* repeats a source's exact words and uses quotation marks to set the words off from the rest of the text. A *paraphrase*, a restatement of the quotation in your own words, requires that you completely rewrite the idea, not just remove or replace a few words.

   As Key 8.9 illustrates, a paraphrase may not be acceptable if the wording is too close to the original. To avoid picking up too much of the original quote, read the quote several times, and then use your own words to communicate the thought without looking back at the quote.

> PLAGIARISM
>
> The act of using someone else's exact words, figures, unique approach, or specific reasoning without giving appropriate credit.

Avoid plagiarism by learning how to paraphrase.

QUOTATION

From Searle, John R. "I Married a Computer." Rev. of *The Age of Spiritual Machines*, by Ray Kurzweil. *New York Review of Books* 8 Apr. 1999: 34+.

"We are now in the midst of a technological revolution that is full of surprises. No one thirty years ago was aware that one day household computers would become as common as dishwashers. And those of us who used the old Arpanet of twenty years ago had no idea that it would evolve into the Internet."

UNACCEPTABLE PARAPHRASE

The current technological revolution is surprising. Thirty years ago, no one expected computers to be as common today as air conditioners. What once was the Arpanet has evolved into the Internet, and no one expected that.

ACCEPTABLE PARAPHRASE

John Searle states that we live in a technologically amazing time of change in which computers have "become as common as dishwashers" (37). Twenty years ago, no one could have predicted the Arpanet would become the Internet (37).

Source: Lynn Quitman Troyka and Douglas Hesse, *Simon & Schuster Handbook for Writers*, Fourth Canadian Edition (Toronto, ON: Pearson Education Canada, 2006) 519–520.

You are less likely to have problems when you integrate your own analysis into your writing and when you connect ideas from different sources.

- **Use a citation even for an acceptable paraphrase.** Take care to credit any source that you quote, paraphrase, or use as evidence. To credit a source, write a footnote or endnote that describes it, using the format preferred by your instructor.
- **Understand that lifting material off the internet is plagiarism.** Words in electronic form belong to the writer just as words in print form do. If you cut and paste sections from a source document into your draft, you are probably committing plagiarism.

Key 8.10 will help you identify what instructors regard as plagiarized work.

Students who plagiarize place their academic careers at risk, in part because the cheating is easy to discover. Increasingly, instructors are using antiplagiarism software to investigate whether strings of words in student papers match those in a database. Make a commitment to hand in your own work and to uphold the highest standards of academic integrity. The potential consequences of cheating are not worth the risk. The Get Analytical exercise on page 252 will help you analyze your attitudes about academic integrity and plagiarism.

Citing Sources

You may be asked to submit different kinds of source lists when you hand in your paper:

- The *References* list, also called the *List of Works Cited*, includes only the sources you actually cited in your paper.
- The *Bibliography* includes all the sources you consulted, whether or not they were cited in the paper.

Plagiarism takes many forms.

key 8.10

Instructors consider work to be plagiarized when you . . .

- Submit a paper from a website that sells or gives away research papers
- Buy a paper from a non-internet service
- Hand in a paper written by a fellow student or a family member
- Copy material in a paper directly from a source without proper quotation marks or source citations
- Paraphrase material in a paper from a source without proper source citation
- Submit the same paper in more than one class, even if the classes are in different terms or even different years

- The *Annotated Bibliography* includes all the sources you consulted as well as an explanation or critique of each source.

Your instructor will tell you which documentation style to use and whether to list notes at the end of the paper (endnotes) or the bottom of the page (footnotes). The general styles of documentation are discipline-specific (for more details, see resource lists at the end of this chapter):

- The Modern Language Association (MLA) format is generally used in the humanities, including history, literature, the arts, and philosophy.
- The American Psychological Association (APA) style is the appropriate format in psychology, sociology, business, economics, nursing, criminology, and social work.
- An alternate documentation style is found in the 15th edition of the *Chicago Manual of Style*, published by the University of Chicago Press.
- The Council of Science Editors (CSE)—formerly called the Council of Biology Editors (CBE)—style is used to cite scientific sources.
- The Columbia Online Style (COS) is often used to cite online sources.

Consult a post-secondary-level writers' handbook for an overview of these documentation styles.

Solicit feedback

Because it is difficult to be objective about your own work, asking for someone else's perspective can be a practical help. Talk with your instructor about your draft, or ask a study partner to read it and answer specific analytical questions like these:

- Is my thesis clear and does my evidence back it up?
- Are the ideas logically connected?
- Are there places where my writing style, choice of words, paragraph structure, or transitions detract from what I am trying to say?
- Am I missing anything?

Be open-minded about the comments you receive. Consider each carefully, and then make a decision about what to change.

Feedback from an instructor, classmate, or writing centre tutor can be invaluable as you revise your writing. These students catch a moment to review each other's work.

Avoid Plagiarism

Complete the following to explore your views on the growing problem of plagiarism:

- Why is plagiarism considered an offence that involves both stealing and lying? Describe how you look at it:

  _____

  _____

  _____

- Citing sources indicates that you respect the ideas of others. List two additional ways in which accurate source citation strengthens your writing and makes you a better student:

  1. _____

  2. _____

- What specific penalties for plagiarism are described in your college or university handbook? Explain whether you feel that these penalties are reasonable or excessive and whether they will keep students from plagiarizing:

  _____

  _____

  _____

- Many experts believe that researching on the internet is behind many acts of plagiarism. Do you agree? Why or why not?

  _____

  _____

- How do you react when others plagiarize and you don't? Does it affect how you feel about them?

  _____

  _____

Revising

When you revise, you critically evaluate the content, organization, word choice, paragraph structure, and style of your first draft. You evaluate the strength of your thesis and whether your evidence proves it, and you look for logical holes. You can do anything you want at this point to change your work. You can move information from the end of your paper to the front, tweak your thesis to reflect the evidence you presented, or choose a different organizational structure. This is also the time to incorporate ideas from peer reviewers or your instructor.

Key 8.11 shows a paragraph from the first draft of the business ethics paper, with revision comments added.

Engage your analytical thinking skills to evaluate the content and form of your paper. Ask yourself these questions as you revise:

- Does the paper fulfill the requirements of the assignment?
- Do I prove my thesis?

Incorporate revision comments to strengthen your paper.

Like Texas Instruments, Johnson & Johnson developed a code of ethics that *written in plain English,*
~~employees rely on to make decisions.~~ *is a cornerstone of its corporate culture* A simple one-page document that has

(add more detail here)

been in place for more than 60 years, "Our Credo," as the code is called, states

customers, employees, communities, stockholders
J & J's ethical responsibilities to ~~everyone it does business with.~~ It has been trans-

lated into 36 languages for employees, customers, suppliers, governments, and

to consult
shareholders in every market in which it operates, from North America

the
to the far reaches of Africa, Europe, Latin America, the Middle East, and ∧

Asia/Pacific *region* (add footnote—Johnson & Johnson: Our Credo).

When Johnson & Johnson updated its credo in the mid-1970s, executives

it continued to represent company values.
examined every word and phrase to make sure ~~they still applied~~ "These meetings

infused the values in the minds of all of us managers," explained Bob Kniffin,

who was *at the time.*
∧ Vice President of External Affairs. J & J's managers had no way of knowing that

prepare them *one of the most*
the exercise they were engaged in would ~~give them the skills~~ to handle a difficult

ever faced by an American company.
challenges Only a few years later, many of the same executives who *scrutinized* ~~examined~~ the

company's credo struggled with how to protect consumers, company employees ∧

and shareholders when bottles of Tylenol were poisoned on store shelves and

innocent people died.

- Will my audience understand my thesis and how I've supported it?
- Does the introduction prepare the reader and capture attention?
- Is the body of the paper organized effectively?
- Does each paragraph have a *topic sentence* that is supported by the rest of the paragraph? (See Chapter 5 for more on topic sentences.)
- Is each idea and argument developed, explained, and supported by examples?
- Are my ideas connected to one another through logical transitions?
- Do I have a clear, concise, simple writing style?
- Does the conclusion provide a natural ending without introducing new ideas?

Check for clarity and conciseness

Now check for sense, continuity, and clarity. Focus also on tightening your prose and eliminating wordy phrases. Examine once again how paragraphs

STRESSBUSTER

ALICIA BRETT   St. Francis Xavier University, Antigonish, Nova Scotia

What part of the writing process (researching, planning, drafting, revising, editing) causes you the most stress, and why? What techniques do you use to minimize stress when writing longer papers? If you had to give an oral presentation in front of your class, would you be stressed? How would you overcome this challenge?

Drafting is the most difficult part of the writing process for me. Planning is not a problem, but when I have all my thought maps and summaries prepared, I still don't know where to begin. I often find myself staring at a blank page. When there is nothing left to do but write, I sit down and remind myself that I have to start with something—anything—so that I can edit and revise. Then the words start coming, and by following my framework, things start to fall into place. If I've thought about the assignment and how I want the concepts to be organized, then I know where to add information, citations, and examples so that the essay flows. It's hard to take ideas and find the right words with which to convey them; however, mediocre words will do for the time being. Tweaking the paper comes later.

To keep stress at a minimum when writing long papers, I break down the assignment into chunks of work, and when I complete each, I reward myself by doing something fun, like watching TV with friends. When I sit down to work and I'm having an especially rough time, I go for a quick walk and think of everything but the paper. Then I'm ready to think when I return.

Oral presentations stress me out. If I were to give a presentation to my class, I would make sure that I knew the material well beforehand. I'd practise, to myself and to others, and ask my practice audience to think of questions for me. That way, I could adjust the parts that may be unclear in my presentation. Also, if my professor or classmates had questions, I'd be less likely to be caught off guard by them. I would also think about hand gestures and body positioning; the words are important, but so is the delivery.

---

flow into one another by evaluating the effectiveness of your *transitions*—the words, phrases, or sentences that connect ideas. Make your transitions signal what comes next.

Editing

Editing comes last, after you are satisfied with your thesis, ideas, organization, and writing style. It involves correcting technical mistakes in spelling, grammar, and punctuation, as well as checking for consistency in such elements as abbreviations and capitalization. If you use a computer, start with the grammar-check and spell-check features to find mistakes, realizing that you still need to check your work manually. Look also for *sexist language*, which characterizes people according to gender stereotypes and often involves the male pronouns *he* or *his* or *him*.

Peer editing can sharpen your writing. Kristina Torres is convinced that her relationship with fellow student Adam Cole helped make her a better writer. She has worked with Adam for more than three years to

Revise and Edit with the Help of a Checklist

get practical!!

SUCCESSFUL PRACTICAL INTELLIGENCE

When finishing a paper, you have a lot to keep track of. To avoid forgetting important steps, try using a checklist like the one below to organize your work.

Date due	Task	Is it complete?
	Check the body of the paper for clear thinking and adequate evidence.	
	Finalize introduction and conclusion.	
	Check spelling, usage, and grammar.	
	Check paragraph structure.	
	Make sure language is familiar and concise.	
	Check punctuation and capitalization.	
	Check transitions.	
	Eliminate sexist language.	
	Get feedback from peers and/or instructors.	

- Use this checklist for your next paper. Then respond: Did it help you stay focused on tasks and organize your time? Did it help you do your best work?

_____

_____

- On separate sheets, use what you learned in this chapter to create two additional checklists—one for planning your paper and the other for writing your first draft.

fine-tune her work. In one case, Adam helped Kristina cut a 40-page paper in half. "It's hard to do that on your own," she said, "because you get really attached to a line or a section. You need to have someone who can help you step back and take another look at it."[8]

Codes of Ethics Encourage Companies to Do What Is Right

Open to the business section of any newspaper and you are likely to find at least one story of a corporate executive on trial and facing jail or a company paying huge fines or court settlements to the government, consumers, or
investors. In the last few years, stories of alleged wrongdoing at Enron, WorldCom, Tyco International, Computer
Associates, Sotheby's, and Adelphi Communications, to name just a few, have been front-page news. In an
environment where so many executives are behaving badly and where corporate reputations are being tarnished,
companies are struggling with how to set expectations of ethical behaviour. Most major corporations, including
Texas Instruments and Johnson & Johnson, now believe that creating a corporate code of ethics is a critical
first step in the process of sensitizing employees to how they should act under normal circumstances and
during crises.

Business ethics, like personal ethics, are based on values that define actions as right or wrong, good or bad,
proper or improper. Sometimes ethical decisions are clear—for example, almost no one would argue that it is
ethically wrong for an auto maker to hide a major safety defect in order to avoid the cost of recalling thousands of
vehicles—but often they are not. (Should the same manufacturer issue a recall if the defect is likely to affect only
1 in 10 000 cars?) Business decisions in today's complex, competitive marketplace often involve choices that put
a company's morals to the test.

The Josephson Institute of Ethics defines six key concepts to help managers evaluate competing choices
(Josephson Institute of Ethics, 2002). These are trustworthiness (honesty, integrity, promise-keeping, loyalty),
respect (civility, courtesy and decency, dignity and autonomy, tolerance and acceptance), responsibility (accountability, pursuit of excellence, self-restraint), fairness (procedural fairness, impartiality, equity), caring (compassion,
consideration, giving, sharing, kindness), and citizenship (law abiding, community service, protection of
environment). These pillars are among the factors that underlie the ethics codes at Texas Instruments and
Johnson & Johnson.

Texas Instruments places ethics at the core of its corporate culture. First published 45 years ago, TI's code
sets ethical expectations, based on principles and values, for employees to consider every time they make a
decision or take action. To encourage adherence to the highest ethical standards, TI gives each employee
a business-card sized "Ethics Test" to carry at all times (Texas Instruments, 1988). The test—with seven clear
bullet points—is based on TI's core principles and on legal and societal values:

- Is the action legal?
- Does it comply with our values?
- If you do it, will you feel bad?
- How will it look in the newspaper?
- If you know it's wrong, don't do it!
- If you're not sure, ask.
- Keep asking until you get an answer.

To support employees who face ethics-related challenges in an ever-changing and increasingly competitive
business environment, TI established an ethics office in the late 1980s. The function of the office is to make sure
business practices continue to reflect company values, to communicate and reinforce ethical expectations to
every employee, and to give employees feedback on ethics-related problems (Texas Instruments, 1988).

Like Texas Instruments, Johnson & Johnson developed a code of ethics, written in plain English, that is a
cornerstone of its corporate culture. A simple one-page document that has been in place for more than 60 years,
"Our Credo," as the code is called, states J & J's ethical responsibilities to its customers, its employees, the
communities in which it operates, and its stockholders. It has been translated into 36 languages for employees,
customers, suppliers, governments, and shareholders to consult in every market in which it operates, from
North America to the far reaches of Africa, Europe, Latin America, the Middle East, and the Asia/Pacific region
(Johnson & Johnson, 2004).

(continued)

McNamara (1999) describes Johnson & Johnson's updating of its credo in the mid-1970s along with subsequent events. Executives examined every word and phrase to make sure it continued to represent company values. "These meetings infused the values in the minds of all of us managers," explained Bob Kniffin, who was Vice President of External Affairs at the time. J & J's managers had no way of knowing that the exercise they were engaged in would prepare them to handle one of the most difficult challenges ever faced by an American company: Only a few years later, many of the same executives who scrutinized the company's credo struggled with how to protect consumers, company employees, and shareholders when bottles of Tylenol were poisoned on store shelves and innocent people died.

Experts inside and outside the company believed that the examination of the company's credo that had taken place in these meetings guided J & J's decision to recall every bottle of Tylenol and repackage the product at a cost of $100 million. According to Kniffin, who was a key player in the crisis, the ethical road was set before the crisis began. "In a crisis, there's no time for moral conclusions," he said. Those must be done beforehand (quoted in McNamara, 1999).

Corporate codes of ethics are effective only if they are followed. (Even Enron had a code of ethics that was set aside by the board of directors to allow the company to complete unscrupulous deals.) While products and marketing strategies change frequently to meet competitive pressures, core values never change, nor does the expectation (in companies like TI and J & J) that managers will weigh business decisions and actions against these values. The old joke about "business ethics" being a contradiction in terms does not apply at these companies—not only because they have taken the time to institutionalize a code of ethics and to use it to evaluate job candidates, but also because employees are expected to follow its guidelines, even when it hurts the bottom line. When employees choose to break the law, they are dismissed and the authorities are notified. This happened to J & J in 2007 when the head of its medical devices unit was believed to have made improper payments to secure business abroad (Seelye, 2007).

Taking the idea of a written ethics code to another dimension, financial services companies are considering adopting an industry-wide code to set uniform standards of right and wrong for every company (Berman, 2005). That would mean that even in the toughest competitive situations—where millions of dollars in commissions were up for grabs—everyone would be playing by the same ethical rules.

References

Berman, D. K. (2005, March 10). Does Wall Street finally need an ethics code? *Wall Street Journal,* p. C1.
Johnson & Johnson. (2004). *Our credo.* Retrieved February 16, 2005, from *http://www.jnj.com/our_company/ our_credo/index.htm*
Josephson Institute of Ethics. (2002). The six pillars of character. In *Making ethical decisions* [Electronic version]. Retrieved February 22, 2005, from *http://www.josephsoninstitute.org/MED/MED-intro+toc.htm*
McNamara, C. (1999). *Complete guide to ethics management: An ethics toolkit for managers* [Electronic version]. Retrieved February 16, 2005, from *http://www.managementhelp.org/ethics/ethxgde.htm*
Seelye, K. Q. (2007, February 13). J & J says improper payments were made. *New York Times,* p. D1.
Texas Instruments. (1988). The TI ethics quick test. Retrieved March 4, 2005, from *http://www.ti.com/corp/docs/company/citizen/ethics/quicktest.shtml*

Proofreading, the last editing stage, involves reading every word for accuracy. Look for technical mistakes, run-on sentences, and sentence fragments. Look for incorrect word usage and unclear references. A great way to check your work is to read it out loud.

Your final paper reflects all the hard work you put in during the writing process. Ideally, when you are finished, you have a piece of work that shows your writing and thinking ability and that clearly communicates and proves your thesis. Key 8.12, the final version of the business ethics paper, is a product of this writing process. The reference sources follow APA style.

The writing skills you develop during your post-secondary education will be reflected in the documents you give to prospective employers, and these, in turn, will impact the success of your job search. June Brown, of Olive Harvey College, explains how good writing is at the centre of your efforts:

> The written documents you leave with a company may be your most lasting calling card. If your documents are incorrect, messy, or poorly organized, they will leave a negative impression. No matter how well you do in a face-to-face meeting, your cover letter, résumé, and other work-related documents are a record that memorializes who you are. Make sure it is your best work.[9]

How can you deliver an *effective* oral presentation?

In school, you may be asked to deliver a speech, take an oral exam, or present a team project. When you ask a question or make a comment in class, you are using public speaking skills. On the job, you will need these skills to deliver presentations to clients, run meetings, and give speeches.

The public speaking skills that you learn for *formal* presentations help you make a favourable impression in *informal* settings, such as when you meet with an instructor, summarize a reading for your study group, or have a planning session at work. When you are articulate, others take notice.

Prepare as for a writing assignment

Speaking in front of others involves preparation, strategy, and confidence. Planning a speech is similar to planning a piece of writing; you must know your topic and audience and think about presentation strategy, organization, and word choice. Specifically, you should:

- **Think through what you want to say and why.** What is your purpose—to make or refute an argument, present information, entertain? Have a goal for your speech.
- **Plan.** Take time to think about who your listeners are and how they are likely to respond. Then, get organized. Brainstorm your topic—narrow it with prewriting strategies, determine your thesis, write an outline, and do research.
- **Draft your thoughts.** Draft your speech. Illustrate ideas with examples, and show how examples lead to ideas. As in writing, have a clear beginning and end. Start with an attention-getter and conclude with a wrap-up that summarizes your thoughts and leaves your audience with something to remember.
- **Integrate visual aids.** Think about building your speech around visual aids including charts, maps, slides and photographs, and props. Learn software programs to create presentation graphics.

Practise your performance

The element of performance distinguishes speaking from writing. Here are tips to keep in mind:

- **Know the parameters.** How long do you have? Where are you speaking? Be aware of the setting—where your audience will be and what the available props are (e.g., a podium, table, a blackboard).

- **Use index cards or notes.** Reduce your final draft to "trigger" words or phrases that remind you of what you want to say and refer to the cards and to your visual aids during your speech.

- **Pay attention to the physical.** Your body position, voice, and clothing contribute to the impression you make. Your goal is to look and sound good and to appear relaxed. Try to make eye contact with your audience, and walk around if you are comfortable presenting in that way.

- **Practise ahead of time.** Do a test run with friends or alone. If possible, practise in the room where you will speak. Audiotape or videotape your practice sessions and evaluate your performance.

- **Be yourself.** When you speak, you express your personality through your words and presence. Don't be afraid to add your own style to the presentation. Take deep breaths. Smile. Know that you can speak well and that your audience wants to see you succeed. Finally, envision your own success.

Successful Intelligence Wrap-Up

At their heart, researching and writing are about communicating information. When you research, you tap the knowledge of others in the hope of learning something new and valuable. When you write, others read your information and perspective and learn from you. Here's how you have built skills in Chapter 8:

Analytical

You discovered how to select and use the best combination of library and internet sources for research assignments. You explored how to analyze the reliability of specific internet sources. In the Get Analytical exercise, you analyzed your views on plagiarism. In reading the section on writing, you examined the parts and sequence of the writing process.

Creative

In the Get Creative exercise, you used creative skills to explore the pros and cons of internet searching. You considered how to brainstorm topic ideas for a research paper. Considering creative prewriting strategies, such as freewriting and asking journalists' questions, may have inspired new ideas about how you will develop your thesis the next time you write.

Practical

You solidified your understanding of how to conduct a keyword information search of library and internet sources, and sharpened your sense of when to prioritize each type of source. You went through the steps in the writing process including planning, drafting, revising, and editing. In the Get Practical exercise, you used a checklist to make sure you took care of all tasks related to a paper. In the section on plagiarism, you explored specific rules for proper citation.

meraki
μερακι
(meh-ra-kee)

In Greece, when someone says you are acting with *meraki*, he is a giving you a compliment. It means that you are putting your heart, soul, creativity, and intelligence into a task so that your work reflects what's inside you. While the word is traditionally used to describe cooking a wonderful meal and setting an elaborate table, you can use it to refer to accomplishing results that are at your highest level and are uniquely yours.

As a researcher and writer, set a goal of filling your work with your thoughts and analysis, your creativity and organizational ability, your tenacity and skill in tracking down information, and your special way with language. Know in advance that no one else will hand in writing that is exactly like yours, and no one else will experience your satisfaction when the writing hits the mark.[10]

"How can I know what I think until I read what I write?"

NEW YORK TIMES COLUMNIST JAMES RESTON, DURING THE 1962 NEWSPAPER STRIKE

Building World-Class Skills
for Post-secondary, Career and Life Success

SUCCESSFUL INTELLIGENCE
Think, Create, Apply

Be a planner. Engage analytical, creative, and practical skills as you work through the planning stage of writing.

Step 1. Think it through: *Analyze your writing goal.* Imagine that you have been asked to write an essay on a time when you turned a difficulty into an opportunity. First, write a brief description of your topic:

_____

_____

Next, think about your purpose and audience. How might you frame your purpose if you were writing to a person who is going through a tough time and needs inspiration? How would your purpose change if you were writing to an instructor who wanted to know what you learned from a difficult experience? Write your purpose and intended audience here.

_____

_____

_____

_____

Step 2. Think out of the box: *Prewrite to create ideas.* On a separate sheet of paper, use prewriting strategies to start the flow of ideas.

- Brainstorm your ideas.
- Freewrite.
- Ask journalists' questions.

Step 3. Make it happen: *Write a thesis statement.* With the thesis statement, you make your topic as specific as possible and you clearly define your purpose. Write your thesis statement here:

_____

_____

_____

TEAMWORK

Create Solutions Together

Team research. Join with three other classmates and decide on two relatively narrow research topics that interest all of you and that you can investigate by spending no more than an hour in the library. The first topic should be current and in the news—for example, safety problems in sport utility vehicles (SUVs), body piercing, or the changing nature of the Canadian family. The second topic should be more academic and historical—for example, the polio epidemic in the 1950s, the Irish potato famine, or multiculturalism in Canada.

Working alone, team members will use your school's library and the internet to research both topics. Set a research time limit of no more than one hour per topic. The goal should be to collect a list of sources for later investigation. When everyone is finished, the group should come together to discuss the research process. Ask each other questions such as:

- How did you "attack" and organize your research for each topic?
- What research tools did you use to investigate each topic?
- How did your research differ from topic to topic? Why do you think this was the case?
- How did your use of library and internet resources differ from topic to topic?
- Which research techniques yielded the best results? Which techniques led to dead ends?

Next, compare the specific results of everyone's research. Analyze each source for what it is likely to yield in the form of useful information. Finally, come together as a group and discuss what you learned that might improve your approach to library and internet research.

WRITING

Journal and Put Skills to Work

Record your thoughts on a separate piece of paper or in a journal.

Learning from other writers. Identify a piece of powerful writing that you have recently read. (It could be a work of literature, a biography, a magazine or newspaper article, or even a section from one of your college or university texts.) Describe, in detail, why it was powerful. Did it make you feel something, think something, or take action? Why? What can you learn about writing from this piece that you can apply to your own writing?

Real-life writing: Proposing a new student organization. You see a need for a student organization that does not exist at your school. Using your research and writing skills, draft a proposal to the dean of student affairs that accomplishes the following goals:

- States your thesis that students would benefit from the new student organization

- States at least two specific arguments to support your thesis

- Reflects evidence you collected by surveying students who share your interest and by searching the web for other post-secondary institutions that have such an organization.

- States what the organization needs from the school—for example, a place to meet or an academic adviser

Use the stages in the writing process to perfect your proposal, and then ask others to read it over. Finally, consider sending it. Stay open to the possibility of a positive response.

PERSONAL PORTFOLIO

Prepare for Career Success

Writing sample: A job interview cover letter. To secure a job interview, you will, at some point, have to write a letter describing your background and explaining your value to the company. For your portfolio, write a one-page, three-paragraph cover letter to a prospective employer. (The letter will accompany your résumé.) Be creative—you may use fictitious names, but select a career and industry that interest you. Use the format shown in the sample letter in Key 8.13.

- **Introductory paragraph:** Start with an attention-getter—a statement that convinces the employer to read on. For example, name a person the employer knows who told you to write, or refer to something positive about the company that you read in the paper. Identify the position for which you are applying, and tell the employer that you are interested in working for the company.

- **Middle paragraph:** Sell your value. Try to convince the employer that hiring you will help the company in some way. Centre your "sales effort" on your experience in school and the workplace. If possible, tie your qualifications to the needs of the company. Refer indirectly to your enclosed résumé.

- **Final paragraph:** Close with a call to action. Ask the employer to call you, or tell the employer to expect your call to arrange an interview.

Exchange your first draft with a classmate. Read each other's letter and make notes in the margins that try to improve the letter's impact and persuasiveness, as well as its writing style, grammar, punctuation, and spelling. Discuss each letter and make whatever corrections are necessary to produce a well-written, persuasive letter. Create a final draft for your portfolio.

A cover letter should express your job interest and summarize why you are a strong candidate.

First name Last name
1234 Your Street
City, Province Postal Code

November 1, 201X

Ms. Prospective Employer
Prospective Company
5432 Their Street
City, Province Postal Code

Dear Ms. Employer:

On the advice of Mr. X, career centre adviser at Y University, I am writing to inquire about the position of production assistant at C101.5 Radio. I read the description of the job and your company on the career centre's employment-opportunity bulletin board, and I would like to apply for the position.

I will graduate this spring with a degree in communications. Since my second year when I declared my major, I have wanted to pursue a career in radio. For the last year I have worked as a production intern at CCOL Radio, the campus's station, and have occasionally filled in as a disc jockey on the evening news show. I enjoy being on the air, but my primary interest is production and programming. My enclosed résumé will tell you more about my background and experience.

I would be pleased to talk with you in person about the position. You can reach me anytime at (555) 555-5555 or by email at xxxx@xx.com. Thank you for your consideration, and I look forward to meeting you.

Sincerely,

Sign Your Name Here

First name Last name
Enclosure(s) *(use this notation if you have included a résumé or other item with your letter)*

SUGGESTED READINGS

American Psychological Association. *Publication Manual of the American Psychological Association*. 5th ed. Washington: American Psychological Association, 2001.

Becker, Howard S. *Tricks of the Trade: How to Think about Your Research While You're Doing It*. Chicago: University of Chicago Press, 1998.

Booth, Wayne C., Gregory G. Columb, and Joseph M. Williams. *The Craft of Research*. 2nd ed. Chicago: University of Chicago Press, 2003.

Cameron, Julia. *The Right to Write: An Invitation into the Writing Life*. New York: Putnam, 2000.

Council of Science Editors. *Scientific Style and Format: The CSE Manual for Authors, Editors, and Publishers*. 7th ed. Reston, VA: Council of Science Editors, 2006.

Gibaldi, Joseph, and Phyllis Franklin. *MLA Handbook for Writers of Research Papers*. 6th ed. New York: Modern Language Association of America, 2003.

LaRocque, Paula. *Championship Writing: 50 Ways to Improve Your Writing*. Oak Park, IL: Marion Street Press, 2000.

Markman, Peter T., and Roberta H. Markman. *10 Steps in Writing the Research Paper*. 6th ed. New York: Barron's Educational Series, 2001.

Strunk, William, Jr., and E. B. White. *The Elements of Style*. 4th ed. New York: Allyn and Bacon, 2000.

Troyka, Lynn Quitman, and Douglas Hess. *Simon & Schuster Handbook for Writers*. 4th Canadian ed. Toronto: Pearson Education Canada, 2006.

University of Chicago Press Staff. *Chicago Manual of Style*. 15th ed. Chicago: University of Chicago Press, 2003.

Walker, Janice R., and Todd Taylor. *The Columbia Guide to Online Style*. 2nd ed. New York: Columbia University Press, 2006.

Walsch, Bill. *Lapsing into a Comma: A Curmudgeon's Guide to the Many Things That Can Go Wrong in Print—and How to Avoid Them*. New York: Contemporary Books, 2000.

Williams, Joseph M. *Style: Ten Lessons in Clarity and Grace*. Chicago: University of Chicago Press, 2003.

INTERNET RESOURCES

Dr. John Lye from Brock University's English Language and Literature Department offers this webpage of links to help students with all their documentation questions. He also offers other links on improving your writing:
www.brocku.ca/english/jlye/genlinks.php

The University of Toronto offers their students these practical tips on writing essays:
www.utoronto.ca/writing/

Jack Lynch from Rutgers University offers great advice and many useful links for disorganized writers:
http://andromeda.rutgers.edu/~jlynch/Writing/links.html

Need more information about the issue of plagiarism? Check out this handy site:
www.plagiarism.org

The University of Guelph's Learning Commons offers a practical tutorial on academic integrity:
www.academicintegrity.uoguelph.ca

1. Conference Board of Canada, *Employability Skills 2000+*, http://www.conferenceboard.ca/education/learning-tools/pdfs/esp2000.pdf.

2. Andrea L. Foster, "Information Navigation 101," *Chronicle of Higher Education*, March 9, 2007, http://chronicle.com/free/v53/i27/27a03801.htm; Duncan Riley, "World Wide Blog Count for May: Now over 50 Million Blogs," *Blog Herald*, May 25, 2005, www.blogherald.com/2005/05/25/world-wide-blog-count-for-may-now-over-60-million-blogs.

3. Lori Leibovich, "Choosing Quick Hits over the Card Catalog," *The New York Times*, August 10, 2000.

4. Cited in David Hochman, "In Searching We Trust," *New York Times*, March 14, 2004.

5. Robert Harris, "Evaluating Internet Research Sources," VirtualSalt, November 17, 1997, http://www.virtualsalt.com/evalu8it.htm (accessed September 3, 2008).

6. *Keys to Lifelong Learning Telecourse* [Videocassette], directed by Mary Jane Bradbury, Intrepid Films, 2000.

7. Analysis based on Lynn Quitman Troyka, *Simon & Schuster Handbook for Writers* (Upper Saddle River, NJ: Prentice Hall, 1996), 22–23.

8. Thomas Bartlett, "Undergraduates Heed the Writer's Muse: English Departments Add Programs as More Students Push to Write Fiction and Poetry," *Chronicle of Higher Education*, March 15, 2002, http://chronicle.com/weekly/v48/i27/2703901.htm.

9. *Keys to Lifelong Learning Telecourse*.

10. Christopher J. Moore, *In Other Words: A Language Lover's Guide to the Most Intriguing Words around the World* (New York: Walker, 2004), 103.

Slay the Math Anxiety Dragon

Math anxiety is a special form of test anxiety, based on common misconceptions about math such as the notion that people are born with or without an ability to think quantitatively or that men are better at math than women. Students who feel they can't do math may give up without asking for help. On exams, these students may experience a range of physical symptoms—including sweating, nausea, dizziness, headaches, and fatigue—that reduce their ability to concentrate and leave them feeling defeated.

The material in this Study Break is designed to help you deal with the kind of math-related anxiety that affects your grades on exams. As you learn concrete ways to calm your nerves and discover special techniques for math tests, you will feel more confident in your ability to succeed.

Use special techniques for math tests

Use the general test-taking strategies presented in this chapter as well as the techniques below to achieve better results on math exams.

- **Read through the exam first.** When you first get an exam, read through every problem quickly and make notes on how you might attempt to solve the problems.
- **Analyze problems carefully.** Categorize problems according to type. Take the "givens" into account and, before you begin, write down any formulas, theorems, or definitions that apply. Focus on what you want to find or prove.
- **Estimate before you begin** to come up with a "ballpark" solution. Work the problem and check the solution against your estimate. The two answers should be close. If they're not, recheck your calculations. You may have made a calculation error.

Gauge your level of math anxiety

Use the math anxiety questionnaire on the next page to get an idea of your math anxiety level.

Improve your math performance with these techniques.

- Break the calculation into the smallest possible pieces. Go step-by-step and don't move on to the next step until you are clear about what you've done so far.
- Recall how you solved similar problems. Past experience can provide valuable clues.

Are you anxious about math?

Rate each of the following statements on a scale of 1 (Strongly Disagree) to 5 (Strongly Agree).

1. _____ I cringe when I have to go to math class.
2. _____ I am uneasy when asked to go to the board in a math class.
3. _____ I am afraid to ask questions in math class.
4. _____ I am always worried about being called on in math class.
5. _____ I understand math now, but I worry that it's going to get really difficult soon.
6. _____ I tend to zone out in math class.
7. _____ I fear math tests more than any other kind.
8. _____ I don't know how to study for math tests.
9. _____ Math is clear to me in math class, but when I go home it's like I was never there.
10. _____ I'm afraid I won't be able to keep up with the rest of the class.

SCORING KEY

40–50   Sure thing, you have math anxiety.

30–39   No doubt! You're still fearful about math.

20–29   On the fence.

10–19   Wow! Loose as a goose!

Source: Freedman, Ellen. (March 1997). *Test Your Math Anxiety* [online]. Available:www.mathpower.com/anxtest.htm (May 2004).

The best way to overcome math-related anxiety is through practice. Keeping up with your homework, attending class, preparing well for tests, and doing extra problems will help you learn the material and boost your confidence.

Following are 10 additional ways to reduce math anxiety and do well on tests.

1. Overcome your negative self-image about math by remembering that even Albert Einstein wasn't perfect.
2. Ask questions of your teachers and your friends, and seek outside assistance when needed.
3. Math is a foreign language—practise it often.
4. Don't study mathematics by trying to memorize information and formulas.
5. READ your math textbook.
6. Study math according to your personal learning style.
7. Get help the same day you don't understand something.
8. Be relaxed and comfortable while studying math.
9. "TALK" mathematics. Discuss it with people in your class. Form a study group.
10. Develop a sense of responsibility for your own successes and failures.

Source: Adapted from Freedman, Ellen. *Ten Ways to Reduce Math Anxiety* [online]. Available:www.mathpower.com/reduce.htm (May 2004).

- Draw a picture to help you see the problem. Visual images such as a diagram, chart, probability tree, or geometric figure may help clarify your thinking.
- Be neat. Sloppy numbers can mean the difference between a right and a wrong answer. A "4" that looks like a "9" will be marked wrong.
- Use the opposite operation to check your work. Work backward from your answer to see if you are right.
- Look back at the question to be sure you completed everything. Did you answer every part of the question? Did you show all required work?

Decide how well these techniques work for you. Use what you just learned about yourself and math to answer the following questions:

- What did you learn from the math anxiety questionnaire? Describe your current level of math anxiety.

_____

_____

_____

- What effect do you think your attitude toward math will have on your future?

_____

_____

_____

- Which suggestions for reducing math anxiety are you likely to use? How do you think they will help you feel more comfortable with math?

_____

_____

_____

- Which suggestions for improving your performance on math tests are you likely to use?

_____

_____

_____

- What other ways can you think of to improve your math performance?

_____

_____

_____

SELF-STUDY QUIZ

MULTIPLE-CHOICE QUESTIONS

Circle or highlight the answer that seems to fit best.

1. The activity that lies at the heart of critical thinking is
   A. solving problems.
   B. taking in information.
   C. reasoning.
   D. asking questions.

2. *Primary sources* are defined as
   A. periodicals.
   B. original documents.
   C. expert opinions on experimental results.
   D. resource materials.

3. When in class, you should choose a note-taking system that
   A. suits the instructor's style, the course material, and your learning style.
   B. you've used in other classes successfully.
   C. matches what you use when you study outside of class.
   D. is recommended by your instructor.

4. *Association* means
   A. considering how information is updated.
   B. finding the differences between two sets of information.

   C. considering new information on its own terms.
   D. considering new information in relation to information you already know.

5. A library search strategy takes you from
   A. specific reference works to general reference works.
   B. general reference works to specific reference works.
   C. encyclopedias to almanacs.
   D. encyclopedias to the internet.

6. When answering an essay question on a test
   A. spend most of your time on the introduction because the grader sees it first.
   B. skip the planning steps if your time runs short.
   C. use the four steps of the writing process but take less time for each step.
   D. write your essay and then rewrite it on another sheet or booklet.

Complete the following sentences with the appropriate word(s) or phrase(s) that best reflect what you learned in the chapter. Choose from the items that follow each sentence.

1. The three parts of the path of critical thinking are _____, _____, and _____. (recall/idea to example/example to idea; taking in information/asking questions about information/using information; taking in information/using information/communicating information)

2. A broad range of interests and a willingness to take risks are two common characteristics of _____. (creativity, critical thinking, cause and effect)

3. When you begin to read new material, what you already know gives you _____ that help you understand and remember new ideas. (ideas, contexts, headers)

4. In the Cornell note-taking system, Section 2 is called the _____ and is used for filling in comments and diagrams as you review. (cue column, summary area, main body)

5. A _____ is a memory technique that works by connecting information you are trying to learn with simpler or familiar information. (mnemonic device, acronym, idea chain)

6. _____ encourages you to put your _____ ideas on paper and is an important part of the _____ process. (Freewriting/uncensored/planning, Editing/polished/planning, Researching/censored/editing)

The following essay questions will help you organize and communicate your ideas in writing, just as you must do on an essay test. Before you begin answering a question, spend a few minutes planning (brainstorm possible approaches, write a thesis statement, jot down main thoughts in outline or think link form). To prepare yourself for actual test conditions, limit writing time to no more than 30 minutes per question.

1. Describe the steps of the reading strategy SQ3R. What is involved in each step? How does each step contribute to your understanding of your reading material?

2. Write an essay that supports or rejects all or part of the following statement: *"The tests you take in college or university not only help ensure that you acquire important skills and knowledge, but also help prepare you for the day-to-day learning demands that are associated with twenty-first-century careers."* If possible, support your position with references to career areas that interest you.

RELATING TO OTHERS
Communicating in a diverse world

9

> "*Successfully intelligent people question assumptions and encourage others to do so. We all tend to have assumptions about the way things are or should be . . . but creatively intelligent people question many assumptions that others accept, eventually leading others to question those assumptions as well.*"
>
> ROBERT J. STERNBERG

For many students, the college experience brings exposure to new and diverse values, lifestyles, backgrounds, and people. Being open to what is new and different around you can inspire you to question your thinking and beliefs, and ultimately can lead to building respect for others and strong teamwork skills. In this chapter, you will investigate how analytical, creative, and practical abilities can help you build the cultural competence and communication and relationship skills that add to your success as a person and as a student.

Being able to "recognize and respect people's diversity, individual experiences and perspectives" is highlighted by the Conference Board of Canada's *Employability Skills 2000+* profile.[1] Furthermore, the Canadian Charter of Rights and Freedoms offers everyone in Canada "freedom of thought, belief and expression."[2] Diversity isn't just part of your academic experience, it's part of every Canadian's life.

In this chapter you will explore answers to the following questions:

- How can you develop cultural competence? 274
- How can minority students make the most of college or university? 280
- How can you communicate effectively? 281
- How do you make the most of personal relationships? 291
- Successful Intelligence Wrap-Up 295

Analytical

- Evaluating the assumptions that underlie prejudice and stereotypes
- Analyzing how you communicate with others
- Examining how you manage conflict and criticism

Creative

- Brainstorming ways to defuse conflict and anger
- Taking risks that build relationships
- Creating new ideas about what diversity means

Practical

- How to relate to others with cultural competence
- How to communicate effectively
- How to criticize constructively

How can you develop *cultural competence*?

As you learned in Chapter 2, *cultural competence* refers to the ability to understand and appreciate differences among people and to change your behaviour in a way that enhances, rather than detracts from, relationships and communication. According to the National Center for Cultural Competence, to develop cultural competence you must accomplish the following five stages:[3]

1. Value diversity.
2. Identify and evaluate personal perceptions and attitudes.
3. Be aware of what happens when different cultures interact.
4. Build knowledge about other cultures.
5. Use what you learn to adapt to diverse cultures as you encounter them.

As you develop cultural competence, you heighten your ability to analyze how people relate to one another. Most important, you develop practical skills that enable you to connect to others by bridging the gap between who you are and who they are.[4]

Value diversity

Valuing diversity means having a basic respect for, and acceptance of, the differences among people. Every time you meet someone new, you have a choice about how to interact. You won't like everyone you meet, but if you value diversity, you will choose to treat people with tolerance

The value of an open-minded approach to diversity in Canada.

YOUR ROLE	SITUATION	CLOSED-MINDED ACTIONS	OPEN-MINDED ACTIONS
Fellow student	For an assignment, you are paired with a student old enough to be your mother.	You assume the student will be clueless about the modern world. You think she might preach to you about how to do the assignment.	You get to know the student as an individual. You stay open to what you can learn from her experiences and knowledge.
Friend	You are invited to dinner at a friend's house. When he introduces you to his partner, you realize that he is gay.	You are turned off by the idea of two men in a relationship. You make an excuse to leave early. You avoid your friend after that.	You have dinner with the two men and make an effort to get to know more about them, individually and as a couple.
Employee	Your new boss is of a different racial and cultural background than yours.	You assume that you and your new boss don't have much in common. You think he will be distant and uninterested in you.	You rein in your stereotypes. You pay close attention to how your new boss communicates and leads. You adapt to his style and make an effort to get to know him better.

and respect, avoiding assumptions about them and granting them the right to think, feel, and believe without being judged. Being open-minded in this way will help your relationships thrive, as shown in Key 9.1.

Identify and evaluate personal perceptions and attitudes

Whereas people may value the *concept* of diversity, attitudes and emotional responses may influence how people act when they confront the *reality* of diversity in their own lives. As a result, many people have prejudices that lead to damaging stereotypes.

Prejudice

Almost everyone has some level of **prejudice**, meaning that they prejudge others, usually on the basis of characteristics such as gender, race, sexual orientation, and religion. People judge others without knowing anything about them because of the following:

- **Influence of family and culture.** Children learn attitudes, including intolerance, superiority, and hate, from their parents, peers, and community.
- **Fear of differences.** It is human to fear, and to make assumptions about the unfamiliar.
- **Experience.** One bad experience with a person of a particular race or religion may lead someone to condemn all people with the same background.

Stereotypes

Prejudice is usually based on **stereotypes**—assumptions made without proof or critical thinking about the characteristics

PREJUDICE

A preconceived judgment or opinion, formed without just grounds or sufficient knowledge.

STEREOTYPE

A standardized mental picture that represents an oversimplified opinion or uncritical judgment.

of a person or group of people. Stereotyping emerges from the following:

- **A desire for patterns and logic.** People often try to make sense of the world by using the labels, categories, and generalizations that stereotypes provide.
- **Media influences.** The more people see stereotypical images—the airhead beautiful blonde, the jolly fat man—the easier it is to believe that stereotypes are universal.
- **Laziness.** Labelling group members according to a characteristic they seem to have in common takes less energy than exploring the qualities of individuals.

Stereotypes stall the growth of relationships because pasting a label on a person makes it hard for you to see the real person underneath. Even stereotypes that seem "positive" may not be true and may get in the way of perceiving people as individuals. Key 9.2 shows some "positive" and "negative" stereotypes.

Use your analytical abilities to question your own ideas and beliefs and to weed out the narrowing influence of prejudice and stereotyping. Giving honest answers to questions like the following is an essential step in the development of cultural competence:

- How do I react to differences?
- What prejudices or stereotypes come to mind when I see people in real life or the media who are a different colour than I am? From a different culture? Making different choices?
- Where did my prejudices and stereotypes come from?
- Are these prejudices fair? Are these stereotypes accurate?
- What harm can having these prejudices and believing these stereotypes cause?

With the knowledge you build as you answer these questions, move on to the next stage: Looking carefully at what happens when people from different cultures interact.

Stereotypes involve generalizations that may not be accurate.

POSITIVE STEREOTYPE	NEGATIVE STEREOTYPE
Women are nurturing.	Women are too emotional for business.
White people are successful in business.	White people are cold and power-hungry.
Gay men have a great sense of style.	Gay men are sissies.
People with disabilities have strength of will.	People with disabilities are bitter.
Older people are wise.	Older people are set in their ways.
Asians are good at math and science.	Asians are poor leaders.

Expand Your Perception of Diversity

get creative!

SUCCESSFUL INTELLIGENCE
CREATIVE

Heighten your awareness of diversity by examining your own uniqueness.

Being able to respond to people as individuals requires that you become more aware of the diversity that is not always on the surface. Brainstorm 10 words or phrases that describe you. The challenge: Keep references to your ethnicity or appearance (brunette, gay, Aboriginal, wheelchair-dependent, and so on) to a minimum, and fill the rest of the list with characteristics others can't see at a glance (laid-back, only child, 24 years old, drummer, marathoner, interpersonal learner, and so on).

1. _____   6. _____

2. _____   7. _____

3. _____   8. _____

4. _____   9. _____

5. _____   10. _____

Use a separate piece of paper to make a similar list for someone you know well—a friend or family member. Again, stay away from the most obvious visible characteristics. See if anything surprises you about the different image you create of this familiar person.

Be aware of what happens when cultures interact

As history has shown, when people from different cultures interact, they often experience problems caused by lack of understanding, by prejudice, and by stereotypic thinking. At their mildest, these problems create roadblocks that obstruct relationships and communication. At their worst, they set the stage for acts of discrimination and hate crimes.

Discrimination

Discrimination refers to actions that deny people equal employment, education, and housing opportunities, or that treat people as second-class citizens. If you are the victim of discrimination, it is important to know that the Canadian Charter of Rights and Freedoms is on your side: You cannot be denied basic opportunities and rights because of your race, creed, colour, age, gender, national or ethnic origin, religion, marital status, potential or actual pregnancy, or potential or actual illness or disability (unless the illness or disability prevents you from performing required tasks and unless accommodations are not possible).

Despite these legal protections, discrimination is common and often appears on campuses. Students may not want to work with students of other races. Members of campus clubs may reject prospective members because of religious differences. Outsiders may harass students attending

LGBTQ (initials representing *lesbian, gay, bisexual, transgender, queer*) alliance meetings. Instructors may judge students according to their weight, accent, or body piercings.

Hate crimes

⟨ HATE CRIME ⟩

A crime motivated by a hatred of a specific characteristic thought to be possessed by the victim.

When prejudice turns violent, it often manifests itself in **hate crimes** directed at racial, ethnic, and religious minorities, and at homosexuals. The Criminal Code of Canada defines hate crimes as crimes "motivated by bias, prejudice or hate based on race, national or ethnic origin, language, colour, religion, sex, age, mental or physical disability, sexual orientation, or any other similar factor."[5] According to Statistics Canada's pilot survey of hate crime, based on data from 2001 and 2002:[6]

- 57% of hate crimes are motivated by the victim's race or ethnicity.
- The most likely targets of hate crimes in Canada are Jews, Blacks, and Muslims.
- The most common incidents categorized as hate crimes include vandalism (the most common hate crime in Canada), assault, uttering threats, arson, and hate propaganda.

These statistics include only reported incidents, so they tell only a part of the story—many more crimes likely go unreported by victims fearful of what might happen if they contact authorities.

Build cultural knowledge

The successfully intelligent response to discrimination and hate, and the next step in your path toward cultural competence, is to gather knowledge. You have a personal responsibility to learn about people who are different from you, including those you are likely to meet on campus.

What are some practical ways to begin?

- *Read* newspapers, books, magazines, and websites.
- *Ask questions* of all kinds of people, about themselves and their traditions.
- *Observe* how people behave, what they eat and wear, how they interact with others.
- *Travel internationally* to unfamiliar places where you can experience first-hand different ways of living.
- *Travel locally* to equally unfamiliar places where you will encounter a variety of people.
- *Build friendships* with fellow students or co-workers you would not ordinarily approach.

Building knowledge also means exploring yourself. Talk with family, read, and seek experiences that educate you about your own cultural heritage. Then share what you know with others.

Adapt to diverse cultures

Here's where you take everything you have gathered—your value of diversity, your self-knowledge, your understanding of how cultures interact, your information about different cultures—and put it to work with practical actions. With these actions you can improve how you relate to others and perhaps even change how people relate to one another on a larger scale. Think carefully and creatively about what kinds of actions feel right to you. Make choices that you feel comfortable with, that cause no harm, and that may make a difference, however small.

Dr. Martin Luther King Jr. believed that careful thinking could change attitudes. He said:

> The tough-minded person always examines the facts before he reaches conclusions: in short, he postjudges. The tender-minded person reaches conclusions before he has examined the first fact; in short, he prejudges and is prejudiced. . . . There is little hope for us until we become tough minded enough to break loose from the shackles of prejudice, half-truths, and down-right ignorance.[7]

Try the following suggestions. In addition, let them inspire your own creative ideas about what else you can do in your daily life to improve how you relate to others.

Look past external characteristics. If you meet a woman with a disability, get to know her. She may be an accounting major, a daughter, and a mother. She may love baseball, politics, and science fiction novels. These characteristics—not just her physical person—describe who she is.

Put yourself in other people's shoes. Shift your perspective and try to understand what other people feel, especially if there's a conflict. If you make a comment that someone interprets as offensive, for example, think about why what you said was hurtful. If you can talk about it with the person, you may learn even more about how he or she interpreted what you said and why.

Adjust to cultural differences. When you understand someone's way of being and put it into practice, you show respect and encourage communication. If a friend's family is formal at home, dress appropriately and behave formally when you visit. If an instructor maintains a lot of personal space, keep a respectful distance when you visit during office hours. If a study group member takes offence at a particular kind of language, avoid it when you meet.

Help others in need. Newspaper columnist Sheryl McCarthy wrote about an African-American who, in the midst of the 1992 Los Angeles riots, saw an Asian-American man being beaten and helped him to safety: "When asked why he risked grievous harm to save an Asian man he didn't even know, the African-American man said, 'Because if I'm not there to help someone else, when the mob comes for me, will there be someone there to save me?'"[8]

Stand up against prejudice, discrimination, and hate. When you hear a prejudiced remark or notice discrimination taking place, think about what you can do to encourage a move in the right direction. You may choose to make a comment, or to get help by approaching an authority such as an instructor or dean. Sound the alarm on hate crimes—let authorities know if you suspect that a crime is about to occur, join campus protests, and support organizations that encourage tolerance.

Recognize that people everywhere have the same basic needs. Everyone loves, thinks, hurts, hopes, fears, and plans. When you are trying to find common

Make a Difference

Find personal ways to connect with other cultures.

Rewrite three strategies in the Adapt to Diverse Cultures section on pages 278–280 as specific actions to which you commit. For example, "Help others in need" might become "Sign up to tutor in the Writing Centre." Circle or check the number when you have completed each task or, if it is ongoing, when you have begun the change.

1. _____

2. _____

3. _____

ground with diverse people, remember that you are united first through your essential humanity.

How can *minority students* make the most of college or university?

Who fits into the category of "minority student" at your school? The term *minority* includes students of colour; students who are not part of the majority Christian religions; and LGBTQ students. Most colleges and universities have special organizations and support services that centre on minority groups. Among these are specialized student associations, cultural centres, arts groups with a minority focus, residence halls for minority students, minority fraternities and sororities, and political-action groups. Your level of involvement with these groups depends on whether you are comfortable within a community of students who share your background or whether you want to extend your social connections.

Define your experience

When you start school and know no one, it's natural to gravitate to people with whom you share common ground. You may choose to live with a roommate from the same background, sit next to other minority students in class, and attend minority-related social events and parties. However, if you define your *entire* post-secondary experience by these ties, you may be making a choice that limits your understanding of others, thereby limiting your opportunities for growth. Many minority students adopt a balanced approach, involving themselves in activities with members of their group, as well as with the college mainstream.

To make choices as a minority student on campus, ask yourself these questions:

- Do I want to limit my social interactions as much as possible to people who share my background? How much time do I want to spend pursuing minority-related activities?

- Do I want to minimize my ties with my minority group and be "just another student"? Will I care if other minority students criticize my choices?

- Do I want to achieve a balance in which I spend part of my time among people who share my background and part with students from other groups?

You may feel pressured to make certain choices based on what your peers do—but if these decisions go against your gut feelings, they are almost always a mistake. Your choice should be right for you, especially because it will determine your college experiences. Plus, the attitudes and habits you develop now may have implications for the rest of your life—in your choice of friends, where you decide to live, your work, and even your family. Think long and hard about the path you take, and always follow your head and heart.

So far, this chapter has focused on the need to accept and adapt to diversity and the realities of Canadian multiculturalism in many forms. However, some forms of diversity are subtler, including differences in the way people communicate. While one person may be direct and disorganized, another may be analytical and organized, and a third may hardly say a word. Just as there is diversity in skin colour and ethnicity, there is also diversity in the way people communicate.

How can you *communicate effectively?*

Spoken communication that is clear promotes success at school, at work, and in personal relationships. Successfully intelligent communicators analyze and adjust to communication styles, learn to give and receive criticism, analyze and make practical use of body language, and work through communication problems.

Note that language barriers may arise with cross-cultural communication. When speaking with someone who is struggling with your language, make the conversation easier by choosing words the person is likely to know, avoiding slang expressions, being patient, and using body language to fill in what words can't say. Also, invite questions—and ask them yourself—so that you both can be as clear as possible.

Adjust to communication styles

When you speak, your goal is for listeners to receive the message as you intended. Problems arise when one person has trouble "translating" a message that comes from someone with a different style of communication.

Your knowledge of the Personality Spectrum (see Chapter 3) will help you understand different styles of communication. Particular communication styles tend to accompany dominance in particular dimensions. Recognizing specific styles in yourself and others will help you communicate more effectively.

Identifying your styles

Following are some communication styles that tend to be associated with the four dimensions in the Personality Spectrum. No one style is better than another. Successful communication depends on understanding your personal style and becoming attuned to the styles of others.

Thinker-dominant communicators focus on facts and logic. As speakers, they tend to rely on logic to communicate ideas and prefer quantitative concepts to those that are conceptual or emotional. As listeners, they often do best with logical messages. They may also need time to process what they have heard before responding. Written messages—on paper or via email—are often useful because writing can allow for time to put ideas together logically.

Organizer-dominant communicators focus on structure and completeness. As speakers, they tend to deliver well-thought-out, structured messages that fit into an organized plan. As listeners, they often appreciate a well-organized message that defines tasks in clear, concrete terms. As with thinkers, a written format is often an effective form of communication to or from an organizer.

Giver-dominant communicators focus on concern for others. As speakers, they tend to cultivate harmony and work toward closeness in their relationships. As listeners, they often appreciate messages that emphasize personal connection and address the emotional side of the issue. Whether speaking or listening, they often favour direct, face-to-face interaction over written messages.

Adventurer-dominant communicators focus on the present. As speakers, they tend to convey a message as soon as the idea arises and then move on to the next activity. As listeners, they appreciate up-front, short, direct messages that don't get sidetracked. Like givers, they tend to communicate and listen more effectively in person.

What is your style? Use this information not as a label but as a jumping-off point for your self-exploration. Just as people tend to demonstrate characteristics from more than one Personality Spectrum dimension, communicators may demonstrate different styles.

Put your knowledge of communication styles to use

Analyze your style by thinking about the communication styles associated with your dominant Personality Spectrum dimensions. Compare them to how you tend to communicate and how others seem to respond to you. Then, use creative and practical thinking skills to decide what works best for you as a communicator.

Speakers adjust to listeners

Listeners may interpret messages in ways you never intended. Think about how you can address this problem as you read the following example involving a Giver-dominant instructor and a Thinker-dominant student (the listener):

> Instructor: "Your essay didn't communicate any sense of your personal voice."
>
> Student: "What do you mean? I spent hours writing it. I thought it was on the mark."

- Without adjustment: The instructor ignores the student's need for detail and continues to generalize. Comments like, "You need to elaborate. Try writing from the heart. You're not considering your audience," will probably confuse and discourage the student.

- With adjustment: Greater logic and detail will help. For example, the instructor might say: "You've supported your central idea clearly, but you didn't move beyond the facts into your interpretation of what they mean. Your essay reads like a research paper. The language doesn't sound like it is coming directly from you."

Listeners adjust to speakers

As a listener, you can improve understanding by being aware of stylistic differences and translating the message into one that makes sense to you. The following example of an Adventurer-dominant employee speaking to an Organizer-dominant supervisor shows how adjusting can pay off.

> Employee: "I'm upset about the email you sent me. You never talked to me and just let the problem build into a crisis. I don't feel I've had a chance to defend myself."

- Without adjustment: If the supervisor is annoyed by the employee's insistence on direct personal contact, he or she may become defensive: "I told you clearly what needs to be done, and my language wasn't a problem. I don't know what else there is to discuss."

- With adjustment: In an effort to improve communication, the supervisor responds by encouraging the in-person, real-time exchange that is best for the employee. "Let's meet after lunch so you can explain to me how we can improve the situation."

Although adjusting to communication styles helps you speak and listen more effectively, you also need to understand the nature of criticism and learn to handle criticism as a speaker and listener.

Know how to give and receive criticism

Understanding types of criticism

Criticism can be either **constructive** or non-constructive. *Constructive criticism* involves goodwill suggestions for improvement, promoting the hope that things will be better. In contrast, *non-constructive criticism* focuses on what went wrong, doesn't offer alternatives or help, and is often delivered negatively, creating bad feelings and defensiveness.

Consider a case in which someone has continually been late to study group sessions. The group leader can comment in either of these ways:

- **Constructive.** The group leader talks privately with the student: "I've noticed that you've been late a lot. Because our success depends on what each of us contributes, we are all depending on your contribution. Is there a problem that is keeping you from being on time? Can we help?"

CONSTRUCTIVE CRITICISM

Criticism that promotes improvement or development.

- **Non-constructive.** The leader watches the student arrive late and says, in front of everyone, "Nice to see you could make it. If you can't start getting here on time, we might look for someone else who can."

Which comment would encourage you to change your behaviour? When offered constructively and carefully, criticism can help bring about important changes.

While at school, your instructors will constructively criticize your class work, papers, and exams. On the job, constructive criticism comes primarily from supervisors and co-workers. No matter the source, positive comments can help you grow as a person. Be open to what you hear, and always remember that most people want to help you succeed.

Offering constructive criticism

When offering constructive criticism, use the following strategies to be effective:

- **Criticize the behaviour rather than the person.** Avoid personal attacks. "You've been late to five group meetings" is much preferable to "You're lazy."
- **Define the problematic behaviour specifically.** Try to focus on the facts, substantiating with specific examples and minimizing emotions. Avoid additional complaints—people can hear criticisms better if they are discussed one at a time.
- **Suggest new approaches and offer help.** Talk about practical ways of handling the situation. Work with the person to develop creative options. Help the person feel supported.
- **Use a positive approach and hopeful language.** Express the conviction that changes will occur and that the person can turn the situation around.

Receiving criticism

When you find yourself on criticism's receiving end, use the following techniques:

- **Analyze the comments.** Listen carefully, then evaluate what you heard. What does it mean? What is the intent? Try to let unconstructive comments go without responding.
- **Request suggestions on how to change your behaviour.** Ask, "How would you like me to handle this in the future?"
- **Summarize the criticism and your response to it.** Make sure everyone understands the situation.
- **Use a specific strategy.** Use problem-solving skills to analyze the problem, brainstorm ways to change, choose a strategy, and take practical action to make it happen.

Criticism, as well as other thoughts and feelings, may be communicated non-verbally. You will become a more effective communicator if you understand body language.

Understand body language

Body language has an extraordinary capacity to express people's real feelings through gestures, eye movements, facial expressions, body positioning and

Communication ⬅

Using techniques corresponding to your stronger intelligences boosts your communication skills both as a speaker and as a listener.

INTELLIGENCE	SUGGESTED STRATEGIES	WHAT WORKS FOR YOU? WRITE NEW IDEAS HERE
Verbal–Linguistic	• Find opportunities to express your thoughts and feelings to others—either in writing or in person. • Remind yourself that you have two ears and only one mouth. Listening is more important than talking.	
Logical–Mathematical	• Allow yourself time to think through solutions before discussing them—try writing out a logical argument on paper and then rehearsing it orally. • Accept the fact that others may have communication styles that vary from yours and that may not seem logical.	
Bodily–Kinesthetic	• Have an important talk while walking or performing a task that does not involve concentration. • Work out physically to burn off excess energy before having an important discussion.	
Visual–Spatial	• Make a drawing or diagram of points you want to communicate during an important discussion. • If your communication is in a formal classroom or work setting, use visual aids to explain your main points.	
Interpersonal	• Observe how you communicate with friends. If you tend to dominate the conversation, brainstorm ideas about how to communicate more effectively. • Remember to balance speaking with listening.	
Intrapersonal	• When you have a difficult encounter, take time alone to evaluate what happened and to decide how you can communicate more effectively next time. • Remember that in order for others to understand clearly, you may need to communicate more than you expect to.	
Musical	• Play soft music during an important discussion if it helps you, making sure it isn't distracting to the others involved.	
Naturalistic	• Communicate outdoors if that is agreeable to all parties. • If you have a difficult exchange, imagine how you might have responded differently had it taken place outdoors.	

Give Constructive Criticism

Imagine how you would offer constructive criticism.

Briefly describe a situation in your life that could be improved if you were able to offer constructive criticism to a friend or family member. Describe the improvement you want:

_____

_____

Imagine that you have a chance to speak to this person. First describe the setting—time, place, atmosphere—where you think you would be most successful:

_____

_____

Now develop your "script." Keeping in mind what you know about constructive criticism, analyze the situation and decide on what you think would be the best approach. Freewrite what you would say. Keep in mind the goal you want your communication to achieve.

_____

_____

_____

_____

_____

_____

Finally, if you can, make your plan a reality. Will you do it?   Yes   No

If you do have the conversation, note here: Was it worth it?   Yes   No

posture, touching behaviours, vocal tone, and use of personal space. Why is it important to know how to analyze body language?

Non-verbal cues shade meaning. What you say can mean different things depending on body positioning or vocal tone. The statement "That's a great idea" sounds positive. However, said while sitting with your arms and legs crossed and looking away, it may communicate that you dislike the idea. Said sarcastically, the tone may reveal that you consider the idea a joke.

Culture influences how body language is interpreted. For example, in North America, looking away from someone may be a sign of anger or distress; in Japan, the same behaviour is usually a sign of respect.

Non-verbal communication strongly influences first impressions. First impressions emerge from a combination of verbal and non-verbal cues. Non-verbal elements, including tone of voice, posture, eye contact, and speed and style of movement, usually come across first and strongest.

Although reading body language is not an exact science, the following practical strategies will help you use it to improve communication.

- Pay attention to what is said through non-verbal cues. Focus on your tone, your body position, and whether your cues reinforce or contradict your words. Then do the same for those with whom you are speaking. Look for the level of meaning in the physical.
- Note cultural differences. Cultural factors influence how an individual interprets non-verbal cues. In cross-cultural conversation, discover what seems appropriate by paying attention to what the other person does on a consistent basis, and by noting how others react to what you do.
- Adjust body language to the person or situation. What body language might you use when making a presentation in class? Meeting with your adviser? Confronting an angry co-worker? Think through how to use your physicality to communicate successfully.

Communicate across cultures

As you meet people from other countries and try to form relationships with them, you may encounter communication issues that are linked to cultural differences.[9] As you recall from Chapter 2, these problems often stem from the different communication styles that are found in high-context and low-context cultures.

In North American and other low-context cultures, communication is linked primarily to words and to the explicit messages sent through these words. In contrast, in high-context cultures, such as those in the Middle and Far East, words are often considered less important than such factors as context, situation, time, formality, personal relationships, and non-verbal behaviour.

Key 9.3 will help you see how 12 world cultures fit on the continuum of high- to low-context communication styles. Key 9.4 summarizes some major communication differences you should be aware of when talking with someone from a different culture. Being attuned to culture-based communication differences will help you interact comfortably with people who come from different parts of the world.

Language barriers may also arise when communicating cross-culturally. When speaking with someone who is struggling with your language, make the conversation easier by choosing words the person is likely to know, avoiding slang expressions, being patient, and using body language to fill in what words can't say. Also, invite questions—and ask them yourself—so that you both can be as clear as possible.

One of the biggest barriers to successful communication is conflict, which can result in anger and even violence. With effort, you can successfully manage conflict and stay away from those who cannot.

The continuum of high- and low-context cultures.

LOW-CONTEXT CULTURES   **HIGH-CONTEXT CULTURES**

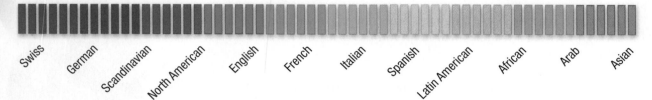

Swiss   German   Scandinavian   North American   English   French   Italian   Spanish   Latin American   African   Arab   Asian

Manage conflict

Conflicts, both large and small, arise when there is a clash of ideas or interests. You may have small conflicts with a housemate over a door left unlocked. You may have major conflicts with your partner about finances or with an instructor about a failing grade. Conflict, as unpleasant as it can be, is a natural element in the dynamic of getting along with others. Prevent it when you can—and when you can't, use problem-solving strategies to resolve it.

Some ways communication differs in high- and low-context cultures.

FACTORS AFFECTING COMMUNICATION	LOW-CONTEXT CULTURES	HIGH-CONTEXT CULTURES
Personal Relationships	The specific details of the conversation are more important than what people know about each other.	Personal trust is the basis for communication, so sharing personal information forms a basis for strong, long-lasting relationships.
Time	People expect others to be punctual and to meet schedules.	Time is seen as a force beyond the person s control. Therefore lateness is common, and not considered rude.
Formality	A certain degree of civility is expected when people meet, including hand-shakes and introductions.	People often require formal introductions that emphasize status differences. As a result, a student will speak with great respect to an instructor.
Eye Contact	Expect little direct eye contact.	• Arab natives may use prolonged, direct eye contact. • Students from Japan and other Far Eastern countries are likely to turn their eyes away from instructors as a sign of respect.
Personal Space	In North America, people converse while remaining between 4 and 12 feet apart.	People from Latin America and the Middle East may sit or stand between 18 inches and 4 feet away from you.

Source: Adapted from Louis E. Boone, David L. Kurtz, and Judy R. Block. *Contemporary Business Communication*, 2nd ed. Upper Saddle River, NJ: Prentice Hall, 1997, p. 72.

Conflict prevention strategies

These two strategies can help you prevent conflict from starting in the first place.

Being assertive. No matter what your dominant learning styles, you tend to express yourself in one of three ways—aggressively, assertively, or passively. Aggressive communicators focus primarily on their own needs and can become impatient when needs are not satisfied. **Assertive** communicators are likely both to get their message across and to give listeners the opportunity to speak, without attacking others or sacrificing their own needs. Passive communicators focus primarily on the needs of others and often deny themselves power, causing frustration.

Key 9.5 contrasts the characteristics of these three. Assertive behaviour strikes a balance between aggression and passivity and promotes the most productive communication. Aggressive and passive communicators can use practical strategies to move toward a more assertive style of communication.

ASSERTIVE

Able to declare and affirm one's own opinions while respecting the rights of others to do the same.

- Aggressive communicators might take time before speaking, use "I" statements, listen to others, and avoid giving orders.
- Passive communicators might acknowledge anger, express opinions, exercise the right to make requests, and know that their ideas and feelings are important.

Send "I" messages. "I" messages help you communicate your needs rather than attacking someone else. Creating these messages involves some simple rephrasing: "You didn't lock the door!" becomes "I felt uneasy when I came to work and the door was unlocked." Similarly, "You never called last night" becomes "I was worried when I didn't hear from you last night."

Assertiveness fosters successful communication.

key 9.5

AGGRESSIVE	ASSERTIVE	PASSIVE
Loud, heated arguing	Expressing feelings without being nasty or overbearing	Concealing one's own feelings
Blaming, name-calling, and verbal insults	Expressing oneself and giving others the chance to express themselves	Feeling that one has no right to express anger
Walking out of arguments before they are resolved	Using "I" statements to defuse arguments	Avoiding arguments
Being demanding: "Do this"	Asking and giving reasons: "I would appreciate it if you would do this, and here's why . . ."	Being noncommittal: "You don't have to do this unless you really want to . . ."

Successful Intelligence Connections Online

Listen to author Sarah Kravits describe how to use analytical, creative, and practical intelligence to manage conflict.

Go to the *Keys to Success* Companion Website at www.pearsoned.ca/carter to listen or download as a podcast.

"I" statements soften the conflict by highlighting the effects that the other person's actions have on you, rather than focusing on the person or the actions themselves. These statements help the receiver feel freer to respond, perhaps offering help and even acknowledging mistakes.

Conflict resolution

All too often, people deal with conflict through avoidance (a passive tactic that shuts down communication) or escalation (an aggressive tactic that often leads to fighting). Conflict resolution demands calm communication, motivation, and careful thinking. Use your analytical, creative, and practical thinking skills to apply the problem-solving plan from Chapter 4.

Trying to calm anger is an important part of resolving conflict. All people get angry at times—at people, events, and themselves. However, excessive anger can contaminate relationships, stifle communication, and turn friends and family away.

Manage anger

Strong emotions can get in the way of happiness and success. It is hard to concentrate on your Canadian history course when you are raging over being cut off in traffic or can't let go of your anger with a friend. Psychologists report that angry outbursts may actually make things worse. When you feel yourself losing control, try some of these practical anger-management techniques.

- **Relax.** Breathe deeply. Slowly repeat a calming phrase or word like "Take it easy" or "Relax."

- **Change your environment.** Take a break from what's upsetting you. Go for a walk, go to the gym, see a movie. Come up with some creative ideas about what might calm you down.

- **Think before you speak.** When angry, most people tend to say the first thing that comes to mind, even if it's hurtful. Inevitably, this escalates the hard feelings and the intensity of the argument. Instead, wait to say something until you are in control.

- **Do your best to solve a problem, but remember that not all problems can be solved.** Instead of blowing up, think about how you can handle what's happening. Analyze a challenging situation, make a plan, resolve to do your best, and begin. If you fall short, you will know you made an effort and be less likely to turn your frustration into anger.

- **Get help if you can't keep your anger in check.** If you consistently lash out, you may need the help of a counsellor. Many schools have mental health professionals available to students.

Your ability to communicate and manage conflict has a major impact on your relationships with friends and family. Successful relationships are built on self-knowledge, good communication, and hard work.

How do you make the most of *personal relationships?*

Personal relationships with friends, classmates, spouses and partners, and parents can be sources of great satisfaction and inner peace. Relationships have the power to motivate you to do your best in school, on the job, and in life.

When things go wrong with relationships, however, nothing in your world may seem right. You may be unable to eat, sleep, or concentrate. Because of this, relationship strategies can be viewed as all-around survival strategies that add to your mental health. Sigmund Freud, the father of modern psychiatry, defined mental health as the ability to love and to work.

Use positive relationship strategies

Here are some strategies for improving your personal relationships.

Prioritize personal relationships. Life is meant to be shared. In some marriage ceremonies, the bride and groom share a cup of wine, symbolizing that the sweetness of life is doubled by tasting it together and the bitterness is cut in half when shared by two.

Spend time with people you respect and admire. Life is too short to hang out with people who bring you down or encourage you to do things that go against your values. Develop relationships with people whose choices you admire and who inspire you to fulfill your potential.

If you want a friend, be a friend. If you treat others with the kind of loyalty and support that you appreciate yourself, you are likely to receive the same in return.

Work through tensions. Negative feelings can fester when left unspoken. Instead of facing a problem, you may become angry about something else or irritable in general. Get to the root of a problem by discussing it, compromising, forgiving, and moving on.

Take risks. It can be frightening to reveal your deepest dreams and frustrations, to devote yourself to a friend, or to fall in love. However, if you open yourself up, you stand to gain the incredible benefits of companionship, which for most people outweigh the risks.

Find a pattern that suits you. Some students date exclusively and commit early. Some students prefer to socialize in groups. Some students date casually. Be honest with yourself—and others—about what you want in a relationship, and don't let peer pressure change your mind.

If a relationship fails, find ways to cope. When an important relationship becomes strained or breaks up, use coping strategies to help you move on. Some people need time alone; others need to be with friends and family. Some seek counselling. Some throw their energy into school or exercise. Some cry. Whatever you do, believe that in time you will emerge from the experience stronger.

Manage communication technology

Modern technology has revolutionized the way people communicate with one another. Not even 30 years ago the telephone, ground mail, and telegrams were the only alternatives to speaking in person. Today, in addition to those existing methods, you can call or text on a mobile phone; you can write a note via email or instant-message from a computer or a PDA such as a BlackBerry or Treo; you can communicate through internet-based venues such as blogs and chat rooms; and you can learn about one another by frequenting social networking sites such as MySpace or Facebook.

© Jason Stitt—Fotolia.com

Younger students, who grew up with technology, tend to use it most. A recent Kaiser Family Foundation study found that 8- to 18-year-olds averaged 6 1/2 hours a day in various media interactions, including texting, cellphones, and networking sites. AOL reports that among Americans aged 16 to 21, 66 percent prefer instant-messaging to email.[10]

Communication technologies have many advantages. You can communicate faster, more frequently, and with more people at one time than ever before. You can be instant-messaging several friends at once while talking on your regular phone, texting on your cellphone, and answering periodic emails. You can also communicate with more control and initiative than you may have in person, which may help you build confidence for face-to-face situations.

However, there are drawbacks. It's easy to misunderstand the tone or meaning of instant messages (IMs), emails, and text messages. Many of these communication methods are addictive—you might look at the clock and realize you've spent 3 hours IM-ing your friends instead of studying for an upcoming test. In addition, spending too much time communicating electronically can limit your real-time personal connections and ultimately derail relationships. Finally, revealing too much about yourself on social networking sites may come back to haunt you. Increasingly, employers are checking MySpace and Facebook for information about prospective job candidates.[11] Before posting words or images, consider whether you may regret your action later on. Once this information is in cyberspace, you cannot pull it back.

Ultimately, students will all have their own personal communication "recipe," consisting of how much they want to communicate and what methods of communication suit them best. The best way for you to create your ideal recipe is to analyze situations carefully, think creatively, and make practical decisions about how to move forward. How do you prefer to communicate with others? What forms of communication do you overuse, and what are the effects? Keep everything in moderation, and let modern communication methods *enhance* in-person interaction rather than replace it.

Avoid destructive relationships

On the far end of the spectrum are relationships that turn destructive. University and college campuses see their share of violent incidents. The more informed you are, the less likely you are to add to these sobering statistics.

Sexual harassment

The facts. Sexual harassment covers a wide range of behaviour, divided into the following types:

- **Quid pro quo harassment** refers to a request for some kind of sexual favour or activity in exchange for something else. It is a kind of bribe or threat. ("If you don't do X for me, I will fail you/fire you/make your life miserable.")
- **Hostile environment harassment** indicates any situation where sexually charged remarks, behaviour, or displayed items cause discomfort. Harassment of this type ranges from lewd conversation or jokes to the display of pornography.

Both men and women can be victims of sexual harassment, although the most common targets are women. Sexist attitudes can create an environment in which men feel they have the right to make statements that degrade women. Even though physical violence is not involved, the fear and mental trauma associated with harassment are harmful.

How to cope. If you feel degraded by anything that goes on at school or work, address the person who you believe is harassing you. If you are uncomfortable doing that, speak to an authority. Try to avoid assumptions—perhaps the person is unaware that the behaviour is offensive. On the other hand, the person may know exactly what is going on and even enjoy your discomfort. Either way, you are entitled to ask the person to stop.

Violence in relationships

The facts. Violent relationships among students are increasing. Here are some chilling statistics from the Canadian Federation of Students:[12]

- The most common form of violence in Canada is male against female. It accounts for almost half of all violent crime in Canada.
- Eighty-seven percent of female victims know their attacker.

Women in their teens and twenties, who make up the majority of women in university and college, are more likely to be victims of domestic violence than are older women. Here's why: First, when trouble occurs, students are likely to turn to friends rather than counsellors or the law. Second, peer pressure makes them uneasy about leaving the relationship. And finally, some inexperienced women may believe that the violence is normal.

How to cope. Start by recognizing the warning signs of impending violence, including possessive, jealous, and controlling behaviour; unpredictable mood swings; personality changes associated with alcohol and drugs; and outbursts of anger. If you see a sign, think about ending the relationship.

If you are being abused, your safety and sanity depend on seeking help. Call a shelter or abuse hotline and talk to someone who understands. Seek counselling at your school or at a community centre. If you need medical attention, go to a clinic or hospital emergency room. If you believe that your life is in danger, get out. Then, get a restraining order that requires your abuser to stay away from you.

Rape and date rape

The facts. Any intercourse or anal or oral penetration perpetrated by a person against another person's will is defined as rape. Rape is primarily a controlling, violent act of rage, not a sexual act.

DATE RAPE
Sexual assault perpetrated
by the victim's escort
during an arranged
social encounter.

Rape, especially acquaintance rape or **date rape**, is a problem on many campuses. Any sexual activity during a date that is against one partner's will constitutes date rape, including situations where one partner is too drunk or drugged to give consent. Currently appearing on campuses is a drug called Rohypnol, also known as "Roofies," that is sometimes used by date rapists to sedate victims. Rohypnol is difficult to detect in a drink. The Canadian Federation of Students offers more sobering numbers on this issue:

- One in five Canadian women is the victim of a sexual assault.
- One in four women of college/university age (18–24) has been sexually assaulted by a date or boyfriend.
- One in five college-/university-aged women admitted being coerced into intercourse with their date/boyfriend.

This last statistic is particularly disturbing because, in 1999, the Supreme Court of Canada ruled that under Canadian law, "no means no":

> A belief that silence, passivity or ambiguous conduct constitutes consent is a mistake in law and provides no defence. An accused cannot say he thought "no" meant "yes." The complainant either consented or not.[13]

How to cope. Beware of questionable situations or drinks when on a date with someone you don't know well or who you suspect is unstable or angry. If you are raped, get medical attention immediately. Don't shower or change clothes; doing so destroys evidence. Next, talk to a close friend or counsellor. Consider reporting the incident to the police or to campus officials, if it occurred on campus. Finally, consider pressing charges, especially if you can identify your assailant. Whether or not you take legal action, continue to get help through counselling, a rape survivor group, or a hotline.

Choose communities that enhance your life

Personal relationships often take place in the context of communities, or groups, that include people who share your interests—for example, martial arts groups, bridge clubs, sororities, fraternities, athletic teams, political groups, etc. It is common to have ties to several communities, often with one holding your greatest interest.

Try to affiliate with communities that are involved in life-affirming activities. You will surround yourself with people who are responsible and character-rich and who may be your friends and professional colleagues for the rest of your life. You may find among them your future husband, wife, or partner; best friend; the person who helps you land your first job; your doctor, accountant, real estate agent, and so on. So much of what you accomplish in life is linked to your network of personal contacts, so start now to make positive connections.

If you find yourself drawn toward communities that are negative and even harmful, such as gangs or groups that haze new members, stop and think before you get in too deep. Be aware of cliques that bring out negative qualities including aggression, hate, and superiority. Use critical thinking to analyze why you are drawn to these groups. In many people, fears and insecurities spur these relationships. Look into yourself to understand the attraction and to resist the temptation to join. If you are

STRESSBUSTER

NANCY E. SHAW   St. Lawrence College, Kingston, Ontario

Have you ever felt that you were stereotyped or prejudged in some way? How did that make you feel? Did it cause you stress? How did you deal with the situation?

I try hard to be true to myself all the time, whether I'm choosing what courses to take next semester or what toppings I want on my sub. Unfortunately, it's not always that easy. When it come to my choice of clothes, sometimes I like to wear skirts, heels, and makeup, but more often I just want to wear jeans and my coziest sweater.

Since I've been at college, I've noticed that on the days I dress up that guys hold doors for me, let me off the bus first, and ask me for the time even though they're wearing watches. Why don't I get that kind of attention on a dress-down day? Aren't I the same person no matter what I'm wearing? Why do guys assume that a girl in heels is going to want their company more than a girl in skateboarding shoes?

It stresses me out to think that I have to get out of bed an hour earlier in the morning and put on $10 worth of makeup if I want a cute classmate to talk to me. I feel that I'm the victim of a stereotype: that girls who don't dress to impress don't want attention.

My way of dealing with this is by reminding myself that a guy who talks to me because I'm dressed nicely probably won't be as good a friend as someone who talks to me because he likes the same class I do. No matter what the magazines say that Britney and Buffy wore last week, it's my personality that's going to attract good people. Those guys who only talk to the girls with the good hair, good nails and belly-button rings are missing out on a good thing.

already involved and want out, believe in yourself and be determined. Never consider yourself a "victim."

Successful Intelligence Wrap-Up

As you go through life, you have a choice—often many times a day—about how to relate to people and ideas that cross your path. When you make a successfully intelligent choice, considering a new person or perspective with an open and questioning mind, you give yourself the opportunity to learn and grow. Here's how you have built skills in Chapter 9:

Analytical

In the section about cultural competence, you gathered the tools you need to analyze your attitudes toward people, cultures, and values that differ from yours. You explored the ways in which you and others communicate and the effects of various styles. You examined various responses to criticism, conflict, and anger, using the Get Analytical exercise to analyze how to use constructive criticism to improve a specific personal situation.

Creative

In the Get Creative exercise, you used brainstorming techniques to broaden your perspective on your own diversity as well as that of a classmate. You expanded your range of ideas for how to accept and support different people and cultures. The section on communication may have inspired ideas about ways to communicate with others that promote understanding, make the best of criticism, and minimize conflict.

Practical

You considered practical strategies for avoiding prejudice, stereotyping, and discrimination. In the Get Practical exercise, you applied strategies for adapting to diverse cultures to your own life in specific, practical ways. You reinforced your knowledge of practical strategies for communicating effectively with others, nurturing personal relationships, and staying safe in your interpersonal interactions.

taraadin

(tah-rah-den)

The Arabic word *taraadin* includes the concept of "compromise" but contains another level of meaning. Specifically, it refers to a "win-win" solution to a problem, an agreement that brings positive effects to everyone involved.[14]

With the cultural competence that enables you to accept and adjust to the diverse people around you, you have the knowledge necessary to come up with win-win solutions. With the ability to analyze communication and think practically about how to make the best of opportunities to communicate, you have the power to make those solutions happen. Not every problem can be resolved happily for all concerned, but when you can bring about *taraadin* in your life, you will benefit as much as will those around you.

"We cannot live for ourselves alone. Our lives are connected by a thousand invisible threads, and along these sympathetic fibres, our actions run as causes and return to us as results."

AUTHOR HERMAN MELVILLE

PERSONAL TRIUMPH

TOOKA SHAHRIARI   Graduate of the University of British Columbia, Vancouver, BC

Connecting with others can be difficult, especially if you start out with a different cultural background. Tooka Shahriari spoke no English when she came to Canada as a teenager. Through hard work and getting involved in activities, she found her niche. Read the account, then use a separate piece of paper to answer the questions in the Building World-Class Skills feature on page 298.

Our first attempt to leave Iran not only failed, but it cost our family a lot of hard-earned money. We were cheated by the people we paid to get us out. A year later, when I was 13, my mother, aunt and I went to Turkey where we waited for another 12 months for our Canadian immigration papers. Our destination was Vancouver, where my brother and sister were living. My father, who had been taken political prisoner during the Iran–Iraq war, was not permitted to leave Iran. In Turkey, the three of us lived in one room in a boarding house—no kitchen or bathroom. A few months after arriving, I broke my leg. I thought life would never get better for me.

Our flight to Vancouver had a stopover in Calgary and because we didn't speak any English we thought Calgary was Vancouver! Luckily, attentive immigration officials put us back on the plane. I clearly remember spending hours in the shower those first few days making up for a year of cold sponge baths.

I arrived at junior high school in March and immediately began ESL classes. I was so sad because my English progress was slow and I wanted to go to high school in September. A poster in the hall advertising a three-month program of building trails around a northern lake caught my eye. But I didn't know enough English to write the application essay. Instead I wrote, "I want to learn English and make friends." I was one of 12 students chosen and what a lucky break that was. I was totally immersed in English while learning trail-building skills in the beautiful outdoors. I credit that experience for giving me the head start I needed for success in high school.

University was a far greater challenge for me than high school. Every student feels nervous leaving the support of nurturing teachers and familiar friends but the immigrant student experiences much stress learning difficult new concepts in a second language. As well, we must plan career goals that fit in with family expectations. Getting involved in campus politics was a positive way for me to enrich my university life. When I told my brother I was thinking of running for secretary of the student society, he said, "why secretary?" So I ran for president and won! I made lasting friendships with students as we worked together in common goals.

I think success at college or university is easier to achieve if you have clear goals. I knew from a young age that I wanted to work in health care. So when my studies in the first two years seemed overwhelmingly difficult I focused on my goal and wasn't afraid to ask for help. Seeking out the support of one or two of your professors or TAs is a wise thing to do. Teachers want hard-working students to succeed, but you have to make the first move! Also, it gets easier. I found third and fourth year easier in many ways because I had already learned the "ins and outs" in my first two years.

Today, working in my chosen profession, I am very grateful to my family, friends, and teachers for helping me realize my dreams.

SUCCESSFUL INTELLIGENCE

Think, Create, Apply

Learn from the experiences of others. Look back to Tooka Shahriari's Personal Triumph on page 297. After you've read her story, relate her experience to your own life by completing the following:

Step 1. Think it through: *Analyze your experience and compare it to Tooka's.* When in your life have you felt like an outsider, and how does this feeling relate to Tooka's experience? What was the key to finding her place in this new world? What was yours?

Step 2. Think out of the box: *Create a challenge.* Think about the activities and organizations at your school with which you would most feel "at home." Then imagine that none of those are available—and that you are required to get involved with three organizations or activities that you would never naturally choose. How would you challenge yourself? Name the three choices and describe what you think you could gain from your experiences. Consider trying one—for real!

Step 3. Make it happen: *Use practical strategies to connect with others.* Choose one of those organizations or activities that feel natural to you. Then choose one from your list of those that would be a challenge. Now try them both. Contact a person involved with each organization or activity and ask them for details—when the group meets, what the group does, what the time commitment would likely be, what the benefit would be. Then join both in the coming semester, making an effort to get to know others who are involved.

TEAMWORK

Create Solutions Together

Problem solving close to home. Divide into groups of two to five students. Assign one group member to take notes. Discuss the following questions, one at a time:

1. What are the three greatest problems Canada faces with regard to how people get along with and accept others?

2. What could we do to deal with these three problems?

3. What can each individual student do to make improvements? (Talk about what you specifically feel that you can do.)

When all groups have finished, gather as a class and hear each group's responses. Observe the variety of problems and solutions. Notice whether more than one group came up with one or more of the same problems. If there is time, one person in the class, together with your instructor, could gather the responses to Question 3 into an organized document that you can send to your school or local paper.

WRITING

Journal and Put Skills to Work

Record your thoughts on a separate piece of paper or in a journal.

Journal entry: Your experience with prejudice. Have you ever been discriminated against, or encountered any other type of prejudice? Have you been on the other end and acted with prejudice yourself? Describe what happened, your feelings about the situation, and any action that you have taken as a result.

Real-life writing: Improve communication. Few students make use of the wealth of ideas and experience that academic advisers can offer. Think of a question you have—regarding a specific course, major/program of study, or academic situation—that your adviser might help you answer. Craft an email in appropriate language to your adviser, and send it. Then, to stretch your communication skills, rewrite the same email twice more: once in a format you would send to an instructor, and once in a format appropriate for a friend. Send either or both of these if you think the response would be valuable to you.

PERSONAL PORTFOLIO

Prepare for Career Success

Complete the following in your electronic portfolio or on separate sheets of paper.

Compiling a résumé. What you have accomplished in various work and school situations will be important for you to emphasize as you strive to land a job that is right for you. Your roles—on the job, in school, at home, or in the community—help you gain knowledge and experience.

On one electronic page or on a sheet of paper, list your education and skills information. On another, list job experience. For each job, record job title, the dates of employment, and the tasks that the job entailed (if the job had no particular title, come up with one yourself). Be as detailed as possible—it's best to write down everything you remember. When you compile your résumé, you can make this material more concise. Keep this list current by adding experiences and accomplishments as you go along.

Using the information you have gathered, draft a résumé for yourself. Remember that there are many ways to construct a résumé; consult other resources for different styles. You may want to reformat your résumé according to a style that your career counsellor or instructor recommends, that best suits the career area you plan to enter, or that you like best.

Keep your résumé draft on hand—and on a computer disk. When you need to submit a résumé with a job application, update the draft and print it out on high-quality paper.

Here are some general tips for writing a résumé:

- Always put your name and contact information at the top. Make it stand out.

- State an objective if it is appropriate—if your focus is specific or you are designing this résumé for a particular interview or career area.

- List your post-secondary education, starting from the latest and working backward, including summer school, night school, seminars, and accreditations.

- List jobs in reverse chronological order (most recent job first). Include all types of work experience (full-time, part-time, volunteer, internship, and so on).

- When you describe your work experience, use action verbs and focus on what you have accomplished, rather than on the description of assigned tasks.

- Include keywords that are linked to the description of the jobs for which you will be applying.

- List references on a separate sheet. You may want to put "References available upon request" at the bottom of your résumé.

- Use formatting (larger font sizes, different fonts, italics, bold, and so on) and indents selectively to help the important information stand out.

- Get several people to look at your résumé before you send it out. Other readers will have ideas that you haven't thought of and may find errors that you have missed.

SUGGESTED READINGS

Dublin, Thomas, ed. *Becoming American, Becoming Ethnic: College Students Explore Their Roots.* Philadelphia: Temple University Press, 1996.

Feagin, Joe R., Hernan Vera, and Nikitah O. Imani. *The Agony of Education: Black Students at White Colleges and Universities.* New York: Routledge, 1996.

Gonzales, Juan L., Jr. *The Lives of Ethnic Americans.* 2nd ed. Dubuque, IA: Kendall/Hunt, 1994.

Hockenberry, John. *Moving Violations.* New York: Hyperion, 1996.

Levey, Marc, Michael Blanco, and W. Terrell Jones. *How to Succeed on a Majority Campus: A Guide for Minority Students.* Belmont, CA: Wadsworth Publishing Co., 1997.

Qubein, Nido R. *How to Be a Great Communicator: In Person, on Paper, and at the Podium.* New York: John Wiley & Sons, 1996.

Schuman, David. *Diversity on Campus.* Dubuque, IA: Kendall/Hunt, 2001.

Suskind, Ron. *A Hope in the Unseen: An American Odyssey from the Inner City to the Ivy League.* New York: Broadway Books, 1999.

Takaki, Ronald. *A Different Mirror: A History of Multicultural America.* Boston: Little, Brown & Company, 1994.

Tannen, Deborah. *You Just Don't Understand: Women and Men in Conversation.* New York: Perennial Currents, 2001.

Tatum, Beverly Daniel. *"Why Are All the Black Kids Sitting Together in the Cafeteria?" and Other Conversations about Race: A Psychologist Explains the Development of Racial Identity.* Philadelphia: Basic Books, 2003.

Terkel, Studs. *Race: How Blacks and Whites Think and Feel about the American Obsession.* New York: Free Press, 1995.

Trotter, Tamera, and Joycelyn Allen. *Talking Justice: 602 Ways to Build and Promote Racial Harmony.* Saratoga, CA: R & E Publishers, 1993.

INTERNET RESOURCES

Prentice Hall Student Success Supersite (see success stories from students from a diversity of backgrounds):
www.prenhall.com/success

Canadian Charter of Rights and Freedoms is available online:
http://laws.justice.gc.ca/en/charter

Learn about how diversity makes Canada a better place at Canada's Cultural Gateway:
www.culture.ca

The history of multiculturalism in Canada and the importance of respecting our differences:
www.pch.gc.ca/progs/multi/respect_e.cfm

More information about student issues such as date rape is available through the Canadian Federation of Students website:
www.cfs-fcee.ca/html/english/home/index.php

ENDNOTES

1. Conference Board of Canada, *Employability Skills 2000+*, http://www.conferenceboard.ca/education/learning-tools/pdfs/esp2000.pdf.

2. Canadian Charter of Rights and Freedoms, http://laws.justice.gc.ca/en/charter.

3. "Conceptual Frameworks/Models, Guiding Values and Principles," National Center for Cultural Competence, 2002 [online]. Available at: http://gucchd.georgetown.edu//nccc/framework.html (accessed May 2004).

4. Information in the sections on the five stages of building competence is based on Mark A. King, Anthony Sims, and David Osher, "How Is Cultural Competence Integrated in Education?" Cultural Competence [online], www.air.org/cecp/cultural/Q_integrated.htm#def (accessed May 2004).

5. Criminal Code of Canada, http://laws.justice.gc.ca/en/C-46.

6. Statistics Canada, "Pilot Survey of Hate Crime," *The Daily*, June 1, 2004.

7. Martin Luther King, Jr., from his sermon, "A Tough Mind and a Tender Heart," *Strength in Love* (Philadelphia: Fortress Press. 1986), 14.

8. Sheryl McCarthy, *Why Are the Heroes Always White?* (Kansas City, MO: Andrews McMeel, 1995), 137.

9. Information for this section from Philip R. Harris and Robert T. Moran, *Managing Cultural Differences*, 3rd ed. (Houston, TX: Gulf Publishing Company, 1991); and Lennie Copeland and Lewis Griggs, *Going International: How to Make Friends and Deal Effectively in the Global Marketplace* (New York: Random House, 1985).

10. Betsy Israel, "The Overconnecteds," *New York Times Education Life*, November 5, 2006, 20.

11. Ibid.

12. Canadian Federation of Students Fact Sheet, *No Means No: Violence against Women, Date Rape and Drugs*, 1999.

13. Ibid.

14. Christopher J. Moore, *In Other Words: A Language Lover's Guide to the Most Intriguing Words around the World* (New York: Walker, 2004), 69.

PERSONAL WELLNESS
Taking care of yourself

10

"Successfully intelligent people have the ability to delay gratification. People who are unable to delay gratification seek rewards for achieving short-term goals but miss the larger rewards they could receive from accomplishing more important, long-term goals."

ROBERT J. STERNBERG

How well you do in school is directly related to your physical and mental health, in large part because healthy people are more able to manage life's stresses as they arise. The more capable you are of managing stress, the more energy you will have to perform well academically. This chapter examines ways to manage stress through health maintenance, to handle stress-related health issues, and to make effective decisions about drugs, alcohol, tobacco, and sex.

Approach all the topics in this chapter with successful intelligence. Analyze your situations and choices, brainstorm creative options, and take practical actions that work for you. Taking care of your personal health and well-being is another key to success as outlined by the Conference Board of Canada's *Employability Skills 2000+* profile.

In this chapter you will explore answers to the following questions:

- How can you maintain a healthy body and mind? 304

- How can you make effective decisions about alcohol, tobacco, and drugs? 315

- How can you make effective decisions about sex? 322

- *Successful Intelligence Wrap-Up 326*

Analytical

- Evaluating how you react to stress
- Analyzing how your sleep and eating patterns affect you
- Analyzing the effects of alcohol, tobacco, and drug use

Creative

- Brainstorming healthy ways to have fun
- Creating new eating habits
- Coming up with ways to fit exercise into your day

Practical

- How to work toward healthier personal habits
- How to seek support for stress and health issues
- How to make effective decisions about substances and sex

How can you maintain a *healthy* body and mind?

Being as physically and mentally healthy as possible is a crucial stress-management tool. You are making a difference in your health, recent studies say, by simply being in school. Scientists and researchers who study aging report that, statistically, more education is linked to longer life. Some potential causes for this link may be that education teaches cause-and-effect thinking, helping people to plan ahead and make better choices for their health, and that educated people tend to be better equipped **to delay gratification**, reducing risky behaviour.[1]

No one is able to make healthy choices and delay gratification all the time. However, you can pledge to do your best. Focus on your physical health through what you eat, how you exercise, how much you sleep, reviewing your vaccinations, and taking steps to stay safe. Focus on your mental health by recognizing mental health problems related to stress or other causes, and understanding ways to get help.

TO DELAY
GRATIFICATION

To forgo an immediate pleasure or reward in order to gain a more substantial one later.

Choose the right food and eating habits

Making intelligent choices about what you eat can lead to more energy, better general health, and an improved quality of life. However, this is easier said than done, for two reasons in particular. One is that the *food environment* in which most people live—characterized by an overabundance of unhealthful food choices combined with the fact that the cheapest choices are often not the best—does not support people's efforts to choose well.[2]

The second reason is that college or university life can make it tough to eat right. Students spend hours sitting in class or studying, and they tend to eat on the run, build social events around food, and eat as a reaction to stress. Many new students find that the "freshman 15"—referring to 15 pounds that people say freshmen tend to gain in the first year of school—is an unpleasant reality.

Take practical actions for healthy eating

The two key ideas for healthy eating are *balance* (varying your diet) and *moderation* (eating reasonable amounts). It can be tough, however, to eat in a balanced and moderate way when unbalanced and overly generous food choices are consistently available to you. To incorporate these concepts into your day-to-day life, break them down into specific actions like the following.

Target your ideal weight. Your college health clinic has charts of ideal weight ranges for men and women with different body builds and heights. You can also find this information on internet sites such as the Centers for Disease Control and Prevention, which has a calculator for **body mass index (BMI)**, at www.cdc.gov/nccdphp/dnpa/bmi/index.htm. You can also calculate your ideal weight at http://bodyandhealth.canada.com under Tools.

Vary what you eat. Make sure your food choices go beyond one or two food groups. Focus especially on getting a variety of vegetables and fruits into your daily diet. Canada's Food Guide recommends the amounts of food that should be eaten in particular food groups; you can find it at www.hc-sc.gc.ca/fn-an/food-guide-aliment/index_e.html.

Evaluate your eating habits. Evaluate a day's food intake by writing down everything that you ate during that day and calculating the total calories. You may even want to log a week's worth of eating. If your eating habits fall short of your ideal plan, make changes in your eating and exercise to move in a more healthful direction.

Limit fat and cholesterol. Watch the fat and cholesterol content of your food choices. When you cook with fats, use "good" fats like olive and canola oils. When you can, minimize your intake of fried foods and foods that contain *trans fats* (an unsaturated fat, usually produced when plant oils are partially hydrogenated, which has been shown to increase the risk of heart disease).

Cut down on sugar consumption. Try to limit foods that contain mostly empty calories, like candy and sugar soda. Try fresh or dried fruit when you need something sweet, or choose a sugar-free treat. If you normally eat dessert with lunch or dinner, try to do so less frequently.

BODY MASS INDEX (BMI)
A number calculated from your weight and height, which provides a reliable indicator of body fatness.

Successful Intelligence Connections Online

Listen to author Sarah Kravits describe how to use analytical, creative, and practical intelligence to shift your attitudes about food.

Go to the *Keys to Success* Companion Website at www.pearsoned.ca/carter to listen or download as a podcast.

Limit alcohol consumption. Don't be fooled—alcohol is surprisingly calorie-heavy. With a non-lite beer averaging about 150 calories and sweet mixed drinks even more, heavy drinkers can pack on the pounds quickly.

Define small, specific tasks. Pledge to stop drinking soda or to give up French fries. Record your plans on paper so they become real. Check in with yourself to note your progress.

Reduce portion size. A "serving" of cooked pasta is about one-half cup, for example, and cheese about 30 grams. Read packaging carefully—that big bag of M&Ms that you split with a friend, for example, is actually 10 servings, not 2! Many restaurants serve supersized portions that could feed two or three people. When you eat out, don't feel obligated to clear your plate. Take home what you don't finish, or ask for a half portion when you order.

Snack smart. Avoid high-fat, high-sugar foods. Choose snacks with fewer than 200 calories, such as a frozen fruit juice bar or a container of low-fat fruit yogurt.

Plan your meals. Try to eat at regular times and in a regular location. Attempt to minimize late-night eating sprees during study sessions. Avoid skipping meals, since it may make you more likely to overeat later.

Identify "emotional triggers" for your eating. If you eat to relieve stress or handle disappointment, try substituting a positive activity. If you are upset about a course, spend more time studying, talk with your instructor, or write in your journal.

Get help. If you need to lose weight, find a support group, such as Weight Watchers or an on-campus organization, that can help you stay on target.

Set reasonable goals. Losing weight and keeping it off will take time and patience. Start by aiming to lose 5 to 10 percent of your current weight; for example, if you weigh 200 pounds, your weight-loss goal is 10 to 20 pounds. Work toward your goal at a pace of approximately 1 to 2 pounds a week. When you reach it, set a new goal if you need to, or begin a maintenance program.

Get your school to help students make better choices. If it's tough to achieve your goals at your school, become an activist for a "healthy food environment." Advocate for menu improvement and more nutritious choices in the dining halls. Ask to have nutrition information posted in eating areas. See if vending machines can be updated with more healthful options and fewer junk foods.

Understand the effects of obesity

Obesity is a problem of epidemic proportion in Canada. A common measure to determine obesity is the body mass index, which is based on weight and height. The term *obese* refers to having a BMI of 30 or more; *overweight* refers to having a BMI of 25 to 29. If your index is 30 or greater, you are probably carrying 14 or more extra kilograms. Government statistics indicate how widespread—and serious—obesity is:

- Between one-third and one-half of Canadians are overweight.
- You decide if there is a gender "double standard": 50 percent of women are on diets, compared with 23 percent of men.
- Sixty-three percent of college-/university-aged Canadians are concerned about their intake of fat.
- Canadians are eating more fast food. Only 27 percent of Canadians eat a "homemade" meal each day, compared to half of Canadians a decade ago.

Obesity is a major risk factor in the development of adult-onset diabetes, coronary heart disease, high blood pressure, stroke, cancer, and other illnesses. In addition, obese people often suffer social and employment discrimination and may find daily life difficult. Studies have shown that overweight job applicants tend to be reviewed more negatively during interviews, and that overweight employees tend to be paid less than normal-weight people in the same jobs and have a reduced chance of promotion.[3]

Use an online BMI calculator to see if you would be considered either overweight or obese. If you would, consider taking specific actions to improve your health, such as consulting health professionals, enrolling in a reputable and reasonable weight-loss program, and incorporating a regular exercise plan into your life. Striving for the goal of reducing your BMI will improve not only your physical well-being but your mental health as well, and perhaps even your job prospects.

Exercise

Being physically fit makes you healthier, adds energy for things that matter, and helps you handle stress. During physical activity, the brain releases endorphins, chemical compounds that have a positive and calming effect on the body. For maximum benefit, make regular exercise a way of life.

Choosing between types of exercise

There are three general categories of exercises. The type you choose depends on your exercise goals, available equipment, your time and fitness level, and other factors.

- *Cardiovascular training* strengthens your heart and lung capacity. Examples include running, swimming, in-line skating, aerobic dancing, and biking.
- *Strength training* strengthens different muscle groups. Examples include using weight machines and free weights, and doing push-ups and abdominal crunches.
- *Flexibility training* increases muscle flexibility. Examples include stretching and yoga.

Some exercises such as lifting weights or biking fall primarily into one category. Others combine elements of two or all three. For maximum benefit and a comprehensive workout, try alternating exercise methods through **cross-training**. For example, if you lift weights, also use a

CROSS-TRAINING
Alternating types of exercise and combining elements from different types of exercise.

stationary bike for cardiovascular work. If possible, work with a fitness consultant to design an effective program.

Making exercise a priority

Student life, both in school and out, is crammed with responsibilities. You can't always spend two hours a day at the gym, and you may not have the money to join a health club. The following suggestions will help you make exercise a priority:

- Walk to classes and meetings on campus. When you reach your building, use the stairs.
- Find out about using your school's fitness centre.
- Do strenuous chores such as shovelling snow, raking, or mowing.
- Play team recreational sports at school or at a local YMCA.
- Use home exercise equipment such as weights, a treadmill, or a stair machine.
- Work out with a friend or family member to combine socializing and exercise.

Get enough sleep

During sleep, your body repairs itself while your mind sorts through problems and questions. A lack of sleep, or poor sleep, causes poor concentration and irritability, which can mean a less-than-ideal performance at school and at work. Irritability can also put a strain on personal relationships. Making up for lost sleep with caffeine may raise your stress level and leave you more tired than before.

On average, adults need about seven hours of sleep a night, but people in their late teens and early twenties may need eight to nine hours. Gauge your needs by how you feel. If you are groggy in the morning or doze off during the day, you may be sleep-deprived.

Barriers to a good night's sleep

University and college students often get inadequate sleep. Long study sessions may keep you up late, and early classes get you up early. Socializing, eating, and drinking may make it hard to settle down. Some barriers to sleep are within your control, and some are not.

What is out of your control? Barriers such as outside noise may keep you up. Earplugs, playing relaxing music, or moving away from the noise (if you can) may help.

What is within your control? Late nights out, your eating and drinking choices, and your study schedule are often (although not always) within your power to change. Schedule your studying so that it doesn't pile up at the last minute.

Tips for quality sleep

Sleep expert Gregg D. Jacobs recommends the following steps to better sleep:[4]

- Reduce consumption of alcohol and caffeine. Caffeine may keep you awake, especially if you drink it late in the day. Alcohol causes you to sleep lightly, making you feel less rested when you awaken.

Find Health Resources

What resources does your school offer to support your efforts to stay healthy? Write down names, locations, phone numbers, hours, and any other pertinent information for the following:

- Free counselling offered to students: _____

  _____

- Exercise facility: _____

  _____

- Other resource: _____

  _____

Finally, if you don't already have plans to work out at school, make a trip to the exercise facility of your choice this week and see what it has to offer.

- **Exercise regularly.** Regular exercise, especially in the afternoon or early evening, promotes sleep.
- **Take naps.** Studies have shown that taking short afternoon naps can reduce the effects of sleep deprivation.
- **Be consistent.** Try to establish somewhat regular times to wake up and go to bed.
- **Complete tasks an hour or so before sleep.** Give yourself a chance to wind down.
- **Establish a comfortable sleeping environment.** Wear something comfortable, turn down the lights, and keep the room cool. Use earplugs, soft music, or a white noise machine if you're dealing with outside distractions.

Review your immunizations

Immunizations are not just for kids. Adults often need them to prevent diseases in particular circumstances or because they didn't receive a full course of shots as children. The Public Health Agency of Canada's National Advisory Committee on Immunization produces guidelines on immunization. The latest at the time of publication of this text was 2006, with errata and updates published in 2008.[5] Review the sections in that publication on Immunization of Adults and, if applicable, Immunization of Children and Adults with Inadequate Immunization Records. Following the immunization guidelines may prevent major illness or literally save your life. If you think you need any vaccines, check with your doctor or the college or university health service.

Stay safe

Staying safe is another part of staying well and reducing stress. Crime is a reality on campus as it is in any community. Alcohol- and drug-related offences may occur more frequently than other crimes on campus. Some colleges and universities are participating in a program known as Campus Crime Watch. Much like Neighbourhood Watch, it's a community-based crime prevention program. Find out if your school is a member.

Making intelligent choices is a crucial part of staying safe. Take the following practical measures to prevent incidents that jeopardize your well-being.

Be aware of safety issues. Every college has its particular issues—problematic areas of the campus, particular celebrations that get out of hand, bad habits such as students propping open security doors. With awareness, you can steer clear of problems and even work to improve them.

Avoid situations that present clear dangers. Don't walk or exercise alone at night, especially in isolated areas. Don't work or study alone in a building. If a person looks suspicious, contact someone who can help.

Avoid drugs or overuse of alcohol. Anything that impairs judgment makes you vulnerable to assault. Avoid driving while impaired or riding with someone who has taken drugs or alcohol.

Avoid people who make you uneasy. If a fellow student gives you bad feelings, avoid situations that place you alone together. Speak to an instructor if you feel threatened.

Be cautious about giving out personal information online. If you have a MySpace or Facebook page, be careful about the text and photos you post. If you feel that someone is harassing you by email or IM, contact an adviser or counsellor who can help you address the problem.

Recognize mental health problems

It is not enough to have a healthy body. Your well-being also depends on a healthy mind. Staying positive about who you are, making hopeful plans for the future, and building resilience to cope with setbacks will all help you target positive mental health. Students in post-secondary institutions are exposed to a number of stressful situations that can cause *burnout*: physical or emotional exhaustion that results from long-term exposure to stresses. Although you may not be able to eliminate a stressful situation entirely, you may be able to find some ways to relieve the stress or improve the situation. Key 10.1 provides some examples of techniques to avoid burnout.

However, some people experience emotional disorders that make it more difficult than usual to cope with life's stressful situations. If you recognize yourself in any of the following descriptions, take practical steps to improve your health. Most student health centres and campus counselling centres provide both medical and psychological help or referrals for students with emotional disorders.

Depression

Almost everyone has experienced sadness or melancholy after the death of a friend or relative, the end of a relationship, or a setback such as a

Techniques to avoid burnout.

IF YOU ARE IN THIS SITUATION...	AND ENCOUNTER THESE STRESSES...	TRY THESE STRESS RELIEVERS.
You share a room with two first-year students.	Your roommates stay up late every night. Their music keeps you awake and sets your nerves on edge.	Talk with your roommates right away and brainstorm solutions. Offer to wear a sleeping blindfold if they will use stereo headphones when you go to bed.
During your first semester, you join the tennis team, write for the school paper, and carry a full course load.	You miss deadlines, fall asleep in class, and fail a test. Your stress level is high, but you are not sure what to do.	Use the prioritizing skills you learned in Chapter 2 to decide how much you can handle. Then, write a schedule that focuses on your academics and also allows time for activities and relaxation.
You live with your parents and commute to school.	Your parents make it hard to be independent. They question your schedule and even your friends. Your insides feel tight as a drum.	If you explain your feelings and your parents still treat you like a kid, re-evaluate your plan. Consider working part- or full-time and renting an apartment with a friend near school.
You carry a full course load and work part-time to pay your bills.	There's no balance in your life. All you do is work—at your studies and your job. You feel overwhelmed so you drink every night.	Consider dropping a course or cutting back your work hours. Ask the financial aid office about loans that will help you meet expenses. Finally, cut back on your drinking.

job loss. Statistics Canada's Canadian Community Health Survey reports that Canadians are just as likely to suffer from depression as they are from either heart disease or diabetes.[6] While people of all ages can suffer from depression, youth between the ages of 15 and 24 are the most likely to suffer with some form of depression. Despite this alarming reality, only about a third of depression sufferers seek professional help. A depressive disorder is an illness; it is not a sign of weakness or a mental state that can be escaped by just trying to "snap out of it." This illness requires a medical evaluation and is treatable.

A depressive disorder is "a 'whole-body' illness, involving your body, mood, and thoughts."[7] Sociologist Dr. Andrée Demers of the Université de Montréal says students suffering from stress, lack of sleep, and/or depression "tend to exhibit lack of concentration, absenteeism and many leave school before they graduate."[8] Among the symptoms of depression are the following:

- Feeling constantly sad, worried, or anxious
- Difficulty with decisions or concentration
- No interest in classes, people, or activities
- Frequent crying
- Hopeless feelings and thoughts of suicide
- Constant fatigue

Know the causes and symptoms of depression.

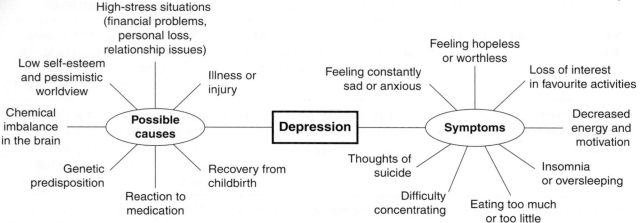

Source: Depression, National Institutes of Health publication 02-3561, National Institutes of Health, 2002.

- Sleeping too much or too little
- Low self-esteem
- Eating too much or too little
- Physical aches and pains
- Low motivation

Depression can have a genetic, psychological, physiological, or environmental cause, or a combination of causes. Key 10.2 describes these causes along with symptoms of depression.

If you recognize any of these feelings in yourself, seek help. Start with your school's counselling office or student health program. You may be referred to a specialist who will help you sort through your symptoms and determine treatment. For some people, adequate sleep, a regular exercise program, a healthy diet, and stress decompression are the solution. For others, medication is important. If you are diagnosed with depression, know that your condition is common, even among college students. Be proud that you have taken a step toward recovery.

Suicide prevention. At its worst, depression can lead to suicide. SAVE (Suicide Awareness Voices of Education), an organization dedicated to suicide prevention education, lists these suicide warning signs[9]:

- Thinking about suicide
- Increased substance use or abuse or change in substance
- Having no sense of purpose or belonging
- Anger
- Feeling of being trapped
- Feeling that there is nothing to live for
- Withdrawal from family, friends, work, school, activities, hobbies
- Anxiety

- High risk-taking behaviour
- Dramatic changes in mood

The website also provides these additional warning signs:

- Talking about suicide
- Statements about hopelessness or worthlessness: "The world would be better off without me"
- Loss of interest in people, things, or activities
- Preoccupation with suicide or death
- Making final arrangements such as visiting or calling family and friends and giving things away
- Sudden sense of happiness or calm (A decision to commit suicide often brings a sense of relief, making others believe that the person "seemed to be on an upswing.")

If you recognize these symptoms in someone you know, do everything you can to get the person to a doctor. Be understanding and patient as you urge action. If you recognize these symptoms in yourself, be your own best friend by reaching out for help.

Eating disorders

Millions of people develop serious and sometimes life-threatening eating disorders every year. The most common disorders are anorexia nervosa, bulimia, and binge eating.

Anorexia nervosa. This condition, occurring mainly in young women, creates an intense desire to be thin, which leads to self-starvation. People with anorexia become dangerously thin through restricting food intake, constant exercise, and use of laxatives, all the time believing they are overweight.

Bulimia. People who binge on excessive amounts of food, usually sweets and fattening foods, and then purge through self-induced vomiting, have bulimia. They may also use laxatives or exercise obsessively. Bulimia can be hard to notice because bulimics are often able to maintain a normal appearance. The causes of bulimia, like those of anorexia, can be rooted in a desire to fulfill a body-type ideal or can come from a chemical imbalance.

Binge eating. Like bulimics, people with a binge-eating disorder eat large amounts of food and have a hard time stopping. However, they do not purge afterwards. Binge eaters are often overweight and feel that they cannot control their eating. As with bulimia, depression and other psychiatric illnesses may contribute to the problem.

Because eating disorders are a common problem on college or university campuses, most student health clinics and campus counselling centres can provide both medical and psychological help.

Mental health issues, stress, and other pressures may lead to substance abuse. The following sections explore the use and abuse of potentially addictive substances.

Stress Management

Everyone handles stress differently—the strategies linked to your stronger intelligences help you improve your coping skills.

INTELLIGENCE	SUGGESTED STRATEGIES	WHAT WORKS FOR YOU? WRITE NEW IDEAS HERE
Verbal–Linguistic	• Keep a journal of what makes you stressed. • Make time to write letters or email friends or talk with them.	
Logical–Mathematical	• Think through problems critically using a problem-solving process and devise a plan. • Analyze possible positive effects that may result from the stress.	
Bodily–Kinesthetic	• Choose a physical activity that helps you release tension—running, yoga, team sports—and do it regularly. • Plan fun physical activities for your free time—go for a hike, take a bike ride, go dancing with friends.	
Visual–Spatial	• Take as much time as you can to enjoy beautiful things—art, nature, etc. Visit an exhibit, see an art film, shoot a roll of film with your camera. • Use a visual organizer to plan out a solution to a stressful problem.	
Interpersonal	• Spend time with people who care about you and are very supportive. • Practise being a good listener to others who are stressed.	
Intrapersonal	• Schedule down time when you can think through what is stressing you. • Allow yourself five minutes a day for visualizing a positive way in which you want a stressful situation to evolve.	
Musical	• Play music that "feeds your soul." • Write a song about what stresses you out—or about anything that transports your mind.	
Naturalistic	• Spend as much time as possible in your most soothing places in nature. • Listen to tapes of outdoor sounds to help you relax.	

How can you make effective decisions *about alcohol, tobacco, and drugs?*

Abusing alcohol, tobacco, and drugs adds significantly to stress levels and can cause financial struggles, emotional traumas, family and financial upheaval, health problems, and even death. As you read the information in this section, think about the effects of your actions on yourself and others, and continually look for new and better ways to make positive, life-affirming choices.

Alcohol

Alcohol is a depressant that slows vital body functions and is the most frequently abused drug on campus. Even a few drinks affect thinking and muscle coordination. Heavy drinking can damage the liver, digestive system, and brain cells and can impair the central nervous system. Prolonged use also leads to **addiction**, making it seem impossible to quit. A survey of Canadian campuses by the Centre for Addiction and Mental Health in 2004 concluded that roughly one-third of Canadian students exhibit behaviours associated with drinking dependency, such as "being unable to stop, failing to perform normal everyday activities or needing a drink first thing in the morning."[10] The study also claims that there are many costs to alcohol abuse. For example, "alcohol-related harms were evident in the survey with 10% reporting alcohol-related assault, 9.8% reporting alcohol-related sexual harassment and 14.1% reporting . . . unplanned sexual relations due to alcohol."[11] In addition, alcohol contributes to the deaths of thousands of people every year through both alcohol-related illnesses and accidents involving drunk drivers.

Of all alcohol consumption, **binge drinking** is associated with the greatest problems, and is consistently an issue on college or university campuses. In a National Survey on Drug Use and Health (NSDUH), 41.9 percent of respondents 18 to 25 years of age reported binge drinking in the month before the survey; 32.9 percent of respondents 26 to 34 years of age reported binge drinking in that same time period.[12]

If you drink, think carefully about the effects on your health, safety, and academic performance. The Get Analytical exercise on page 317, a self-test, will help you analyze your habits. If you think you have a problem, use your creative and practical thinking skills to come up with a viable solution. The information in the section Facing Addiction on pages 318–322 introduces possible options.

Tobacco

The good news is that smoking is on the decline in Canada. This may be due to the increase in public education or in smoking bans. However, the bad news is that about 5 million Canadians over the age of 15 still smoke. That's according to Statistics Canada's 2005 Canadian Tobacco Use

> **ADDICTION**
> Compulsive physiological need for a habit-forming substance.

> **BINGE DRINKING**
> Having five or more drinks (for men) or four or more (for women) at one sitting.

Monitoring Survey. The group with the highest rate of smoking in Canada? 29 percent of men and 23 percent of women aged 20 to 24.[13]

When people smoke, they inhale nicotine, a highly addictive drug found in all tobacco products. Nicotine's immediate effects may include an increase in blood pressure and heart rate, sweating, and throat irritation. Long-term effects may include the following:

- High blood pressure
- Bronchitis and emphysema
- Stomach ulcers
- Heart disease
- For pregnant women, increased risk of infants with low birth weight, premature births, or stillbirths
- Damage to the cells that line the air sacs of the lungs, potentially leading to lung cancer or mouth, throat, and other cancers (lung cancer causes more deaths in Canada than any other type of cancer)[14]

In recent years, the health dangers of **secondhand smoke** have been recognized. This awareness has led many colleges (and local jurisdictions) to ban smoking in classrooms and other public spaces and even in dorm rooms. More and more companies, aware of the risk, are banning smoking in the workplace or even refusing to hire people who smoke.[15]

If you want to quit smoking, your best bet may be to combine medicine with emotional support and habit change. Practical suggestions include these strategies:[16]

- Try a nicotine replacement strategy such as a patch or nicotine gum, and be sure to use it consistently.
- Get support and encouragement from a health care provider, a telephone-based support program such as the Canadian Cancer Society's Smokers' Helpline, a support group such as Nicotine Anonymous, and friends and family.
- Avoid situations that increase your desire to smoke, such as places or events where other smokers gather.
- Find other ways to lower stress and occupy your hands, such as exercise or a hobby you enjoy.
- Set goals. Set a quit date and tell friends and family. Make and keep medical appointments.

The positive effects of quitting—increased life expectancy, lung capacity, and energy—may inspire any smoker to consider making a lifestyle change. Quitting provides financial benefits as well, even if you quit later in life. *MSN Money* reports that "a 40-year-old pack-a-day smoker who quits and puts the savings into a 401(k) [similar to Canada's Registered Retirement Savings Plan] earning 9% a year will have $250,000 by age 70." In addition, there are savings connected to health care costs, cleaning costs (home and car), dental costs, and insurance costs (health and life insurance agencies charge smokers a higher rate).[17]

To assess the level of your potential addiction, you may want to take the self-test in the Get Analytical exercise on page 317, replacing the words "alcohol," "drinking," or "taking drugs" with "cigarettes" or "smoking." Think about your results, weigh your options, and make a responsible choice.

SECONDHAND SMOKE

Smoke in the air exhaled by smokers or given off by cigarettes, cigars, or pipes.

Evaluate your Substance Abuse

Even one "yes" answer may indicate a need to look carefully at your habits. Three or more "yes" answers indicate that you may benefit from discussing your use with a counsellor.

WITHIN THE LAST YEAR:

Y N 1. Have you tried to stop drinking or taking drugs but found that you couldn't do so for long?

Y N 2. Do you get tired of people telling you they're concerned about your drinking or drug use?

Y N 3. Have you felt guilty about your drinking or drug use?

Y N 4. Have you felt that you needed a drink or drugs in the morning—as an "eye-opener"—in order to cope with a hangover?

Y N 5. Do you drink or use drugs alone?

Y N 6. Do you drink or use drugs every day?

Y N 7. Have you found yourself regularly thinking or saying, "I need" a drink or any type of drug?

Y N 8. Have you lied about or concealed your drinking or drug use?

Y N 9. Do you drink or use drugs to escape worries, problems, mistakes, or shyness?

Y N 10. Do you find you need increasingly larger amounts of drugs or alcohol in order to achieve a desired effect?

Y N 11. Have you forgotten what happened while drinking or using drugs because you had a blackout?

Y N 12. Have you been surprised by how much you were using alcohol or drugs?

Y N 13. Have you spent a lot of time, energy, and/or money getting alcohol or drugs?

Y N 14. Has your drinking or drug use caused you to neglect friends, your partner, your children, or other family members, or caused other problems at home?

Y N 15. Have you gotten into an argument or a fight that was alcohol- or drug-related?

Y N 16. Has your drinking or drug use caused you to miss class, fail a test, or ignore schoolwork?

(continued)

(Y) (N) 17. Have you rejected planned social events in favour of drinking or using drugs?

(Y) (N) 18. Have you been choosing to drink or use drugs instead of performing other activities or hobbies you used to enjoy?

(Y) (N) 19. Has your drinking or drug use affected your efficiency on the job or caused you to fail to show up at work?

(Y) (N) 20. Have you continued to drink or use drugs despite any physical problems or health risks that your use has caused or made worse?

(Y) (N) 21. Have you driven a car or performed any other potentially dangerous tasks while under the influence of alcohol or drugs?

(Y) (N) 22. Have you had a drug- or alcohol-related legal problem or arrest (possession, use, disorderly conduct, driving while intoxicated, etc.)?

Source: Compiled and adapted from the *Criteria for Substance Dependence and Criteria for Substance Abuse in the Diagnostic and Statistical Manual of Mental Disorders,* Fourth Edition, published by the American Psychiatric Association, Washington, D.C.; and from materials entitled "Are You An Alcoholic?" developed by Johns Hopkins University.

Drugs

Although alcohol remains the most abused drug by young people in Canada, use of illicit drugs can also be a problem. Drug users rarely think through the possible effects when choosing to take a drug. However, many of the so-called "rewards" of drug abuse are empty. Drug-using peers may accept you for your drug use and not for who you are. Problems and responsibilities may multiply when you emerge from a high. The pain of withdrawal may not compare to the pain of the damage that long-term drug use can do to your body. Key 10.3 shows the most commonly used drugs and their potential effects.

You are responsible for analyzing the potential consequences of what you introduce into your body. Ask questions like the following:

* Why do I want to do this?
* Am I taking drugs to escape from other problems?
* What positive and negative effects might my behavior have?
* Why do others want me to take drugs, and what do I really think of these people?
* How would my drug use affect the people in my life?

Facing addiction

People with addictions have lost control. If you think you may be addicted, take the initiative to seek help. Because substances often cause physical and chemical changes and psychological dependence, habits are

Drugs have potent effects on the user.

DRUG	DRUG CATEGORY	USERS MAY FEEL...	POTENTIAL PHYSICAL EFFECTS	DANGER OF DEPENDENCE
Cocaine (also called *coke, blow, snow*) and **crack cocaine** (also called *crack* or *rock*)	Stimulant	Alert, stimulated, excited, energetic, confident	Nervousness, mood swings, sexual problems, stroke or convulsions, psychosis, paranoia, coma at large doses	Strong
Alcohol	Depressant	Sedated, relaxed, loose	Impaired brain function, impaired reflexes and judgment, cirrhosis, impaired blood production, greater risk of cancer, heart attack, and stroke	Strong with regular, heavy use
Marijuana and hashish (also called *pot, weed, herb*)	Cannabinol	Euphoric, mellow, little sensation of time, paranoid	Impaired judgment and coordination, bronchitis and asthma, lung and throat cancers, anxiety, lack of energy and motivation, hormone and fertility problems	Moderate
Heroin (also called *smack, dope, horse*) and **codeine**	Opiate	Warm, relaxed, without pain, without anxiety	Infection of organs, inflammation of the heart, convulsions, abscesses, risk of needle-transmitted diseases such as hepatitis and HIV	Strong, with heavy use
Lysergic acid diethylamide (LSD) (also called *acid, blotter, trips*)	Hallucinogen	Heightened sensual perception, hallucinations, distortions of sight and sound, little sense of time	Impaired brain function, paranoia, agitation and confusion, flashbacks	Insubstantial
Hallucinogenic mushrooms (also called *shrooms, magic mushrooms*)	Hallucinogen	Strong emotions, hallucinations, distortions of sight and sound, "out of body" experience	Paranoia, agitation, poisoning	Insubstantial
Glue, aerosols (also called *whippets, poppers, rush*)	Inhalants	Giddy, light-headed, dizzy, excited	Damage to brain, liver, lungs, and kidneys; suffocation; heart failure	Insubstantial

(continued)

Continued.

DRUG	DRUG CATEGORY	USERS MAY FEEL...	POTENTIAL PHYSICAL EFFECTS	DANGER OF DEPENDENCE
Ecstasy (also called *X, XTC, vitamin E*)	Stimulant	Heightened sensual perception, relaxed, clear, fearless	Fatigue, anxiety, depression, heart arrhythmia, hyperthermia from lack of fluid intake during use	Insubstantial
Ephedrine (also called *chi powder, zest*)	Stimulant	Energetic	Anxiety, elevated blood pressure, heart palpitations, memory loss, stroke, psychosis, insomnia	Strong
Gamma hydroxyl butyrate (GHB) (also called *G, liquid ecstasy, goop*)	Depressant	Uninhibited, relaxed, euphoric	Anxiety, vertigo, increased heart rate, delirium, agitation	Strong
Ketamine (also called *K, Special K, vitamin K*)	Anesthetic	Dreamy, floating, having an "out of body" sensation, numb	Neuroses, disruptions in consciousness, reduced ability to move	Strong
OxyContin (also called *Oxy, OC, legal heroin*)	Analgesic (containing opiate)	Relaxed, detached, without pain or anxiety	Overdose death can result when users ingest or inhale crushed time-release pills, or take them in conjunction with alcohol or narcotics	Moderate, with long-term use
Anabolic steroids (also called *roids, juice, hype*)	Steroid	Increased muscle strength and physical performance, energetic	Stunted growth, mood swings, male-pattern baldness, breast development (in men) or body hair development (in women), mood swings, liver damage, insomnia, aggression, irritability	Insubstantial
Methamphetamine (also called *meth, speed, crank*)	Stimulant	Euphoric, confident, alert, energetic	Seizures, heart attack, strokes, vein damage (if injected), sleeplessness, hallucinations, high blood pressure, paranoia, psychosis, depression, anxiety, loss of appetite	Strong, especially if taken by smoking

Source: "Drug Facts," n.d., SafetyFirst, Drug Policy Alliance (www.safety1st.org/drugfacts.html).

tough to break, and quitting may involve a painful withdrawal. Asking for help isn't an admission of failure but a courageous move to reclaim your life.

Even one "yes" answer on the self-test may indicate that you need to evaluate your alcohol or drug use and to monitor it more carefully. If you answered "yes" to three or more questions, you may benefit from talking to a professional about your use and the problems it may be causing.

Working through substance-abuse problems can lead to restored health and self-respect. Helpful resources like the following can help you generate options and develop practical plans for recovery:

Counselling and medical care. You can find help from school-based, private, government-sponsored, or workplace-sponsored resources. Ask your school's counselling or health centre, your personal physician, or a local hospital for a referral.

STRESSBUSTER

SOUMIK KANUNGO   Champlain St. Lambert CEGEP, St. Lambert, Quebec

Healthy habits help people deal with the general stresses associated with student life. What do you think are healthy stress management habits and effective stress management techniques?

In order to deal with stress, we must look at what causes it. It can range from problems in the family, moving into a new school environment, having too much work to do in too short a time, or even from a minor change in one's life.

The ways in which I would suggest to reduce and manage stress are creating a timetable of daily activities and following it, talking to friends about your problems, and taking a break from stressful activities and relaxing.

Creating a timetable and following it is probably the best way to deal with stress. It allows a person to be better organized, and to be able to accomplish everything that they want to on any given day.

Talking to friends is also a great way to deal with the general stresses of student life. It gives you the chance to get advice from a friend who might have faced the same problem before, and your friends will be there to support you and to help you manage your stress.

Sometimes people need to take some free time and relax, and you should definitely do that from time to time. It will help you to relieve some stress and to enjoy life more. You can set aside an amount of time where you can do anything you want. You can have fun, watch television, call a friend, go on the internet, walk outside, exercise, or do anything else that you enjoy.

Stress is definitely a big part of life. In order to overcome it we can't ignore it, but have to deal with it using one of these effective techniques.

Detoxification ("detox") centres. If you have a severe addiction, you may need a controlled environment in which to separate yourself completely from drugs or alcohol. Some are outpatient facilities. Other programs provide a 24-hour environment to help you get through the withdrawal period.

Support groups. Alcoholics Anonymous (AA) is the premier support group for alcoholics. Based on a 12-step recovery program, AA membership costs little or nothing. AA has led to other support groups for addicts such as Overeaters Anonymous and Narcotics Anonymous. Many Canadian schools have AA, NA, or other group sessions on campus.

When people address their problems directly instead of avoiding them through substance abuse, they can begin to grow and improve. Working through substance-abuse problems can lead to a restoration of health and self-respect.

How can you make effective decisions *about sex*?

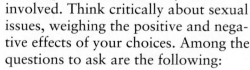

Sexual relationships involve body and mind on many levels. Being informed about sexual decision-making, birth control options, and sexually transmitted infections (STIs) will help you make decisions that are right for you.

Sex and critical thinking

What sexuality means to you and the role it plays in your life are your own business. However, the physical act of sex goes beyond the private realm. Individual sexual conduct can have consequences such as unexpected pregnancy and the transmission of STIs. These consequences affect everyone involved in the sexual act and, often, their families.

Your self-respect depends on making choices that maintain your health and safety, as well as those of the person with whom you are involved. Think critically about sexual issues, weighing the positive and negative effects of your choices. Among the questions to ask are the following:

- Is this what I really want? Does it fit with my values?

- Do I feel ready?

- Is this the right person/moment/ situation? Does my partner truly care for me and not just for what we might be doing? Will this enhance our emotional relationship or cause problems later?

Find More Fun

get creative!

SUCCESSFUL CREATIVE INTELLIGENCE

Broaden your repertoire of fun things to do.

Sometimes, college and university students get involved in potentially unsafe activities because it seems like there isn't anything else to do. Use your creativity to make sure you have a variety of enjoyable activities to choose from when you hang out with friends. Check out your resources: What possibilities can you find at your student union, student activities centre, local arts organizations, athletic organizations, various clubs, or nature groups? Could you go hiking? Paint pottery? Check out a baseball game? Run a 5K? Try a new kind of cuisine? Volunteer at a children's hospital ward? See a play?

Expand your horizons. List here 10 specific activities available to you, and pledge to try one or more in the next month.

1. _____
2. _____
3. _____
4. _____
5. _____

6. _____
7. _____
8. _____
9. _____
10. _____

- Do I have what I need to prevent pregnancy and exposure to STIs? If not, what may be the consequences (pregnancy or disease)? Are they worth it?

Birth control

Using birth control is a choice, and it is not for everyone. For some, using any kind of birth control is against their religious beliefs. Others may want to have children. Many sexually active people, however, choose one or more methods of birth control.

In addition to preventing pregnancy, some birth control methods also protect against sexually transmitted infections. Key 10.4 describes the most established methods of birth control, with effectiveness percentages and STI prevention based on proper and regular use.

Evaluate the pros and cons of each method for yourself as well as for your partner. Consider cost, ease of use, reliability, comfort, and protection against STIs. Communicate with your partner and together make a choice that is comfortable for both of you. For more information, check your library, the internet, or a bookstore; talk to your doctor; or ask a counsellor at the student health centre.

Sexually transmitted infections

Sexually transmitted infections spread through sexual contact (intercourse or other sexual activity that involves contact with the genitals). All are

Make an educated decision about birth control.

METHOD	APPROXIMATE EFFECTIVENESS	PREVENTS STIs?	DESCRIPTION
Abstinence	100%	Only if no sexual activity occurs	Just saying no. No intercourse means no risk of pregnancy. However, alternative modes of sexual activity can still spread STIs.
Condom	85% (95% with spermicide)	Yes, if made of latex	A sheath that fits over the penis and prevents sperm from entering the vagina.
Diaphragm, cervical cap, or shield	85%	No	A bendable rubber cap that fits over the cervix and pelvic bone inside the vagina (the cervical cap and shield are smaller and fit over the cervix only). The diaphragm and cervical cap must be fitted initially by a gynecologist. All must be used with a spermicide.
Oral contraceptives ("the Pill")	99% with perfect use, 92% for typical users	No	A dosage of hormones taken daily by a woman, preventing the ovaries from releasing eggs. Side effects can include headache, weight gain, and increased chances of blood clotting. Various brands and dosages; must be prescribed by a gynecologist.
Injectable contraceptives (Depo-Provera)	97%	No	An injection that a woman must receive from a doctor every few months. Possible side effects may resemble those of oral contraceptives.
Vaginal ring (NuvaRing)	92%	No	A ring inserted into the vagina that releases hormones. Must be replaced monthly. Possible side effects may resemble those of oral contraceptives.
Spermicidal foams, jellies, inserts	71% if used alone	No	Usually used with diaphragms or condoms to enhance effectiveness, they have an ingredient that kills sperm cells (but not STIs). They stay effective for a limited period of time after insertion.
Intrauterine device (IUD)	99%	No	A small coil of wire inserted into the uterus by a gynecologist (who must also remove it). Prevents fertilized eggs from implanting in the uterine wall. May or may not have a hormone component. Possible side effects include increased or abnormal bleeding.
Tubal ligation	Nearly 100%	No	Surgery for women that cuts and ties the fallopian tubes, preventing eggs from travelling to the uterus. Difficult and expensive to reverse. Recommended for those who do not want any, or any more, children.
Vasectomy	Nearly 100%	No	Surgery for men that blocks the tube that delivers sperm to the penis. Like tubal ligation, difficult to reverse and recommended only for those who don't want any, or any more, children.
Rhythm method	Variable	No	Abstaining from intercourse during the ovulation segment of the woman's menstrual cycle. Can be difficult to time and may not account for cycle irregularities.
Withdrawal	Variable	No	Pulling the penis out of the vagina before ejaculation. Unreliable, because some sperm can escape in the fluid released prior to ejaculation. Dependent on a controlled partner.

Source: "Birth Control," 2005, MayoClinic.com (www.mayoclinic.com/health/birth-control/BI99999).

To stay safe, know these facts about sexually transmitted infections.

DISEASE	SYMPTOMS	HEALTH PROBLEMS IF UNTREATED	TREATMENTS
Chlamydia	Discharge, painful urination, swollen or painful joints, change in menstrual periods for women	Can cause pelvic inflammatory disease (PID) in women, which can lead to sterility or ectopic pregnancies; infection; miscarriage or premature birth.	Curable with full course of antibiotics; avoid sex until treatment is complete.
Gonorrhea	Discharge, burning while urinating	Can cause PID, swelling of testicles and penis, arthritis, skin problems, infections.	Usually curable with antibiotics; however, certain strains are becoming resistant to medication.
Genital herpes	Blisterlike itchy sores in the genital area, headache, fever, chills	Symptoms may subside and then reoccur, often in response to high stress levels; carriers can transmit the virus even when it is dormant.	No cure; some medications, such as Acyclovir, reduce and help heal the sores and may shorten recurring outbreaks.
Syphilis	A genital sore lasting one to five weeks, followed by a rash, fatigue, fever, sore throat, headaches, swollen glands	If it lasts over four years, it can cause blindness, destruction of bone, insanity, or heart failure; can cause death or deformity of a child born to an infected woman.	Curable with full course of antibiotics.
Human papilloma virus (HPV, or genital warts)	Genital itching and irritation, small clusters of warts	Can increase risk of cervical cancer in women; virus may remain in body and cause recurrences even when warts are removed.	Treatable with drugs applied to warts or various kinds of wart removal surgery. Vaccine (Gardasil) newly available; most effective when given to women before exposure to HPV.
Hepatitis B	Fatigue, poor appetite, vomiting, jaundice, hives	Some carriers will have few symptoms; others may develop chronic liver disease that may lead to other diseases of the liver.	No cure; some will recover, some will not. Bed rest may help ease symptoms. Vaccine is available.

HIV/AIDS

Four main phases of progression of HIV to AIDS; initial symptoms can resemble the flu or go completely unnoticed; symptoms, which become more serious as the infection progresses and the immune system becomes weaker, include persistent fever and diarrhea, weight loss, fatigue, and other symptoms.

Phase 4 is AIDS. As the immune system becomes weaker it can no longer defend against other diseases and infections, resulting in death. No cure; individual drug treatments vary to prolong lives, but can cause severe side effects.

---

highly contagious. The only birth control methods that offer protection are the male and female condoms (latex or polyurethane only) that prevent skin-to-skin contact. Most STIs can also spread to infants of infected mothers during birth. Have a doctor examine any irregularity or discomfort as soon as you detect it. Key 10.5 describes common STIs.

AIDS and HIV

The most serious of the STIs is AIDS (acquired immune deficiency syndrome), which is caused by the human immunodeficiency virus (HIV). Not everyone who tests positive for HIV will develop AIDS, but AIDS has no cure and results in eventual death. HIV can lie undetected in the body for up to 10 years before surfacing, and a carrier can spread it during that time. Medical science continues to develop drugs to combat AIDS and its related illnesses. However, the drugs can cause severe side effects, many have not been thoroughly tested, and none offer a cure.

HIV is transmitted through two types of bodily fluids: fluids associated with sex (semen and vaginal fluids) and blood. People have acquired HIV through sexual relations, by sharing hypodermic needles for drug use, and by receiving infected blood transfusions. You cannot become infected unless one of those fluids is involved. Therefore, it is unlikely you can contract HIV from toilet seats, hugging, kissing, or sharing a glass.

The best defence against AIDS or other STIs is to not have sex or to be in a long-term monogamous relationship with someone who has tested negative. Condoms are the next best choice. The U.S. Department of Health and Human Services reports: "*There's absolutely no guarantee even when you use a condom.* But most experts believe that the risk of getting AIDS and other sexually transmitted diseases can be greatly reduced if a condom is used properly. . . . Sex with condoms *isn't* totally 'safe sex,' but it *is* 'less risky' sex."[18]

Always use a latex condom, because natural skin condoms may let the virus pass through. If a lubricant is used, use K-Y® Brand Jelly or a spermicide because petroleum jelly can destroy the latex in condoms and diaphragms. Although some people dislike using condoms, it's a small price to pay for preserving your life.

Successful Intelligence Wrap-Up

College or university pressures can be enormous—but successfully intelligent thinking gives you the power to manage your wellness in the face of those pressures. If you do your best to make choices that have a positive impact, you have a strong chance of enjoying physical and mental health over the long haul. Here's how you have built skills in Chapter 10:

Analytical

You examined the effect that stress has on performance. You analyzed how eating, exercise, and sleeping patterns can affect your health. You used the Get Analytical exercise to examine your relationship with drugs, alcohol, and tobacco. You explored the pros and cons of choices regarding substances and sex.

Creative

Considering ways to incorporate more healthful behaviours into your life may have inspired new ideas about how to eat, exercise, adjust your schedule, or manage stress. In the Get Creative exercise, you brainstormed new ideas about how to have fun in safe and positive ways. You explored creative ways to handle substance problems.

Practical

You gathered a wealth of eating, exercise, and sleeping strategies from which you can choose those that work best for you. In the Get Practical exercise, you tracked down resources in your college and community that can support your personal wellness efforts. You considered practical ways to get help if your mental health demands it. You noted specific ways to adjust, if necessary, your use of alcohol, drugs, and tobacco.

zhongyong (Mandarin) 中庸
(djung-yung)

This long-standing Chinese concept can be loosely translated as "the doctrines of the mean" (*zhong* means "middle" and *yong* means "normal"). In other words, it recommends that one live moderately, using common sense to avoid extremes. It is similar to the phrase often attributed to the Greek philosopher Socrates: "Everything in moderation."[19]

Zhongyong applies to every aspect of your personal wellness. If you avoid extremes in your actions and choices, if you use common sense to make practical and intelligent decisions about how you live, you will have the best chance to manage stress and maintain good health. And remember, when you do swing too far, there is no shame in asking for help. Maintaining balance challenges people regardless of wealth, fame, or level of accomplishment, and trained and caring people stand ready to help bring balance back. Here's to your wellness.

"When we change our perception we gain control. . . . When we commit to action, to actually doing something rather than feeling trapped by events, the stress in our life becomes manageable."

GREG ANDERSON, CANCER SURVIVOR AND FOUNDER OF THE AMERICAN WELLNESS PROJECT

SUCCESSFUL INTELLIGENCE

Think, Create, Apply

Take steps toward better health. Put your successful intelligence to work in improving your physical health.

Step 1. Think it through: *Analyze your habits.* Pick a topic—eating, drinking, sleeping, sexual activity—that is an issue for you. To examine why it is a problem, identify behaviours and attitudes and note their positive and negative effects.

Example: *Issue:* binge drinking

Behaviour: I binge drink probably three times a week.

Attitude: I don't think it's any big deal. I like using it to escape.

Positive effects: I have fun with my friends. I feel confident, accepted, social.

Negative effects: I feel hung over and foggy the next day. I miss class. I'm irritable.

Your turn: *Issue:* _____

Behaviour: _____

Attitude: _____

Positive effects: _____

Negative effects: _____

Question to think about: Is it worth it?

Step 2. Think out of the box: *Brainstorm ways to change.* First think about what you want to be different, and why. Then come up with changes you could make. Be creative!

How you might change your behaviour: _____

How you might change your attitude: _____

Positive effects you think these changes would have: _____

Step 3. Make it happen: *Put a practical health improvement plan into action.* Choose two actions to take—one that would improve your attitude and one that would improve your behaviour—that you think would have the most positive effect for you. Commit to these actions with specific plans and watch the positive change happen.

Attitude improvement plan: _____

Behaviour improvement plan: _____

TEAMWORK
Create Solutions Together

Actively dealing with stress. By yourself, make a list of stressors—whatever events or factors cause you stress. As a class, discuss the stressors you have listed. Choose the five most common. Divide into five groups according to who would choose what stressor as his or her most important (redistribute some people if the group sizes are unbalanced). Each group should discuss its assigned stressor, brainstorming solutions and strategies. List your best coping strategies and present them to the class. Groups may want to make extra copies of the lists so that every member of the class has five, one for each stressor.

WRITING
Journal and Put Skills to Work

Record your thoughts on a separate piece of paper, in a journal or in a computer file.

Addiction. At one time or another, many people have had to cope with some kind of addiction. Describe how you feel about addiction in any form—to alcohol, drugs, food, sex, the internet, or gambling. How has addiction ensnared you, if at all? How did you deal with it? If you have never faced an addiction nor been close to someone who did, describe how you think you would work through the problem if it ever happened to you.

PERSONAL PORTFOLIO
Prepare for Career Success

Complete the following in your electronic portfolio or on separate sheets of paper.

Wellness at work. In the working world, mental and physical health is a big issue. One reason is that many companies are putting pressure on their employees to do more in less time. Resulting issues such as increased work burdens, additional tasks, late nights, and keeping your cellphone on for work calls on weekends or at off hours create an environment that places workers under a great deal of stress. Another reason is that health care costs are on the rise for companies, in terms of both paying for health insurance and dealing with the cost of lost work time when employees are out sick. Two specific actions will help you manage your health and work situation effectively:

1. Make sure that, for any current or prospective job, you understand the company's health-related policies. On a sheet of paper, write down answers to the following questions if you have a job right now, or keep the questions handy for when you do enter the workplace:

   - What health care is available for full-time employees? Part-time? Freelance?

   - What is the policy regarding sick days—how many per year? Paid or unpaid?

   - In what ways does the company promote wellness for employees? Clinic care, wellness programs, discounts on insurance for specific criteria?

2. Come up with plans to address minor health issues that may not be enough to justify staying home from work or school, but still hamper your functioning.

In the table that follows, enter drugstore or home remedies that can help you in each of these situations (use the blank row to enter any health situation you encounter that is not listed here). Make sure the remedies are in your medicine cabinet, and always stick to the dosage recommended on the packaging. If a problem worsens or continually recurs, make an appointment with a health professional to discuss it.

Problem	Helpful home remedy	Helpful drugstore item
Head cold		
Twisted knee or ankle		
Burned hand		
Stomach problem		
Sleep deprivation		
Sinus headache		

Finally, name where you can go on campus for health issues and include the phone number or e-mail: _____

SUGGESTED READINGS

Grayson, Paul A., Phil Meilman, and Philip W. Meilman. *Beating the College Blues*. New York: Checkmark Books, 1999.

Johanson, Sue. *Sex, Sex and More Sex*. Reganbooks, 2004.

Kadison, Richard D., and Theresa Foy DiGeronimo. *College of the Overwhelmed: The Campus Mental Health Crisis and What to Do About It*. San Francisco: Jossey-Bass, 2004.

Kuhn, Cynthia, et al. *Buzzed: The Straight Facts about the Most Used and Abused Drugs from Alcohol to Ecstasy*. 2nd ed. New York: W. W. Norton, 2003.

Mayo Clinic Family Health Book: The Ultimate Home Medical Reference. 3rd ed. New York: HarperResource, 2003.

Physician's Desk Reference. The Physician's Desk Reference Family Guide Encyclopedia of Medical Care. New York: Ballantine Books, 1999.

Schuckit, Marc Alan. *Educating Yourself about Alcohol and Drugs: A People's Primer*. New York: HarperCollins, 1998.

Selkowitz, Ann. *The College Student's Guide to Eating Well on Campus*. Bethesda, MD: Tulip Hill Press, 2000.

Ward, Darrell. *The Amfar AIDS Handbook: The Complete Guide to Understanding HIV and AIDS*. New York: W. W. Norton, 1998.

INTERNET RESOURCES

Prentice Hall Student Success Supersite (fitness and well-being information):
www.prenhall.com/success

Canadian Cancer Society (general information, prevention, and early detection tips):
www.cancer.ca

Learn more about AIDS Awareness from the Canadian Foundation for AIDS Research:
www.canfar.ca

Think you might be addicted? Check out the Canadian Centre on Substance Abuse website:
www.ccsa.ca

Sue Johanson: Get more information about sex and issues regarding sexuality at Sue Johanson's FAQ. This website maintained by the W Network:
www.wnetwork.com/expert_tips/love/sue_faq/index.asp

ENDNOTES

1. Gina Kolata, "A Surprising Secret to a Long Life: Stay in School," *New York Times*, January 3, 2007.

2. Information in this section based on materials from Dr. Marlene Schwartz of the Rudd Center for Food Policy and Obesity at Yale University.

3. Centers for Disease Control, National Center for Health Statistics, "Prevalence of Overweight and Obesity among Adults: United States, 2003–2004," January 30, 2007, http://www.cdc.gov/nchs/products/pubs/pubd/hestats/overweight/overwght_adult_03.htm.

4. Herbert Benson, M.D., and Eileen M. Stuart, R.N. C. M.S., et al., *The Wellness Book* (New York: Simon & Schuster, 1992), 292.

5. National Advisory Committee on Immunization, *Canadian Immunization Guide*, 7th ed., Public Health Agency of Canada, 2006, http://www.phac-aspc.gc.ca/publicat/cig-gci/index-eng.php.

6. Statistics Canada, "Canadian Community Health Survey: Mental Health and Well-being," *The Daily*, September 3, 2003, http://www.statcan.ca/Daily/English/030903/d030903a.htm.

7. National Institutes of Health Publication, No. 94-3561, National Institutes of Health, 1994.

8. Centre for Addiction and Mental Health, "Heavy Drinking, Levels of Stress High among University Students – Canadian Campus Survey," September 15, 2005, http://www.camh.net/News_events/News_releases _and_media_advisories_and_backgrounders/canadian _campus_survey0905.html (accessed September 5, 2008).

9. Suicide Awareness Voices of Education, "Symptoms and Danger Signs," in Depression and Suicide Information, http://www.save.org/index.cfm?fuseaction=home.viewPage&page_ID=705F4071-99A7-F3F5-E2A64A5A8BEAADD8 (accessed September 5, 2008).

10. Centre for Addiction and Mental Health, "Heavy Drinking."

11. Ibid.

12. National Survey on Drug Use and Health (NSDUH), "The NSDUH Report: Binge Alcohol Use among Persons 12 to 20: 2002 and 2003 Update," August 26, 2005, http://www.oas.samhsa.gov/2k5/youthBinge/youthBinge.htm.

13. Statistics Canada, *Canadian Tobacco Use Monitoring Survey*, 2005, Health Canada, http://www.hc-sc.gc.ca/hl-vs/tobac-tabac/research-recherche/stat/ctums-esutc_2005-eng.php.

14. Public Health Agency of Canada, Centre for Chronic Disease Prevention and Control, "Cancer: Lung Cancer," December 29, 2003, http://www.phac-aspc.gc.ca/ccdpc-cpcmc/cancer/publications/lung_e.html.

15. Hilary Smith, "The High Cost of Smoking," 2007, *MSN Money*, http://moneycentral.msn.com/content/Insurance/Insureyourhealth/P100291.asp.

16. American Cancer Society, "Guide to Quitting Smoking," October 27, 2006, http://www.cancer.org/docroot/PED/content/PED_10_13X_Guide_for_Quitting_Smoking.asp.

17. Smith, "The High Cost of Smoking."

18. U.S. Department of Health and Human Services, "A Condom Could Save Your Life," Publication #90-4239.

19. Christopher J. Moore, *In Other Words: A Language Lover's Guide to the Most Intriguing Words around the World* (New York: Walker, 2004), 85.

11

"Successfully intelligent people realize that the environment in which they find themselves may or may not enable them to make the most of their talents. They actively seek an environment where they can not only do competent work but make a difference."

ROBERT J. STERNBERG

D ealing with finances and thinking through career plans should be a high priority for every post-secondary student. How will you manage your money now and in the future? What careers and work environments will make the most of your strengths while providing the money you need for your chosen lifestyle? This chapter will show you how you can use successful intelligence to make effective decisions about money, careers, job searches, and balancing the demands of work and school.

In this chapter you will explore answers to the following questions:

Analytical

- Analyzing your money-related attitudes and goals
- Examining your spending and saving patterns
- Evaluating your strengths and career interests

Creative

- Coming up with day-to-day money-saving ideas
- Creating new ways to connect how you learn to career areas
- Brainstorming ways to search for a job on the internet

Practical

- How to use a monthly budget
- How to save money for short-term and long-term financial goals
- How to search for and win a job

How can you prepare for *career success*?

Students are in different stages when it comes to thinking about careers. Like many people, you may not have thought too much about it yet. You may have had a career for years and be looking for a change. Maybe you've decided on a particular career but are now having second thoughts. Regardless of your starting point, now is the time to make progress.

Everything in this book, particularly the guidelines provided by the Conference Board of Canada, is geared toward workplace success. Skills such as critical thinking, teamwork, writing skills, and long-term planning all prepare you to thrive in any career. Use the following strategies to start getting more specific in your preparation for career success.

Investigate career paths

Change happens in the working world all the time. You can get a good idea of what's out there—and what you think of it all—by exploring potential careers and building knowledge and experience.

Career possibilities extend far beyond what you can imagine. Brainstorm about career areas. Ask instructors, relatives, mentors, and fellow students about careers they are familiar with. Check your library for books on careers or biographies of people who worked in fields that interest you. Explore careers you discover through movies, newspapers, novels, or non-fiction.

What can I do in this area that I like and do well?	Do I respect the company or the industry? The product or service?
What are the educational requirements (certificates or degrees, courses)?	Does this company or industry accommodate special needs (child care, sick days, flex-time)?
What skills are necessary?	Will I belong to a union?
What wage or salary and benefits can I expect?	Are there opportunities near where I live (or want to live)?
What kinds of personalities are best suited to this kind of work?	What other expectations exist (travel, overtime, etc.)?
What are the prospects for moving up to higher-level positions?	Do I prefer the service or the production end of this industry?

Use your critical-thinking skills to broaden your investigation. Look at Key 11.1 for some of the questions you might ask as you talk to people or investigate materials. You may discover that:

A wide array of job possibilities exists for most career fields. For example, the medical world consists of more than doctors and nurses. Emergency medical technicians respond to emergencies, administrators run hospitals, researchers test new drugs, pharmacists prepare prescriptions, and so on.

Within each job, there is a variety of tasks and skills. You may know that an instructor teaches, but you may not see that instructors also often write, research, study, design courses, give presentations, and counsel. Push past your first impression of any career and explore what else it entails.

Common assumptions about salaries don't always hold. Finance, medicine, law, and computer science aren't the only high-paying careers. Don't jump to conclusions until you have investigated. And remember to place earnings in perspective: Even if you earn an extraordinary salary, you may not be happy unless you truly enjoy and learn from what you are doing.

Your school's career centre may offer job listings, occupation lists, assessments of skills and personality types, questionnaires to help you pinpoint areas that may suit you, and information about different careers and companies. Visit the centre early in your post-secondary career, and work with a counsellor there to develop a solid career game plan.

Consider your personality and strengths

Because who you are as a learner relates closely to who you are as a worker, your assessment results from Chapter 3 will give you helpful clues in the search for the right career. The Multiple Pathways to Learning assessment points to information about your natural strengths and challenges, which can lead you to careers that involve these strengths. Review Key 3.5 on pages 87–88 to see majors/programs of study and internships that tend to suit different intelligences, and look at Key 11.2 to see how those intelligences may link up with various careers.

Multiple intelligences may open doors to careers.

Multiple Intelligence	Look into a career as . . .
Bodily–Kinesthetic	■ Carpenter or draftsman ■ Physical therapist ■ Mechanical engineer ■ Dancer or actor ■ Exercise physiologist
Intrapersonal	■ Research scientist ■ Computer engineer ■ Psychologist ■ Economist ■ Author
Interpersonal	■ Social worker ■ PR or HR rep ■ Sociologist ■ Teacher ■ Nurse
Naturalistic	■ Biochemical engineer ■ Natural scientist (geologist, ecologist, entomologist) ■ Paleontologist ■ Position with environmental group ■ Farmer or farm management
Musical	■ Singer or voice coach ■ Music teacher ■ Record executive ■ Musician or conductor ■ Radio DJ or sound engineer
Logical–Mathematical	■ Doctor or dentist ■ Accountant ■ Attorney ■ Chemist ■ Investment banker
Verbal–Linguistic	■ Author or journalist ■ TV/radio producer ■ Literature or language teacher ■ Business executive ■ Copywriter or editor
Visual–Spatial	■ Graphic artist or illustrator ■ Photographer ■ Architect or interior designer ■ Art museum curator ■ Art teacher ■ Set or retail stylist

The Personality Spectrum assessment in Chapter 3 is equally as significant, because it focuses on how you work best with others, and career success depends in large part on your ability to function in a team.

Key 11.3 focuses the four dimensions of the Personality Spectrum on career ideas and strategies. Look for your strengths and decide what you may want to keep in mind as you search. Look also at areas of challenge, and try to identify ways to boost your abilities in those areas. Even the most ideal job involves some tasks that are not in your area of comfort.

Use the information in Key 11.3 as a guide, not a label. Although you may not have all the strengths and challenges indicated by your dominant area, thinking through them will still help you clarify your abilities and interests. In addition, remember that you are capable of change, and with focus and effort you can develop your abilities. Use ideas about strengths and challenges as a starting point for your goals about how you would like to grow.

Build knowledge and experience

Having knowledge and experience specific to the career you want to pursue is valuable on the job hunt. Courses, internships, jobs, and volunteering are four great ways to build both.

Courses. When you narrow your career exploration to a couple of areas of interest, try to take a course or two in those areas. How you react to the material gives you clues as to how you feel about the area in general. Find out what courses you have to take to major in the field, what jobs are available in the field, what credentials (degrees or training) you need for particular jobs, and so on.

Internships. Companies that offer internships are looking for people who will work hard in exchange for experience they can't get in the classroom. An internship may or may not offer pay. Your career centre may be able to help you explore summer internship opportunities or those during the school year. Stick to areas that interest you, and look for an internship that you can handle while still being able to fulfill your financial obligations. An **internship** is a great way to gain real-world experience and show initiative.

Jobs. No matter what you do to earn money while you are in college or university, whether it is in your area of interest or not, you may discover career opportunities that appeal to you. Someone who takes a third-shift legal proofreading job to make extra cash might discover an interest in law. Someone who answers phones for a newspaper company might be drawn into journalism. Be open to the possibilities around you.

Volunteering. Offering your services to others in need can introduce you to careers and increase your experience. Some schools have programs to help you find volunteering opportunities. Include volunteer activities on your résumé. Many employers look favourably on volunteering.

Even after you've completed a college or university degree, training program, course, book, or job, the key is to continually build on what you know. With the world's fast-paced changes in mind, today's employers value those who seek continual improvement in their skills and knowledge.

INTERNSHIP

A temporary work program in which a student can gain supervised practical experience in a particular professional field.

Personality Spectrum in the working world.

DIMENSION	STRENGTHS ON THE JOB	CHALLENGES ON THE JOB	LOOK FOR JOBS/ CAREERS THAT FEATURE...
Thinker	• Problem solving • Development of ideas • Keen analysis of situations • Fairness to others • Efficiency in working through tasks • Innovation of plans and systems • Ability to look strategically at the future	• A need for private time to think and work • A need, at times, to move away from established rules • A dislike of sameness— systems that don't change, repetitive tasks • Not always open to expressing thoughts and feelings to others	• Some level of solo work/think time • Problem solving • Opportunity for innovation • Freedom to think creatively and to bend the rules • Technical work • Big-picture strategic planning
Organizer	• High level of responsibility • Enthusiastic support of social structures • Order and reliability • Loyal • Able to follow through on tasks according to requirements • Detailed planning skills with competent follow-through • Neatness and efficiency	• A need for tasks to be clearly, concretely defined • A need for structure and stability • A preference for less rapid change • A need for frequent feedback • A need for tangible appreciation • Low tolerance for people who don't conform to rules and regulations	• Clear, well-laid-out tasks and plans • Stable environment with consistent, repeated tasks • Organized supervisors • Clear structure of how employees interact and report to one another • Value of and reward for loyalty
Giver	• Honesty and integrity • Commitment to putting energy toward close relationships with others • Finding ways to bring out the best in self and others • Peacemaker and mediator • Able to listen well, respect opinions, and prioritize the needs of co-workers	• Difficulty in handling conflict, either personal or between others in the work environment • Strong need for appreciation and praise • Low tolerance for perceived dishonesty or deception • Avoidance of people perceived as hostile, cold, or indifferent	• Emphasis on teamwork and relationship building • Indications of strong and open lines of communication among workers • Encouragement of personal expression in the workplace (arrangement of personal space, tolerance of personal celebrations, and so on)
Adventurer	• Skilfulness in many different areas • Willingness to try new things • Ability to take action • Hands-on problem-solving skills • Initiative and energy • Ability to negotiate • Spontaneity and creativity	• Intolerance of being kept waiting • Lack of focus on detail • Impulsiveness • Dislike of sameness and authority • Need for freedom, constant change, and constant action • Tendency not to consider consequences of actions	• A spontaneous atmosphere • Less structure, more freedom • Adventuresome tasks • Situations involving change • Encouragement of hands-on problem solving • Travel and physical activity • Support of creative ideas and endeavours

Skills employers seek.

SKILLS	WHY?
Communication	Both good listening and effective communicating are keys to workplace success, as is being able to adjust to different communication styles.
Critical thinking	An employee who can assess workplace choices and challenges critically and recommend appropriate actions stands out.
Teamwork	All workers interact with others on the job. Working well with others is essential for achieving work goals.
Goal setting	Teams fail if goals are unclear or unreasonable. Benefit is gained from setting realistic, specific goals and achieving them reliably.
Acceptance	The workplace is becoming increasingly diverse. A valuable employee is able to work with and respect all kinds of people.
Leadership	The ability to influence others in a positive way earns you respect and helps advance your career.
Creativity	The ability to come up with new concepts, plans, and products is valuable in the workplace.
Positive attitude	If you show that you have a high level of commitment to all tasks, you may earn the right to tackle more challenging projects.
Integrity	Acting with integrity at work—communicating promptly, being truthful and honest, following rules, giving proper notice, respecting others—enhances your value.
Flexibility	The most valuable employees understand the constancy of change and have developed the skills to adapt to its challenge.
Continual learning	The most valuable employees stay current on changes and trends by reading up-to-the-minute media and taking workshops and seminars.

Know what employers want

When you apply for a job, it is important to realize that prospective employers look for particular skills and qualities that mark you as a promising candidate. Most employers require you to have a **skillset** that includes specific technical skills, but in the current rapidly changing workplace, more general life skills may be even more crucial to your success. Following are some details about what employers will be looking for.

Big-picture skills

In the modern workplace, workers will hold an average of 10 jobs through their most productive working years.[1] The high rate of job and workplace change means that abilities such as successful thinking and teamwork are the most crucial to workplace success. Key 11.4 describes the particular skills and qualities that tell an employer you are likely to be an efficient and effective employee.

SKILLSET

A combination of the knowledge, talent, and abilities that are needed to perform a specific job.

Emotional intelligence

Another quality employers seek is emotional intelligence. In his book *Working with Emotional Intelligence*, psychologist Daniel Goleman states that emotional intelligence can be even more important than IQ and knowledge. He defines emotional intelligence as a combination of these factors:[2]

- **Personal competence.** This includes self-awareness (knowing your internal states, preferences, resources, intuitions), self-regulation (being able to manage your internal states, impulses, and resources), and motivation (the factors that help you reach your goals).
- **Social competence.** This includes empathy (being aware of the feelings, needs, and concerns of others) and social skills (your ability to create desirable responses in those with whom you interact).

Your emotional and social intelligence can empower or limit your career success during every single workday. Consider the following scenario: Say you arrive at work distracted by a personal problem and tired from studying late the night before. Your supervisor is overloaded with a major project due that day. The person you work most closely with will be arriving late due to a car problem. In other words, everyone is strung out. What does an emotionally and socially intelligent person do?

- Knowing your mental state, you prioritize your task list so that you can concentrate on what is most pressing and leave the rest for a day when you are more energetic.
- Sensing your supervisor's stress, you put a memo on her desk saying that you are available to support her as she nails down the loose ends on her urgent project.
- You call your co-worker on his cellphone while he settles the car problem and let him know the status at work, preparing him to prioritize and to support the supervisor.
- You ask another co-worker to bring in a favourite mid-morning snack to keep everyone going on what looks to be a very long day.

The current emphasis on teamwork has heightened the importance of emotional and social intelligence in the workplace. The more adept you are at working comfortably and productively with others, the more likely you are to succeed.

Expect change

The working world is always in flux, responding to technological developments, global competition, and other changes. Reading newspapers and magazines, scanning business sites on the internet, and watching television news all help you keep abreast of what you face as you make career decisions. Spend your time staying on top of two issues: growing and declining career areas, and workplace trends.

Growing and declining career areas

Try to stay on top of what careers are growing most rapidly. Rapid workplace change means that a growth area today may be declining tomorrow—witness the sudden drop in internet company jobs and

Connect Values to Career

Use your values as a career exploration guide.

First, look at the following list of "value words." Put a checkmark by those qualities that are most important to you as a working person. Circle your top five.

- Accepting
- Adventurous
- Ambitious
- Calm
- Caring
- Conscientious
- Co-operative
- Creative

- Decisive
- Demonstrating leadership
- Efficient
- Enthusiastic
- Focused on learning
- Honest/fair
- Independent

- Kind
- Loyal
- Organized
- Powerful
- Prompt
- Serious
- Trustworthy
- Wealthy

Keeping your top values in mind, answer the following questions:

The kind of work I enjoy most is _____

I can't see myself working as a _____

Self-fulfillment at work consists of _____

Being in charge of others makes me feel _____

Being responsible makes me feel _____

Working independently makes me feel _____

Working in a team makes me feel _____

Imagining that I'm being promoted after two years on a job, I think my employer would say it is because of these exemplary characteristics:

_____

_____

Source: Adapted from Gary Izumo et al., *Keys to Career Success.* Upper Saddle River, NJ: Prentice Hall, 2002, pp. 67–69.

---

fortunes in 2001. Service Canada keeps up-to-date labour market information available on their website at www.labourmarketinformation.ca. Check in periodically to keep up on current trends.

Workplace trends. What's happening now? To save money, corporations are hiring more temporary employees (temps) and fewer full-time employees. When considering whether to take a permanent job or a temporary job, consider the effects of each. Permanent jobs offer benefits (employer contribution to pension plan, paid vacations, and health insurance) and stability, but less flexibility. Temporary jobs offer flexibility, few obligations, and often more take-home pay, but have limited benefits. Also, in response to the changing needs of the modern workforce, companies are offering more "quality of life" benefits such as telecommuting, job sharing, and on-site child care.

Personal change

Even difficult personal changes can open doors that you never imagined were there. For example, Canadian country singer Shania Twain's parents were both killed in a car accident when she was just 21 years old. She was left to take care of her two teenage brothers. Despite this, she did not give up her dream of becoming a singer/songwriter. She took whatever singing jobs she could to help pay for rent and food.

Adjusting to changes, both large (leaving an industry for a new career) and small (changing the software you use daily on the job) means putting successful intelligence to work. With the information you collect from newspapers and magazines, internet sites, and television news, you can analyze what you are facing in the workplace. Based on your analysis you can create options for yourself, either within your own workplace or elsewhere, and take practical action.

With what you know about general workplace success strategies, you can search effectively for a job in a career area that works for you.

How can you conduct an effective *job search*?

Many different routes can lead to satisfying jobs and careers. In the career areas that interest you, explore what's possible and evaluate potential positive and negative effects so that you can make an educated decision about what suits you best. Maximize your opportunities by using the resources available to you, making a strategic search plan, and knowing some basics about résumés and interviews.

Use available resources

NETWORKING

The exchange of information or services among individuals, groups, or institutions.

Use your school's career planning and placement office, your **networking** skills, classified ads, online services, and employment agencies to help you explore possibilities both for jobs you need right away and for post-graduation career opportunities.

Your school's career planning and placement office. Generally, the career planning and placement office deals with post-graduation job placements, whereas the student employment office, along with the financial aid office, has more information about working while in school. At either location you might find general workplace information, listings of job opportunities, sign-up sheets for interviews, and contact information for companies.

The career office may hold frequent informational sessions on different topics. Your school may also sponsor job or career fairs that give you a chance to explore job opportunities. Start exploring your school's career office early in your college life. The people and resources there can help you at every stage of your career and job exploration process.

Networking. Networking is one of the most important job-hunting strategies. With each person you get to know, you build your network and tap into someone else's. With whom can you network? You can network with friends and family members, instructors, administrators, alumni, employers, co-workers and others.

Classified ads. Some of the best job listings are in newspapers. Individual ads describe the kind of position available and give a telephone number or post office box for you to contact. Some ads include additional information such as job requirements, a contact person, and the salary or wages offered. You can run your own classified ads if you have a skill to advertise.

Online services. The internet has exploded into one of the most fruitful sources of job listings. There are many different ways to hunt for a job on the web:

- Look up career-focused and Canadian job listing websites such as www.monster.ca, www.canjobs.com, www.actualjobs.com, http://workingcanada.com, or Canada's job bank at Human Resources and Social Development Canada, http://jb-ge.hrdc-drhc.gc.ca (also accessible at www.jobbank.gc.ca). In addition to listing and describing different jobs, sites like these offer resources on career areas, résumés, online job searching, and more.

- Check the webpages of individual associations and companies, which may post job listings and descriptions.

- If nothing happens right away, keep at it. New job postings appear; new people sign on to look at your résumé. Plus, sites change all the time. Do a general search using the keywords "hot job sites" or "job search sites" to stay current on what sites are up and running.

Be strategic

After you've gathered enough information to narrow your career goals, plan strategically to achieve them by mapping out your long-term timeline and keeping track of specific actions.

Making a big-picture timeline

Make a career timeline that illustrates the steps toward your goal, as shown in Key 11.5. Mark years and half-year points (and months for the first year), and write in the steps when you think they should happen. If your plan is five years long, indicate what you plan to do by the fourth, third, and second years, and then the first year, including a six-month goal and a one-month goal for that first year.

Using what you know about strategic planning, fill in the details about what you will do throughout your plan. Set goals that establish whom you will talk to, what courses you will take, what skills you will work on, what jobs or internships you will investigate, and any other research you need to do. Your path may change, of course; use your timeline as a guide rather than as an inflexible plan.

The road to a truly satisfying career can be long. Seek support as you work toward goals. Confide in supportive people, talk positively

Career timeline.

1 month	Enter university on part-time schedule
3 months	Meet with adviser to discuss desired major and required courses
6 months	Declare major in Child Studies
1 year	Switch to full-time class schedule
2 years	Pick up courses during spring and summer
3 years	Graduate with B.A.
4 years	Transfer to teacher's college
5 years	Work part-time as classroom aide as part of teacher's college training
	Graduate with teaching certificate
6 years	Have a job teaching high school

to yourself, and read books about career planning such as those listed at the end of this chapter.

Keep track of details

After you establish your time frame, make a plan for pursuing the jobs or careers that have piqued your interest. Organize your approach according to what you need to do and how much time you have to do it. Do you plan to make three phone calls per day? Will you fill out three job applications a week for a month? Keep a record—on index cards, in a computer file, or in a notebook—of the following:

- People you contact
- Companies to which you apply
- Jobs you rule out (e.g., jobs that become unavailable or that you find don't suit your needs)
- Responses to your communications (phone calls to you, interviews, written communications), information about the person who contacted you (name, title), and the time and the dates of contact

Sample file card.

Job/company:	Child-care worker at Morningside Daycare
Contact:	Kim McKay, Morningside Daycare, 136 Rockwood Avenue, St. Catharines ON L2P 3R8
Phone/fax/email:	(905) 555-3353 phone, (905) 555-3354 fax, no email
Communication:	Saw ad in paper, sent résumé and cover letter on October 1
Response:	Call from Kim to set up interview — Interview on Oct. 15 at 2 p.m., seemed to get a positive response, said she would contact me again by the end of the week
Follow-up:	Sent thank-you note on Oct. 16

Keeping accurate records enables you to both chart your progress and maintain a clear picture of the process. You never know when information might come in handy again. If you don't get a job now, another one could open up at the same company in a couple of months. In that case, well-kept records enable you to contact key personnel quickly and efficiently. Key 11.6 illustrates a sample file card.

Your résumé, cover letter, and interview

Information on résumés, targeted résumés, cover letters, and interviews fills entire books. You'll find specific sources listed at the end of the chapter. To get you started, here are a few basic tips on giving yourself the best possible chance at a job. (Also see information on cover letters in Building World-Class Skills in Chapter 8 [including the example in Key 8.13] and on résumés in that section of Chapter 9.)

Produce an effective résumé and cover letter. Your résumé should always be typed or printed on high-quality bond paper that is heavier than used for ordinary copies. Design your résumé neatly, using an acceptable format (books or your career office can show you some standard formats). Include a cover letter along with your résumé that tells the employer what job you are interested in and why he or she should hire you.

Proofread. Check them carefully for errors and have someone else proofread them as well. Errors in your résumé or cover letter could suggest to the employer that you will be careless in your job as well.

Use keywords. Prospective employers often use a computer to scan résumés. The computer program will select résumés if they contain enough *keywords*—words relating to the job opening or industry. Résumés without enough keywords probably won't even make it to the human resources desk. When you construct your résumé, make sure to include as many keywords as you can. For example, if you are seeking a computer-related job, list computer programs you use and other specific technical proficiencies. To figure out what keywords you need, check out job descriptions, job postings, and other current résumés.[3]

Take the interview seriously. Be clean, neat, and appropriately dressed. Choose a nice pair of shoes—people notice. Bring an extra copy of your résumé and any other materials that you want to show the interviewer, even if you have already sent a copy ahead of time. Avoid chewing gum or smoking. Offer a confident handshake. Make eye contact. Show your integrity by speaking honestly about yourself. After the interview, no matter what the outcome, follow up right away with a formal but pleasant thank-you note.

Being on time to your interview makes a positive impression—and being late will almost certainly be held against you. If you are from a culture that does not consider being late a sign of disrespect, remember that your interviewer may not agree.

Having a job may not only be a thought for the future; it may be something you are concerned about right now. Many students need to work and take classes at the same time to fund their education. Although you may not necessarily work in an area that interests you, you can hold a job that helps you pay the bills and still allows you to make the most of your school time.

What does *money* mean in your life?

According to Health Canada, worrying about finances is a major stressor for many Canadians. Adding the high cost of college or university tuition to the normal list of financial obligations means that, for the vast majority of post-secondary students, money is tight. Finances can be especially problematic for self-supporting students who may have to cover living and family expenses while coming up with funds for tuition, books, and other college or university fees.

The way you handle money and the level of importance it has for you reflects your values, your goals, and your self-image. It influences your career choice and where you choose to live. For example, if your goal is to earn a high salary and you have strong mathematical and business sense, you might choose investment banking as a career. Jobs in this field are generally located in cities with a high cost of living. In contrast, if you are not focused on high earnings and your talents lie in a field with lower annual salaries, you may be able to live comfortably on your earnings in less expensive locations.

Approaching money management with successful intelligence can help relieve money-related stress and increase control. Engage your successful intelligence in this process by analyzing who you are as a money manager and the relationship between your money and your time.

Your unique way of managing money

The way you interact with money is as unique as you are: You might be a spender or a saver. You might think about money only in the present tense, or you might frequently plan for the future. You might charge everything, only purchase things that you can buy with cash, or do something in between. You might measure your success in life in terms of how much money you have or define your worth in non-material terms.

Influences on who you are as a money manager might include the following:

- **Your values.** You tend to spend money on what *you* think is most important.

- **Your personality.** Thinkers may focus on planning, Organizers may balance bank accounts down to the penny, Givers may prioritize spending money to help others, Adventurers may spend impulsively and deal with the consequences later.

- **The culture of your family.** Some cultures see money as a collective resource to be shared within families, others prize individual accumulation as a sign of independence.

- **Your family and peer group.** You tend to either follow or react against how your parents and immediate family handle money. Your classmates and friends also influence your attitudes and behaviour.

- **Other factors.** Aspects such as ethnicity, class, level of education, and marital status play a role in how you manage money.

Money coach Connie Kilmark notes that you cannot change how you handle money until you analyze your attitudes and behaviours. "If managing money was just about math and the numbers, everyone would know how to manage their finances sometime around the fifth grade," she says.[4] She encourages her clients to take a hard look at how they feel about money as they work to develop effective money-management attitudes and skills. Once you do the same, you can make real-life money decisions based on what works best for you.

Money spent costs you the time it took to earn it

When you spend money, you exchange the time you spent earning it for a product or service. For example, you are thinking about purchasing a $200 cellphone. If you have a job that pays you $10 an hour after taxes, you would have spent 20 hours of work—a full week at a part-time job—to buy the phone. Ask yourself: Is it worth it? If the answer is no, put the money away and use it for something that is of more value to you. Every hour you work has a value—consider how to exchange those hours for what matters most to you.

Put your wallet away today; earn money for tomorrow.

DAY-TO-DAY EXPENSE	APPROXIMATE COST	POTENTIAL SAVINGS
Gourmet coffee	$4 per day, 5 days a week, totals $20 per week	$80 per month; $960 for the year—invested in a 5% interest account for a year, would amount to over $1,000
Cigarettes	$10 per day, 7 days a week (for a pack-a-day habit), totals $70 per week	$280 per month; $3360 for the year—invested in a 5% interest account for a year, would amount to over $3500
Ordering in meals	$15 per meal, twice per week, totals $30 per week	$120 per month; $1440 for the year—invested in a 5% interest account for a year, would amount to nearly $1550

This concept can hit home when you look at where your money goes from day to day. Cutting back on regular expenses can make a significant difference (see Key 11.7). If it takes you a month of work to earn $1000 at your part-time job, you need to decide whether you would rather spend that money on coffee or see it grow in a savings account.

Going to college or university may cost more hours of work than almost anything else you purchase, and it takes hours away from your day that you might otherwise spend earning money. It is an expensive investment. However, you are spending tuition and time in order to better your chances of long-term financial success. Your finances may be tight now, but they are likely to improve in the years ahead. If you look back at the statistics in Key 1.1 on page 5, you will recall that college graduates tend to earn more in the workplace than non-graduates. You are making a sound investment in your future.

What you give up to get something, in economic terms, is called *opportunity cost*. For most students, the opportunity cost of going to college is worth it. The Multiple Intelligence Strategies table on page 357 is designed to clarify the concept of opportunity cost through descriptions of different budgeting strategies.

Continue to engage your successful intelligence as you use analytical, creative, and practical skills to set and achieve both short- and long-term financial goals.

How can you manage *short-term financial goals?*

You make financial decisions nearly every day. Managing your income and expenses, juggling work and school, handling credit card use, and financing your education require frequent money-management actions. Look back at Chapter 2 where the exploration of majors/programs of study was broken down into a series of short-term goals. In like fashion, the following sections will help you think of day-to-day money management in terms of short-term *financial* goals. These goals also support long-term financial goals as they help you manage and save your money.

Short-term goal #1: Learn to manage income and expenses through budgeting

Creating a practical monthly **budget** that works requires that you tap every aspect of successful intelligence. You gather information about your resources (money flowing in) and expenditures (money flowing out) and *analyze* the difference. Next, you come up with *creative ideas* about how you can make changes. Finally, you take *practical action* to adjust spending or earning so that you come out even or ahead.

Your biggest expense right now is probably the cost of your education, including tuition and room and board. However, that expense may not hit you fully until after you graduate and begin to pay back your student loans. For now, include in your budget only the part of the cost of your education you are paying while you are in school.

Figure out your income

Add up all of the money you receive during the year—the actual after-tax money you have in your hand to pay your bills. Common sources of income include the following:

- Take-home pay from a regular full-time or part-time job during the school year
- Take-home pay from summer and holiday employment
- Money you earn as part of a work-study program
- Money you receive from your parents or other relatives for your college expenses
- Scholarships or grants

If you have savings specifically earmarked for your education, decide how much you will withdraw every month for school-related expenses.

Figure out what you spend

Start by recording every cheque or electronic withdrawal going toward fixed expenses like rent, phone, and internet service. Then, over the next month, record personal expenditures in a small notebook. Indicate any expenditure over five dollars, making sure to count smaller expenditures if they are frequent (for example, a bus pass for a month, coffee or lunch purchases per week).

Some expenses, like automobile and health insurance, may be billed only a few times a year. In these cases, convert the expense to monthly by dividing the yearly cost by 12. Common expenses include the following:

- Rent or mortgage
- Tuition that you are paying right now (the portion remaining after all forms of financial aid, including loans, scholarships, and grants, are taken into account)
- Books, lab fees, and other educational expenses
- Regular bills (electric, gas, oil, phone, water)
- Food, clothing, toiletries, and household supplies
- Child care
- Transportation and auto expenses (gas, maintenance)
- Credit cards and other payments on credit (car payments)

BUDGET
A plan to coordinate resources and expenditures; a set of goals regarding money.

- Insurance (health, auto, homeowner's or renter's, life)
- Entertainment items (cable TV, movies, eating out, books and magazines, music downloads)
- Computer-related expenses, including the cost of your online service
- Miscellaneous unplanned expenses

Use the total of all your monthly expenses as a baseline for other months, realizing that your expenditures will vary depending on what is happening in your life and even the season (for example, the cost to heat your home may be much greater in the winter than in the summer).

Evaluate the difference

Focusing again on your current situation, subtract your monthly expenses from your monthly income. Ideally, you have money left over—to save or to spend. However, if you are spending more than you take in, use your analytical thinking skills to ask some focused questions.

Examine your expenses. Did you forget to budget for recurring expenses such as the cost of semi-annual dental visits? Or was your budget derailed by an emergency expense that you could not foresee, such as a major car repair?

Examine your spending patterns and priorities. Did you spend money wisely during the month, or did you overspend on luxuries? If you are using your credit card frequently, are you being hit by high interest payments or late fees?

Examine your income. Do you bring in enough to suit your needs? Do you need to look for another source of income—a job or financial aid?

Adjust expenses or earning

After you have analyzed the causes of any budget shortfall, brainstorm solutions that address those causes. Solutions can involve either increasing resources or decreasing spending. To increase resources, consider taking a part-time job, increasing hours at a current job, or finding scholarships or grants. To decrease spending, prioritize your expenditures and trim the ones you don't need to make. In addition, work to save money in small ways on a day-to-day basis. Small amounts can eventually add up to big savings. Here are some suggestions for cutting corners:

- Share living space.
- Rent movies or borrow them from friends or the library.
- Eat at home more often.
- Use grocery and clothing coupons.
- Take advantage of sales, buy store brands, and buy in bulk.
- Find discounted play and concert tickets (students often receive discounts).
- Walk or use public transportation.
- Bring lunch from home.
- Shop in secondhand stores or swap clothing with friends.
- Communicate via IM, email or snail mail.

How one student mapped out a monthly budget.

- Wages: $10 an hour (after taxes) × 20 hours a week = $200 a week × 4⅓ weeks (one month) = $866
- Withdrawals from savings (from summer earnings) made each month = $200
- Total income per month = $1066

MONTHLY EXPENDITURES

School-related expenses (books, supplies, any expense not covered by financial aid)	$80
Public transportation	$90
Phone	$72
Food (groceries and takeout)	$305
Credit card payments	$100
Rent (including utilities)	$650
Entertainment (music, movies, tickets to events)	$90
Miscellaneous expenses, including clothing and personal items	$75
Total monthly spending:	**$1462**
$1066 (income) − $1,462 (expenses) = − $396	*$396 over budget*

- Ask a relative to help with child care, or create a babysitting co-op.
- Save on the cost of electricity by cutting back on air conditioning and switching to compact fluorescent lightbulbs (CFLs) in your lamps at home.

Key 11.8 shows a sample budget of an unmarried student living with two other students in off-campus housing with no meal plan. Included are all regular and out-of-pocket expenses with the exception of tuition, which the student will pay back after graduation in student loan payments. In this case, the student is $396 over budget. How would you make up the shortfall?

Rely on your dominant Multiple Intelligences to plan your budget. For example, whereas logical–mathematical learners may take to a classic detail-oriented budgeting plan, visual learners may want to create a budget chart, or bodily–kinesthetic learners may want to make budgeting more tangible by dumping receipts into a big jar and tallying them at the end of the month.

Short-term goal #2: Juggle work and school

With the cost of education rising all the time, the working student has become the norm. In fact, more than two-thirds of post-secondary students have some kind of job while in school. Many people want to work and many need to work to pay for school. Use your decision-making skills to gather information about what

Brainstorm Day-to-Day Ways to Save Money

Think about all the ways you spend money in a month's time. Where can you trim a bit? What expense can you do without? Where can you look for savings or discounts? Can you barter a product or service for one that a friend can provide? Give yourself a day or two to brainstorm a list of ideas on a sheet of paper or computer. Write your five most workable ideas here:

1. _____
2. _____
3. _____
4. _____
5. _____

Give these a try and see how they can help you put some money toward your savings. To make the experiment tangible, put cash into a jar daily or weekly in the amounts that these changes are saving you. See what you have accumulated at the end of one month—and bank it.

you need; analyze the potential effects of working; create options; and choose one that works for you.

Establish your needs

Think about what you need from a job before you begin your job hunt. Ask questions like these:

- How much money do I need to make—weekly, per term, for the year?
- What time of day is best for me? Should I consider night or weekend work?
- Can my schedule handle a full-time job, or should I look for part-time work?
- Do I want hands-on experience in a particular field? What do I like and dislike doing?
- Does location matter? Where do I want to work and how far am I willing to commute?
- How flexible a job do I need?
- Can I, or should I, find work at my school or as part of a work-study program?

Analyze effects of working while in school

Working while in school has pros and cons. In addition to the money you earn, your job may have positive effects such as the following:

- General and career-specific experience
- Contacts who might be able to help you in the future

- Enhanced school and work performance (working up to 15 hours a week may encourage students to manage time more effectively and build confidence)

Potential negative effects of working while in school include:

- Time commitment, for the job and perhaps for a commute, that reduces available study time
- Reduced opportunity for social and extracurricular activities
- Having to shift gears mentally from work to classroom

Some part-time jobs build skills that you can use after graduation.

Successful Intelligence Connections Online

Listen to author Sarah Kravits describe how to use analytical, creative, and practical intelligence to find the best possible part-time job for you.

Go to the *Keys to Success* Companion Website at www.pearsoned.ca/carter to listen or download as a podcast.

Create and choose options

With the information you have gathered and analyzed, you can look carefully at what is available on and off campus and apply for the job or jobs that suit your needs best. Continue to evaluate after you start a job. If it doesn't benefit you as much as you had anticipated, consider making a change, either within that job or by changing jobs. Your goal is to juggle two major responsibilities—school and work—in order to do well in your studies and meet your expenses.

Short-term goal #3: Manage credit card use

Post-secondary students often receive dozens of credit card offers. These offers—and the cards that go along with them—are a double-edged sword: They are a handy alternative to cash and can help build a strong credit history if used appropriately, but they also can plunge you into debt. Recent statistics from a survey of undergraduates illustrate the situation:[5]

- 42% of students in their first year of post-secondary education hold a credit card. By the final year, 90% of students have at least one, and 56% have four or more.
- Students who hold credit cards carry an average outstanding balance of $2169.
- Just under half of student credit card holders carry a balance of over $1000. Nearly 25% of students carry over $3000 in debt, and 7% carry over $7000.
- 74% of students report charging school supplies on their cards. Nearly 24% report using their cards to pay tuition.
- 44% of student card holders report that although they pay more than the minimum every month, they always carry a balance. Just 21% report that they pay the full balance due every month.

Often cash-poor, post-secondary students charge books and tuition on cards (or "plastic") as well as expenses like car repairs,

food, and clothes. Before they know it, their debt becomes unmanageable. It's hard to notice trouble brewing when you don't see your wallet taking a hit.

How credit cards work

Every time you charge a textbook, a present, or a pair of pants, you are creating a debt that must be repaid. The credit card issuer earns money by charging interest, often 18 percent or higher, on unpaid balances. Here's an example of how quickly debt can mount. Say you have a $3000 unpaid balance on your card at an annual interest rate of 18 percent. If you make the $60 minimum payment every month, it will take you *eight years* to pay off your debt, assuming that you make no other purchases. The math—and the effect on your wallet—is staggering:

- Original debt—$3000
- Cost to repay credit card loan at an annual interest rate of 18% for 8 years—$5760
- Cost of using credit—$5760 − $3000 = $2760

As you can see, by the time you finish, you will have repaid nearly *twice* your original debt.

To avoid unmanageable debt that can lead to a personal financial crisis, learn as much as you can about credit cards, starting with the important concepts in Key 11.9. Use credit wisely while you are still in school. The habits you learn today can make a difference to your financial future.

Managing credit card debt

Prevention is the best line of defence. To avoid excessive debt, ask yourself questions before charging: Would I buy it if I had to pay cash? Can I pay off the balance in full at the end of the billing cycle? If I buy this, what purchases will I have to forgo?

The majority of Canadians have some level of debt, and many people go through periods when they have a hard time keeping up with their bills. Falling behind on payments, however, could result in a poor credit rating that makes it difficult for you to make large purchases or take out loans. If you are having trouble keeping up with your payments, seek out the advice of a credit counsellor. Their services are often free.

David Thompson, a credit counsellor in Ottawa, says students need to be careful when using credit cards. Abusing credit cards can damage your credit rating, which can affect you when applying for jobs in the future. Two companies in Canada track and collect credit information: Equifax Canada and TransUnion Canada. They document your credit history, including your payment history and any missed payments.[6]

WHAT TO KNOW ABOUT . . .	. . . AND HOW TO USE WHAT YOU KNOW
Account balance—a dollar amount that includes any unpaid balance, new purchases and cash advances, finance charges, and fees. Updated monthly on your card statement.	Charge only what you can afford to pay at the end of the month. Keep track of your balance. Hold on to receipts and call customer service if you have questions about recent purchases.
Annual fee—the yearly cost some companies charge for owning a card.	Look for cards without an annual fee or, if youve paid your bills on time, ask your current company to waive the fee.
Annual percentage rate (APR)—the amount of interest charged on your unpaid balance, meaning the cost of credit if you carry a balance in any given month. The higher the APR, the more you pay in finance charges.	Credit card companies compete by charging different APRs. Shop around, especially on the web. Two sites with competitive APR information are www.studentcredit.com and www.bankrate.com. Also, watch out for low, but temporary, introductory rates that skyrocket to over 20 percent after a few months. Look for *fixed* rates (guaranteed not to change).
Available credit—the unused portion of your credit line. Determine available credit by deducting your current card balance from your credit limit.	It is important to have credit available for emergencies, so avoid charging to the limit.
Billing cycle—the number of days between the last statement date and the current statement date.	Knowledge of your billing cycle can help you juggle funds. For example, if your cycle ends on the 3rd of the month, holding off on a large purchase until the 4th gives you an extra month to pay without incurring finance charges.
Cash advance—an immediate loan, in the form of cash, from the credit card company. You are charged interest immediately and may also pay a separate transaction fee.	Use a cash advance only in emergencies because the finance charges start as soon as you complete the transaction. It is a very expensive way to borrow money.
Credit limit—the debt ceiling the card company places on your account (e.g., $1500). The total owed, including purchases, cash advances, finance charges, and fees, cannot exceed this limit.	Credit card companies generally set low credit limits for college students. Many students get around this limit by owning more than one card, which increases the credit available but most likely increases problems as well.
Credit line—a revolving amount of credit that can be used, paid back, then used again for future purchases or cash advances.	Work with the credit line of one card, paying the money you borrow back at the end of each month so you can borrow again.
Delinquent account—an account that is not paid on time or for which the minimum payment has not been met.	Avoid having a delinquent account at all costs. Not only will you be charged substantial late fees, but you also risk losing your good credit rating, affecting your ability to borrow in the future. Delinquent accounts remain part of your credit record for many years.
Due date—the date your payment must be received and after which you will be charged a late fee.	Avoid late fees and finance charges by mailing your payment a week in advance.

Continued.

WHAT TO KNOW ABOUT . . .	. . . AND HOW TO USE WHAT YOU KNOW
Finance charges—the total cost of credit, including interest and service and transaction fees.	Your goal is to incur no finance charges. The only way to do that is to pay your balance in full by the due date on your monthly statement.
Grace period—the interest-free time period between the date of purchase and the date your payment for that purchase is due once it appears on your statement. For example, a purchase on November 4 may first appear on your November 28 statement with payment due 25 days later.	It is important to know that interest-free grace periods apply only if you have no outstanding balance. If you carry a balance from month to month, all new purchases are immediately subject to interest charges.
Minimum payment—the smallest amount you can pay by the statement due date. The amount is set by the credit card company.	Making only the minimum payment each month can result in disaster if you continue to charge more than you can realistically afford. When you make a purchase, think in terms of total cost, not monthly payments.
Outstanding balance—the total amount you owe on your card.	If you carry a balance over several months, additional purchases are immediately hit with finance charges. Pay cash instead.
Past due—your account is considered "past due" when you fail to pay the minimum required payment on schedule.	Three credit bureaus note past due accounts on your credit history: Experian, TransUnion, and Equifax. You can contact each bureau for a copy of your credit report to make sure there are no errors.

A few basics will help you stay in control:

- Choose your card wisely—students are often eligible for cards with a lower interest rate, cards with no annual fee, cards with useful rewards, or cards with a grace period (no penalty for late payments up to a certain number of days).
- Pay bills regularly and on time and always make at least the minimum payment.
- If you get into trouble, deal with it in three steps:
  (1) admit that you made a mistake, even though you may be embarrassed
  (2) address the problem immediately to minimize damages: call the **creditor** and see if you can pay your debt gradually using a payment plan
  (3) Then, try to avoid what got you into trouble.
- Cut up a credit card or two if you have too many.

If you clean up your act, your credit history will gradually clean up as well.

CREDITOR

A person or company to whom a debt is owed, usually money.

Budgeting ←

Looking into the strategies associated with your strongest intelligences helps you identify effective ways to manage your money.

INTELLIGENCE	SUGGESTED STRATEGIES	WHAT WORKS FOR YOU? WRITE NEW IDEAS HERE
Verbal–Linguistic	• Talk over your budget with someone you trust. • Write out a detailed budget outline. If you can, keep it on a computer where you can change and update it regularly.	
Logical–Mathematical	• Focus on the numbers; using a calculator and amounts as exact as possible, determine your income and spending. • Calculate how much money you'll have in 10 years if you start now to put $500 in an RRSP account each year.	
Bodily–Kinesthetic	• Consider putting money, or a slip with a dollar amount, each month in different envelopes for various budget items—rent, dining out, etc. When the envelope is empty or the number is reduced to zero, your spending stops.	
Visual–Spatial	• Set up a budgeting system that includes colour-coded folders and coloured charts. • Create colour-coded folders for papers related to financial and retirement goals—investments, accounts, etc.	
Interpersonal	• Whenever budgeting problems come up, discuss them right away. • Brainstorm a solid five-year financial plan with one of your friends.	
Intrapersonal	• Schedule quiet time and think about how you want to develop, follow, and update your budget. Consider financial-management software. • Think through the most balanced allocation of your assets—where you think your money should go.	
Musical	• Include a category of music-related purchases in your budget—going to concerts, buying CDs—but keep an eye on it to make sure you don't go overboard.	
Naturalistic	• Remember to include time and money in your budget to enjoy nature. • Sit in a spot you like. Brainstorm how you will achieve your short- and long-term financial goals.	

How can you work toward *long-term financial goals?*

Being able to achieve long-term financial goals—buying a car or a house, having money for expenses that go beyond everyday costs, saving money for retirement and for emergencies— requires that you think critically about what you do with your money for the long term.

The short-term goals you just examined—budgeting, working while in school, managing credit use, and finding financial aid—all contribute to your long-term goals because they help you spend wisely and maximize your savings.

Save and invest your money

Having financial security requires that you live beneath your means— in other words, that you spend *less* than you earn. Then the money accumulated can go into savings accounts and investments, helping you with regular expenses, long-term financial plans, and emergencies (financial advisers recommend that you have cash in an "emergency fund" amounting to three to six months' income). Use the following tools to help your money grow.

Use bank accounts wisely

Paying your bills and saving money require that you form your own relationship with a financial institution such as a bank. Choose a bank with convenient locations, hours that fit your schedule, account fees that aren't too high, and a convenient network of automatic teller machines (ATMs).where you can use your debit card to access your funds. Many banks now have phone or online payment services that help you bank from your home, as well as services that allow you to set up the automatic payment of bills directly from your account each month.

The two specific services you need when you use a bank are chequing and savings accounts.

Chequing accounts. Most banks offer more than one chequing plan. Some accounts include cheque-writing fees, a small charge on every cheque you write or on any cheques above a certain number per month. Some accounts have free chequing, meaning unlimited cheque writing without extra fees—but you often have to maintain a minimum balance in your account to qualify.

Some accounts charge a monthly fee that is standard or varies according to your balance. Interest chequing pays you a low rate of interest, although you may have to keep a certain balance or have a savings account at the same bank.

Savings accounts. The most basic savings account, the interest savings account, pays a rate of interest to you determined by the bank. Many interest savings accounts do not have a required balance, but the interest rate they pay is very low.

Map Out Your Budget

Step 1: Estimate your current expenses in dollars per month, using the following table. This may require tracking expenses for a month, if you don't already keep a record of your spending. The grand total is your total monthly expenses.

Expense	Amount Spent
Rent/mortgage or room and board payment	$
Utilities (electric, heat, gas, water)	$
Food (shopping, eating out, meal plan)	$
Telephone (land line and mobile phone)	$
Books, lab fees, other educational expenses	$
Loan payments (educational or bank loans)	$
Car (repairs, insurance, payments, gas)	$
Public transportation	$
Clothing/personal items	$
Entertainment	$
Child care (caregivers, clothing/supplies, etc.)	$
Medical care/insurance	$
Other	$
TOTAL	$

Step 2: Calculate your average monthly income. If it's easiest to come up with a yearly figure, divide by 12 to derive the monthly figure. For example, if you have a $6000 scholarship for the year, your monthly income would be $500 ($6000 divided by 12).

Income Source	Amount Received
Regular work salary/wages (full-time or part-time)	$
Grants or work-study programs	$
Scholarships	$
Assistance from family members	$
Other	$
TOTAL	$

Step 3: Subtract the grand total of your monthly expenses from the grand total of your monthly income:

Income per month	$
Expenses per month	− $
CASH FLOW	$

Step 4: If you have a negative cash flow, you can increase income, decrease spending, or both. List here two workable ideas about how you can get your cash flow back in the black:

1. _____

2. _____

STRESSBUSTER

SONYA BEEL   Sprott-Shaw Community College, Duncan, British Columbia

How do you manage the conflicting demands of work and school? How do you find positive ways to manage this stress?

I decided to go back to school after my third son was born. I have three children, all under 10 years of age, which meant that I waited eight years to get my career training started. I was a little nervous about taking out a student loan, especially since I had to get one from outside of the province, but that was the only way I could get the money for my education.

I have a part-time job on weekends. My spouse, Tony, works full-time at a door factory. With him working full-time, and me working part-time, things were very comfortable financially. Unfortunately, he was laid off in September and was out of work for six weeks. I have never been so scared. What would I do? How could I feed three small boys, pay the rent, and cover all the expenses on a part-time salary? Every day, I kept telling myself that it would get easier and less stressful. For a little peace of mind, I talked to my family and friends about it. The staff at the school was very helpful, and would let me know what resources were available to me.

The biggest stressbusters I have are my children, even though they do cause a lot of financial worry. I try to play with them every night after their bath. It really seems to help me forget, for a few hours, all the stress I feel about having a young family, a job, and school. If you have similar stress and children, I recommend that you take a few hours every day, get out the toys, and play with your kids.

Successful Intelligence Wrap-Up

Many money and career decisions are made too quickly or based on criteria that aren't really important—often with troublesome results. As a successfully intelligent thinker, you can buck that trend by planning ahead in ways that will benefit you down the road, enabling you to say, years from now, "I made a good choice." Here's how you have built skills in Chapter 11:

Analytical

You looked carefully at what promotes career success, and used your values to guide you in career exploration in the Get Analytical exercise. You examined what money means in your life and how you manage it. You broke down the step-by-step process of budgeting. You explored the effects of working in school as well as the potential results of working toward long-term financial goals.

Creative

As you explored the section on careers and job searches, you may have come up with new career ideas or creative ways to look for a job. The material on budgeting may have inspired new ideas about how to manage what you earn and spend. In the Get Creative exercise, you brainstormed day-to-day ways to save money. Considering long-term financial goals may have introduced new thoughts about how to plan ahead with your money.

Practical

You took in the details of how to perform an effective job search. You reviewed a step-by-step plan for budgeting month by month, and put some ideas into action by mapping out your personal budget in the Get Practical exercise. You gathered specific strategies for managing credit card use. You explored the practical value of committing to save for your near future (major purchases) and far future (retirement).

Sacrifici

In Italy, parents often use the term *sacrifici*, meaning "sacrifices," to refer to tough choices that they make to improve the lives of their children and family members. They may sacrifice a larger home so that they can afford to pay for their children's sports and after-school activities. They may sacrifice a higher-paying job so that they can live close to where they work. They give up something in exchange for something else that they have decided is more important to them.

Think of the concept of *sacrifici* as you analyze the sacrifices you can make to get out of debt, reach your savings goals, and prepare for a career that you find satisfying. Many of the short-term sacrifices you are making today will help you do and have what you want in the future.

"Standing still is the fastest way of moving backwards in a rapidly changing world."

LAUREN BACALL

Building World-Class Skills for Post-secondary, Career, and Life Success

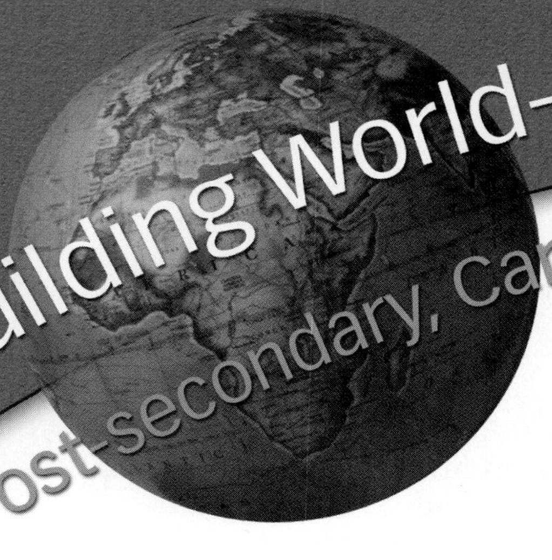

SUCCESSFUL INTELLIGENCE

Think, Create, Apply

Your relationship with money. Getting a handle on money anxiety starts with an honest examination of how you relate to it.

Step 1. Think it through: ***Analyze yourself as a money manager.*** Look back to the section Your Unique Way of Managing Money on page 347 for a description of what influences how people handle money. Make some notes about your personal specifics in the following areas.

I most value spending money on: ______________________________

____

My money "personality" can be described as: ______________________

____

My culture tends to view money as: ____________________________

____

My family and friends tend to handle money in this way: __________

____

Step 2. Think out of the box: ***Generate ideas about what you want to do with your money.*** If you had enough for expenses and then some, what would you do with the extra? Would you save it, spend it, a little of both? Imagine what you would do if you had an extra $10 000 to spend this year. Describe your plan on a separate sheet of paper.

Step 3. Make it happen: ***Look for practical ways to move toward the scenario you imagined.*** How can you make that $10 000 a reality? You may need to change how you operate as a money manager. You may need to make sacrifices in the short term. Come up with two specific plans here about changes and sacrifices that will move you toward your goal:

1. _____

2. _____

When you put these ideas to work, save or invest the money to reach for your goal.

TEAMWORK

Create Solutions Together

Building interview skills. Divide into pairs—each student will have a turn interviewing the other about themselves and their career aspirations. Follow these steps.

1. Independently, take three minutes to brainstorm questions you'll ask the other person. Focus on learning style, interests, and initial career ideas. You might ask questions like these:

   - If you could have any job in the world, what would it be?
   - What do you think would be the toughest part of achieving success in that profession?
   - Who are you as a learner and worker—what is your learning style?
   - What sacrifices are you willing to make to realize your dreams?
   - What is your greatest failure, and what have you learned from it?
   - Who is a role model to you in terms of career success?

2. Person A interviews Person B for five to ten minutes and takes notes.

3. Switch roles: Person B interviews Person A and takes notes. Remember that each person uses his/her own questions developed in Step 1.

4. Share with each other what interesting ideas stand out to you from the interviews. If you have any, offer constructive criticism to your interviewee about his or her interview skills.

5. Finally, submit your notes to your instructor for feedback.

This exercise will build your ability to gather information from others and to answer questions during an interview. You will use this skill throughout your professional life. Probe deeply when interviewing others so that you develop the ability to draw out the best in someone. Be as interested—and interesting—as you can.

WRITING

Journal and Put Skills to Work

Record your thoughts on a separate piece of paper, in a journal or in a computer file.

Your money personality. Describe who you are as a money manager, and where you think your behaviours and attitudes came from. What do you buy? Are you careful or reckless? Inattentive or detail-focused? How do you handle credit? How do you feel about how you handle money?

Real-life writing: Apply for aid. Start by reading the information on financial aid on pages xxiii–xxiv in Quick Start to College and University. Then, use internet or library resources to find two non-federally-funded scholarships, available through your post-secondary institution, for which you are eligible. They can be linked to academic areas of interest, associated with particular talents that you have, or offered by a group to which you or members of your family belong. Get applications for each and fill them out. Finally, write a one-page cover letter for each, telling each committee why you should receive this scholarship. Have someone proofread your work, *send the applications*, and see what happens.

PERSONAL PORTFOLIO

Prepare for Career Success

Complete the following in your electronic portfolio or on separate sheets of paper.

Being specific about your job needs. As you consider specific job directions and opportunities, you will have to begin thinking about a variety of job-related factors that different employers offer and that may affect your job experience and personal life. Among these factors are the following:

- Benefits (including health insurance, vacation)
- Integrity of company (What is its reputation?)
- Integrity of organization in its dealings with employees
- Promotion prospects/your chances for advancement
- Job stability
- Training and educational opportunities (Does the company offer in-house training? Will it pay for job-related courses or degrees?)
- Starting salary
- Quality of employees
- Quality of management
- Nature of the work you will be doing (Will you be required to travel extensively? Will you be expected to work long hours? Will you be working in an office or in the field?)
- Your official relationship with the company (Will you be a full-time or part-time employee or an independent contractor?)
- Job title
- Location of your primary workplace
- Company size
- Company's financial performance over time

Think about how important each factor is in your job choice. Then rate each on a scale of one to ten, with one being the least important and ten being the most important. As you consider each factor, keep in mind that even if you consider something very important, you may not get it right away if you are just beginning your career.

Finally, consider the results of a recent survey of college students conducted by the National Association of Colleges and Employers. When asked their top two reasons for choosing an employer, students named *integrity of organization in its dealings with employees* as number one and *job stability* as number two. How do these top choices compare to your own?[7]

SUGGESTED READINGS

Adams, Robert Lang, et al. *The Complete Résumé and Job Search Book for College Students.* Holbrook, MA: Adams Publishing, 1999.

Beatty, Richard H. *The Resume Kit.* 5th ed. New York: John Wiley & Sons, 2003.

Boldt, Laurence G. *Zen and the Art of Making a Living: A Practical Guide to Creative Career Design.* New York: Arkana, 1999.

Bolles, Richard Nelson. *What Color Is Your Parachute? 2003: A Practical Manual for Job Hunters and Career Changers.* Berkeley, CA: Ten Speed Press, 2003.

Detweiler, Gerri. *The Ultimate Credit Handbook.* 3rd ed. New York: Plume, 2003.

Goleman, Daniel. *Emotional Intelligence.* New York: Bantam Books, 1997.

Goleman, Daniel. *Working with Emotional Intelligence.* New York: Bantam Books, 2000.

Kennedy, Joyce Lain. *Job Interviews for Dummies.* Foster City, CA: IDG Books Worldwide, 2000.

Tyson, Eric. *Personal Finance for Dummies.* Foster City, CA: IDG Books Worldwide, 2000.

INTERNET RESOURCES

For information on online job searches and targeting your résumé, check out Monster.ca:
www.monster.ca

The University of Saskatchewan offers students tips on money management:
http://students.usask.ca/moneymatters

Advice on how to write a résumé can be found at The Resume Edge:
www.resumeedge.com

What's the latest on what Canadian employers want? Find out from the Conference Board of Canada:
www.conferenceboard.ca

If you're looking for varied and current labour market information, as well as what skills you have to offer potential employers, check out Canada Prospects:
www.canadaprospects.com/products/cp_nav/home.cfm

Prentice Hall Student Success Supersite—Money Matters:
www.prenhall.com/success/MoneyMat/index.html

ENDNOTES

1. U.S. Department of Labor, Bureau of Labor Statistics, "Number of Jobs Held, Labor Market Activity, and Earnings Growth among the Youngest Baby Boomers: Results from a Longitudinal Survey," news release, August 25, 2006, http://www.bls.gov/news.release/pdf/nlsoy.pdf.

2. Daniel Goleman, *Working with Emotional Intelligence* (New York: Bantam Books, 1998), 26–27.

3. Network Services and Consulting Corporation, "Resume Keyword Search," n.d., www.enetsc.com/ResumeTips23.htm (accessed September 6, 2008).

4. Cited in Jim Hanson, "Your Money Personality: It's All in Your Head," December 25, 2006, University Credit Union, http://hffo.cuna.org/12433/article/1440/html.

5. Nellie Mae, "Undergraduate Students and Credit Cards in 2004," May 2005, http://www.nelliemae.com/library/research_12.html.

6. Colin Campbell, "The Danger of Debt" [on-line]. Available at: http://www.carleton.ca/ottawainsight/2002/pfinance/s4.html. Downloaded October 30, 2002.

7. Eduardo Porter and Greg Winter, "'04 Graduates Learned Lesson in Practicality," *New York Times,* May 30, 2004.

CREATING YOUR LIFE
Building a successful future

12

"Successfully intelligent people are flexible in adapting to the roles they need to fulfill. They recognize that they will have to change the way they work to fit the task and situation at hand, and then they analyze what these changes will have to be and make them."

ROBERT J. STERNBERG

This chapter will help you analyze how well you did this term, think through upcoming academic decisions, and connect your post-secondary education to the rest of your life. You will see how the skills and attitudes you acquire in school fuel future success. You will consider what your role is as a member of broader communities and what it means to be an active participant. You will gather tools that will help you apply the power of successful intelligence to your life now and after college. Finally, you will create a personal mission, exploring how to use it to guide your dreams.

In this chapter you will explore answers to the following questions:

- How can you continue to activate your successful intelligence? 368

- How will what you've learned in this course bring success? 371

- How can you make a difference in your community? 375

- How can you create and live your personal mission? 378

- Successful Intelligence Wrap-Up 381

Chapter 12's
Successful Intelligence Skills

Analytical

- Examining your development of the 20 self-activators
- Analyzing how the skills in this course promote life success
- Examining how your character, contributions, and values inform your life goals

Creative

- Creating new ways to continue to learn throughout life
- Brainstorming ways to make a difference locally and globally
- Creating positive thoughts and dreams

Practical

- How to respond to change with flexibility
- How to preserve the environment and help others
- How to construct a personal mission

How can you continue to *activate your successful intelligence?*

Throughout this text you have connected analytical, creative, and practical thinking to academic and life skills. You have put them together in order to solve problems and make decisions. You have seen how these skills, used consistently and balanced, can help you succeed.

You are only just beginning your career as a successfully intelligent learner. You will continue to discover the best ways to use your analytical, creative, and practical thinking skills to achieve goals that are meaningful to you. In the section Building World-Class Skills in Chapter 1, you completed a self-assessment to examine your levels of development in Robert Sternberg's 20 self-activators. Here are more details to remind you of these characteristics that will keep you moving ahead toward your goals. According to Sternberg, successfully intelligent people do the following:[1]

1. *They motivate themselves.* They make things happen, spurred on by a desire to succeed and a love of what they are doing.
2. *They learn to control their impulses.* Instead of going with their first quick response, they sit with a question or problem. They allow time for thinking and let ideas surface before making a decision.
3. *They know when to persevere.* When it makes sense, they push past frustration and stay on course, confident that success is in their sights. They also are able to see when they've hit a dead end—and, in those cases, to stop pushing.

4. *They know how to make the most of their abilities.* They understand what they do well and capitalize on it in school and work.

5. *They translate thought into action.* Not only do they have good ideas, but they are able to turn those ideas into practical actions that bring ideas to fruition.

6. *They have a product orientation.* They want results; they focus on what they are aiming for rather than on how they are getting there.

7. *They complete tasks and follow through.* With determination, they finish what they start. They also follow through to make sure all the loose ends are tied and the goal has been achieved.

8. *They are initiators.* They commit to people, projects, and ideas. They make things happen rather than sitting back and waiting for things to happen to them.

9. *They are not afraid to risk failure.* Because they take risks and sometimes fail, they often enjoy greater success and build their intellectual capacity. Like everyone, they make mistakes—but tend not to make the same mistake twice.

10. *They don't procrastinate.* They are aware of the negative effects of putting things off, and they avoid them. They create schedules that allow them to accomplish what's important on time.

11. *They accept fair blame.* They strike a balance between never accepting blame and taking the blame for everything. If something is their fault, they accept responsibility and don't make excuses.

12. *They reject self-pity.* When something goes wrong, they find a way to solve the problem. They don't get caught in the energy drain of feeling sorry for themselves.

13. *They are independent.* They can work on their own and think for themselves. They take responsibility for their own schedule and tasks.

14. *They seek to surmount personal difficulties.* They keep things in perspective, looking for ways to remedy personal problems and separate them from their professional lives.

15. *They focus and concentrate to achieve their goals.* They create an environment in which they can best avoid distraction and they focus steadily on their work.

16. *They spread themselves neither too thin nor too thick.* They strike a balance between doing too many things, which results in little progress on any of them, and too few things, which can reduce the level of accomplishment.

17. *They have the ability to delay gratification.* While they enjoy the smaller rewards that require less energy, they focus the bulk of their work on the goals that take more time but promise the most gratification.

18. *They have the ability to see the forest and the trees.* They are able to see the big picture as well as the important details.

19. *They have a reasonable level of self-confidence and a belief in their ability to accomplish their goals.* They believe in themselves enough to get through the tough times, while avoiding the kind of overconfidence that stalls learning and growth.

20. *They balance analytical, creative, and practical thinking.* They sense what to use and when to use it. When problems arise, they combine all three skills to arrive at solutions.

These characteristics are your personal motivational tools. Consult them when you need a way to get moving. You may even want to post them somewhere in your home, in the front of a notebook, on your computer, or in your PDA.

Use the following Get Analytical exercise to see how you have developed your command of the self-activators over the course of the term.

GET ANALYTICAL!

Evaluate Your Self-Activators

To see how you use successful intelligence in your daily life, assess how developed you perceive your self-activators to be.

1	2	3	4	5
Not at all like me	Somewhat unlike me	Not sure	Somewhat like me	Definitely like me

Please circle the number that best represents your answer:

1. I motivate myself well.   1 2 3 4 5

2. I can control my impulses.   1 2 3 4 5

3. I know when to persevere and when to change gears.   1 2 3 4 5

4. I make the most of what I do well.   1 2 3 4 5

5. I can successfully translate my ideas into action.   1 2 3 4 5

6. I can focus effectively on my goal.   1 2 3 4 5

7. I complete tasks and have good follow-through.   1 2 3 4 5

8. I initiate action—I move people and projects ahead.   1 2 3 4 5

9. I have the courage to risk failure.   1 2 3 4 5

10. I avoid procrastination.   1 2 3 4 5

11. I accept responsibility when I make a mistake.   1 2 3 4 5

12. I don't waste time feeling sorry for myself.   1 2 3 4 5

13. I independently take responsibility for tasks.   1 2 3 4 5

14. I work hard to overcome personal difficulties.   1 2 3 4 5

15. I create an environment that helps me to concentrate on my goals.   1 2 3 4 5

16. I don't take on too much work or too little.   1 2 3 4 5

17. I can delay gratification in order to receive the benefits.　　1 2 3 4 5

18. I can see both the big picture and the details in a situation.　1 2 3 4 5

19. I am able to maintain confidence in myself.　　1 2 3 4 5

20. I can balance my analytical, creative, and practical
    thinking skills.　　1 2 3 4 5

When you complete the assessment, look back at pages 27–28 in Chapter 1 for your original scores. What development do you see? List five changes that feel significant:

1. _____

2. _____

3. _____

4. _____

5. _____

As you grow, there is always room for improvement. Choose one self-activator that you feel still needs work. Analyze the specific reasons why it remains a challenge. For example, does a need to please others lead to taking on too much work, or is it a lack of taking time to map out responsibilities and time commitments? Write a brief analysis here, and let this analysis guide you as you work to build your strength in this area:

_____

_____

_____

How will what you've learned in this course *bring success*?

 ou leave this course with far more than a final grade, a notebook full of work, and some credit hours on your transcript. You have gathered important attitudes and skills, developed flexibility, and opened the door to lifelong learning.

New attitudes and skills prepare you to succeed

The attitudes and skills you gained this semester are your keys to success now and in the future (see Key 12.1). As you move through your post-secondary years, keep motivation high by reminding yourself that you

Student success skills are career and life success skills.

ACQUIRED SKILL	IN SCHOOL, YOU'LL USE IT TO...	IN YOUR CAREER, YOU'LL USE IT TO...
Investigating resources	... find who and what can help you have the post-secondary experience you want	... get acclimated at a new job—find the people, resources, and services that can help you succeed
Knowing and using your learning style	... select study strategies that make the most of your learning style	... select jobs and career areas that suit what you do best
Setting goals	... complete assignments and achieve educational goals	... accomplish work tasks and reach career goals
Managing time	... get to classes on time, juggle school and work, turn in assignments when they are due	... finish tasks on or before your supervisor says they are due, balance different on-the-job duties
Critical thinking	... think through writing assignments, solve math problems, see similarities and differences among ideas in literature, history, sociology, etc.	... find ways to improve product design, increase market share, present ideas to customers and employees, and so on
Reading	... read course texts and readings	... read operating manuals, work guidebooks, media materials in your field, and continuing education materials
Note taking	... take notes in class and in study groups	... take notes in work meetings and during important phone calls
Test taking	... take quizzes, tests, and final exams	... take tests for certification in particular work skills
Writing	... write essays and reports	... write memos, letters, reports, or media material
Building successful relationships	... get along with instructors, students, student groups	... get along with supervisors, co-workers, and team members
Staying healthy	... manage stress and stay healthy so that you can make the most of school	... manage stress and stay healthy so that you can operate at your best at work
Managing money	... stay on top of school costs and make decisions that earn you the money you need	... budget the money you are earning so that you can pay your bills and save for the future
Establishing and maintaining a personal mission	... develop a big-picture idea of what you want from your education	... develop a big-picture idea of what you want to accomplish in your life and make choices that guide you toward those goals

are creating tools that will benefit you in everything you do.

Flexibility helps you adapt to change

As a citizen of the twenty-first century, you are likely to move in and out of school, jobs, and careers in the years ahead. You are also likely to experience important personal changes. How you react to the changes you experience, especially if they are unexpected and difficult, is almost as important as the changes themselves in determining your future success. The ability to "make lemonade from lemons" is the hallmark of people who always land on their feet.

Successfully intelligent thinking will help you adapt to and benefit from both planned and unexpected changes. Your goal is flexibility as you analyze each change, generate and consider options, make decisions, and take practical actions. With flexibility and resourcefulness, you can adapt to the loss of a job or to getting an exciting job offer, a personal health crisis or a happy change in family status, failing a course or winning an academic scholarship.

Seeking experiences that broaden your horizons is part of lifelong learning. These students are learning both academic and life lessons during their travel in China.

Although sudden changes may throw you off balance, the unpredictability of life can open new horizons. Margaret J. Wheatley and Myron Kellner-Rogers, leadership and community experts and founders of the Berkana Institute, explain that people "often look at this unpredictability with resentment, but . . . unpredictability gives us the freedom to experiment. It is this unpredictability that welcomes our creativity."[2] Here are some strategies they recommend for making the most of unpredictable changes:

- Look for what happens when you meet someone or something new. Be aware of new feelings or insights that arise. Observe where they lead you.

- Be willing to be surprised. Great creative energies can come from the force of a surprise. Instead of turning back to familiar patterns, explore new possibilities.

- Use your planning as a guide rather than a rule. If you allow yourself to follow new paths when changes occur, you are able to grow from what life gives you.

- Focus on what is rather than what is supposed to be. Planning for the future works best as a guide when combined with an awareness of the realities of your situation.

College promotes lifelong learning

As a student, your main focus is on learning—on acquiring knowledge and skills in the courses you take. Though you will graduate knowing much more than you did when you started college, you are not finished learning. On the contrary, with knowledge in many fields doubling every two to three years and with your personal interests and needs changing every day, what you learn in college is just the beginning of lifelong learning. With the *habit* of learning you will be able to achieve your career and personal goals—those that you set out for yourself today and those that you cannot anticipate but that will be part of your future.

You can make learning a habit through asking questions and being open to exploring new ideas and possibilities. Here are some ways to make that happen:

Investigate new interests. When information and events catch your attention, take your interest one step further and find out more. Instead of dreaming about it, just do it.

Read, read, read. Reading expert Jim Trelease says that people who don't read "base their future decisions on what they used to know. If you don't read much, you really don't know much. You're dangerous."[3] Decrease the danger to yourself and others by opening a world of knowledge and perspectives through reading. Ask friends which books have changed their lives. Keep up with local, national, and world news through newspapers and magazines.

Pursue improvement in your studies and career. After graduation, continue your education both in your field and in the realm of general knowledge. Stay on top of ideas, developments, and new technology in your field by seeking out **continuing education** courses. Sign up for career-related seminars. Take single courses at a local college or community learning centre. Some companies offer additional on-the-job training or pay for their employees to take courses that will improve their knowledge and skills.

Spend time with interesting people. When you meet someone new who inspires you and makes you think, keep in touch. Form a study group, a film club, or a walking club. Host a potluck dinner party and invite people from different corners of your life—family, school, work, or neighbourhood. Learn something new from everyone you meet.

Talk to people from different generations. Younger people can learn from the experienced, broad perspective of those belonging to older generations; older people can learn from the fresh and often radical perspective of those younger than themselves. Communication builds mutual respect.

Delve into other cultures. Talk with a friend who has grown up in a culture different from your own. Invite him or her to dinner. Eat food from a country you've never visited. Initiate conversations with people of

CONTINUING EDUCATION
Courses that students can take without having to be part of a degree program.

different races, religions, values, and ethnic backgrounds. This is not difficult in a multicultural country like Canada. Travel internationally and locally. Take a course that deals with some aspect of cultural diversity. Try a semester or year abroad.

Nurture a spiritual life. You don't have to attend a house of worship to be spiritual, although that may be part of your spiritual life. Wherever you find spirituality and soul—in music, organized religion, friendship, nature, cooking, sports, or anything else—these will help you find balance and meaning.

Experience the arts. Art is "an adventure of the mind" (Eugène Ionesco, playwright); "a means of knowing the world" (Angela Carter, author); something that "does not reproduce the visible; rather, it makes visible" (Paul Klee, painter); "a lie that makes us realize truth" (Pablo Picasso, painter); a revealer of "our most secret self" (Jean-Luc Godard, filmmaker). Through art forms you can discover new ideas and shed light on old ones. Seek out whatever moves you—music, visual arts, theatre, photography, dance, domestic arts, performance art, film and television, poetry, prose, and more.

Make your own creations. Take a class in drawing, writing, or quilting. Learn to play an instrument. Write poems for your favourite people or stories to read to your children. Concoct a new recipe. Design and build a set of shelves for your home. Create a memoir of your life. Express yourself, and learn more about yourself, through art.

Lifelong learning is the master key that unlocks every door you encounter on your journey. If you keep it firmly in your hand, you will discover worlds of knowledge—and a place for yourself within them.

You are part of a world community of people who depend on one another. Giving what you can of your time, energy, and resources to those who need help makes you a valued community member.

How can you *make a difference* in your community?

Everyday life is demanding. You can become so caught up in your own issues that you neglect to pay attention to anything else. However, you can make a difference in your **community**—by helping others; being an active, involved citizen; and doing your share for the environment.

You can help others

What you do for others has enormous impact. Giving others hope, comfort, or help can improve their ability to cope. Reaching out to others can also enhance your career. Being involved in causes and the community shows caring and community spirit, qualities that companies look for in people they hire.

COMMUNITY

(1) A group of people living in the same locality.

(2) A group of people having common interests.

(3) A group of people forming a distinct segment of society.

Appreciate yourself, and plan to expand your horizons.

On a piece of paper, list 25 things you like about yourself. You can name anything—things you can do, things you think, things you've accomplished, things you like about your physical self, and so on.

Next, list 25 things you would like to do in your life. These can be anything from trying Indian food to travelling to Ellesmere Island in Canada's Arctic. They can be things you'd like to do tomorrow or things that you plan to do in 20 years. At least five items on each list should involve your current and future education.

Finally, come up with five things you can plan for the next year that combine what you like about yourself and what you want to do. If you like your strength as a mountain biker and you want to explore a province you've never seen, plan a mountain biking trip. If you like your writing and you want to be a published author, write an essay to submit to a magazine. Be creative. Let everything be possible.

1. _____

2. _____

3. _____

4. _____

5. _____

You can help others by volunteering, participating in service learning, and setting an example in how you live your life.

Volunteering. Look for a volunteering activity that you can fit into your schedule. Key 12.2 lists organizations that provide volunteer opportunities; you might also look into more local efforts or private clearinghouses that set up smaller projects.

Service learning. In the past few years, looking for a way to help students become involved citizens as well as successful learners, many colleges have instituted *service learning* programs. These are sometimes referred to as citizenship courses or volunteer hours. The basic concept of service learning is to provide the community with service and the students with knowledge, creating positive change for both and including specific opportunities for students to reflect on and analyze their experiences.[4] Service learning builds a sense of civic responsibility, helps students learn useful skills through doing, and promotes values exploration and personal change. Service learning is a "win–win" situation—everyone has something to gain.

Look into volunteering opportunities that these organizations offer.

- Amnesty International
- Women's shelters
- Big Brothers and Big Sisters
- Canadian Blood Services
- Canadian AIDS Society
- Churches, synagogues, temples, and affiliated organizations such as the YM/YWCA
- Educational support organizations

- Environmental awareness/support organizations such as Greenpeace
- Free the Children
- Food banks
- Hospitals
- Hotlines
- Kiwanis/Knights of Columbus/Lions Club/Rotary
- Libraries

- Meals on Wheels
- Nursing homes
- Planned Parenthood
- Scouting organizations
- Share Our Strength/other food donation organizations
- Shelters and organizations supporting the homeless

You can get involved locally and nationally

Being an active citizen is another form of involvement. On a local level, you might take part in your community's debate over saving open space from developers. On a provincial level, you might contact legislators about building sound barriers along a highway that runs through your town. On a national level, you might write letters to your MP to urge support of an environmental, energy, or health bill. Work for political candidates who adopt the views you support, and consider running for office yourself—in your city, provincially, or nationally.

Most important, vote in every election. Your votes and your actions can make a difference—and getting involved will bring you the power and satisfaction of being a responsible Canadian citizen. Having the right to vote places you in a privileged minority among people around the world who have no voice in how they live.

You can help to preserve your environment

Your environment is your home. When you help to maintain a clean, safe, and healthy place to live, your actions have an impact not only on your immediate surroundings but also on others around you and on the future of the planet. Every environmentally aware person, saved bottle, and reused bag is a step in the right direction. Take responsibility for what you can control—your own habits—and develop sound practices that contribute to the health of the environment.

Recycle anything that you can. Many communities have some kind of recycling program. If you live on campus, your college may have its own recycling program set up. What you can recycle—plastics, aluminum, glass, newspapers, magazines, other scrap paper—depends on how extensive the program is. Products that use recycled materials are often more expensive, but if they are within your price range, try to reward the company's dedication by purchasing them.

Respect the outdoors. Use products that reduce chemical waste. Pick up after yourself. Through volunteering, voicing your opinion, or making monetary donations, support the maintenance of parks and the preservation of natural, undeveloped land. Be creative: One young woman planned a cleanup of a local lakeside area as the main group activity for the guests at her birthday party (she joined them, of course). Everyone benefits when each person takes responsibility for maintaining the fragile earth.

Reduce your "footprint." Your *environmental footprint* refers to the effect your day-to-day actions have on the earth and its resources. Every step you take to use less energy or make less trash helps to reduce your footprint. Ways to use less energy include turning off lights and appliances when not in use, using energy-saving lightbulbs and appliances, walking or biking instead of driving, using public transportation, driving an energy-efficient or hybrid automobile, or using alternative energy sources for your home (solar power, wind power). Ways to make less trash include composting, buying products that minimize packaging, and growing food in a garden.

Set an example. As with helping others, setting an example is a great way to make a difference yourself while inspiring others to make positive changes. Television producer Laurie David and singer-songwriter Sheryl Crow went on a two-week tour of colleges, in a bus powered by biodiesel fuel, to open a dialogue with students about global warming. Decide how you can set an example in your life.

Successful Intelligence Connections Online

Listen to author Sarah Kravits describe how to use analytical, creative, and practical intelligence to support the environment in your daily life.

Go to the *Keys to Success* Companion Website at www.pearsoned.ca/carter to listen or download as a podcast.

Your future accomplishments, and those of your family and community, are possible only if the environment continues to sustain life and economic activity. Ensuring a clean environment that supports your hopes and dreams may be part of the larger picture of your personal mission.

Remember that valuing yourself is the base for valuing all other things. Improving the earth is possible when you value yourself and think you deserve the best living environment possible. Part of valuing yourself is doing whatever you can to create the life you want to live. Activating your successful intelligence and developing your personal mission are two ways to guide yourself to that life.

How can you *create and live* your personal mission?

If the trees are your goals, then the forest is the big picture of what you are aiming for in life—your personal mission. To define your mission, craft a *personal mission statement.*

Dr. Stephen Covey, author of *The Seven Habits of Highly Effective People*, defines a mission statement as a philosophy outlining what you want to be (character), what you want to do (contributions and achievements), and the principles by which you live (your values). He describes the statement as "a personal constitution, the basis for making major, life-directing decisions."[5]

Here is a mission statement written by Carol Carter, one of the authors of *Keys to Success*.

> My mission is to use my talents and abilities to help people of all ages, stages, backgrounds, and economic levels achieve their human potential through fully developing their minds and their talents. I aim to create opportunities for others through work, service, and family. I also aim to balance work with people in my life, understanding that my family and friends are a priority above all else.

How can you start formulating a mission statement? Try using Covey's three aspects of personal mission as a guide. Think through the following:

- **Character.** What aspects of character do you think are most valuable? When you consider the people you admire most, which of their qualities stand out?
- **Contributions and achievements.** What do you want to accomplish in your life? Where do you want to make a difference?
- **Values.** How do the values you established in your work in Chapter 2 inform your life goals? What in your mission could help you live according to what you value most highly? For example, if you value community involvement, your mission may reflect a life goal of holding elected office, which may translate into an interim goal of running for class office at college.

Because what you want out of life changes as you move from one phase to the next—from single person to spouse, from student to working citizen—your personal mission should remain flexible and open to revision. If you frame your mission statement carefully so that it truly reflects your goals, it can be your guide in everything you do, helping you to live with integrity and to work to achieve your personal best.

Live with integrity

Having integrity puts your **ethics** into day-to-day action. When you act with integrity, you earn trust and respect from others. If people can trust you to be honest, to be sincere in what you say and do, and to consider the needs of others, they will be more likely to encourage you, support your goals, and reward your work.

Living with integrity helps you believe in yourself and in your ability to make good choices. A person of integrity isn't a perfect person, but is one who makes the effort to live according to values and principles, continually striving to learn from mistakes and to improve. Take responsibility for making the right moves, and you will follow your mission with strength and conviction.

Aim for your personal best in everything you do. As a lifelong learner, you will always have a new direction in which to grow and a new challenge to face. Seek constant improvement in your personal, educational, and professional life. Dream big, knowing that incredible

ETHICS
A system of moral values; a sense of what is right to do.

STRESSBUSTER

JENNIFER ARMOUR   University of Guelph, Guelph, Ontario

Do thoughts of your future path after school cause you stress? What steps are you taking now to prepare yourself for life after graduation?

Of course thoughts about my future frustrate me and cause me stress all the time! I don't think a day goes by that I don't worry about what I'm going to do after I graduate or someone asks, "So what exactly are you going to do with this degree?" Unfortunately, our society never thinks positively about the workforce, which creates a tremendous amount of pressure on students. One is more inclined to hear, "It's so hard to find a job nowadays," "The unemployment rate rose again," and "All that money for an education when there aren't any job opportunities in your field." Honestly, I really don't know what kinds of jobs are going to be available after graduation since the world is constantly changing. My plan, though, is to remain positive and ambitious, and not be afraid to take risks.

To prepare myself for the real world, I'm focusing on the areas I'm interested in and looking for connections that may open doors in the future. I'm also looking into some entry-level positions to familiarize myself with certain aspects of my field, so I'll be better prepared when it comes time to find a job. I ask questions and study hard because I believe the knowledge I've acquired will make me an asset to the workforce. If I could give one piece of advice to anyone about the future, it would be to have the courage to pursue your dreams even when they seem unattainable. So just remember that you are not alone in your worries about the future. Make the most out of each day and reach for your goals because they will lead to greater things.

things are possible for you if you think positively and act with successful intelligence. Enjoy the richness of life by living each day to the fullest, developing your talents and potential into the achievement of your most valued goals.

Dave E. Redekopp, Barrie Day, and Marnie Robb of Edmonton's Life-Role Development Group sum up the main points of this chapter with their "High Five" checklist:[6]

- **Change is constant.** Remember to be flexible. It will help you adapt to the changes that will occur in your personal or professional life.

- **Follow your heart.** Create and live out your personal mission.

- **Focus on the journey.** While goal setting is important, it's also important to enjoy what life offers you.

- **Stay learning.** Remember that learning is a lifelong process. It helps us grow as people.

- **Be an ally.** Spend time with friends and family and remember to get involved in your local community.

Explore Your Personal Mission

Work toward a concrete description of your most important life goals.

As a way of exploring what you most want out of life, consider one or more of the following questions, which ask you to look back at the life you imagined you would have. Freewrite some answers on a separate piece of paper.

1. You are at your retirement dinner. You have had an esteemed career in whatever you ended up doing in your life. Your best friend stands up and talks about the five aspects of your character that have taken you to the top. What do you think they are?

2. You are preparing for a late-in-life job change. Updating your résumé, you need to list your contributions and achievements. What would you like them to be?

3. You have been told that you have one year to live. Talking with your family, you reminisce about the values that have been central to you in your life. Based on that discussion, how do you decide you want to spend your time in this last year? How will your choices reflect what is most important to you?

Thinking about your answers, draft a personal mission statement here, up to a few sentences long, that reflects what you want to achieve in life. Focus on the practical—on what you want to do and the effects you want to have on the world.

Successful Intelligence Wrap-Up

As a lifelong learner, you will always have a new direction in which to grow and a new challenge to face. Seek improvement in your personal, educational, and professional life. Dream big, knowing that incredible things are possible. Live each day to the fullest, using your successful intelligence to achieve your most valued goals. Here's how you have built skills in Chapter 12:

Analytical

You explored how you will continue to use the skills you acquired in this course. With the Get Analytical exercise, you examined how you now use successful intelligence in your daily life. You considered the role you play in your community and the effect your actions can have both locally and nationally. You analyzed what you consider important to include in your personal mission.

Creative

Reading the material about how college skills promote lifelong learning may have inspired new ideas about how you can learn throughout your life. In the Get Creative exercise, you brainstormed positive thoughts about yourself as well as plans for the near and far future. The material on making a difference in the community may have sparked thoughts about actions you can take to change your community for the better.

Practical

You revisited Sternberg's 20 self-activators, practical skills for living with successful intelligence. You explored specific ways to be flexible in the face of change. You noted ways to help others and protect the environment. In the Get Practical exercise, you used specific thought-provoking questions to prepare materials that will help you develop a personal mission statement.

hozh'q

(hoe-shk)

The Navajo would translate *hozh'q* as "the beauty of life, as seen and created by a person." The word incorporates many concepts, including health and well-being, balance, and happiness. The Navajo perceive that *hozh'q* can start with one person and extend outward indefinitely, having a unifying effect on other people, on the world, and even on the universe. Because the Navajo consider the unity of experience as the ultimate life goal, *hozh'q* is a way of life.[7]

Do, or do not. There is no "try."

YODA (*THE EMPIRE STRIKES BACK*)

PERSONAL TRIUMPH

CRAIG KIELBURGER

In 2008, Craig Kielburger was awarded the Order of Canada by Governor General Michaëlle Jean for his outstanding passion for social justice. That's not the only award he's earned. He's won the Nelson Mandela Human Rights Award, The Roosevelt Freedom Medal, and many others.

Some people find their mission in life while in college or university. For others, it happens later in life. For some, they create their passion and their life's work in Grade 7. There are few people more dedicated to their personal mission than Canadian Craig Kielburger. There are even fewer that are examples of how one can create and live their personal mission.

While Craig now has his degree in Peace and Conflict Studies from the University of Toronto, it all began for Craig when he was in Grade 7 and living in Thornhill, Ontario. One morning he read the story of Iqbal Masih, a Pakistani boy who was forced into child labour when he was just four years old. He worked over 70 hours a week weaving rugs. When he was 12, Iqbal was murdered when he tried to protest against his working conditions. Craig was so moved by this story of a boy his own age that he made copies of the article for his classmates and asked if anyone would help him become an advocate for children's rights around the world. As a result of this, he and his classmates founded Free the Children, a not-for-profit organization. That was 1995. Today, Free the Children is the largest organization of children helping children in the world. More than one million people in 45 countries are members.

His work leads him to many different parts of the world and allows him the opportunity to meet many interesting and famous people. He's shared the public stage with Oprah Winfrey, Bill Clinton, Nelson Mandela, Desmond Tutu, and the Dalai Lama.

Despite his busy schedule, Craig and his brother Marc also write a weekly column in the *Toronto Star* called Global Voices to help connect with not only Canadian students, but students all over the world. Craig has high hopes for the column (online at www.thestar.com/news/globalvoices). The website "provides youth with an opportunity to express their opinions, their views and get perspectives on these very issues. We hope that this inspires more students to get educated, to raise their voices and to take action on shaping the world in which they live."

In the last few years, students at many colleges and universities have become involved in Free the Children. Students at the University of Western Ontario, the University of Calgary, and Mount Allison University have chapters or have held fundraisers. Check to see if there is a chapter on your campus. If there isn't, perhaps you can start one.

If you're interested in getting involved, Free the Children offers both summer and two-year internships. If this sounds like a journey you'd be interested in taking, check them out online at www.freethechildren.com.

Building World-Class Skills
for Post-secondary, Career, and Life Success

SUCCESSFUL INTELLIGENCE
Think, Create, Apply

Learn from the experiences of others. Look back to Craig Kielburger's Personal Triumph on page 383. After you've read his story, relate his experience to your own life by completing the following:

Step 1. Think it through: *Analyze your experience and compare it to Craig's.* What one event caused Craig to become interested in social justice? Is there something that you feel passionate about that you could develop into your passion to help others in your community?

Step 2. Think out of the box: *Imagine ways to contribute.* Think about the ways in which you could serve. How might your talents and skills give something to others? Brainstorm ideas about how you could use what you do well to help others in your community? How can you take your skills and talents to try new things that might make a difference in your community?

Step 3. Make it happen: *Make a practical plan to get involved.* Decide on a specific way to help others, then form a plan to pursue this goal. As you think about your decision, consider how Craig inspired others to join him in his mission. Write down what you intend to do and the specific steps you will take to do it and live your personal mission.

TEAMWORK
Create Solutions Together

Giving back. In your group, research volunteering opportunities in your community. Each group member should choose one possibility to research. Answer questions such as the following: What is the situation or organization? What are its needs? Do any volunteer positions require an application, letters of reference, or background checks? What is the time commitment?

Is any special training involved? Are there any problematic or difficult elements to this experience?

When you have the information, meet together so that each group member can describe each volunteering opportunity to the other members. Choose one that you feel you will have the time and ability to try next semester. Name your choice and tell why you selected it.

WRITING
Journal and Put Skills to Work

Record your thoughts on a separate piece of paper, in a journal, or on a computer file.

Journal entry: Your communities. Thinking about the definition of community in the margin on page 375, list the communities to which you belong—professional, family, spiritual, academic, athletic, political, and so on. Choose one community and write about your interaction with it—what it gives you, what you give to it, and whether you want to change the nature of your involvement.[8]

Real-life writing: Personal mission. Thinking about your answers to the Get Practical exercise on page 381, draft a personal mission statement here, up to a few sentences long, that reflects what you want to achieve in life. Focus on the practical—on what you want to do and the effects you want to have on the world.

PERSONAL PORTFOLIO
Prepare for Career Success

Revisit the wheel of successful intelligence. Without looking at your self-assessments from Get Analytical, Get Creative, and Get Practical from Chapter 1 or the wheel in Get Practical in Chapter 4, analyze where you are after completing this course by taking the three assessments again.

Assess yourself as an analytical thinker.

For each statement, circle the number that feels right to you, from 1 for "not at all true for me" to 5 for "very true for me."

1. I recognize and define problems effectively.   1 2 3 4 5

2. I see myself as a "thinker," "analytical," "studious."   1 2 3 4 5

3. When working on a problem in a group setting, I like   1 2 3 4 5
   to break down the problem into its components and
   evaluate them.

4. I need to see convincing evidence before accepting   1 2 3 4 5
   information as fact.

5. I weigh the pros and cons of plans and ideas   1 2 3 4 5
   before taking action.

6. I tend to make connections among pieces of information by categorizing them.   1 2 3 4 5

7. Impulsive, spontaneous decision making worries me.   1 2 3 4 5

8. I like to analyze causes and effects when making a decision.   1 2 3 4 5

9. I monitor my progress toward goals.   1 2 3 4 5

10. Once I reach a goal, I evaluate the process to see how effective it was.   1 2 3 4 5

Total your answers here: _____

Assess yourself as a creative thinker.

For each statement, circle the number that feels right to you, from 1 for "not at all true for me" to 5 for "very true for me."

1. I tend to question rules and regulations.   1 2 3 4 5

2. I see myself as "unique," "full of ideas," "innovative."   1 2 3 4 5

3. When working on a problem in a group setting, I generate a lot of ideas.   1 2 3 4 5

4. I am energized when I have a brand-new experience.   1 2 3 4 5

5. If you say something is too risky, I'm ready to give it a shot.   1 2 3 4 5

6. I often wonder if there is a different way to do or see something.   1 2 3 4 5

7. Too much routine in my work or schedule drains my energy.   1 2 3 4 5

8. I tend to see connections among ideas that others do not.   1 2 3 4 5

9. I feel comfortable allowing myself to make mistakes as I test out ideas.   1 2 3 4 5

10. I'm willing to champion an idea even when others disagree with me.   1 2 3 4 5

Total your answers here:_____

Assess yourself as a practical thinker.

For each statement, circle the number that feels right to you, from 1 for "not at all true for me" to 5 for "very true for me."

1. I can find a way around any obstacle.   1 2 3 4 5

2. I see myself as a "doer," the "go-to" person, I "make things happen."   1 2 3 4 5

3. When working on a problem in a group setting, I like   1 2 3 4 5
   to set up the plan and monitor how it is carried out.

4. Because I learn well from experience, I don't tend   1 2 3 4 5
   to repeat a mistake.

5. I finish what I start and don't leave loose ends hanging.   1 2 3 4 5

6. I pay attention to my emotions in academic and   1 2 3 4 5
   social situations to see if they help or hurt me as
   I move toward a goal.

7. I can sense how people feel, and can use that   1 2 3 4 5
   knowledge to interact with others effectively in order
   to achieve a goal.

8. I manage my time effectively.   1 2 3 4 5

9. I find ways to adjust to the teaching styles of my   1 2 3 4 5
   instructors and the communication styles of my peers.

10. When involved in a problem-solving process,   1 2 3 4 5
    I can shift gears as needed.

Total your answers here: _____

After you have finished, fill in your new scores in the blank wheel of
successful intelligence in Key 12.3. Compare this wheel with your
previous wheel on page 117 of Chapter 4. Look at the changes: Where
have you grown? How has your self-perception changed?

- Note three *creative ideas* you came up with over the term that aided
  your exploration or development:

  Creative idea: _____

  _____

  Creative idea: _____

  _____

  Creative idea: _____

  _____

- Note three *practical actions* you took that moved you toward your
  goals:

  Practical action: _____

  _____

  Practical action: _____

  _____

  Practical action: _____

  _____

Use this new wheel of successful intelligence to evaluate your progress.

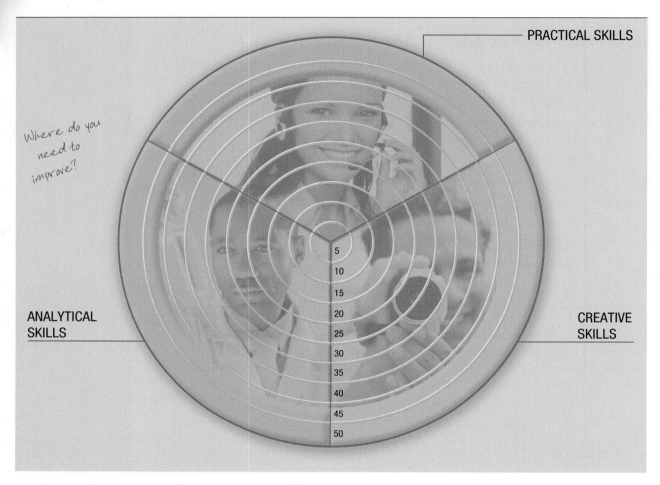

PRACTICAL SKILLS

Where do you need to improve?

ANALYTICAL SKILLS

CREATIVE SKILLS

5
10
15
20
25
30
35
40
45
50

Source: Based on "The Wheel of Life" model developed by the Coaches Training Institute © Co-Active Space 2000.

Let what you learn from this new wheel inform you about what you have accomplished and what you plan to accomplish. Continue to grow your analytical, creative, and practical skills and use them to manage the changes that await you in the future.

SUGGESTED READINGS

Blaustein, Arthur I. *Make a Difference: America's Guide to Volunteering and Community Service.* San Francisco: Jossey-Bass, 2003.

Delany, Sarah, and Elizabeth Delany, with Amy Hill Hearth. *Book of Everyday Wisdom.* New York: Kodansha America, 1996.

Jones, Laurie Beth. *The Path: Creating Your Mission Statement for Work and for Life.* New York: Hyperion, 1998.

Moore, Thomas. *Care of the Soul: How to Add Depth and Meaning to Your Everyday Life.* New York: HarperCollins, 1998.

Wheatley, Margaret J., and Myron Kellner-Rogers. *A Simpler Way.* San Francisco: Berrett-Koehler Publishers, 1998.

INTERNET RESOURCES

Volunteer Canada is dedicated to volunteerism in Canada:
www.volunteer.ca

Helping out in your community can be easy as donating blood:
www.bloodservices.ca

Help out someone in need of guidance and support. Big Brothers and Big Sisters can always use an extra person:
www.bbbsc.ca

Need help with career development? Check out Edmonton's Life Role Development Group:
www.life-role.com

ENDNOTES

1. List and descriptions based on Robert J. Sternberg, *Successful Intelligence* (New York: Plume, 1997), 251–269.

2. Margaret J. Wheatley and Myron Kellner-Rogers, "A Simpler Way," *Weight Watchers Magazine* 30.3 (1997): 42–44.

3. Linton Weeks, "The No-Book Report: Skim It and Weep," *Washington Post*, May 14, 2001.

4. National Service Learning Clearinghouse, "Service Learning Is...," 2004 [online], http://www.servicelearning.org/article/archive/35 (accessed May 2004).

5. Stephen Covey, *The Seven Habits of Highly Effective People* (New York: Simon &Schuster, 1989), 70–144, 309–318.

6. Adapted from Dave E. Redekopp, Barrie Day, and Marnie Robb' s *The High Five of Career Development*, n.d., http://www.life-role.com/documents/High%20Five.pdf.

7. Christopher J. Moore, *In Other Words: A Language Lover's Guide to the Most Intriguing Words around the World* (New York: Walker, 2004), 116.

8. Adapted from Katherine Woodward Thomas, *Calling in the One* (New York: Three Rivers Press, 2004), 298–299.

STUDY BREAK: GET READY FOR EXAMS

Demonstrate What You Know in an Oral Exam

In an oral exam, your instructor asks you to verbally present your responses to exam questions or to discuss a pre-assigned topic. Oral exam questions may be similar to essay questions on written exams. They may be broad and general, or they may focus on a narrow topic that you are expected to explore in depth.

The material in this Study Break is designed to help you master the skills you need in order to perform well during an oral exam. These skills have lifelong benefits. The more comfortable you are speaking in front of instructors, the more prepared you will be for any kind of public speaking situation—in school, in the community, and at work.

Keep in mind that if you have a documented learning disability that limits your ability to express yourself effectively in writing, you may need to take all your exams orally. Speak with your adviser and instructors to set up an oral exam schedule.

Use preparation strategies

Because oral exams require that you speak logically and to the point, your instructors will often give you the exam topic in advance and may even allow you to bring your notes to the exam room. Other instructors ask you to study a specified topic and they then ask questions about the topic during the exam.

Speaking in front of others—even an audience of one, your instructor—involves developing a presentation strategy before you enter the exam room:

Learn your topic. Study for the exam until you have mastered the material. Nothing can replace subject mastery as a confidence booster.

Plan your presentation. Dive into the details. Brainstorm your topic if it is pre-assigned, narrow it with the prewriting strategies you learned in Chapter 8, determine your central idea or argument, and write an outline that will be the basis of your talk. If the exam uses a question-and-answer format, make a list of the most likely questions, and formulate the key points of your response.

Use clear thinking. Make sure that your logic is solid and that your evidence supports your thesis. Work on an effective beginning and ending that focus on the exam topic.

Draft your thoughts. To get your thoughts organized for the exam, make a draft, using "trigger" words or phrases that will remind you of what you want to say.

Practise your presentation

The element of performance distinguishes speaking from writing. As in any performance, practice is essential. Use the following strategies to guide your efforts:

Know the parameters. How long do you have to present your topic? Where will you be speaking? Will you have access to a podium, table, chair, or whiteboard?

Use index cards or notes. If your instructor doesn't object, bring note cards to the presentation. Don't put them in front of your face, however; it's tempting to hide behind them.

Pay attention to the physical. Your body positioning, voice, eye contact, and what you wear contribute to the impression you make; therefore, try to look good and sound good.

Time your practice sessions to determine whether you should add or cut material. If you are given your topic in advance, make sure you can state your points in the allotted time. During the exam, make sure you don't speak too quickly.

Try to be natural. Use words you are comfortable with to express concepts you know. Be yourself as you show your knowledge and enthusiasm for the topic.

Be prepared for questions

After your formal presentation, your instructor may ask you topic-related questions. Your responses and the way you handle the questions will affect your grade. Here are some strategies for answering questions effectively:

Take the questions seriously. The exam is not over until the question-and-answer period ends.

Jot down keywords from the questions. This is especially important if the question has several parts, and you intend to address one part at a time.

Ask for clarification. Ask the instructor to rephrase a question you don't understand.

Think before you speak. Take a moment to organize your thoughts and to write down keywords for the points you want to cover.

Answer only part of a question if that's all you can do. Emphasize what you know best and impress the instructor with your depth of knowledge. If you draw a blank, simply tell the instructor that you don't know the answer.

Control your nervousness during an exam

If you are nervous, there are things you can do to help yourself:

Keep your mind on your presentation, not yourself. Focus on what you want to say and how you want to say it.

Take deep breaths right before you begin, and carry a bottle of water. Deep breathing will calm you, and the water will ease a dry mouth.

Visualize your own success. Create a powerful mental picture of yourself acing the exam. Then visualize yourself speaking with knowledge, confidence, and poise.

Establish eye contact with your instructor and realize that he or she wants you to succeed. You'll relax when you feel that your instructor is on your side.

Decide how well these techniques work for you

Practice makes perfect, especially when it comes to public speaking. Gauge your ability to speak effectively during an oral exam with the following team exercise:

- Team up with another student to prepare for a written essay, then quiz each other as if you were taking an actual oral exam. How did your partner evaluate your presentation? What were your strengths? Your weaknesses?

- Do you think that your answers demonstrated all you know about the subject or that you could have done better in writing? If you answered the latter, what obstacles prevented you from doing your best in your oral presentation?

- Describe three actions you will take to improve your next presentation.

  1. _____
  2. _____
  3. _____

SELF-STUDY QUIZ

MULTIPLE-CHOICE QUESTIONS

Circle or highlight the answer that seems to fit best.

1. Students who are vulnerable to being stereotyped may
   A. call attention to themselves as members of a minority group.
   B. be self-conscious because they see themselves as underachievers.
   C. feel superior to others because of their minority status.
   D. distance themselves from the qualities they think others associate with their group and avoid asking for help because they fear perpetuating a group stereotype.

2. The goal of stress management is to
   A. eliminate all stress from your life.
   B. focus only on school-related stress.
   C. learn to blame all stressful situations on others.
   D. develop strategies for handling the stresses that are an inevitable part of life.

3. *Emotional intelligence* is defined by Daniel Goleman as a combination of
   A. empathy and social skills.
   B. self-regulation and motivation.
   C. Thinker qualities and Giver qualities.
   D. personal competence and social competence.

4. *Networking* can be defined as
   A. visiting your instructor during office hours.
   B. the exchange of information or services among individuals, groups, or institutions.
   C. discovering your ideal career.
   D. making a strategic plan.

5. Being flexible in the face of change involves
   A. changing your direction when you encounter obstacles in your life and work.
   B. acknowledging the change and assessing what new needs it brings.
   C. reacting in a way that you have seen work for others.
   D. focusing on an aspect of your life not affected by the change.

6. To be open to unpredictability,
   A. put your energy into building existing relationships.
   B. make a plan and stick with it even in the face of change.
   C. focus on what is rather than on what is supposed to be.
   D. don't let surprises throw you off.

Complete the following sentences with the appropriate word(s) or phrase(s) that best reflect what you have learned. Choose from the items that follow each sentence.

1. _____ factors play an important role in how _____ are interpreted. (Personal/body movements, Biological/verbal cues, Cultural/non-verbal cues)

2. _____ criticism involves goodwill suggestions for improvement. (Non-constructive, Direct, Constructive)

3. The three most common eating disorders are _____, _____, and _____. (anorexia nervosa/food allergies/binge drinking, anorexia nervosa/bulimia/binge eating, constant dieting/eating too much fat/bulimia)

4. Two effective ways to build career knowledge and experience are _____ and _____. (job hunting/networking, internships/volunteering, learning style/critical thinking)

5. The debt ceiling a credit card company places on your account is called a _____. (cash advance, account balance, credit limit)

The following essay questions will help you organize and communicate your ideas in writing, just as you must do on an essay test. Before you begin answering a question, spend a few minutes planning (brainstorm possible approaches, write a thesis statement, jot down main thoughts in outline or think link form). To prepare yourself for actual test conditions, limit writing time to no more than 30 minutes per question.

1. Discuss the mind–body connection—specifically, the impact of diet, exercise, sleep, and medical care on the development and management of stress. Describe the changes you hope to make in your stress-management plan as a result of the information you have read in this textbook.

2. Choose three important skills you have developed during this course. Explain how they will contribute to your success for the remainder of your post-secondary experience and beyond.

Answer Key

For Self-Study Quizzes

Chapter 4, page 134

MULTIPLE-CHOICE QUESTIONS	FILL-IN-THE-BLANK QUESTIONS
1. D	1. commitment
2. A	2. initiative
3. D	3. learning preferences/personality traits
4. A	4. interests/abilities
5. C	5. mission
6. A	6. flexible

Chapter 8, page 270

MULTIPLE-CHOICE QUESTIONS	FILL-IN-THE-BLANK QUESTIONS
1. D	1. taking in information/asking questions about information/using information
2. B	2. creativity
3. A	3. contexts
4. D	4. cue column
5. B	5. mnemonic device
6. C	6. Freewriting/uncensored/planning

Chapter 12, page 393

MULTIPLE-CHOICE QUESTIONS	FILL-IN-THE-BLANK QUESTIONS
1. D	1. Cultural/non-verbal cues
2. D	2. Constructive
3. D	3. anorexia nervosa/bulimia/binge eating
4. B	4. internships/volunteering
5. B	5. credit limit
6. C	

INDEX

Clarkson, Adrienne, 93
Clinton, Bill, 383
Cole, Adam, 254–255
Coleman, Daniel, 114
Columbia Online Style
    (COS), 251
commitment, 13–14
common sense, 113
Commonwealth Edison, 242
communication,
    adventurer-dominant, 282
    assertive, 289, 290
    cultural, 287
    effective, 281
    giver-dominant, 282
    non-verbal, 287
    organizer-dominant, 282
    styles, 281–282
    technology, 292
    thinker-dominant, 282
    usage, 282–283
community involvement, 6,
    375–376
compact fluorescent lightbulbs
    (CFLs), 351
Conference Board of Canada,
    6, 33, 69, 82, 99, 137,
    165, 169, 201, 233, 273,
    303, 334
conflict prevention strategies, 289
conflict resolution, 290
constructive criticism,
    283–284
    strategies, 284
Cornell note-taking (T-note) system,
    174–175, 178
COS. See Columbia Online Style
    (COS)
Council of Science Editors (CSE)
    (prev. Council of Biology
    Editors (CBE)), 251
cover letter, 264, 345
Covey, Dr. Stephen, 378, 379
cramming (for tests), 207
creativity, 108–109, 375
    strategies, 111–112
Credibility, Accuracy,
    Reasonableness, Support
    (CARS) test, 240,
    241–242
credit cards, 353–354
    managing debts, 354, 356
Criminal Code of Canada, 278
critical reading, 154–155
    note taking, 157
    questioning, 156
    see also reading comprehension
    summarizing, 157–158, 160
    text highlighting, 156–157

criticism,
    types, 283
Crosby, Stills, Nash, and
    Young, 103
Crow, Sheryl, 378
CSE. See Council of Science
    Editors (CSE) (prev.
    Council of Biology
    Editors (CBE))
cultural competence, 274
    knowledge and, 278–279
cultural diversity, 38
    adapting to, 278–279
    high-context, 38–39
    low-context, 39
    valuing, 274–275

D
Dalai Lama, 383
date rape, 293–294
David, Laurie, 378
Day, Barrie, 380
decision making, 118
    problem solving and, 119
    strategies, 122
Dell, Michael, 111
Demers, Dr. Andrée, 311
depression, 310–311
    causes of, 312
detoxification, 322
Devil Wears Prada,
    The (movie), 139
digital revolution, 4
discipline, 18–19
discrimination, 277–278
    standing up to, 279
distractions, 172
divided attention, 172
Dodson, John E., 55
Dogpile.com, 238
Douglas, Claire, 155
drafting, 247–249
    feedback, 251
drugs, 310, 318, 319–320
Duvalier, François "Baby Doc," 93
Dweck, Carol, 8

E
eating disorders, 313
eating,
    binge, 313
Ebbinghaus, Herman, 187
education,
    foundation, 22
    income and, 5
    minority students, 280–281
    post-secondary, 4, 5, 20,
        169, 367
    values and, 35–36

emotional intelligence quotient
    (EQ), 114
emotional intelligence, 340
Employability Skills 2000+
    profile, 6, 7, 33, 69, 82,
        99, 273, 303
environmental footprint, 378
environmental practices,
    377–378
EQ. See emotional intelligence
    quotient (EQ)
Equifax Canada, 354
essay questions, 220–221
Excite, 238
exercise, 307
    prioritize, 308
    types, 307–308

F
face fears, 15–16
FaceBook, 292, 310
facts versus opinions,
    104–105
failure, 19–20
fairness, 37
fill-in-the-blank questions, 219
financial goals, 348–351
flash cards, 190, 207
flexibility, 373, 380
Foot, David, 19
Forseth, Kevin, 45
Frank, Steven, 212
Free the Children, 383
freewriting, 245
    rough draft, 248
Friedman, Thomas, 4
Frostburg State University,
    Maryland, 102

G
Gardner, Howard, 71,
    72, 73
Geldof, Bob, 104
Glass, Colby, 106
global economy, 22, 24
global marketplace, 5
globalization, 22
Go.com, 238
goal setting, 33
    achieving, 42–43
    linkages, 41–42
    long-term, 39–40
    planners for, 46–47
    practical thinking and, 115
    prioritizing, 42, 48–49
    reasonable, 52
    short-term, 40–41
    stress and, 55–56
Godard, Jean-Luc, 375

Thompson, David, 354
Three Women, The (painting), 191
time management, 43–44,
    85, 203
    flexibility, 52, 85–86
    personal needs, 44
    returning students and, 209
    stress and, 55–56
timelines, 181
    big picture, 343–344
Timm, Paul, 45
to-do list, 51
tobacco, 315–316
Toronto Star, 383
Torres, Kristina, 254–255
TransUnion Canada, 354
Treaty of Versailles, 188
Trelease, Jim, 374
true-or-false questions, 218
trust, 37
Turnbull, Helen, 39
Tutu, Desmond, 383
Twain, Shania, 342

U
U.S. Department of Health and
    Human Services, 326
uniform resource locator (URL),
    240, 246
uniqueness, 70–71
Université de Montréal, 311
University of British Columbia,
    83, 297

University of Calgary, 383
University of Chicago Press, 251
University of Florence, 93
University of Guelph, 380
University of Michigan, 238
University of Montreal, 93
University of Southern
    California, 195
University of Toronto, 383
University of Western Ontario,
    London, 383
URL. *See* uniform resource
    locator (URL)

V
values, 34
    cultural diversity and, 38
    education and, 35–36
    evaluating, 35–36
    identifying, 34–35
verbal signposts, 173
vocabulary, 146, 148
volunteering, 337, 376, 377
von Oech, Roger, 109

W
Wall Street Journal, 100
weblogs, 237
*WebQuester: A Guidebook
    to the Web,* 240
websites, 237, 239, 383
    evaluating, 240
Weight Watchers, 306

Wheatley, Margaret J., 373
Wikipedia, 240
Winfrey, Oprah, 383
*Working with Emotional
    Intelligence,* 340
workplace trends, 341–342
World is Flat, The, 4
World War I, 188
World Wide Web (WWW), 238
writing, 233
    brainstorming for, 243, 245
    drafting, 247–248
    editing, 254–255
    logistics of, 243
    process, 243, 245–247
    proofreading, 257–258
    research, 246–247
    revising, 252–254
    strategies for, 245
WWW. *See* World Wide
    Web (WWW)

Y
Yahoo!, 238
Yerkes, Dr. Robert M., 55
Yipp, Victor, 242
York University, Toronto, 155
Yoruba peoples, 92
Young, Neil, 103
Yuen, Lenora M., 52

Z
Zull, James, 187

PHOTO CREDITS

Photo objects throughout this text from Fotolia and Hemera Technology.

2, Wyatt McSpadden/The New York Times; 32, © Copyright 2000 PhotoDisc, Inc.; 93, Wonderfuke/Masterfile; 42, iStockphoto; 45, Kevin Forseth; 56, AP Photo/Matt Rourke; 68, Tara Todras-Whitehill/The New York Times; 93, CP Photo/Fred Chartrand; 98, Suzy Allman/The New York Times; 105, © vikki martin/Alamy; 136, Tony Cenicola/The New York Times; 168, Suzanne DeChillo/The New York Times; 195, Timothy Clary/AFP/Getty Images; 200, Josh Anderson/The New York Times; 212, Ozier Muhammad/NY Times; 232, Don Ipock/The New York Times; 251, Suzanne DeChillo/The New York Times; 272, Marilynn Yee/The New York Times; 292, © Jason Stitt—Fotolia.com; 295, Nancy E. Shaw; 302, Andrea Mohin/ The New York Times; 321, Soumik Kanungo; 344, © Copyright 2000 PhotoDisc, Inc.; 366, Alamy Images; 373, © Hemis/Corbis; 377, CP Photo/Jonathan Hayward; 380, Jennifer Armour; 383, Photo courtesy of Free The Children, www.freethechildren.com.